Studying Dialect

PERSPECTIVES ON THE ENGLISH LANGUAGE
Series Editors: Lesley Jeffries and Dan McIntyre

DISCOURSE AND GENRE: USING LANGUAGE IN CONTEXT
Stephen Bax

THINKING ABOUT LANGUAGE: THEORIES OF ENGLISH
Siobhan Chapman

STUDYING LANGUAGE: ENGLISH IN ACTION
Urszula Clark

ENGLISH LITERARY STYLISTICS
Christiana Gregoriou

STUDYING THE HISTORY OF EARLY ENGISH
Simon Horobin

DISCOVERING LANGUAGE: THE STRUCTURE OF MODERN ENGLISH
Lesley Jeffries

CRITICAL STYLISTICS: THE POWER OF ENGLISH
Lesley Jeffries

THE LANGUAGE OF EARLY ENGLISH LITERATURE: FROM CÆDMON TO MILTON
Sara M. Pons-Sanz

PRAGMATICS AND THE ENGLISH LANGUAGE
Jonathan Culpeper and Michael Haugh

STUDYING DIALECT
Rob Penhallurick

Perspectives on the English Language

Series Standing Order
ISBN 978–0–333–96146–9 hardcover
ISBN 978–0–333–96147–6 paperback
(*outside North America only*)

You can receive future titles in this series as they are published by placing a standing order. Please contact your bookseller or, in the case of difficulty, write to us at the address below with your name and address, the title of the series and one of the ISBNs quoted above.

Customer Services Department, Macmillan Distribution Ltd, Houndmills, Basingstoke, Hampshire, RG21 6XS, UK

Studying Dialect

Rob Penhallurick

Reader in English Language,
University of Swansea

First published 2018 by
PALGRAVE

Palgrave in the UK is an imprint of Macmillan Publishers Limited, registered in England, company number 785998, of 4 Crinan Street, London, N1 9XW.

Palgrave is a global imprint of the above companies and is represented throughout the world.

Palgrave® and Macmillan® are registered trademarks in the United States, the United Kingdom, Europe and other countries.

ISBN 978–0–230–20581–9   paperback

A catalogue record for this book is available from the British Library.

A catalog record for this book is available from the Library of Congress.

Contents

List of Figures

Table

Editors' Preface

We are delighted to introduce this volume in the Perspectives on the English Language series. It is a unique sociolinguistic publication because it tells the story of one of the most fascinating sub-fields of Linguistics - dialectology – and simultaneously teaches the reader how to go about doing the work it describes.

Dialects (and accents) have long been of interest to the world at large as well as to universities and Penhallurick traces the history of how they have been studied from the sixteenth century up to the present day. This means that he not only introduces the lexicography of early periods, and the early dialectology of the age of recordings, but also summarises some of the more recent debates, linking his discussion to the development of cartography and dialect-mapping and taking account of the most recent developments in the field. All the important landmarks, from the Survey of English Dialects to Labov's famous New York studies and Peter Trudgill's ground-breaking work on the dialect of Norwich, are to be found here, and are supplemented by insightful discussion of the most recent work in perceptual dialectology and geolinguistics.

The result is a clear and lucid history of the field from its earliest beginnings, written in an accessible style and effectively illustrated with a diverse range of examples. Each chapter includes information on where to read further in the relevant topic, explanations of the principal terminology of the field and what the reader can actually do to carry out their own work. Each chapter also introduces significant ideas, theories and methods so that readers are aware of the basis of the ideas that inform the dialect studies decribed.

Preface

This book is about regional dialectal variation in the English language around the world. More precisely, it is a comprehensive introduction to the study of dialectal variation in English. It tells the story of research into the dialects of English from the first works that explored dialectal vocabulary in the sixteenth century up to the IT-enabled approaches of the present day.

It is arranged into ten thematic chapters, but the chapters also proceed in a chronological order. It is written in clear, readable style, with technical terms explained as we go along and summed up at the end of each chapter. It narrates the histories of all the main areas in the study of English dialects, explaining and evaluating each approach in turn, as well as highlighting the continuities between them. We encounter dialect dictionaries and glossaries, dialect maps and linguistic atlases, sociolinguistic and geolinguistic work, and research into cultural attitudes towards English dialects.

The book is an indispensable companion for undergraduate and postgraduate students taking courses in linguistics, especially in dialectology, sociolinguistics, and geolinguistics, and of interest to anyone who is curious about dialects of English and their nature, and who is keen to learn about how scholars have developed our knowledge of language variation. *Studying Dialect* will help students preparing to do their own research into dialectal variation, who will be carrying out assignments and projects on varieties of English. At the end of each chapter there is concise guidance on further reading, and for each theme there are suggestions about small-scale research projects that can be undertaken by individuals.

Before we go any further, we should begin with a succinct definition of what is meant by the term *dialect*, even though I should also say that the whole of this book is occupied with working out a definition of the term *dialect*. The *Oxford English Dictionary* (OED) defines *dialect* as:

> A form or variety of a language which is peculiar to a specific region, especially one which differs from the standard or literary form of the language in respect of vocabulary, pronunciation, idiom, etc.; (as a mass noun) provincial or rustic speech. Also more generally: a particular language considered in terms of its relationship with the family of languages to which it belongs.

This definition covers the idea that a dialect is a regionally specific subdivision of a language, a point emphasized in my opening sentence above. It also hints at a common cultural perception of regional dialect as rural and traditional, and then interestingly it suggests that a language too can be considered a regionally specific subdivision (a dialect) in the context of a grouping of related languages (a language family). This is an allusion to the fact that dialects of a language can over time evolve into separate languages. The difference between calling something a *dialect* rather calling it a *language* refers to a difference of degree. The OED adds another sense to the definition:

> Manner of speaking, language, speech; especially the mode of speech peculiar to, or characteristic of, a particular person or group; phraseology, idiom; jargon; a particular variety of any of these.

This does not mention region but concentrates on the social attributes of a dialect as the characteristic speech of an identifiable community of speakers. The OED traces the arrival in English of the word *dialect* to the sixteenth century, probably borrowed from French, but going back to Latin and ancient Greek. All of the shades of meaning in these definitions feature in this book, and it is mostly, though not exclusively, concerned with spoken rather than written dialect. (Note that in linguistics the term *variety* is often used as a synonym for *dialect*, particularly when referring to national types of a language, such as American English or Australian English.)

However, for something rather more succinct, I recommend this as our starting-point definition:

> By a *dialect* we here only mean, *first, a local difference of speech* ... and, *secondly, an evident relation of all these forms of local speech to one another.*

This is from the first major study of English accents and dialects in Britain, published in 1889 (the italics are in the original), and written by Alexander J. Ellis, the man who gave the name *dialectology* to the academic discipline concerned with studying dialect. (Note that the term *accent* refers only to pronunciation, and not to the vocabulary or grammar of a dialect.) Ellis's definition neatly sums up the following: that a dialect is geographically specific, and that it is different from other dialects; and that, conversely, a dialect is also in many aspects connected by similarity and kinship to other dialects. This encourages us to picture threads of linkage between diverse dialects, to imagine words, grammar, and pronunciations travelling across territories and over time between dialects, and it takes us into the realm of studying linguistic change, one of the primary themes in dialect study.

There are other big themes in the history of dialect study, other reasons why so many people have investigated regional variation in language, including these: in order to compile a record or archive of local forms; to determine what is local, distinguishing regional features from the more widespread; to discover more about language history; to discover more and understand better the early literature of a language; to understand the qualities and behaviour of linguistic diversity better; and to contribute to linguistic theory. In sum, we find a concern with identity (individual, local, national), history, and the nature of language and linguistic change. The ten chapters of this book provide an introductory, explanatory guide to all of these themes.

Chapters 1 and 2 focus on dialect lexicography, that is, research into the regional vocabulary of English with the aim of producing dialect dictionaries and glossaries, works that range from brief lists of local words and meanings gathered by individuals to multi-volume national-scale ventures. The findings of the early dialect lexicographers fed into the centuries-long process that split the language into *Standard English* and *non-standard English*, or, put another way, the general versus the local. Chapter 1 looks at the pioneers of this type of scholarship, from the sixteenth to the end of the nineteenth century. Chapter 2 looks at the spread of the dialect lexicography of English across the world and at its continuing vitality in the digital age. Also in Chapter 2 there is a guide to descriptive works on the grammars of English dialects, from the nineteenth century to the present day.

Chapters 3, 4, and 5 give an expository account of another great tradition in dialect study, the making of linguistic atlases. This is arguably the most basic impulse in dialect study – putting the geographical distributions of regional forms onto maps. Like the lexicographers, the early dialect cartographers wanted to describe for the first time the regional forms of language, to record them for posterity and as a matter of national pride, but they were also interested in language history and in theories about linguistic change through time. Chapter 3 looks at the first linguistic atlas projects, which took place in the late nineteenth century in mainland Europe. Chapter 4 describes the aims of these massive works and their influence on the dialect study of English in the twentieth and twenty-first centuries. Also in Chapter 4 there are overviews of research on the acoustics and discourse of English dialects. Chapter 5 gives a full history of the dialect cartography of English in North America and Britain, and ends with an assessment of the enabling effects of the IT revolution on linguistic geography.

In the 1960s, dialect study was transformed by a new emphasis and a wave of innovative methods, and by a new academic discipline: sociolinguistics. Chapter 6 traces the origins of sociolinguistics, in particular the brand of sociolinguistics associated with dialect research, and then takes a close look at the first major sociolinguistic dialect study, William Labov's survey in 1966 of New York City English. The sociolinguistic approach clarified aspects of regional language variation somewhat set aside in previous work, highlighting the fact that a given regional dialect not only differs from other regional dialects, but contains difference and variation within itself – linguistic variation which correlates with variation in social class, age, ethnicity, education, and gender among the members of a speech community, as well as with the relative formality/informality of the speaking context. Variationist sociolinguistics also directed the attention of scholars much more towards urban dialects.

Chapter 7 steers us through the great wealth of sociolinguistic studies in English-speaking lands that followed Labov's lead, taking in work on African-American Vernacular English and the attempt to develop a theory of grammar based in analysis of the inherent variability of language. We also look at the social-network approach that emerged in the 1970s, which emphasizes the ways in which speech communities and everyday interactions between their members can (depending on the circumstances) either maintain local speech norms or foster innovations.

Sometimes in academic circles when a new generation of scholars espouses a new approach, it can involve criticism of older approaches – a bit like when a builder arrives at your house to give you a quote on some work and tells you how bad the workmanship of the builders you employed previously is. If they could, the previous builders would no doubt respond. Both new and old might have a point. The advent of sociolinguistics in dialect study caused something of an upheaval, and there was dispute between some adherents of new and old schools in the 1970s and 1980s. In Chapter 8, I tell the tale of the Great Argument in Dialect Study, and also I try to explain precisely how peace eventually broke out, leaving dialect scholars better equipped to deal with a wider range of interests.

The final two chapters of the book bring the story up to date, looking at two trends in contemporary dialect study which also illustrate the reconciliation and merging of the dialectological with the sociolinguistic approach.

Chapter 9 provides a short history of societal attitudes and perceptions regarding dialectal variation in English (a history documented back to the twelfth century), before outlining the key research in recent dialect study that explores these cultural beliefs, especially the relatively new branch known as perceptual dialectology, which scrutinizes the perceptions and views of non-linguists in order to understand more fully what we mean by *dialect*. Why are speakers attracted to or repelled by different dialects, accents, and linguistic features? Are there communal attitudes which influence the speaking choices that individuals and groups make? Is dialect funny? And thanks to the analytical models of accommodation theory, we can add another perspective to our definition of *dialect*: each of us can shift our mode of speaking between different levels on a standard/non-standard continuum according to our perceptions of the persons that we are conversing with at any given time. A regional dialect not only differs from other regional dialects and differs within itself in correlation with social groupings, but it also varies at different times in its performance by its speakers in response to differing social situations. (A brief aside here to note that there is some overlap between the meanings of *dialect* and of *slang*, in that *slang* refers to non-standard speech just as *dialect* often does. But the term *slang* puts no emphasis on the notion of regional variation, which is an important part of the meaning of *dialect*.)

Chapter 10 looks at geolinguistics, a modern form of dialect study that investigates linguistic change and its relationship with geographical space using insights and methods drawn from human geography, dialectology, and sociolinguistics, with the aim of explaining the effects of population movements like migration and commuting on regional varieties of English.

At times in its history, dialect study has been at the forefront of linguistic research. The early dialect lexicographers, the philological dialectologists of the nineteenth century, and the sociolinguists of the mid twentieth century were all pioneers. In the early twenty-first century, stimulated and aided by the digital revolution, dialect study is flourishing. This book illuminates the fascination that dialects hold for scholars and guides us through the research.

Dialects are strange. When we hear other speakers of our language speaking the language differently, using words and sounds that we ourselves do not use, it is a strange experience. Studying dialect involves getting closer to this strangeness, appreciating others and their language better, and, strangely enough, gradually realizing that our own immediate linguistic surroundings are as rich as these foreign territories, waiting to be explored.

Acknowledgements

I would like to thank the following for their responses to my questions about their work and for their help in facilitating my access to it: David Britain, Allison Burkette, Beat Glauser, Joan Hall, Reinhard Heuberger (*EDD* Online), Fumio Inoue, Juhani Klemola (transcription of SED audio), Bernd Kortmann, Alfred Lameli (*Digitaler Wenker-Atlas*), Jean Le Dû, Chris Montgomery, Alexander Morris, Dennis Preston, Stefano Quaino, Jonnie Robinson, Roger Shuy, and Martijn Wieling (*Gabmap/Voices*).

For their efficiency and considerate assistance in answering queries and providing me with access to and use of materials in their care, my thanks to: Ian Glen of Swansea University Library, David Govier of Manchester City Central Library, the staff of the Bodleian Library, and the staff of the British Library.

For their help and suggestions, I am very grateful to: Rebecca Comairas (why study dialect), John Goodby (English in Ireland), Ute Keller (translations from German and Dutch), Heli Paulasto (advice on corpora), James Penhallurick (image preparation), and Adrian Willmott (everything else). For their support, encouragement, and advice, my thanks to Karen Atherton, Helen Elton, and Andrew Jenkins.

Many thanks also to my very patient and supportive editors at Palgrave and Integra.

From a certain point of view, work on this book began some decades ago when I was introduced to dialect study in the first year of my undergraduate degree. An MA followed, then a PhD, and then a variety of posts working for dialect surveys. During those years, I was lucky enough to be guided by some sympathetic and knowledgeable mentors. For their support and counsel in many ways then and since, I would like especially to thank David Parry, Clive Upton, John Widdowson, and the late Stanley Ellis.

I have benefited from the services of a number of digital and online resources during the writing of this book, including the Digital Public Library of America, the Education Resources Information Center of the US Office of Education, Google Books, HathiTrust Digital Library, Historical Texts, the Internet Archive, the Internet Library of Early Journals, the Joint Information Systems Committee, JSTOR (Journal Storage), and the Münchener DigitalisierungsZentrum. Other more subject-specific resources are acknowledged in the text.

In addition, the author and publishers wish to thank the following for permission to reproduce material:

IPA Chart, http://www.internationalphoneticassociation.org/content/ipa-chart, available under a Creative Commons Attribution-Sharealike 3.0 Unported License. Copyright © 2015 International Phonetic Association.

Taylor and Francis Group for Figure 2.2, a page from the SED *Questionnaire* (Dieth and Orton, 1962, page 86); for Figure 2.4, a page from *SED: Basic Material* Volume IV: *The Southern Counties*, Part III (Orton and Wakelin, 1968, page 871); for Figures 4.10 and 4.11, Maps 29 and 29A from the *Linguistic Atlas of Scotland* Volume 1 (Mather, Speitel and Leslie, 1975); for Figure 5.21, map Ph7 from *The Linguistic Atlas of England* (Orton, Sanderson and Widdowson, 1978); and for Figure 5.26, symbol map of polyphonemes in *nut*, from the *Linguistic Atlas of Scotland* Volume 3 (Mather, Speitel and Leslie, 1986).

Harvard University Press for Figure 2.7, page 653 of the *Dictionary of American Regional English*, Volume I (1985), edited by Frederic G. Cassidy.

The Newfoundland and Labrador Heritage Web Site for Figure 2.8, entry for *chowder* from the online edition of the *Dictionary of Newfoundland English* (1999), reproduced as a screen-grab, and located at http://www.heritage.nf.ca/dictionary/index.php#854.

Jonnie Robinson of the British Library for Figure 3.2, 'Regional Voices: Phonological variation', reproduced as a screen-grab, and located at: http://www.bl.uk/learning/langlit/sounds/regional-voices/phonological-variation/. Map content selection and interpretation by Jonnie Robinson © British Library *Sounds Familiar* website (2007).

Jean Le Dû for Figure 3.10, map 252 from the *Nouvel Atlas Linguistique de la Basse-Bretagne*, Volume 1 (Le Dû, 2001).

De Gruyter for Figure 4.5, spectrogram of *past*, Figure 4.6, map showing Southern breaking, and Figures 10.2 and 10.4, maps showing the main dialect regions of North American English, from *The Atlas of North American English:*

Phonetics, Phonology and Sound Change (2006), by William Labov, Sharon Ash and Charles Boberg; and for Figures 9.5 and 9.6, hand-drawn maps of US dialect regions, from Dennis Preston's essays in *Language and Space: An International Handbook of Linguistic Variation* (2010), Volumes 1 (edited by Auer and Schmidt) and 2 (edited by Lameli, Kehrein and Rabanus) respectively.

Elsevier for Figure 4.9, spectrogram of the phrase *what a good idea*, from Clopper and Smiljanic (2011), 'Effects of Gender and Regional Dialect on Prosodic Patterns in American English', *Journal of Phonetics*, Vol. 39, Issue 2, page 240.

University of Michigan Press for Figure 5.16, speech areas of the Eastern States, from *A Word Geography of the Eastern United States* (1949, 1966) by Hans Kurath.

The University of Tennessee for Figure 5.17, variants of *frying pan*, from 'Some Problems in Editing the Linguistic Atlas of the Upper Midwest' (Figure 15), by Harold B. Allen, in *Dialectology: Problems and Perspectives* (1971), edited by Lorraine Hall Burghardt.

The University of Georgia Press for Figure 5.18, map showing the distribution of *passed*, from the *Linguistic Atlas of the Gulf States*, Volume 7 (1992, page 3), edited by Lee Pederson and Susan L. McDaniel.

Narr Francke Attempto Publishing for Figure 5.24, Map 208 from the *Atlas of English Sounds* (Kolb, Glauser, Elmer and Stamm, 1979).

Cambridge University Press for Figure 6.1, overall stratification of (r) by store, Figure 6.2 class stratification of (r), and Figure 6.3 structure of subjective evaluation form for (r), all from *The Social Stratification of English in New York City* (2006, 2nd edn, pages 47, 152, and 284 respectively) by William Labov; and for Figure 7.1, the Sydney speech community, from Horvath and Sankoff (1987), 'Delimiting the Sydney Speech Community', *Language in Society*, Vol. 16, No. 2, page 190, and Figure 7.2, backing of /a/, from Milroy and Milroy (1985), 'Linguistic Change, Social Network and Speaker Innovation', *Journal of Linguistics*, Vol. 21, No. 2, page 371.

Channel View Publications Ltd / Multilingual Matters for Figure 9.7, South Indiana respondents' perceptions of the southern dialect area of the USA, from Dennis R. Preston (1988, page 384), 'Methods in the Study of Dialect Perception', in *Methods in Dialectology: Proceedings of the Sixth International Conference held at the University College of North Wales, 3rd-7th August 1987*, edited by Alan R. Thomas.

Royal Netherlands Academy of Arts and Sciences for Figure 9.8, 'little arrows' perceptual map of North Brabant, from Antonius A. Weijnen, 'De grenzen tussen de Oost-Noordbrabantse dialecten onderling' ['The borders between the dialects of eastern North Brabant'] (1946).

Duke University Press for Figure 9.9, subjective dialect division of Great Britain, from Fumio Inoue (1996), 'Subjective Dialect Division in Great Britain', *American Speech*, Vol. 71, No. 2, page 149.

Fumio Inoue and Franz Steiner Publishers for Figure 9.10, distribution of British students' evaluative words, and Figure 9.11 distribution of dialects by British students according to dialect images, both from Fumio Inoue (1995, pages 153 and 154 respectively), 'Classification of Dialects by Image: English and Japanese', in *Verhandlungen des Internationalen Dialektologenkongresses: Bamberg, 29.7.--4.8.1990* ['Proceedings of the International Congress of Dialectologists: Bamberg, 29 July--4 August 1990'], edited by Wolfgang Viereck, 3 volumes.

Chris Montgomery for Figure 9.12, Carlisle respondents' placement of a Preston voice sample, from his *Northern English Dialects: A Perceptual Approach* (2007, page 292).

John Wiley and Sons for Figure 10.1, bundles of isoglosses, from Horvath and Horvath (2002), 'The Geolinguistics of /l/ Vocalization in Australia and New Zealand', *Journal of Sociolinguistics*, Vol. 6, No. 3, page 342.

University of Virginia Press for Figure 10.3, directions of the main sound changes in the Northern Cities Shift, from Labov (2012, Figure 5, location 356/page 20, copyright © the Rector and Visitors of the University of Virginia).

Abbreviations

AAVE	African-American Vernacular English
ACE	Macquarie Australian Corpus of English
ADS	American Dialect Society
AES	*Atlas of English Sounds*
AFAM	African-American/Gullah linguistic atlas project
AIS	*Sprach- und Sachatlas Italiens und der Südschweiz*
ALF	*Atlas linguistique de la France*
ALS	American Linguistic Survey
ANAE	*Atlas of North American English*
ARDWG	*American Regional Dialects: A Word Geography*
ATLSP	Atlanta Survey Project
BL	British Library
BM	*Basic Material* (of the SED)
BNC	British National Corpus
CLAE	*Computer Developed Linguistic Atlas of England*
CoRD	Corpus Resource Database
DARE	*Dictionary of American Regional English*
DDS	Detroit Dialect Study
DECTE	The Diachronic Electronic Corpus of Tyneside English
DiWA	*Digitaler Wenker-Atlas*
DNE	*Dictionary of Newfoundland English*
DPLA	Digital Public Library of America
DSA	*Deutscher Sprachatlas*
DSAE	Dictionary Unit for South African English
DSL	*Dictionary of the Scots Language* (*Dictionar o the Scots Leid*)
DWA	*Deutscher Wortatlas*
EDD	*English Dialect Dictionary*

EDG	*English Dialect Grammar*
Edisyn	European Dialect Syntax project
EDS	English Dialect Society
eLib Project	Electronic Libraries Programme Project by the Universities of Birmingham, Leeds, Manchester, and Oxford
ERIC	Education Resources Information Center of the US Office of Education
eWAVE	*Electronic World Atlas of Varieties of English*
F1; F2; F3	formant 1; formant 2; formant 3
FL	faculty of language
F-LOB	Freiburg-LOB Corpus of British English
FRED	Freiburg English Dialect Corpus
Frown	Freiburg-Brown Corpus of American English
GADS	'Great Argument in Dialect Study'
GIS	Geographic Information Systems
HRT	High Rising Terminal or Tone
ICAME	International Computer Archive of Modern and Medieval English
ICE	International Corpus of English
ILEJ	Internet Library of Early Journals
IM	Incidental Material (of the SED)
IPA	International Phonetic Alphabet
IViE	Intonational Variation in English project
Jisc	Joint Information Systems Committee
JSTOR	Journal Storage digital library
LAE	*Linguistic Atlas of England*
LAEME	*Linguistic Atlas of Early Middle English*
LAGS	*Linguistic Atlas of the Gulf States*
LALME	*Linguistic Atlas of Late Mediaeval English*
LAMSAS	Linguistic Atlas of the Middle and South Atlantic States
LANCS	Linguistic Atlas of the North Central States
LANE	*Linguistic Atlas of New England*
LAO	Linguistic Atlas of Oklahoma
LAOS	*Linguistic Atlas of Older Scots*
LAP	Linguistic Atlas Project of the United States
LAPNW	Linguistic Atlas of the Pacific Northwest
LAPW	*Linguistic Atlas of the Pacific West*
LARMS	Linguistic Atlas of the Rocky Mountain States
LAS	*Linguistic Atlas of Scotland*
LAUM	*Linguistic Atlas of the Upper Midwest*
LAUSC	Linguistic Atlas of the United States and Canada
LAVC	Leeds Archive of Vernacular Culture
LAWS	Linguistic Atlas of the Western States

LCV	(Philadelphia Project on) Linguistic Change and Variation
LGW	*Linguistic Geography of Wales*
LOB	Lancaster-Oslo/Bergen Corpus of British English
LSAI	Linguistic Survey of Anglo-Irish
LSS	Linguistic Survey of Scotland
LSWE	Longman Spoken and Written English corpus
MDS	multidimensional scaling
MDZ	Münchener DigitalisierungsZentrum ['Munich Digitization Center']
MFY	Mobilization for Youth Program
MGT	matched-guise technique
MP	Minimalist Program
NALF	*Nouvel atlas linguistique de la France par régions*
NARVS	North American Regional Vocabulary Survey
NC(C)S	Northern Cities (Chain) Shift
NECTE	Newcastle Electronic Corpus of Tyneside English
NWAV	New Ways of Analyzing Variation conference series
NYC	New York City
OE	Old English
OED	*Oxford English Dictionary*
Oxigen	Oxford Intonation Generator project
P&P	principles and parameters
PCA	principal components analysis
PD	perceptual dialectology
PEAS	*Pronunciation of English in the Atlantic States*
PIE	Proto-Indo-European
pWAVE	(or *printWAVE*) *Mouton World Atlas of Variation in English*
REDE	Regionalsprache.de ['Regional language of Germany']
RP	Received Pronunciation
RVT	*Regional Vocabulary of Texas*
SAWD	Survey of Anglo-Welsh Dialects
SD Test	Semantic Differential Test
SEC	socio-economic class
SED	Survey of English Dialects
SGDS	*Survey of the Gaelic Dialects of Scotland*
SKNP	St Kitts/Nevis Project
SOD	Survey of Oklahoma Dialects
SPEED	Spoken English in Early Dialects project
SPSS	*Statistical Package for the Social Sciences*
SR test	subjective reaction test
SSENYC	*Social Stratification of English in New York City*

SV test	self-evaluation test
T2KSWAL	TOEFL 2000 Spoken and Written Academic Language corpus
TLS	Tyneside Linguistic Survey
ToBI	Tones and Break Indices system for transcribing intonation patterns
TOEFL	Test of English as a Foreign Language
TRS	Tape-recorded Survey of Hiberno-English Speech
UG	universal grammar
VARIENG	Research Unit for the Study of Variation, Contacts and Change in English
WGE	*Word Geography of England*
WGEUS	*Word Geography of the Eastern United States*
WSC	Wellington Corpus of Spoken New Zealand English
WWC	Wellington Corpus of Written New Zealand English

* preceding a linguistic item means the item is a hypothetical form
[ ] are used to enclose phonetic symbols
/ / enclose phonemes
( ) are used to enclose linguistic variables

THE INTERNATIONAL PHONETIC ALPHABET (revised to 2015)

© 2015 IPA

CONSONANTS (PULMONIC)

	Bilabial	Labiodental	Dental	Alveolar	Postalveolar	Retroflex	Palatal	Velar	Uvular	Pharyngeal	Glottal
Plosive	p b			t d		ʈ ɖ	c ɟ	k ɡ	q ɢ		ʔ
Nasal	m	ɱ		n		ɳ	ɲ	ŋ	ɴ		
Trill	ʙ			r					ʀ		
Tap or Flap		ⱱ		ɾ		ɽ					
Fricative	ɸ β	f v	θ ð	s z	ʃ ʒ	ʂ ʐ	ç ʝ	x ɣ	χ ʁ	ħ ʕ	h ɦ
Lateral fricative				ɬ ɮ							
Approximant		ʋ		ɹ		ɻ	j	ɰ			
Lateral approximant				l		ɭ	ʎ	ʟ			

Symbols to the right in a cell are voiced, to the left are voiceless. Shaded areas denote articulations judged impossible.

CONSONANTS (NON-PULMONIC)

Clicks		Voiced implosives		Ejectives	
⊙	Bilabial	ɓ	Bilabial	ʼ	Examples:
ǀ	Dental	ɗ	Dental/alveolar	pʼ	Bilabial
ǃ	(Post)alveolar	ʄ	Palatal	tʼ	Dental/alveolar
ǂ	Palatoalveolar	ɠ	Velar	kʼ	Velar
ǁ	Alveolar lateral	ʛ	Uvular	sʼ	Alveolar fricative

VOWELS

xxx

OTHER SYMBOLS

ʍ Voiceless labial-velar fricative
w Voiced labial-velar approximant
ɥ Voiced labial-palatal approximant
ʜ Voiceless epiglottal fricative
ʢ Voiced epiglottal fricative
ʡ Epiglottal plosive

ɕ ʑ Alveolo-palatal fricatives
ɺ Voiced alveolar lateral flap
ʄ Simultaneous ʃ and x

Affricates and double articulations can be represented by two symbols joined by a tie bar if necessary.

t͡s k͡p

æ a•ɶ — ɑ•ɒ
a

Where symbols appear in pairs, the one to the right represents a rounded vowel.

Open

SUPRASEGMENTALS

ˈ	Primary stress	ˌfoʊnəˈtɪʃən
ˌ	Secondary stress	
ː	Long	eː
ˑ	Half-long	eˑ
̆	Extra-short	ĕ
ǀ	Minor (foot) group	
‖	Major (intonation) group	
.	Syllable break	ɹi.ækt
‿	Linking (absence of a break)	

TONES AND WORD ACCENTS

LEVEL		CONTOUR	
e̋ or ˥	Extra high	ě or ˇ	Rising
é ˦	High	ê ˆ	Falling
ē ˧	Mid	e᷄ ˴	High rising
è ˨	Low	e᷅ ˳	Low rising
ȅ ˩	Extra low	e᷈ ˷	Rising-falling
ꜜ	Downstep	↗	Global rise
ꜛ	Upstep	↘	Global fall

DIACRITICS Some diacritics may be placed above a symbol with a descender, e.g. ŋ̊

̥	Voiceless	n̥ d̥	̤	Breathy voiced	b̤ a̤	̪	Dental t̪ d̪
̬	Voiced	s̬ t̬	̰	Creaky voiced	b̰ a̰	̺	Apical t̺ d̺
ʰ	Aspirated	tʰ dʰ	̼	Linguolabial	t̼ d̼	̻	Laminal t̻ d̻
̹	More rounded	ɔ̹	ʷ	Labialized	tʷ dʷ	̃	Nasalized ẽ
̜	Less rounded	ɔ̜	ʲ	Palatalized	tʲ dʲ	ⁿ	Nasal release dⁿ
̟	Advanced	u̟	ˠ	Velarized	tˠ dˠ	ˡ	Lateral release dˡ
̠	Retracted	e̠	ˤ	Pharyngealized	tˤ dˤ	̚	No audible release d̚
̈	Centralized	ë	̴	Velarized or pharyngealized	ɫ		
̽	Mid-centralized	e̽	̝	Raised	e̝ (ɹ̝ = voiced alveolar fricative)		
̩	Syllabic	n̩	̞	Lowered	e̞ (β̞ = voiced bilabial approximant)		
̯	Non-syllabic	e̯	̘	Advanced Tongue Root	e̘		
˞	Rhoticity	ɚ a˞	̙	Retracted Tongue Root	e̙		

xxxi

Studying Dialect Timeline

According to John Considine's chronology of lexicography (2015), the earliest word lists date to *circa* 3200 BC, in Sumerian; European lexicography dates back to the first century BC, in ancient Latin; and the first dialect dictionary to the early years AD, in Chinese. The first English dictionary with a dialectal element was completed *circa* 1565:

1565:	Laurence Nowell's *Vocabularium Saxonicum*.
1604:	Robert Cawdrey's *Table Alphabeticall* is published, the first general monolingual dictionary of English.
1635:	The first public postal service in Britain is introduced.
1674:	John Ray's *A Collection of English Words Not Generally Used* is published, the first dialect dictionary of English on a national scale.
1721:	Nathan Bailey's first *Universal Etymological Dictionary* is published, which includes many dialect words.
1735–6:	*An Alphabet of Kenticisms* is compiled by Samuel Pegge (the elder), one of the first dialect glossaries of English.
1755:	Samuel Johnson's general *Dictionary of the English Language* is published.
1786:	William Jones delivers his lecture to the Asiatic Society in Calcutta, proposing the theory of an Indo-European language family.
1787:	Francis Grose's *A Provincial Glossary* is published.
1807:	The first fare-paying passenger railway service in the world opens in Swansea, South Wales, using horse-drawn vehicles.
1821:	Johann Andreas Schmeller's map of Bavarian dialects is published.

1825:	The first public railway in the world to use steam power is opened at the Stockton and Darlington Railroad by George Stephenson; construction of the Erie Canal is completed.
1828:	Noah Webster's *An American Dictionary of the English Language* is published.
1842:	Following informal meetings in the early 1830s, the Philological Society is founded.
1852:	Following a proposal by Anthony Trollope, roadside letter boxes are introduced in Britain.
1854:	Australia's first steam-powered railway opens.
1857:	The sound-recording era begins with the invention of the phonautograph by the Frenchmen Édouard-Léon Scott de Martinville.
1858:	The *New English Dictionary* or *Oxford English Dictionary* is initiated by the Philological Society.
1860:	South Africa's first steam-powered railway opens.
1863:	New Zealand's first steam-powered public railway opens.
1873:	The English Dialect Society is founded with the aim of producing a comprehensive English Dialect Dictionary; James Murray's *Linguistical Map of Scotland* is published; Prince Louis-Lucien Bonaparte presents his first map of English dialects to the Philological Society.
1876:	August Leskien argues in favour of exceptionless sound laws; Georg Wenker starts collecting data for a linguistic atlas of German; Bismarck unites the postal and telegraph services of the German Empire into one administrative body, the *Reichs-Post und Telegraphenverwaltung*. (A regular German postal service had been in existence since the mid seventeenth century.)
1878:	Hermann Osthoff and Karl Brugmann firmly articulate the 'neogrammarian hypothesis' of exceptionless sound laws.
1886:	First edition of *Hobson-Jobson: A Glossary of Colloquial Anglo-Indian Words and Phrases* is published.
1887:	Alexander J. Ellis prepares his map of English Dialect Districts.
1889:	The American Dialect Society is founded.
1896:	George Hempl's map of American English dialects is published; the English Dialect Society is wound up.
1897:	Jules Gilliéron and Edmond Edmont begin fieldwork for a linguistic atlas of French.
1898–1905:	Joseph Wright's *English Dialect Dictionary* is published.
1905:	Wright's *English Dialect Grammar* is published.
1908:	The world's first road for high-speed automobile traffic opens, the Long Island Motor Parkway, New York City.

1916:	Ferdinand de Saussure's *Cours de linguistique générale* is published.
1924:	The first European public motorway opens between Milan and Como in Italy.
1929:	The Linguistic Atlas of the United States and Canada is initiated.
1931:	First fascicles of *A Dictionary of the Older Scottish Tongue* and *The Scottish National Dictionary* are published.
1933:	The first edition of the *Oxford English Dictionary* completes its publication.
1935:	A linguistic atlas of the British Isles is proposed.
1939–43:	*Linguistic Atlas of New England* is published.
1945:	The first general-purpose programmable electronic computer is built by J. Presper Eckert and John V. Mauchly at the University of Pennsylvania.
1946:	Harold Orton and Eugen Dieth begin planning for the Survey of English Dialects.
1948:	Linguistic Survey of Scotland starts.
1953:	Patrick Leo Henry begins preliminary work on a Linguistic Survey of Anglo-Irish.
1957:	Noam Chomsky's *Syntactic Structures* is published.
1958:	Wallace Lambert and colleagues in Montreal pioneer the matched-guise technique on attitudes to linguistic variation; John Fischer's proto-sociolinguistic article on a New England village is published.
1963:	William Labov publishes his first article, on sound change in progress on the island of Martha's Vineyard.
1964:	The first portable audio-cassette recorders arrive on the market.
1965–70:	Fieldwork for the *Dictionary of American Regional English* takes place.
1966:	Labov's *The Social Stratification of English in New York City* is published; the Detroit Dialect Study begins.
1967:	*Dictionary of Jamaican English* is published.
1968:	Peter Trudgill carries out fieldwork for his study of Norwich English; David Parry begins the Survey of Anglo-Welsh Dialects.
1974:	*A Word Geography of England* is published.
1975:	The first volume of *The Linguistic Atlas of Scotland* is published.
1976:	In their research on Belfast English, Lesley Milroy and James Milroy pioneer the concept of social networks in explanations of linguistic variation and change.
1977:	The era of digital sound recording begins with Sony's PMC-1.
1978:	*The Linguistic Atlas of England* is published.
1981:	First edition of the *Macquarie Dictionary* of Australian English is published; Dennis R. Preston begins modern perceptual dialectology.

1982:   First edition of *Dictionary of Newfoundland English* is published.

1983:   By combining the Advanced Research Projects Agency Network with Transmission Control Protocol and Internet Protocol, researchers begin to assemble the forerunner to the Internet.

1985:   The first volume of the *Dictionary of American Regional English* is published.

1986:   The first volume of the *Linguistic Atlas of the Gulf States* is published.

1990:   Tim Berners-Lee invents the World Wide Web.

1994:   The first volume of Labov's *Principles of Linguistic Change* is published.

1996:   *Dictionary of Caribbean English Usage* and *A Dictionary of South African English on Historical Principles* are published.

1997:   *The Dictionary of New Zealand English* is published.

2000:   After preliminary work beginning in 1994, the *OED* goes online.

2004:   *Dictionary of the Scots Language* goes online.

2004–5:   BBC *Voices* survey takes place.

2006:   *The Atlas of North American English* is published.

2010:   Joseph Wright's *English Dialect Dictionary* goes online at the University of Innsbruck.

2011:   *The Electronic World Atlas of Varieties of English* is launched.

2012:   *Dialect Atlas of Newfoundland and Labrador* is launched.

1 Lexicography: ↗ Study of vocab
From early works to *The English Dialect Dictionary*

This chapter includes the following:

- Introduction to English dialect lexicography.
- Overview of the first lexicographers of English dialects, sixteenth–nineteenth centuries.
- Guide to the first national dialect dictionaries, seventeenth–nineteenth centuries.
- Joseph Wright's *English Dialect Dictionary* (1898–1905).

1.1   Introduction

What does the word *maze* mean and why would anyone be curious about it?

In Standard English, the noun *maze* means a labyrinth or a bewildering mass of things, but this is not the word that Nick Stephens of Cornwall submitted to the BBC's *Voices* web-pages in 2005. He said, '*Yoom maze* for "you're crazy/stupid"', adding, 'Probably could have written a book on this but sadly my grandparents have passed on now.' (See: http://www.bbc.co.uk/cornwall/voices2005/stories/jan2005/voices_from_you2.shtml.)

According to the *Voices* dialect survey, this *maze* is a local word, here in adjectival form, meaning crazy or stupid, and for Nick Stephens it represents the bygone Cornish English of older generations. Another adjectival form of the word in this sense was recorded in one of the early dialect dictionaries of English, Francis Grose's *Provincial Glossary* of 1787, which says that MAZ'D, or MAZED means 'mad' as in 'A mazed man, a crazy, or madman.' Grose was interested in cataloguing words and meanings which were used only locally in England rather than generally across the whole country. This was a trailblazing task in the late eighteenth century. He says that *mazed* is a word from Exmoor, and the source of his information was a short article published in August 1746 (pp. 405–8) in the scholarly monthly *The Gentleman's Magazine* under the title 'An Exmoor Vocabulary'. The pseudonymous compiler of the Vocabulary, 'Devoniensis' (a name which means 'about or from Devon'), says that his aim in describing 'this barbarous dialect' (p. 408) was to provide a service to readers from other parts of the country, for 'perhaps it may afford some help to their understanding our old books' (p. 405). Devoniensis was one of a growing number of scholars in the first half of the eighteenth century showing an interest in local speech because of what it could tell us about older forms of the English language. ('Devoniensis' was the Devonshire-born clerk, William Chapple (1718–81).) So we see that dialectal *maze* has quite a history, and that there have been, historically, a number of reasons to be interested in the word and its meaning, and we also get a hint of an assortment of attitudes towards regional dialectal speech.

In fact, one of the great traditions in dialect study is the exploration of vocabulary. The frequent end-product of such an enquiry is a list of words accompanied at the very least by the words' definitions and an indication of their geographical **provenance**, that is, which parts of the world they are used in. Often these are quite short lists compiled by individuals and published in pamphlets or in specialist journals or on the Internet. These comparatively short lists are **dialect glossaries** (such as the Exmoor Vocabulary by Devoniensis), and any student of dialect, with a bit of time, patience, and practice, can research and produce their own dialect glossary, thereby contributing to the lexicographical tradition in dialect study, **lexicography** being the making of dictionaries and glossaries. And there have been some great **dialect dictionaries** – great in the sense of LARGE, quite a few of them MONUMENTAL, as well as great in terms of their achievement. A glance at any of the bigger dictionaries, such as the 4700-page *English Dialect Dictionary* (1898–1905, edited by Joseph Wright), might provoke the fleeting thought that one would have to be a little *mazed* to take on such a task, in which case there have been a good number of mazed dialect lexicographers.

In dialect lexicography, then, the term *dictionary* usually refers to the larger projects, and *glossary* usually to the smaller in scale.

The investigation of vocabulary is a tradition in the study of dialects of English which can be traced back to the sixteenth century. This chapter and the next will tell the story of this tradition. We will negotiate the rich mass of surveys by looking at the main contributions, their motivations, methods, assumptions, and their achievements.

The term *dialect* itself is defined briefly in the Preface, yet a key theme of Chapters 1 and 2 is the very process by means of which the dialectal or regional became identified in the English language. We will be concerned with dictionaries and glossaries of regional dialect rather than with the treatment of dialectal items in other types of dictionary, although that issue is of some relevance here. Neither will we deal with the lexicography of slang, nor of occupational dialect and jargon, although the borders between these and regional dialect are sometimes quite blurry. We shall concentrate on works which themselves have concentrated on the regional in English **lexis** (vocabulary).

First, we will look at the origins and development of interest in English dialect words and idioms up until the mid nineteenth century, concentrating on Britain. Then we move on to the achievements of the late nineteenth century, a period which saw the culmination of immense activity in dialect lexicography, before (in Chapter 2) considering the twists and turns of the twentieth century and onwards (in Britain and across the English-speaking world) up to the present day. Running alongside this we will trace the evolution of the distinction between the *dialectal* or *non-standard* and the *Standard*, as in *Standard English*, a distinction substantially influenced by the work of lexicographers.

1.2   Early works: sixteenth century to late seventeenth century

From the late sixteenth century onwards there was a gradual identification and separation by lexicographers of the non-standard and the Standard in the English language, a process which climaxed in two massive, parallel projects in the second half of the nineteenth century: Joseph Wright's *English Dialect Dictionary* (*EDD*; 1898–1905), and the *Oxford English Dictionary* (*OED*; 1884–1933). The terms *non-standard* and *Standard English* themselves are comparatively recent labels, dating from 1913 and 1836, respectively, according to the *OED*, and lexicographers of dialect were instrumental in helping to construct the two categories. The labels are an outcome of the process of construction.

From its very beginnings in the fifth century AD, English has been a language characterized by geographical variety. The earliest recorded comment on the regional diversity of English was in a historical chronicle written in Latin in the first quarter of the twelfth century by the monk William of Malmesbury (1125; edition of 1870, p. 209), a passage which was used again at the end of the fourteenth century by John of Trevisa in his English translation of another chronicle, the *Polychronicon* (1387; edition of 1869, p. 163). This short passage criticizes the English spoken in northern England for its uncouth, strident, and incomprehensible nature to the ears of southerners, and it marks the beginnings of a discussion about the relative merits of different varieties of English that continues to the present day. From the end of the sixteenth century through the seventeenth and eighteenth, a general educated opinion arises which, while showing an interest in dialect, also demonstrates a distaste for local, provincial speech when measured against the cultured language of the

Seen as uncultured

higher classes in the south-east of England. This opinion informs an agitation during this time in favour of identifying a regularized, supra-regional, educated English to be used in formal and public contexts. Eventually this campaign becomes concerned not only with lexical and grammatical usage in writing and speech, but extends also to pronunciation, in that attempts are made to exclude provincial accents from definitions of the 'best' English. This 'best' English was eventually to crystallize around the concept of a *Standard English*.

But there is more to the pre-nineteenth-century interest in dialect than this developing opinion. We also see a curiosity about the history of English as the national language of England, a curiosity which necessarily incorporated an awareness of dialect, because in its essence English is characterized by regional diversity. One of the pioneers of the study of early English and of dialect vocabulary was the cleric Laurence Nowell (whose dates are *circa* 1515–70).

1.2.1   Laurence Nowell's *Vocabularium Saxonicum* (1565)

Nowell was an antiquary (a scholar of antiquities), with an interest in place names and in mapping the British Isles. In English studies he is known as the compiler of the *Vocabularium Saxonicum*, the first attempt at a dictionary of **Old English**. (The Old English period is the earliest in the history of the language, stretching from the fifth century to the early twelfth, and the term is often abbreviated to **OE**.) The *Vocabularium Saxonicum* is an unfinished manuscript, which remained unpublished until the edition prepared by Albert Marckwardt in 1952. It is likely that it was completed by about 1565, and was passed on by Nowell in 1567 to his pupil William Lambarde, a scholar and lawyer, who made additions to it. It was a major source for the first published dictionary of Old English, William Somner's *Dictionarium Saxonico-Latino-Anglicum* of 1659 (see Marckwardt, 1947, and 1952, p. 16). Nowell's *Vocabularium* is an early example of a citation dictionary, that is, it provides illustrative citations or quotations for many of the words defined. Nowell used a broad range of written sources from the Old English period, but he also drew upon his knowledge of the regional language of his own time, including in his dictionary 190 local words (the great majority from his native Lancashire) which had survived from Old English in local use but had dropped out of wider currency.

Wakelin (1977, p. 44) illustrates the etymological value of Nowell to dialect researchers (**etymology** being the study of the history and origins of words) by quoting the following entry from the *Vocabularium* (Marckwardt, 1952, p. 90):

Haȝan. Hawes. The frute of the white thorne or hawthorne. Lanc., hagges.

Wakelin points out that twentieth-century dialect forms of *haws* with a medial [g], such as *haigs*, *haggles* or *heagles*, and *haigins* recorded by the *Survey of English Dialects* (Orton and Halliday, 1963, p. 451), are difficult to trace back to the Old English form *haga*, because OE -*ag*- regularly leads to -*aw*- in modern English, in this case giving *haws*. However, the *Vocabularium* provides this -*g*- form above, *hagges*, from Lancashire for as late as 1565, suggesting the survival in regional English of a base form with **gemination** (that is, the doubling of an originally single consonant), **hagga*, from which we can postulate a derivation for the twentieth-century -*g*- forms.

Nowell's editor, Marckwardt (1952, pp. 10–13), recognizes the weaknesses in the *Vocabularium*, such as mistakes regarding Old English grammar, an ignorance of Norse influence, and even errors caused by Nowell's Lancastrian perspective – assigning incorrect meanings to OE words based on contemporary northern forms and meanings. But it should be remembered that the *Vocabularium* was an unfinished work, which nevertheless has assumed a greater importance as an information source for historians of the language in recent decades, because it remained unpublished for 400 years.

For Nowell, the significance of the local words he lists was in their direct lineage from Anglo-Saxon, or Old English as we now usually call it. Much of the major work on English dialect in Britain up until the mid-twentieth-century Survey of English Dialects is characterized by interest in the history of the language. For some scholars before Joseph Wright's *EDD* (1898–1905), the study of dialect was of interest *solely* because it offered a route to a greater understanding of early English and its writers.

1.2.2 Alexander Gil's *Logonomia Anglica* (1619)

Alexander Gil's *Logonomia Anglica* of 1619 includes the first attempt to characterize the main dialect areas of England (pp. 15–18). Written in Latin, it is not a dictionary, but the short section on dialects does list some features of regional English pronunciation, grammar, and vocabulary, such as the noun *witpot* meaning 'sausage' from the west of England (p. 17). Gil (1565–1635), a schoolmaster with an interest in devising a phonetic spelling system for English, identified six dialects: the Common or General, the Northern, Southern, Eastern, Western, and the Poetic. All six are listed under the heading *Dialecti* ('dialects'), though clearly only four are regional. The first refers to features in widespread use across the country, and the last to refined writing. The *Logonomia*, therefore, provides an early instance of the distinguishing of the regional and the supra-regional (literally, 'above the regional') in English.

Furthermore, like Edmund Coote in the spelling manual *The English Schoole-Master* (1596, p. 30), and Christopher Cooper in *The English Teacher* (1687, p. 77), Gil (p. 17) uses the term 'barbarous' to refer to provincial speech (actually *barbariem* in Gil), a term which by this period had the sense 'uncultured, uncivilized, unpolished'. (You will recall that Devoniensis also used it in 1746 to describe the Exmoor dialect.) Edmund Coote (1596, pp. 30–1), a headmaster in Bury St Edmunds, warns against the corruptive influence of local pronunciations on spelling, but in the process provides some interesting information on the contemporary East Anglian accent. The work of Gil, Coote, and Cooper contributes to that body of writing between the sixteenth and eighteenth centuries that argued that a standard variety of English (to use present-day terminology) was needed, and that it should be based on the usages of the cultured south-east. Gil and Coote also take part in the parallel process of identifying and constituting the dialectal. Or perhaps it would be more accurate to say that establishing the standard variety and constituting the dialectal are two aspects of the one process.

Martyn Wakelin, in his survey of 'The Treatment of Dialect in English Dictionaries' (1987, p. 157), points out that from early in the history of English lexicography scholars were attempting to differentiate words considered of lower and higher status, for example, between the 'vulgar' and the 'choicest' words as recorded in Henry Cockeram's *The English Dictionarie* of 1623, the first part of which listed the latter, and the second the former. Among the general dictionaries, Wakelin identifies (p. 157) Stephen Skinner's *Etymologicon Linguæ Anglicanæ* of 1671 and Elisha Coles's *An English Dictionary* of 1676 as the earliest in which a regional element (in the lower-status category) is openly acknowledged. The pattern that develops is of, on the one hand, dictionaries whose prime aim is to designate what we could call either the general or common or even core, and eventually standard, vocabulary of English, and which in doing so may identify a dialectal element, and then, on the other hand, dictionaries whose primary aim is to provide some kind of comprehensive list of dialectal vocabulary, distinguished from the general/standard.

The first attempt to achieve the latter on a national scale is John Ray's *A Collection of English Words Not Generally used*, published in 1674, and in an expanded second edition in 1691.

1.2.3   John Ray's *A Collection of English Words Not Generally Used* (1674)

Ray (1627–1705) was a naturalist, a member of the Royal Society (founded in 1645, and which gave an added impetus to the study of the English language), and already the author of *A Collection of English Proverbs* (1670). Ray based his *Collection of English Words* on his own observations while travelling and on those of several correspondents dotted about the country. The first edition is divided into two main sections: 'North Country words' (pp. 1–56), and 'South and East Country words' (pp. 57–80). The revised edition has the same division, but with each section considerably expanded, giving 121 pages overall. Both editions also contain a mixture of splendid supplements, such as the 'Catalogues of English Birds and Fishes' in the first edition and 'The Making of Salt at Namptwych in Cheshire' in the second. In the preamble 'To The Reader' in the first edition, Ray describes his material as 'Local words (for so I will take leave to call such as are not of general use)' found in 'the Language of the common people'. In a Postscript to the second edition (pp. 169–70), he adds:

> For I intend not this book to be a general *English* Glossary; (of which sort there are many already extant,) but only, as the Title imports, a Catalogue of such [words] as are proper to some Countries [that is, counties], and not universally known or used. (p. 169; spellings modernized)

Here, then, is a slightly different emphasis by Ray compared with commentators such as Gil. Ray certainly talks of the language of 'the vulgar' and 'the common people', but he is keen to identify its vocabulary in detail rather than to censure it. Here in Ray the local is being marked out as distinct from the general or countrywide. These are regional words with a limited provenance (place of origin or use), as opposed to words which in Ray's judgement are in common or widespread use across the land. This judgement is not straightforward to make, as Ray acknowledges in his Preface of 1691:

> These Gentleman [that is, some of his correspondents] being, I suppose North Country Men, and during their abode in the Universities or elsewhere, not happening to hear those Words used in the South, might suppose them to be proper to the North. The same error I committed my self in many Words that I put down for Southern, which afterwards I was advised were of use also in the North ...

It is not possible for Ray to know definitively which words are 'standard' and which are 'non-standard', for these concepts are not adequately formed at this stage, and the information necessary for their fuller development has not yet been sufficiently gathered. Ray at least had some advantage over his predecessors in that a rudimentary national postal service had started in 1635, but it goes without saying that there were as yet no railways nor any of the modern transport systems or communication media that facilitate such data collection in the present day. Ray and his fellow lexicographers of the sixteenth to nineteenth centuries were paving the way towards the concepts of 'standard' and 'non-standard' and gathering the initial information. These scholars were also pioneering the shape and structure of the dictionary format.

In Ray's *Collection*, an **entry** in its most basic form consists of the lexical item in italics, often preceded by either the definite or the indefinite article if a noun, or infinitival 'To' if a verb, and followed by the **gloss** (meaning). The provenance can be told from the heading of the section, that is, 'North Country' or 'South and East Country', and so is rather broad. Sometimes further detail is given, such as a county designation (for example, '*Cheshire*' or '*Chesh.*' or '*Cheshire, Lancashire*, &c [etcetera]'), or 'Var. Dial.' ('various dialects'), or, in apparent contravention of Ray's own rule, 'This is a general Word, common to both North and South.'

Sometimes a brief etymology is given, as in 'a word common to the ancient Saxon, High and low Dutch and Danish' (referring to 'A *Beck*: a small brook' (1674, p. 5)); and sometimes such information is given in Latin, with a reference to 'Skinner', that is, Stephen Skinner's *Etymologicon Linguæ Anglicanæ* (1671).

Great writers are occasionally cited; for example, the entry '*Yewd* or *Yod*: Went, *Yewing*: Going' (1674, p. 55), in the northern section, cites 'Yed, Yeden, Yode' from Chaucer, and quotes three lines from Edmund Spenser's *Faerie Queene*.

From time to time an entry includes a comment on variant pronunciations, or presents a number of sub-entries of items related in some way. For example, the long entry introduced by 'A *Bannock*; An *Oat-cake* kneaded with water only' (1674, p. 4), in the northern section, includes names for 'several sorts of Oaten Bread', and in the following order, *Tharcakes, Clap-bread, Kitchiness-bread, Riddle-cakes, Hand-hoven Bread,* and *Jannock* (pp. 4–5), of which only the last also has its own main entry later in the section.

Figure 1.1 below, showing two facing pages from the southern section, provides more illustration of the *Collection*.

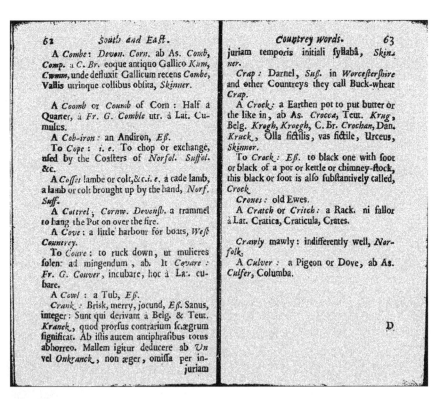

Figure 1.1   Sample pages from John Ray's *A Collection of English Words Not Generally Used* (1674).

Those among us who are a little picky about these things might criticize Ray's dictionary for not being wholly consistent or systematic in its typography and layout (for example, the alphabetical order of *S* is wayward at pages 114–15 of the 1691 edition), in the amount of information given about entries, and in the application of the criteria for inclusion of items. We should also note that his material was not gathered very systematically. But it is unreasonable to expect Ray to match the standards of modern descriptive linguistics. The *Collection* is the first major exploration of largely unmapped territory. Nobody previously had attempted to compile such a list on this national scale, and the *Collection* begins to lay the ground rules for identifying, organizing, and presenting the material. It became a key source and influence for dialect lexicographers for the next 200 years.

1.3   The growth of dialect lexicography: eighteenth century to mid-nineteenth century

From the first half of the eighteenth century, activity in the field of dialect lexicography in Britain (especially England) grows significantly, reaching a flood by the second half of the nineteenth century. Scores of dialect glossaries – works focusing on individual localities or regions – were produced during this time. Among the first, as identified by Wakelin (1977, p. 43), is Samuel Pegge's *Alphabet of Kenticisms* (1735–6; this is Samuel Pegge the elder (1704–96); his son, of the same name, was also a lexicographer). Among the later are William Barnes's *A Glossary of the Dorset Dialect with a Grammar of its Word Shapening And Wording* (1886), Frederic Thomas Elworthy's 900-page *The West Somerset Word-Book* (1886; now available in a free Kindle edition, in which you will find more information on *maze* and *mazed*), and Dartnell and Goddard's *Glossary of Words used in the County of Wiltshire* (1893). As early as 1844, Barnes (1801–86) had published a volume of poems in the Dorset dialect accompanied by a glossary of nearly a hundred pages (also now available in a Kindle edition), and he was a regular contributor to *The Gentleman's Magazine*. At the smaller end of the scale, and a century before in the same journal, are word lists of the Exmoor and Lancashire dialects in the August and October 1746 editions, respectively. In Figure 1.2 we see *Maz'd* in the list compiled by Devoniensis (a list whose purpose was to explain vocabulary from the popular dialect dialogues *The Exmoor Scolding* and *Courtship*, believed to have been composed by the Reverend William Hole (1741–91), archdeacon of Barnstaple), and in Figure 1.3 *Jannock* turns up again.

What are the reasons for this growth in activity?

For the most part it is a continuation and expansion of an existing trend, stimulated by the interest in English as a national language, and in discovering and recording its regional diversity and roots, but combined now with

Figure 1.2   *The Gentleman's Magazine*, August 1746 (Devoniensis, 1746), illustrating 'An Exmoor Vocabulary'.

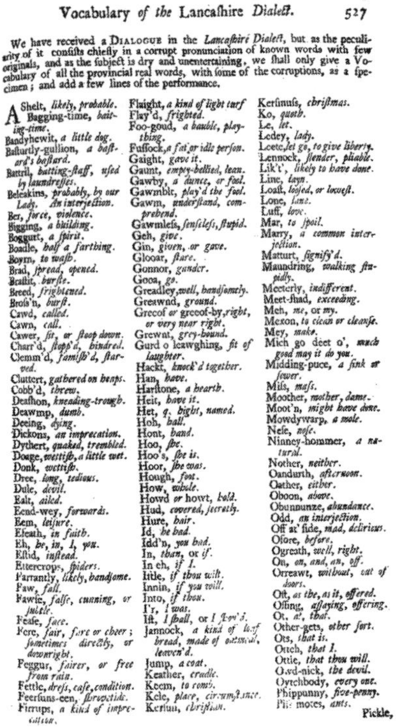

Figure 1.3   *The Gentleman's Magazine*, October 1746 (Bobbin/Collier, 1746b), illustrating 'Vocabulary of the Lancashire Dialect'.

the development of language study as a discipline in itself, and moreover a discipline with aspirations to scientific status. On 2 February 1786, the judge and scholar William Jones delivered an address to the Asiatic Society in Calcutta in which he made succinct remarks about similarities between an ancient language of the Indian subcontinent, Sanskrit, and several European languages. He postulated an original source language for this 'family' of languages, later named the **Indo-European** family, with the source known as **Proto-Indo-European**. With this address, Jones propelled forward a type of scholarship which became known as **comparative philology**, and which dominated language study in Europe in the nineteenth century. The comparative philologists investigated the histories of languages and the connections between these histories. In the case of English, this further consolidated in scholars' minds the importance of studying traditional regional dialects in the endeavour to uncover the early history of the language. (Comparative philology is also discussed in Chapter 4 of the present book.)

Moreover, Graham Shorrocks (2000, p. 86) states that, in addition to the long-existing antiquarian and nationalistic motivations, the industrialization and urbanization of parts of England in the nineteenth century created a market for dialect literature (particularly in Lancashire and Yorkshire) and gave an extra spur to dialect study. He also highlights the role of the clergy in promoting scholarly interest in local speech, as in the example of the Reverend William Gaskell, whose 'Two Lectures on The Lancashire Dialect' are appended to the fifth edition (1854) of Elizabeth Gaskell's novel of industrial Manchester life, *Mary Barton*.

During the course of the nineteenth century the study of dialect and the study of language generally in England and mainland Europe became more systematic. In English lexicography, two enormous projects are launched: the larger has become known as *The Oxford English Dictionary* (OED), and is still ongoing; the other, its sister project, was *The English Dialect Dictionary* (EDD), edited by Joseph Wright and published in six volumes from 1898–1905. Between John Ray and the peak of English dialect lexicography in the *EDD*, chronologically speaking, are another three lexicographers who attempted English dialect dictionaries with national coverage. These were Francis Grose (whose dates are *circa* 1731–91), James Orchard Halliwell (1820–89), and Thomas Wright (1810–77).

1.3.1   Francis Grose's *A Provincial Glossary* (1787)

Grose's *A Provincial Glossary, with a Collection of Local Proverbs and Popular Superstitions*, was published in 1787, a corrected edition following in 1790. I have also used an edition from 1839, titled *A Glossary of Provincial And Local Words used in England*, which incorporates further material collected by Samuel Pegge (the younger, 1733–1800). In the Preface to the 1839 edition (pp. iii–iv), several sources are named, including John Ray's *Proverbs*, 'Tim Bobbin's Lancashire Dialect' (Tim Bobbin is a pseudonym for John Collier, whose *A View of the Lancashire Dialect* first appeared in 1746), 'many of the County Histories', and *The Gentleman's Magazine*. (In fact, the *Magazine*'s 1746 piece on Lancashire dialect was extracted from Bobbin/Collier's *A View*, a work whose popularity can be gauged from Shorrocks's estimate (2000, p. 100) that it went through over one hundred editions. An online reproduction of an 1850 edition of *A View of the Lancashire Dialect* can be found at: http://gerald-massey. org.uk/bamford/b_tim_bobbin.htm. *A View* also exemplifies the practice which accompanies the glossary tradition, that is, the production of monologues and dialogues rendered in dialect, using spellings which attempt to mimic local pronunciations – a rather hit-and-miss process in the days before the invention of the International Phonetic Alphabet (IPA).) Grose's *Glossary* unites these sources 'under one alphabet', as he puts it (p. iii), augmenting them with 'many hundred words collected by the Editor in the different places wherein they are used', for Grose's military service 'occasioned him to reside for some time in most of the counties in England'. (As well as the military, Grose followed artistic and antiquarian pursuits.) 'Several Gentlemen, too respectable to be named on so trifling an occasion' (p. iv), also assisted. In its sources, therefore, Grose's dictionary is more widely ranging than Ray's, but by modern standards it is selective rather than comprehensive, and still not quite systematic.

As in Ray, a number of criteria are used in selecting the provincial and local words in Grose's *Glossary*. (As well as words of general provenance, Ray excluded occupational terms and newly coined London usages, believing that these last items would soon spread all over England.) Grose's provincial words, according to the Preface of 1839, are of three kinds: words which have become obsolete, through disuse and displacement by 'more fashionable terms', but which survive in counties 'remote from the capital, where modern refinements do not easily find their way' (p. iii); words of foreign origin which are hard to recognize as such, being 'so corrupted, by passing through the mouths of illiterate clowns' (p. iii); and 'mere arbitrary words' or 'ludicrous nominations' (p. iii), with very local origins, such as *Churchwarden*, meaning 'cormorant, shag', found in Sussex. Words which differed from those in 'common use' only in pronunciation 'were mostly rejected' (p. iv). *The Gentleman's Magazine* rejected some of John Collier's Lancashire material (1746) for the same reason (see Shorrocks, 2000, p. 87), and here apparently Grose follows the tradition of interpreting such forms as corruptions of 'standard' forms.

In Grose, several familiar threads reappear. Provincial speech is judged to be a repository of the archaic, and therefore the 'utility' of a provincial dictionary, 'universally acknowledged', is as an aid to understanding 'our ancient poets' (1839, p. iii). However, local speech is also quaint and crude in comparison with the 'common use'. The notion being referred to here seems to be metropolitan speech, which is seen as more cultured and more modern, and by implication more subject to change. Local speech is therefore both valued and ridiculed for its conservatism and for its narrowness of outlook. In all of this we see the continued cordoning off of the local from the emerging standard, a process now intertwined with an interest in revealing the history of the national language.

As for the *Glossary* itself, it has no sections or parts, but is one alphabetical list (of some 150 pages in its first edition, expanded to 188 pages by 1839). The basic entry consists of the **headword**, in capitals, followed by the gloss. Some entries have no indication of provenance; some use 'N', 'S', or 'W', to indicate the north, south, or west of England, there being no 'E' because the 'East country scarcely afforded a sufficiency of words to form a division' (1839, p. iv). A good many entries contain more specific designations, usually counties. Occasionally 'C' is used, meaning 'common', that is, a word 'used in several counties in the same sense' (1839, p. iv); very occasionally 'Var. Dial.', meaning 'various dialects', is used for much the same purpose. Entries are usually brief. By the time we get to the 1839 edition, basic etymological information has been occasionally added, and sometimes there are references to the usage of great writers, such as Chaucer and Shakespeare, or the reader is referred to earlier dictionaries, though these references can be very cursory, for example:

> ALE-STAKE, a may-pole. See Bailey's Dict.
> HIGHT, promised. Cumb. See Chaucer.

'Cumb.' is Cumberland; 'Bailey's Dict.' is a reference to Nathaniel Bailey's *An Universal Etymological Dictionary* (1721, to which a Volume II was added in 1727). Bailey's work is a general dictionary, but one which included a substantial dialectal element (this dialectal element was subsequently published in a separate work in 1883 by the English Dialect Society, edited by William E. A. Axon). Wakelin's (1987, pp. 164–5) commentary suggests that Bailey was not over-concerned to distinguish between the dialectal, the colloquial, and the obsolete, but his *Dictionary* nevertheless became an important source for dialect lexicographers. Figures 1.4 and 1.5 are from the 1787 and 1839 editions of Grose, respectively, each showing the final entries under the letter *C*.

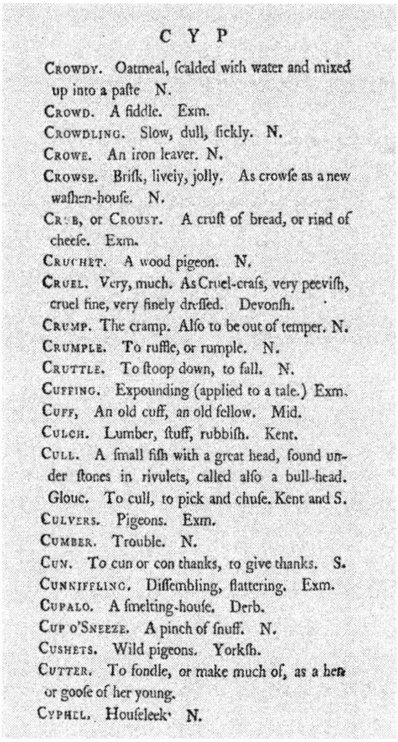

C Y P

CROWDY. Oatmeal, fcalded with water and mixed up into a pafte N.
CROWD. A fiddle. Exm.
CROWDLING. Slow, dull, fickly. N.
CROWE. An iron leaver. N.
CROWSE. Brifk, lively, jolly. As crowfe as a new wafhen-houfe. N.
CR B, or CROUST. A cruft of bread, or rind of cheefe. Exm.
CRUCHET. A wood pigeon. N.
CRUEL. Very, much. As Cruel-crafs, very peevifh, cruel fine, very finely dreffed. Devonfh.
CRUMP. The cramp. Alfo to be out of temper. N.
CRUMPLE. To ruffle, or rumple. N.
CRUTTLE. To ftoop down, to fall. N.
CUFFING. Expounding (applied to a tale.) Exm.
CUFF, An old cuff, an old fellow. Mid.
CULCH. Lumber, ftuff, rubbifh. Kent.
CULL. A fmall fifh with a great head, found under ftones in rivulets, called alfo a bull-head. Glouc. To cull, to pick and chufe. Kent and S.
CULVERS. Pigeons. Exm.
CUMBER. Trouble. N.
CUN. To cun or con thanks, to give thanks. S.
CUNKIFFLING. Diffembling, flattering. Exm.
CUPALO. A fmelting-houfe. Derb.
CUP O'SNEEZE. A pinch of fnuff. N.
CUSHETS. Wild pigeons. Yorkfh.
CUTTER. To fondle, or make much of, as a hen or goofe of her young.
CYPHEL. Houfeleek· N.

Figure 1.4 Some entries under *C* from Francis Grose's *A Provincial Glossary* (1787).

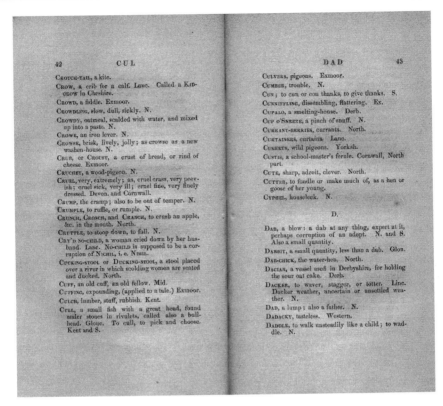

Figure 1.5 Some entries under *C* from Grose's *A Glossary of Provincial And Local Words used in England* (1839).

For those paying attention to our running examples, JANNOCK 'Oaten bread, made into great loaves', from the north, and of course MAZED from Exmoor both occur in the first edition of Grose. BECK or BEEK 'A rivulet or brook', from the north, is also present, as is HAGHES 'Hawes', but with no provenance given.

Despite the brevity of its entries, and the shortage of material from eastern England, Grose's *Glossary* provides fuller coverage than Ray's *Collection*, being compiled from a broader range of sources, as noted above. It can be criticized for its lack of precision in showing provenance and its seemingly haphazard selection of etymologies, but it has the merit of being clearly set out and very easy to use.

1.3.2   The Dictionaries of James Orchard Halliwell (1847) and Thomas Wright (1857)

Before we reach the *EDD*, we will look briefly at two smaller but nonetheless national-scale dialect dictionaries: James Orchard Halliwell's *A Dictionary of*

Archaic and Provincial Words, Obsolete Phrases, Proverbs, and Ancient Customs, From The Fourteenth Century (first published in 1847); and Thomas Wright's *Dictionary of Obsolete And Provincial English* (1857).

As Shorrocks (2000, p. 85) suggests, these titles in themselves amply demonstrate the close link that lexicographers of the time made between the ancient and the dialectal. The primary aim of both Halliwell (antiquary and literary scholar) and Thomas Wright (antiquary and historian) is to aid their readers' understanding of early English writers, by providing a guide to unfamiliar lexis – unfamiliar either because the words have become obsolete, or obsolete in all but local use. While neither Halliwell nor Wright treats any part of his task lightly, both believe that the importance of the provincialisms collected in their dictionaries lies in 'the illustration they afford of our early language' (Halliwell, 1874, p. vii – although I have used the second and eighth editions of Halliwell, from 1850 and 1874, respectively, the quote above is from the reprinted Preface to the first edition of 1847).

Both dictionaries have two volumes. They have very similar layouts: a capitalized headword, followed by the meaning, usually followed by one or more quotations from early writers within which the headword is italicized. Sometimes the geographical provenance, such as the county or regional name, is given before the quotations. Both regularly also provide very brief etymologies, with Wright consistently giving grammatical class after the headword (generally omitted from Halliwell). Sometimes there are references to earlier lexicographers. Halliwell's work, in addition to the dictionary, has a 27-page essay on 'The English Provincial Dialects' (1874, pp. ix–xxxvi). Both Halliwell and Wright acknowledge the assistance of several correspondents in compiling their dictionaries, including each other. In comparison with earlier dictionaries, we see greater depth of coverage (Halliwell (1847) claims to treat 51,027 words in 954 pages, while Wright's dictionary has 1039 pages) and a slightly more systematic treatment of items, but also we get a more definite sense of the secondary importance of the dialectal, as a means of acquiring knowledge of early English.

By the final quarter of the nineteenth century, pressure had built up considerably for a comprehensive dictionary of English dialect in Britain to be assembled. The imperatives that had existed fairly hazily for centuries had come into sharper relief, and English dialect lexicography now embarked on its most ambitious project. There was a reinvigorated interest in adding to and clarifying knowledge of early English, and a burgeoning clamour for deeper study of the traditional dialects of English, as the living archive of the national language. In addition, it became more necessary than ever to distinguish between the core, common, standard vocabulary of English and the regional.

1.4   The late nineteenth century: Joseph Wright and *The English Dialect Dictionary* (1898–1905)

The late nineteenth century saw a boom in comparative philology, which brought with it a greater intensity of interest in the histories and dialects of the languages of Europe. In the 1870s, one group of philologists in Germany, who were given the nickname '**Junggrammatiker**', or '**neogrammarians**', argued that historical sound or phonetic changes that earlier research had shown had occurred in the Indo-European family of languages could be described by means of exceptionless laws. In other words, these phonetic changes, once adequately described, would prove to be absolutely regular, systematic, and comprehensive. This controversial claim, which built on previous work on 'sound laws', further stimulated philological research. Overall the aim was to discover as much as possible about the early histories of languages and to test theories of linguistic change, and this amplified the need to identify, collect, and describe traditional rural dialects. (See Chapter 4 of the present book for more on this.) The first grand dialect atlas projects were begun in Germany and France in the final quarter of the century. In England, in 1842, the Philological Society had been established. This led, in 1864, to the founding of the Early English Text Society, which was followed in 1873 by the formation of the English Dialect Society, whose goal was to produce a national English dialect dictionary.

At its January 1858 meeting, the Philological Society's own Dictionary was formally proposed. As the project proceeded, the *Dictionary*, eventually to be known as the *Oxford English Dictionary* (*OED*), was shaped by two papers 'On Some Deficiencies in our English Dictionaries' delivered by Richard Chenevix Trench (1807–86), language scholar and Dean of Westminster, to the November 1857 meetings of the Society, and published in 1858 and in a second edition in 1860. Trench stated that provincial or local words 'have no right to a place in a Dictionary of the English tongue' (1860, p. 15), unless they were 'once current over the whole land', but 'have now fallen from their former state and dignity, have retreated to remoter districts, and there maintain an obscure existence still; citizens once, they are only provincials now'. He also urged (pp. 66–8) the editors of 'our older authors' to append glossaries to their editions, to assist the makers of the English Dictionary that he envisaged. This was a challenge taken up by the Early English Text Society, but Trench, and the *New English Dictionary* (as the *OED* was then known), also gave the dialect lexicography of English significant new momentum. The prominent scholar and key motivator in things philological in England at this time, W. W. Skeat (1835–1912), gives us a concise explanation:

> In compiling the vocabulary of words admitted into the *New English Dictionary*, it was often extremely difficult to know where to draw the

line. It has sometimes happened that a word which in olden times may fairly be said to have been in general use, or at any rate, in use over a large area, is now only heard in some provincial dialect, being unknown to nearly all the inhabitants of the rest of England; and, on the other hand, a word which was once used, as it would seem from the evidence, in one dialect only, has now become familiar to everybody. It follows from this that the collection of provincial words is absolutely necessary for completing the material with which the lexicographer has to deal; and hence Mr. [Alexander J.] Ellis and others suggested the establishment of an English Dialect Society. (Skeat, 1896, p. xxx)

Skeat wrote its prospectus and the English Dialect Society (EDS) was inaugurated at Cambridge in 1873, and with it the new philological discipline of **dialectology** in Britain. From its start, the overriding aim of the EDS was to produce an all-inclusive English Dialect Dictionary. The project was imbued with a sense of urgency, for it was felt that advances in transport (especially the rail network), the greater mobility of the population generally (as a result of the Industrial Revolution), and the expansion of the education system, would lead to a rapid erosion of the traditional dialects. Anxiety about the effects of social and technological change on regional dialects is a recurrent theme in dialect study, and many scholars down the decades have argued for urgent descriptive work as a response to this concern. Ironically, the improving transport system and postal service (trains began to replace horse-drawn coaches in the 1840s in the delivery of mail) aided the work of the nineteenth-century dialectologists. Technological advance has consistently facilitated the progress of research on dialects.

The second half of the nineteenth century saw these two massive projects underway, the basic aim of the *OED* at this time being to list, define, and tell the histories of the core, standard words of English, and that of the *EDD* being to list, define, tell the histories, and give the provenance of the dialectal words of British English.

During its short existence from 1873 to 1896, the EDS published 80 works in four series: bibliographies, reprinted glossaries (for example, a reprint of Ray in 1874), original glossaries, and miscellanies (Petyt, 1980, p. 77). The *EDD* would draw on these sources, as well as many others, such as county histories, accounts of industries (for example, mining), agricultural surveys, and natural histories (Wakelin, 1977, p. 46). Locating a suitable editor for the dictionary was a problem that took some time to be solved, and throughout the duration of the project, funding, and finding a publisher were also major difficulties – though all such problems are dwarfed by the actual task of compilation. In March 1876, the EDS moved to Manchester. In 1886, Skeat set up a new English Dialect Dictionary Fund, with an offshoot of the EDS now established to run the project. The Reverend A. Smythe Palmer became an interim editor, his task being to receive quotations from correspondents and arrange them for a future editor, with hundreds of helpers in all parts of the United Kingdom collecting new material. By 1887, it seems that Skeat had found his man. On 13 June of that year, he wrote a letter to Joseph Wright (1855–1930), which contained the following proposition:

> We hope to have some day a big Dialect Dictionary. Mr Palmer is provisional editor *pro tem*, for collection of material. But we want a good man for final editor. He should be a phonetician, a philologist, & shd. have some dialect knowledge. I cannot tell whether you consider it within your power or not. Do you think you could do it: & if so, will you undertake it? (As quoted in E. M. Wright, 1932, p. 353)

In her 1932 biography of her husband, Elizabeth Mary Wright suggests that Skeat might have known of Joseph because of his *A Grammar of the Dialect Of Windhill in the West Riding Of Yorkshire*. A very influential work in British dialectology, the *Grammar* was published by the EDS in 1892, but submitted to the Society some time before. Joseph Wright was born in Windhill in 1855, was illiterate until his teenage years, but then enjoyed an academic career of huge achievement. He trained as a philologist under the influence of the neogrammarian school in Germany, completing his doctorate at the University of Heidelberg in 1885. In 1891, he became deputy professor of comparative philology at the University of Oxford, eventually becoming a full professor in 1901. (J. R. R. Tolkien is probably Wright's most famous tutee at Oxford, and *The Lord of the Rings* is the most philological of fantasy works.) He wrote books on Middle High German, Old High German, and Gothic before taking on the *English Dialect Dictionary*.

Wright tackled the funding and publishing problems. The expense of putting out such a work, and the worry that the project was too huge to be completed, deterred publishers from making a full commitment. In the end, and astonishingly, Wright himself took on a big share of the responsibility. The Clarendon Press at Oxford provided him with the premises for a 'Workshop' at a nominal rent, and agreed to print the Dictionary, but, as the Preface to Volume I states (J. Wright, 1898, p. viii), the 'whole responsibility of financing and editing the Dictionary' rested with Wright. A subscription scheme helped cover the costs incurred.

As regards Wright's primary task, A. Smythe Palmer handed over in 1889 the materials collected under his interim editorship. This material consisted of 'slips', which were individual pieces of paper, like index cards, each with one dialect item on it, and giving such details as pronunciation, meaning, counties where the word was used, and citations. Wright calculated that these slips numbered over a million, and that he needed eventually at least twice this amount (E. M. Wright, 1932, p. 355).

The slips were fundamental to Wright's method. On each slip, all the information relevant to a dialect item could be gathered in the one place. All possible sources were to be scoured for items and illustrations of usage, including books and pamphlets in dialect, instances of dialect in general literature (fictive works, as well as guidebooks, county histories, journals, and newspapers), and all the known glossaries (E. M. Wright, 1932, p. 354). Wright sent out thousands of copies of a 'circular' describing the dictionary project and asking for help; he addressed public meetings; and he encouraged his helpers in the field to work together in local committees. The number of his voluntary helpers increased to over 600. In 1893, the EDS moved to Oxford, and Wright became its honorary secretary and literary director. In effect, it seems, the EDS was now synonymous with the dictionary project, and the Society was wound up in 1896. Wright prepared a *Phonetic Alphabet to be used by workers for the English Dialect Dictionary*, and reminded his helpers of the utmost need for careful and legible handwriting (E. M. Wright, 1932, pp. 360–1). Despite his professed interest in getting hold of the 'great deal of dialect which has never yet got itself printed' (reported in E. M. Wright, p. 358), Wright insisted that written authority was required to corroborate each meaning of a form (p. 359). The material from the sources and helpers went onto the slips, and the slips were sorted, edited, corrected, and checked by Wright and his assistants in the Oxford 'Workshop'. These slips formed the basis for the entries in the dictionary. See, for example, Figure 1.6, showing two slips for adverbial **DUFF**, and Figure 1.7, showing the corresponding extract from the *EDD* entries.

The title page of the first volume of *The English Dialect Dictionary* states that it is 'The complete vocabulary of all dialect words still in use, or known to have been in use during the last two hundred years.' This is a bold claim, and indicates the size of the task, and of the finished work. Published between 1898 and 1905 (though see the note in my Bibliography), *The English Dialect Dictionary* comprised six volumes, and nearly 4700 pages of entries. It is massive in comparison with any other dialect dictionary of British English. (With the exception of the online *Dictionary of the Scots Language* (http://www.dsl.ac.uk/), launched in 2004, which combines two earlier multi-volume works, *The Scottish National Dictionary* (Grant and Murison, 1931–76) and *A Dictionary of the Older Scottish Tongue* (Aitken et al., 1931–2002). Note that these works treat Scots as a language in its own right rather than simply as a dialect of English. There is more on Scots in Chapter 5 of the present book.) As Shorrocks (2000, p. 88) says:

One need only compare a few entries from *The English Dialect Dictionary* with entries in earlier dialect dictionaries to note a quite startling increase in systematicity, thoroughness and historical scholarship: the layout of the entries, the supporting quotations, the phonetics, the etymologies, etc.

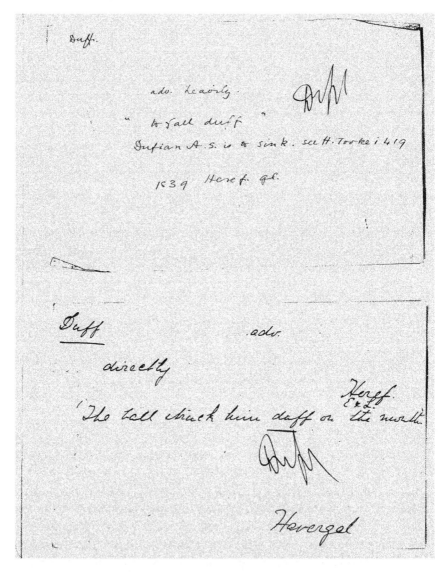

Figure 1.6 Two original slips used by Joseph Wright for the *EDD*. (With thanks to Clive Upton, who provided copies of the slips.)

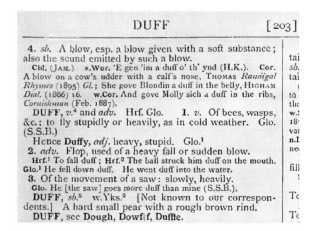

Figure 1.7   Extract from page 203 of the *EDD*, Volume II (1900).

Figure 1.8 is from pages 64–5 of Volume IV (1905), which include the lengthy entry for *maze*. Needless to say, *beck, haggle*, and *jannock* also feature in comprehensive entries, and we are reunited with *yewd/yod(e)* 'went, walked' and *weet-pot* 'sausage'. Like Gil (1619), who used the spelling *witpot*, the *EDD* says (Volume VI, 1905, p. 422) *weet-pot* is from the West Country of England, though is more specific, confining it to Somerset, and adding that although there is written evidence for the word, it was 'Not known to our correspondents'.

Each entry in the *EDD* has the headword in capitals and bold, followed by a grammatical classification. Related forms within the entry are also given in bold, as are cross-references to other entries. The grammatical class is followed by the geographical distribution of the item, giving abbreviations for counties or regions or even countries (for example, 'Sc.' for 'Scotland'). Then follows the meaning. If the item has more than one meaning, these are set out in numbered sub-entries. Variant forms and information on pronunciation are sometimes given, including phonetic transcriptions, alongside the provenance. Following the meaning are the citations from sources, which are sometimes indicated by abbreviations (county name in bold with a superscript number – a key to these is provided at the front of each volume, and Volume VI contained the full Bibliography). Often the entry finishes with etymological information accompanied by citations from literature and/or references to earlier lexicographers.

Since 2006, scholars at the University of Innsbruck have been making available an impressive online version of the *EDD*, at: http://www.uibk.ac.at/anglistik/ projects/speed/startseite_edd_online.html. The Innsbruck project presents the *EDD* anew as an accessible and invaluable searchable database: you can enter in the search-box the item that you are looking for, and if it is in the dictionary,

Figure 1.8 Entry for *maze* from *The English Dialect Dictionary*, Volume IV (1905, pp. 64–5).

the relevant headwords are listed. Via these, you can access the entries. The constituent parts of each entry are colour-coded to aid reading. See Figure 1.9.

The *EDD* is monumental, and without doubt much more systematic than its predecessors. It is, as Wright claims in his Preface, 'a "storehouse" of information for the general reader, and an invaluable work to the present and all future generations of students of our mother-tongue' (1898, p. v), a claim further justified by the electronic Innsbruck edition. It has, nevertheless, been the subject of criticism. Petyt (1980, p. 81) states that 'soon after its publication letters and articles began to point out areas which were undercovered and items which should have been included', but this surely is inevitable, given the nature of the object of study and the size of the task. Petyt adds (p. 81):

> It is not made clear whether items are still in use, and how common they are. And the locality references are far too imprecise: usually they only give the counties where the forms have been attested (or at best something like 'SWYks') and no details are given about who the actual speakers are. No maps are drawn, so the regional distribution of forms is not immediately obvious.

Figure 1.8 (*continued*)

Wakelin (1977, p. 47) makes the same point about the lack of precise geographical information, and also says that the etymologies are 'often suspect'. However, not all of this is reasonable. The precise information about localities and speakers was probably not consistently accessible in the material to hand, and the *EDD* did not aim to be a linguistic atlas. Set in context, the *EDD* represents a major advance. It remains a key work of reference for anyone interested in the history of the dialectal vocabulary of British English. Wright's management of his helpers foreshadows the role of trained fieldworkers in future large-scale dialect surveys; and his use of a reliable phonetic script runs alongside the development of the **International Phonetic Alphabet** (IPA), now a standard tool for all linguists (its first version was published in 1888, with stability achieved by the version of 1899). The twenty-first-century digitization project at Innsbruck testifies to the continuing relevance of the *EDD*. Manfred Markus, the director of the *EDD*'s computerization, says that 'Wright used an admirably precise and scholarly method of linguistic description, from phonetics to the citations' (2007, p. 4), and he stresses the *EDD*'s value as a record of the early part of the Late Modern English period in the history of

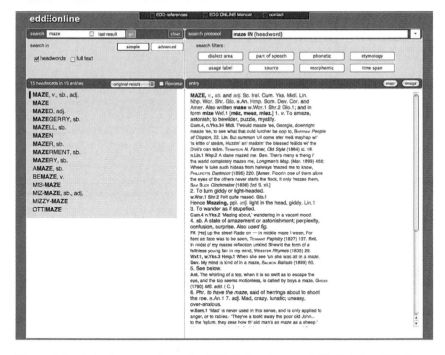

Figure 1.9   Entry for *maze* from the *EDD Online* (accessed 28 October 2016).

the language (1700 onwards) and as a resource for cultural historians as well as linguists. It says something about Wright's achievement that no individual since has attempted to compile an all-encompassing dictionary of dialectal British English. It would be enough to make one as 'maze-'eaded as a sheep' (see Figure 1.8).

1.5   Brief commentary on terms

In this chapter, I have introduced the term *dialectology*. According to the *OED*, the term was first used in English in a translation in 1820. Its first use proper in English appears to have been by Alexander J. Ellis in 1874, in an address he gave as president of the Philological Society. *Dialectology* remains today as the name for the academic discipline most concerned with the study of regional dialects. In its early years, the discipline was a branch of philology. Subsequently it has absorbed influences from several other fields, including anthropology, ethnology, geography, sociology, structuralist linguistics, and sociolinguistics, as you will discover in other chapters of the present book.

Resources and further reading

Studies in Lexicography (1987), a collection of essays edited by the renowned lexicographer Robert Burchfield, is a handy introduction to lexicography in general, but with a bias in its choice of topics towards historical and regional dictionaries, including a typically knowledgeable piece by the dialectologist Martyn Wakelin on 'The Treatment of Dialect in English Dictionaries'. A larger-scale and more recent overview is the authoritative two-volume *Oxford History of English Lexicography* (2009), edited by Tony Cowie, which includes my own essay on 'Dialect Dictionaries', a precursor to the present chapter. Both of these collections therefore offer valuable general context in which to appreciate the lexicography of English dialects. Another short appraisal of dialect lexicography is in Volume 1 of *Language and Space* (2010), edited by Peter Auer and Jürgen Erich Schmidt. This is 'Dialect Dictionaries – Traditional and Modern', written by Claudine Moulin. As well as providing a useful guide to German dictionaries that parallels the account above, the essay is an introduction to the historical development of methods and computerization in dialect lexicography. Two essays by the dialectologist Graham Shorrocks, 'Non-standard Dialect Literature and Popular Culture' (1996) and 'Purpose, Theory and Method in English Dialectology' (2000), give informative, concise commentary on many examples of dialect lexicography and dialect literature published in the period covered by the present chapter. For more detail and discussion on the making, impact, and continuing uses of the *EDD*, see the collection called *Joseph Wright's* English Dialect Dictionary *and Beyond* (2010), edited by Manfred Markus, Clive Upton and Reinhard Heuberger. In connection with this, see also the web-pages of the SPEED (Spoken English in Early Dialects) and *EDD* Online projects at Innsbruck University, where you will find a bibliography of publications on Wright and dialect lexicography by the projects' team members (https://www.uibk.ac.at/anglistik/projects/speed/publications/), including Markus and Heuberger. Ann Thompson's short 2008 article for the *Transactions of the Yorkshire Dialect Society*, 'Joseph Wright's Slips', illustrated with facsimiles, investigates the nine surviving boxes of index cards used in the compilation of the *EDD*. For a full account of Joseph Wright's remarkable life, see the biography (1932) written by his widow, Elizabeth Mary Wright, who herself had previously published the very readable survey of *Rustic Speech and Folk-Lore* (1913), one aim of which was 'to show that rules for pronunciation and syntax are not the monopoly of educated people', for 'Dialect-speaking people obey sound-laws and grammatical rules even more than we do' (p. iii). A century later, David Crystal revisited a selection of words from the *EDD* in *The Disappearing Dictionary* (2015), which has a companion interactive website that aims to update records of their survival: http://www.

disappearingdictionary.com/. Whenever possible – whether you are writing an essay or doing a project or simply because you are interested – it is always best to browse and read the original works alongside the secondary commentaries and introductions that interpret and explain the originals. Thanks to the Internet and digitization, the early works of English dialect lexicography are more accessible than ever before, often at no cost, via resources such as the Digital Public Library of America (DPLA), Forgotten Books, Google Books, the HathiTrust Digital Library, the Internet Archive, the Internet Library of Early Journals (ILEJ), Kindle, the Online Books Page, and Project Gutenberg. Explore these and your own digital library will soon contain treasures large and small, such as scans of the *EDD* volumes or Halliwell's *Dictionary* or Joseph Hunter's *Hallamshire Glossary* (1829) or Jacob Poole's *Glossary of Forth and Bargy*, Wexford, Ireland (1867) or Uncle Jan Treenoodle's (William Sandys) *Specimens of Cornish Provincial Dialect* (1846) or *The Gentleman's Magazine*, and so on. Especially useful is the Internet Archive's free download of Charles Sutton's *Catalogue of the English Dialect Library* (1880), which lists all the books belonging to the English Dialect Society up to the *Catalogue*'s publication. You can search for EDS Library items in the online catalogue of the Manchester Libraries: https://manchester.spydus.co.uk/cgi-bin/spydus.exe/MSGTRN/OPAC/BSEARCH?HOMEPRMS=GENPARAMS. See also Skeat and Nodal's 1877 *Bibliographical List* of works on English dialects. Further and higher education in the United Kingdom is also served by Jisc (Joint Information Systems Committee), in whose Historical Texts database you can find scans of John Ray's and Francis Grose's works, among many others. Take a look too at the *Promptorium Parvulorum*, the 1908 edition of which (by A. L. Mayhew) can be downloaded from the Internet Archive. The original was compiled by Geoffrey the Grammarian in the early fifteenth century. Although it is not a dialect dictionary but the first English-Latin dictionary, its list of English words is in the East Anglian dialect of its author.

2 Lexicography after 1900, and dialect grammars

> **This chapter includes the following:**
>
> - Account of the lexicography of regional English across the world, twentieth to twenty-first centuries.
> - Guides to the SED's *Dictionary and Grammar* (1994) and the *Dictionary of American Regional English* (1985–2014).
> - Introduction to descriptive grammars of dialectal English, nineteenth to twenty-first centuries.

2.1 Introduction

In this chapter, we look at what happened in the lexicography of English dialects after *The English Dialect Dictionary* was published (1898–1905), tracing developments through the twentieth century and on into the early twenty-first. It is quite a surprising story. I use it as a springboard to give also an account of research investigating the grammar of regional English, from the late nineteenth century (and including more works by Joseph Wright) to the present day. Examples and discussion of research on dialect grammar can be found in other parts of the present book (in Chapters 3, 4, 5, 10, and especially 7), as it has been a regular interest of scholars, but the second part of this chapter provides the overview of descriptive dialect grammars of English.

2.2 Lexicography after *The English Dialect Dictionary*

From some perspectives, not least Joseph Wright's, the publication of *The English Dialect Dictionary* meant that a major task had been completed once and for all, and in the nick of time. Wright believed that traditional 'pure dialect speech' was 'rapidly disappearing even in country districts, owing to the spread of education, and to modern facilities for intercommunication' (Wright, 1905c, p. vii; see also Wright, 1898, p. v), and that his work had been done 'none too soon'. The English Dialect Society (EDS) was dissolved in 1896, as the *English Dialect Dictionary* (*EDD*) reached fruition, its aim achieved, though its mantle was to an extent assumed by the Yorkshire Dialect Society, established in 1897 out of a committee formed three years earlier by Wright. The substantial English Dialect Library accumulated by the EDS (see Sutton, 1880) was deposited at the Central Public Library, Manchester, where it is still held in dispersed form. As the American dialectologist Raven I. McDavid, Jr., noted in 1968 (pp. 24, 44), the achievements in the late nineteenth century of Joseph Wright and another great pioneer of British dialectology, A. J. Ellis (see my next chapter), for a while stood in the way of further large-scale work in England, because of a belief that the job had been done. Things were different in Scotland, where a wave of dialect lexicography in the early twentieth century led to the publication in 1931 of the first volumes of *The Scottish National Dictionary* (Grant and Murison, 1931–76) and the *Dictionary of the Older Scottish Tongue* (Aitken et al. 1931–2002), now combined into the online *Dictionary of the Scots Language* (*DSL*). At the same time in the United States, the focus of dialect scholars was also mainly directed towards lexicography. But when the next series of national dialect surveys in Britain got underway in the mid twentieth century, they rather parted company with the dictionary format, with the foremost English dialectologist of the time, Harold Orton, explicitly rejecting it for his Survey of English Dialects (SED). Nevertheless, as we shall see in this chapter, the twentieth century saw great productivity in research into the dialectal vocabulary of English. As things turned out, the *EDD* is both the culmination of 300 years of dialect lexicography and an inspiration for many subsequent projects in Britain and beyond up to the present day. Major dictionaries of non-standard English continued to be produced, and the old custom of smaller-scale glossarial works has carried on vigorously. Before my overview of this abundance of work, we look briefly at why Harold Orton thought that the days of the national dialect dictionary were over.

2.2.1 The Survey of English dialects: no more dictionaries any more

In his lecture *Dialectal English and the Student*, delivered to a meeting of the Yorkshire Dialect Society on 11 May 1946, Harold Orton said that, 'The time is ripe for one more, and possibly the last, co-ordinated, large-scale investigation of all the important English dialects' (1947, p. 2). He gave a short summary of scholarly work in England on dialectal English (pp. 2–3), before settling into a review of dialect dictionaries:

The 'dialect dictionaries' ... mostly reveal only the lexical peculiarities of vernacular English. Further, the earlier ones recorded only the forms and meanings that differed from standard usage. This was unfortunate: for the criterion – whether or not the word occurs in the standard language – is indeed irrelevant. Nowadays, a dictionary of local dialect to be adequate, must certainly include all the words in current use – not only those not in Standard English, but also those that do appear in Standard. The dictionary should aim at completeness, all the words, not merely the unusual, the strange.

(Orton, 1947, pp. 3–4)

Orton in 1946 eschews the dictionary as the goal of the national survey of English dialects that he has in mind – a survey which will describe the **sound systems**, **morphology** (word structure), and **syntax** (sentence structure) of English dialects, and which will also offer the kind of 'complete' picture of vocabulary suggested above (p. 4). On the face of it, this looks like an impossibly ambitious vision. But Orton had something specific in mind. He said (1947, p. 4): 'a dictionary is hardly the best method of presenting this information. Indeed, it would be far best conveyed by means of maps.' The outcome of his survey was to be a linguistic atlas. 'What is now wanted', said Orton (p. 5), 'is a "dialect atlas" of English.' He was conscious that in this respect England was lagging behind other countries in Europe and North America, and that the atlas format had the advantage that it 'shows the distribution of the different vernaculars in a speech area' and enables comparison of 'the distribution of certain test words and phrases over the whole speech unit' (p. 5).

Orton's survey was the Survey of English Dialects (SED), carried out from Leeds University, and his ambition to produce a linguistic atlas of England was realized in the 1970s. Most of the data for the SED was collected by fieldworkers in the 1950s. The 'completeness' that Orton talked of in 1946 with respect to vocabulary was completeness as applied to 'certain test words' rather than to the whole lexis of all the dialects. That is to say, the SED targeted a large (for a dialect survey) but nevertheless very select (compared with the whole non-standard and standard vocabulary of English) list of 'notions' and harvested the words which were used across the country for each notion. For example, for the notion 'slice (of bread)', and by means of face-to-face interviews between fieldworkers and local informants, the SED in total collected the following lexical variants: *bit, butty, hunch, hunk, junk, morsel, piece, round, roundel, shive, slab, slash, slipe, slishe, slithag, slither, square, stull* (Upton, Parry and Widdowson, 1994, p. 370). In this way, one gains a complete set of the words used for each notion, and a map can be produced showing the regional/geographical distributions of the lexical variants across the whole territory. A map could also give information about each word's etymology and its use by different groups of speakers (female, male, older, younger, rural, urban, as well as ethnic groups, and so on). The SED did not, in fact, investigate a wide spectrum of social groups. Orton and his team focused on the speech of the rural elderly age-group, with a historical emphasis much influenced by the philological concerns we witnessed in Chapter 1. While an atlas can thus give a rounded view of **'systems'** of vocabulary, pronunciation, and grammatical notions, realistically (even in the digital age) it cannot easily deal in such a 'systemic' way with the kind of comprehensive list of dialect words that the *EDD* achieved.

As for the apparently impossibly ambitious vision of a complete descriptive inventory of non-standard and Standard English vocabulary, this has become the aim of the ongoing third, and online, edition of the *Oxford English Dictionary* (*OED*).

We dwell some more on the SED, its methods, aims, and history, in Chapter 5 of this book, for it is there that we consider the twentieth-century linguistic atlases of English. And let us note at this point that the description of dialectal vocabulary was one of the interests of the national linguistic atlases which began to appear from the late nineteenth century onwards (see Chapter 3). However, one reason the SED is mentioned here is because of Orton's veto of the dialect dictionary format for the Survey, which to date is indeed the last large-scale study of its kind in England, with the possible exception of the BBC's *Voices* survey of 2004–5. Another reason is that, ironically, one of the last major publications of the SED was *Survey of English Dialects: The Dictionary and Grammar* (edited by Clive Upton, David Parry and John Widdowson, 1994).

2.2.2   *Survey of English Dialects: The Dictionary and Grammar* (1994)

As the Introduction (pp. 3–7) to the *SED Dictionary and Grammar* emphasizes, it is not a conventional dictionary, depending entirely as it does on the Survey's *Basic Material* series of 12 data-volumes (Orton et al., 1962–71), which reproduce all the responses to all the 1300-plus items of the questionnaire used by the fieldworkers for their interviews with local informants. Some 730 of the questions were aimed primarily at collecting lexis (Orton, 1962, p. 15). The SED *Dictionary*, therefore, is a re-presentation of the Survey's lexical database. It is not (like the *EDD*) a 'complete vocabulary of all English dialect words which are still in use' (Wright, 1898, p. v). It is perforce 'an alphabetical listing of the wealth of regional vocabulary' (Upton, Parry and Widdowson, 1994, p. v) which realizes the semantic notions (and only those notions) covered by the Survey's questionnaire.

The idea of a dictionary of the SED was mentioned as early as January 1969 (Keil, 1969), and the project gradually developed in the 1970s and early 1980s under the guidance of Stewart Sanderson of the Institute of Dialect and Folk Life Studies at Leeds University, before it was taken over by the editors. (The main topic of the meeting in 1969 reported by Keil and led by Harold Orton was the computerization of the SED data, an undertaking which was still being discussed fairly unfruitfully throughout the lifetime of the dictionary venture.) The first task was to transfer vocabulary items from all the *Basic Material* (*BM*) to a substantial number of index cards. In the *BM*, these variants are listed according to region and individual locality, and under the heading of each SED notion and question. For example, *Slice* is the notion for question V.6.10 'What do you call the thin piece you cut from the loaf [of bread] with a bread-knife?' Under this heading, then, are the lexical variants obtained in response to the question in each of the 313 localities in the SED network. In the *BM* volumes, the SED localities are divided into four regions: Northern, West Midlands, East Midlands, and Southern, giving us Volumes I–IV, respectively, each volume consisting of three parts, and each part containing a third of the questionnaire and its responses. The index cards were the first stage en route to reordering the dialectal lexis into a single alphabetical list. This first stage was a year-long task of some endurance for a youthful lone research assistant working in the Harold Orton Research Room at Leeds. I know, for I was that research assistant.

Funding was provided by the publishers Croom Helm, but it was not until 1994 that the *Dictionary and Grammar* appeared (published in the end by Routledge), after the project had moved from Leeds to the Centre for English Cultural Tradition and Language run by John Widdowson at the University of Sheffield. Figure 2.1 shows two facing pages from the SED *Dictionary*.

sledder

cart-wheel could slide to prevent the cart from going backwards or too fast on a hill, ⇐ PROP/CHOCK I.11.2. sleːd Nf, sleˡd Nf
3. *n* a DRAG used to slow a wagon I.11.3. sled La Nt L Nf
sledder *n* a DRAG used to slow a cart I.11.3. sledə Db
sledge *1. n When in winter you can't use a cart with wheels, what do you use for carrying heavy loads?* I.9.1. slidʒ Ess Sx, zlidʒ D, sledʒ L, sledʒ Nb Cu Du La Y Ch Db Sa St[*flat bottom, iron skids, same shape as cart*] He Wo Wa Mon Gl O Nt L Lei R Hu C Nf Sf Bk Bd Hrt Ess So Brk K Do Sx. sledʒ Mon O So W Co D Do Ha, ʒledʒ Ha, slɛdʒ Ess So Sr, sledʒ D, stadʒ So, stadʒ Ha, staidʒ D. ⇒ **coop, drag, dray, drug, ground-car, ground-cart, skid(s), slead** ⇒ **sled, sled, sleigh, slide** ⇒ **sled, trail-cart**
2. *n* a DRAG used to slow a wagon I.11.3. sledʒ Nb Cu La Y L
sledge-roof chamber* *n* a BEDROOM in the gable of a house V.2.3. sledʒauf tʃɛˈambə L
sleeper *1. n* a railway sleeper, used as the CURB-STONE in a cow-house I.3.9. slipəˡz Ess
2. *n* a tree STUMP IV.12.4. sleːtəpˀə Nf
sleigh *n* a SLEDGE used to carry loads in winter I.9.1. sleː Ch La[*none locally*], sleɪ Y[*none locally*], sleɪ Ch, *pl* sieːɪz L, ʒleɪ D, zleɪ D
slender *vt* to THIN OUT turnip plants II.4.2. slendəˡ La
slew *1. n* a DRAG used to slow a wagon I.11.3. sɪvː Co
2. *n* on the slew DIAGONALLY, referring to harrowing a field IX.1.8. ɒn ðə sluː K
slewed *n* ASKEW, describing a picture that is not hanging straight IX.1.3. slˀuːd Du; on a slew ɒn ə sluː Y
slewing *v-ing* THROWING a stone VIII.7.7. sluːɪn So [*queried SBM*]
slew-ways-on *adv* DIAGONALLY, referring to harrowing a field IX.1.8. sluweəzɒɪə Y
slice *1. n What do you call the thin piece you cut off from the loaf with the bread-knife?* V.6.10. Eng. ⇒ **bit, butty, hunch, hunk, junk, morsel, piece, round, roundel, shive, slab, slash, slipe, slish** ⇒ **slishe, slishe, slither, sliver, slysh** ⇒ **slishe, square, stull;** ⇒ also **knot, slive**
2. *n* a CUTTING of hay II.9.15. slɒɪs So, slɒɪs So
3. *n* a SHOVEL for a household fire V.3.9. slaɪs Gl
slices *npl* the horizontal BARS of a gate IV.3.6. slaɪsɪz Y[*excluding top bar xl*]
slick *adj* SLIPPERY VII.6.14. slɪk He Mon Gl, sɪɪk Gl
slick-board *n* a PASTE-BOARD V.6.5. slɪkbɔːɪd Gl
slicking *vt-ing* PUTTING your tongue OUT VI.5.4. slɪkn Man

slid *1. n* a DRAG used to slow a wagon I.11.3. slɪd Nf, slʊd Nf
2. *vi* to SLIDE VIII.7.1. slɪd Y
slide *1. vi When children find the footpaths or the playground covered with ice, they will at once begin to ...* VIII.7.1. Eng exc. We. ⇒ **glirry, shirl, skid, skidder, skirl, skirr, slare, slid, slide about, slider, slire, slip, slither, slur, slur about**
2. *n* the SOLE of a horse-drawn plough I.8.9. slɛɪd Sa, slɛɪd D, slɛɪd So Sr, slɔɪd Lei Ess K, slɒɪd St Wo, slɑɪd Wa L Lei Sf, slaɪd Brk
3. *n* a chock chained to a cart, which could be placed behind and under a wheel to prevent the cart from going backwards on a hill, ⇐ PROP/CHOCK I.11.2. slaɪd Mon
4. *n* a DRAG used to slow a cart I.11.3. sleˡd Nf, slaɪd Nth Hu C Bk Bd Hrt, slɔɪd Wa Gl O Sf Hrt Ess, slaɪd Wa Sf Ess, slɒɪd He Mon Gl, slɑɪd Mon
slider *1. n* a DRAG used to slow a wagon I.11.3. slaɪdəˡ Bk, slɒɪdəˡ Bk
2. *vi* to SLIDE VIII.7.1. sɪaɪdəˡː Co
sliding swivel *n* a sliding RING to which a tether is attached in a cow-house I.3.5. slɔɪdɪn swɪvɬ Ess
slight *adj* ILL, describing a person who is unwell VI.13.1(b). slɪt Co
slike *1. vt* to TOP AND TAIL swedes II.4.3. slaɪk Sa
2. *adj* SLIPPERY VII.6.14. slaɪk He, slɔɪk He
sling *1. n* the STRETCHER between the traces of a cart-horse I.5.11. slɪŋ Ess
2. ?pl/pppl to slip a calf, ⇐ SLIPS THE CALF III.1.11. slaŋ Sx
slinger *1. n* a FARM-LABOURER I.2.4. *pl* slɪŋəˡɪz Co [*queried u.r. SBM*]
2. *n* the HANGING-POST of a gate IV.3.3. slɪŋə Man
slingers *n* BROTH V.7.20(a). slɪŋəˡɪz So D
sling-gear-horse *n* a TRACE-HORSE I.6.3. slɪŋɪaɪns Db
slinging *v-ing* THROWING a stone VIII.7.7. slɪŋɪn Y K
sling(s) *n* a SWINGLE-TREE of a horse-drawn plough harness I.8.3.
ʒg: slɪŋ Ess
slɪŋ Ess
·ɪ: slɪŋz Sf
slings *npl* BRACES VI.14.10. slɪŋz Co
sling-tit *n* a TRACE-HORSE I.6.3. slɪŋtɪt Db
slink *1.1. v* to slip a calf, ⇐ SLIPS THE CALF III.1.11. slɪŋk Co; slunk slaŋk K[*before 7 months*]
1.2. vt to slip a calf. slɪŋk Ch K. -*ed* slɪŋkt K; slanked slæŋkt K
2. *vi* referring to a cow, show signs of calving by changes in the pelvic region, ⇐ SHOWS SIGNS OF CALVING III.1.12(b). -*ed* slɪŋkt K Sx, *ppl* ɒːl slaŋk K

Figure 2.1 Sample pages from the *Survey of English Dialects Dictionary and Grammar* (1994, pp. 370–1).

slip

3. vt to SLIP A FOAL III.4.6. slɪŋk K, *-ed* slɪŋkt K
4. n RUBBISH V.1.15. slɪŋk La
5. vi to SPOIL, referring to meat or fish V.7.10. slɪŋk St
slink-butcher *n* a KNACKER III.11.9. slɪŋkbutʃə Db
slink-chap *n* a KNACKER III.11.9. slɪŋktʃap La
slink-dealer *n* a KNACKER III.11.9. slɪŋkdɪələ La
slink-fellow *n* a KNACKER III.11.9. *-s* slɪŋkfɛləz Y
slinkings *n* the AFTERBIRTH that comes from a cow's uterus after a calf is born III.1.13. slɪŋkɪnz K
slinkman *n* a KNACKER III.11.9. slɪŋkmɒn St
slip *1. v* slips the calf *When the cow calves before her time, you say she ....* III.1.11. ⇒ aborted, calved a dead calf, calved before her time, calves before her time, cast calf, cast-calve, cast her calf, casts, casts a calf, casts her calf, casts it, draws her calf, throw, had a slip, has a-warped, has calved before time, has cast, has casted her calf, has cast her calf, has come down before her time, has come down early, has had a slip, has picked, has picked calf, has picked her calf, has picked it, has slipped, has slipped calf, has slipped her calf, slipped it, has slipped the calf, has strat her calf, has stratied calf, has throwed her calf before her time, have slipped her calf, is out of breaking, jacked, pick, pick calf, pick-calved, picked, picked calf, picked her calf, picks, picks a calf, picks calf, picks her calf, picks it, picks its calf, pitched her calf, slanked calf ⇒ slink, slinked her calf, slinked it, slinked the calf, slink her calf, slip calf, slip-calve, slip-calved, slip her calf, slipped, slipped calf, slipped her calf afore time, slipped it, slipped the calf, slips, slips a calf, slips calf, slips her calf, slips him, slips the calf, slung the calf ⇒ sling, slunk ⇒ slink, throwed her calf, warped, warped her calf, warped the calf
2. v to slip a foal *What do you say if the mare gives birth before the proper time?* III.4.6. ⇒ came before time, cast a colt, cast a foal, cast her colt, cast her foal, cast the foal, come down before time, drop a foal, dropped, drop the foal, fling her colt, foal before her time, foaled before her time, foaled before time, had a misfluke, had a slip, has aborted, has a-foaled before her time, has a-slipped foal, has cast a foal, has cast her colt, has cast her foal, has cast it, has dropped her colt, has foaled before her time, has foaled before time, has picked a foal, has picked her colt, has slipped, has slipped a foal, has slip her foal, has slipped a foal, has slipped before time, has slipped colt, has slipped foal, has slipped her foal, has slipped the colt, has strat her colt, has strat her foal, has throwed a colt, has throwed her colt, has throwed the colt, have a slip, he came before his time, it came before time, pick, pick a foal, picked the foal,

pick-foal, pick foal, pick her foal, pick its colt, pick its foal, pick the foal, slink a foal, slinks her foal ⇒ slink, slink it ⇒ slink, slip, slip a colt, slip-foal, slip foal, slip her colt, slip her foal, slip its foal, slipped, slipped a colt, slipped colt, slipped foal, slipped her colt, slipped her foal, slipped the foal, slipping her colt, slip her foal, slip the foal, slip that there foal, slip the colt, slip the foal, slip their foal, throw a foal, throw a foal early, throwed her foal, throw her foal, to cast her colt, warp, warped, warped her colt, warped the foal, warp her foal
3. n a PIGLET III.8.2. slɪp So, slɪp W
4. n a TETHER for a cow I.3.4. slɪp Nf K
5. n a chain tether. slɪp Nf
6. n a tether made of rope or chain. slɪp Nf
7. n a leather tether. slɪp Nf
8. n a bridle for a cow, to which a tie or tether can be clipped. slɪp Nf
9. n a HALTER for a cow I.3.17. slɪp Nf
10. n a TETHERING-ROPE used to tie up a horse I.4.2. slɪp St L Nf K Sx, *pl* slɪps Sa *[queried irr. WMBM]*
11. n the SOLE of a horse-drawn plough I.8.9. slɪp Nf Sf, slɪp D
12. n a movable horizontal rod stretching between the shafts of a cart, fixing them to the cart-body and stopping the cart from tipping, ⇐ ROD/PIN I.10.3. slɪp Cu
13. n a movable iron hoop that slides along a cart-shaft and couples it to the projecting end of the beam on which the cart-body rests, ⇐ ROD/PIN I.10.3. slɪp Cu Du Y
14. n a DRAG used to slow a wagon I.11.3. slɪp L
15. vi to SLIDE VIII.7.1. slɪp Ess *[marked u.r. EMBM]*
16. v to REMOVE STALKS from currants V.7.24. *-ing* slɪpɪn Sx
17. n a decorative APRON V.11.2(b). slɪp C
18. n a NECKERCHIEF VI.14.4. slɪp Do
slip-block *n* the CLOG on a horse's tether I.4.3. slɪpblɒk? Nf
slip-chain *n* a chain used to tie up a horse, ⇐ TETHERING-ROPE I.4.2. slɪptʃeɪn Nt
slip-coat cheese* *n* a kind of cream CHEESE V.5.4(b). *-s* slɪpkʊət tʃˈiːz L
slipe *1.* n a PADDOCK I.1.10. slaɪp C
2. n the MOULD-BOARD of a horse-drawn plough I.8.8. slaɪp Y, slaɪp Y
3. n the SOLE of a horse-drawn plough I.8.9. slaɪp D, slaɪp Y, slaɪp Y Db L, slaɪp Db Nt L Lei R Nth, slaɪp L
4. n a CUTTING of hay II.9.15. slaɪp So, slaɪp

Figure 2.1   *(continued)*

Figure 2.1 shows the layout of the *Dictionary* and the special nature of its material. The first entries at the headwords **sledge**, **slice**, and **slide**, and the first two at **slip**, are 'core' entries, that is, the headword, in bold, is also a notion sought by an SED question, which is reproduced in italics following the headword. Such headwords are from Standard English. Following the number of the question (taken from the SED *Questionnaire* designed by Eugen Dieth and Harold Orton, first published in 1952, and in its sixth and final version in 1962) is a list of the chief variant pronunciations of the headword, in phonetic script, with their regional distribution indicated by abbreviations of the English county names. The editors chose not to list the finer details of phonetic transcription and networks of localities within each county, arguing that these 'would overwhelm the text by their length and complexity' (p. 6), and pointing out that such details are available in the *BM* volumes. This list is followed by another (in bold) which cross-refers to all the other (and generally non-standard) variants obtained in response to the same Dieth-Orton question, each of which is also a headword elsewhere in the *Dictionary* (except for those in italics, most of which are subsumed under other variants). The list under **sledge**, for example, includes **sleigh**, which also appears as a headword in Figure 2.1. This, like the majority of entries, is an 'ordinary' entry. Its meaning is supplied in part by reference to the Dieth-Orton notion (SLEDGE). As with core entries, pronunciations and provenance are given, but the chief cross-reference is to the core entry. Grammatical classifications are given at the start of each entry, and sometimes additional secondary commentary is provided in italics between square brackets. An asterisk indicates an item overlooked for one reason or another in the original *BM* lists.

Figures 2.2–2.6 explain the *Dictionary* and the Survey further by detailing the journey of an item, in this case the noun **circle**, in the sense 'halo round the moon', from field interview to *SED Dictionary* entry. Figure 2.2 is a single page from the Dieth-Orton *Questionnaire* which contains, at Book VII, Section 6, Question 4, the following: 'What can you sometimes see round the moon?' and the notion sought, **Halo.**

Figure 2.3 is a single page from the on-the-spot field-transcription by the fieldworker Michael Barry for the locality of Firle in Sussex of an interview done on 24 June 1959, showing at top left Barry's phonetic rendering of the informant's response of *circle* to question VII.6.4.

Figure 2.4 is a single page from Part III of Volume IV: *The Southern Counties* of the *SED: Basic Material* (Orton and Wakelin, 1968, p. 871), showing in phonetics all the recorded responses in the south of England localities to VII.6.4, including at bottom right the same response (though with slightly adjusted transcription) for Firle, that is, locality number 40.6.

Figure 2.5 shows the same response (with an adjusted final phonetic symbol) at the end of the (ordinary) entry for **circle** in the *SED Dictionary*, and Figure 2.6 shows the core entry of **halo**, which includes a cross-reference to **circle**. The modifications to the phonetic transcription of **circle** are superficial only. The stages illustrated here also tell us a few other things about the SED (also of use when you read Chapter 5, section 3.2 of the present book).

First, note that the notions or keywords, in bold, sought by the questions in Figure 2.2 are of four kinds: lexical, simply in bold, for which the local vocabulary variants were sought; phonological, followed by an asterisk, for which local pronunciations of the keyword were required; morphological, followed by a dagger symbol, seeking information on word structure, as at VII.6.2, where either a singular or a plural form might be elicited; and syntactic, followed by a vertical line with two bars, seeking information on phrase or sentence structure, as at VII.5.3, 5, and 6. The questions are in two styles: either 'naming' questions, some of which begin with three stops, which stand for 'What do you call' or 'What's your word'; or 'completing' questions, which end with three stops, which tell the fieldworker to pause and allow the informant to complete the sentence. A square symbol, as at VII.5.3, means that a picture or other visual aid was to be shown to the informant. In short, and remembering

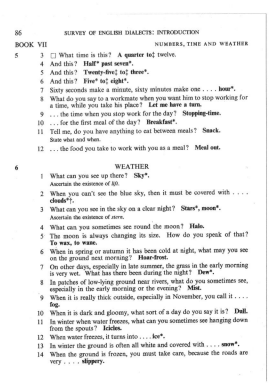

Figure 2.2   A single page from the SED *Questionnaire*, showing question VII.6.4 **Halo** (taken from the reprint of Dieth-Orton in Orton, 1962).

that the final version of the questionnaire had a total of 1322 questions, this was a highly thought-out, extensive apparatus designed to gather a wealth of material across a range of linguistic levels while doing its utmost to avoid overly conditioning or influencing the informants' choice of response.

The Introduction to the SED's *Linguistic Atlas of England* records that 'the questionnaire responses yielded a harvest of over 404,000 items of information' (Orton, Sanderson and Widdowson, 1978, no page number). These items were published in the *Basic Material* volumes, which, as exemplified by Figure 2.4, give the total number of variants of each notion across each region (the south in the case of Figure 2.4) in ordinary orthography first, and then in fine phonetic detail for each locality in the network.

The intervening stage is the field-transcription, and Figure 2.3 shows the standard form used by the SED fieldworkers (and by the fieldworkers for the SED's sister project in Wales, the Survey of Anglo-Welsh Dialects (SAWD)) to record the informants' speech during the interviews. Along the top are the basic details of names and dates. In the left-hand half of the form are boxes in which the fieldworker transcribed in the International Phonetic Alphabet the informant's

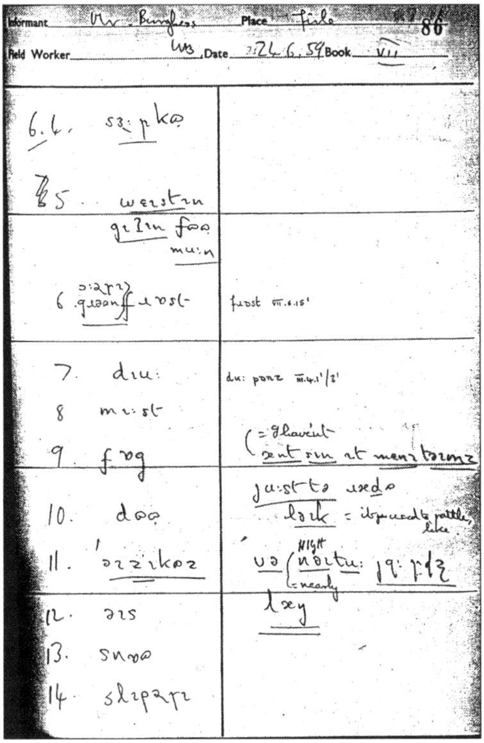

Figure 2.3   Single page of SED field-transcription for Firle, Sussex, 24 June 1959, done by the fieldworker Michael Barry. (Copy provided by Clive Upton.)

responses to the questions. These left-hand columns provided the information for the *BM* volumes. The right-hand column was reserved for 'incidental material' or IM, which Harold Orton (1962, pp. 17–18) defined as 'any significant expressions from the informant's conversation that had relevance to problems under investigation in the Questionnaire'. Orton, who checked and edited the field-recording books himself, added (p. 18): 'Relatively unconditioned by the somewhat artificial circumstances of the interview, this incidental material is particularly valuable for confirming, supplementing, amplifying and even contradicting the evidence of the responses themselves.' That is to say, the IM augments the data in potentially significant ways, counterbalancing in some measure the more careful and self-monitored speech of the question responses. The IM in Figure 2.3 includes an instance of the tag *like* used as a **focusing device** or **utterance-final discourse marker**, in *it used to rattle, like*, and shows Michael Barry cross-referencing some material to other Dieth-Orton questions. Orton intended (in 1962, p. 22) that four 'companion volumes' of IM would be published after the *BM* volumes, but this did not happen. However, as a result of an initiative by Clive

RESPONSES: BOOK VII   871

36 Co   1 staːtʒ. myːn, °~⁽ᵗˣ⁾   2 staːtʒ. myːn   3 staːtʒ. muːn, °~   4
        staːtʒ. muːn, °~⁽ᵗˣ⁾   5 staːtʒ. muːn, °~   6 staːtʒ. muːn   7 staːtʒ.
        muːn, °~

37 D   1–5 staːtʒ. myːn   6 staːtʒ, °~. myːn   7 staːtʒ. myːn, °~   8–9
        staːtʒ. myːn, °~   10–11 staːtʒ. myːn

38 Do   1–5 staːtʒ. muːn

39 Ha   1 staːtʒ, °~. muːn, °~   2 staːtʒ. muːn   3 stəːtʒ. muːn   4 stätʒ
        [ðə staːɾ iːnⁱ *The S. Inn*]. muːn, °~³⁽ᵗˣ⁾   5 staːtʒ. muːn, °~   6 staːtʒ.
        muːn, °~³   7 staːʃtʒ. møːlːn

40 Sx   1 staːʃtʒ. moʊn   2 staːtʒ. moʊn   3 stoʊtʒ. moʊn   [ɑːfmuːnz
        half-ms. (on finger-nails)]   4 staːtʒ. muːn   5 staːtʒ. muːn   6
        staːtʃtʒ. muːn, °~ᵘ VII.6.5

VII.6.4   HALO

Q.   What can you sometimes see round the moon?

Rr.   BALL, BURR, CIRCLE, (COCK'S-)EYE, HALO, RING, WHEEL

Note—For additional exs. of RING, see I.3.5; and of WHEEL, see I.9.5 (and refs.).

31 So   1 ɾɪŋ, s.w. ɛɪloo   2 heɪloo, wiːl [pref.]   3 ɾɛ̃ŋ   4 hɾɪŋ, °~   5 ɾɪn
        [sic]   6 ɾɪŋ   7 soʊkl, ɾɪŋ   8–9 zoʊːkl   10 hɾɪŋ   11 wiːl   12 ɾɪŋ
        13 heːɪlo;, hɾɪŋ, °~

32 W   1 səʊːkl   2 ɾɪŋ   3 səʊːkl   4 ɾɪŋ   5 ɾɪŋ, °~   6 wiːoʊ   7 səʊːɾkoł
        8 wiːoʊ   9 wiːoʊ

33 Brk 1 səʊːɾkoł   2 səʊːɾko   3 wɪoł   4–5 ɾɪŋ

34 Sr   1 səʊːko   2 səʊːko   3 soʊːko   4 səʊːko   5 səʊːko

35 K   1 soʊːkl   2 ɾɪŋ   3 bɒ;   4 ɾɪŋ   5 bɒ;   6 səʊːkl   7 ɾɪŋ, səʊːko ["pref."]

36 Co   1–2 səʊːkl   3 səʊːkl, °kɒksɒɪ   4 səʊːkl, °~   5 ɾɪŋ   6 aɪ   7 səʊːkl

37 D   1 səʊːkl   2–7 ɾɪŋ   8 eːloː, °~   9 boːl   10 zɒʊːkɾəł   11 ɾɪŋ

38 Do   1 ɾɪŋ   2 ɾɪŋ, °~   3 wɪːəł, °~⁽²ˣ⁾   4 ɾɪŋ, wiːˀl, °~   5 ɾɪŋ

39 Ha   1–2 ɾɪŋ   3 wiːl   4 səʊːko   5–6 ɾɪŋ   7 ɾɪŋ

40 Sx   1–2 səʊːɾko   3 s.w. səʊːɾko   4 ɾɪŋ   5 səʊːɾko   6 səʊːɾko

Figure 2.4   Single page from *SED: Basic Material Volume IV: The Southern Counties*, Part III, responses by county and locality to question VII.6.4 (from Orton and Wakelin, 1968, p. 871).

---

chump

chump   *1. n* the human HEAD VI.1.1. tʃʌmp So
2. *vt-1prpl* we CRUNCH apples or biscuits VI.5.12.
-ing tʃʌmpn D

chums   *1. npl* MATES VIII.4.1. tʃʌmz Nf, tʃʊmz Wo
2. *npl* PALS VIII.4.2. tʃʌmz MxL So W Sr K D Sx,
tʃʌmz Nb Nf, tʃʊmz La Y*[old x1]* O*[old]* Brk, tʃʊmz
Gl

chunk   *1. n* a chock placed behind and under a wheel
to prevent a cart from going backwards on a hill, ⇒
PROP/CHOCK I.11.2. tʃʌŋk So
2. *n.* a PIECE OF BREAD AND BUTTER V.6.11(a).
tʃʌŋk Bd; **chunk** of bread tʃʌŋk ə bæɪd Bd, tʃʌŋk ə
bæɪd L; **chunk bread and butter** tʃʌŋk bæɪd ŋ bʌtəʳ
Sr
3. *n.* **chunk bread and jam** a PIECE *OF BREAD
AND BUTTER AND JAM/SUGAR* V.6.11(b). tʃʌŋk
bæɪd ŋ dʒæm Sr

chuns   *npl* CHAPS in the skin VI.7.3. tʃʌnz Db

church-clerk   *n* a SEXTON VIII.5.4. tʃəˀːtʃklaˀːɪk
Ess *[marked u.r. EMBM; see note at clerk]*

churchgarth   *n* a   CHURCHYARD   VIII.5.5.
tʃɜːtʃgaːθ Da*[not usual]*

church-going clothes   *n* SUNDAY-CLOTHES
VI.14.19. tʃəˀːtʃgʌʊɪn klaʊz Ess

church-warden   *n* a SEXTON VIII.5.4. tʃəˀtʃwɔːdn
Mon, tʃəˀtʃwɔːdn Bd, tʃəˀtʃwɔːdən Nf *[marked tr.r.
WM/EMBM]*

churchyard   *n What do you call the place where all
the tombstones are? [Confirm that he means the place
round the church.]* VIII.5.5. Eng. ⇒ burial ground,
cemetery, churchgarth, graveyard, kirkgarth,
kirkyard, parson's acre

churm   *1. n* a CHURN V.5.5. tʃəˀːm Nth*[old]* Bd,
tʃəˀːm C, tʃəˀːm He Gl Bd So W *[not a SBM
headword]*
2. *v* to churn butter. prppl ətʃəˀːmɪn Wa

churn   *1. n Now in the good old days, what was butter
made in?* V.5.5. Eng. ⇒ butter-kiver, butter-tub,
churm, dash-churn, dasher *[northern [k-] forms are
not held separately]*

chuting*   *n* the GUTTER of a roof V.1.6. ʃɾtɪn So D,
ʃʊtɪn D, ʃʊtən So W Do Sx, pl ʃʊtɪɪz Sr, ʃʊʔn Ha, ʃʊtən Mon Gl
So W Do Ha Sx*[old x1]*, ʃuʔn Ha, ʃʊtən Do

cicles   *n* ICICLES VII.6.11. stkłz Ess

cinder   *n* CINDERS V.4.3. stndə Nb Nth, stndəˀ Db
Brk, stndɒˀ He O Nth Brk

cinder-ashes   *n* ASHES from a cold fire V.4.5.
stndəʊæʃɪz Nf

cinder-bing   *n* an   ASH-MIDDEN   V.1.14.   *pl*
stndəbɪŋz L

cinder-dirt   *1. n* ASH in a burning fire V.4.4.
stndədɒˀɪ Ess
2. *n.* ASHES from a cold fire V.4.5. stndədəˀɪ Nf,
stndədɒˀɪ Ess

cinder-heap   *n* an   ASH-MIDDEN   V.1.14.
stndaːɪp C, stndaːɪəp La, stndəˀɾɪp Sa,
stndəbɾɪp Ess, stndɒˀɾɪəːp W

cinder-hole   *n* an ASH-HOLE or other place
beneath a domestic fire in which the ashes are
collected V.3.3. stndəʊɪl Sa, stndəʊəl L

cinder-midden   *n* an   ASH-MIDDEN   V.1.14.
stndəmɪdn Ch

cinder-muck   *1. n* ASH in a burning fire V.4.4.
stndəmɪk Nf
2. *n.* ASHES from a cold fire V.4.5. stndəmʌk
Nf, stndəmɪk Nf

cinder-pit   *n* the ASH-HOLE beneath a domestic
fire V.3.3. stndəpɪt Nf*[not a hole]*, stndəpɛt Sf

cinder-ruck   *n* an   ASH-MIDDEN   V.1.14.
stndəuːk St

cinders   *1. n What do you call the red-hot things
that fall through the grate when the fire is
burning?* V.4.3. Eng. ⇒ cherks, cinder, clinkers,
cokes, embers, gleed(s), greethagh, grubbles,
hot coals, smarags
2. *n.* ASHES from a cold fire V.4.5. stndəz L
[marked tr.r. EMBM]

circle   *1. v* to WHITTLE a stick I.7.19. *-ing*
saˀːklɪn Ess *[marked u.r. EMBM]*
2. *n.* a HALO round the moon VII.6.4. səˀːkł Gl,
səˀːkəł Mon, soˀːko Ess, saˀːkł Ess, sɜˀːkł Man,
sɜˀːɪkł La, saˀːkł Y, səˀːkł Y, səˀːkɪ L, səˀːɪl Db, səˀːɪkł
Y, səˀːkoł Y, soˀːkł He, soˀːɪku Ha, soˀːkł Y Ch Db
Sa St Wa L Hu Bd, saˀːtl Nt, səˀːkł Wo Wa Lei Nth
Bd Hrt Ess K, səˀːkʔł Ess, səˀːɪł Lei, səˀːku Ess
MxL, səˀːɪkł Nb, səˀːɪkł Ch L, səˀːɪkł St, səˀːɪkł Lei
C, səˀːku Sr, səˀːɪkł Sa Wo Gl, səˀːɪkł He Wo Wa
Mon Gl O Bk Bd Ess So W K Co D, zəˀːɪkł So,
zəˀːɪkɾəł D, səˀːɪkəł Mon, səˀːɪku Wo Gl, səˀːɪku
Sr K, səˀːɪkoł W Brk, səˀːɪɾko Brk Sx

cistern   *1. n* a CESS-POOL on a farm I.3.11.
sɪstən Nf, sɛstən Wa
2. *n.* an artificial cess-pool. sɪstən Nth Nf Sf,
sɪstən Nf, sɪstənt Y, sɛstn K, sɛstən Nt Nth Ess
3. *n.* an ASH-MIDDEN at the back of an
earth-closet V.1.14. sɛstən Db
4. *n.* a SALTING-TROUGH III.12.5. sɛstən Lei

clabby   *1. adj* SAD, describing bread or pastry
that has not risen V.6.12. klæbɪ D

clabby   *2. adj* STICKY, describing a child's hands
VIII.8.14. klæbɪ So, klæbɪ D

clacking   *v-ing* GOSSIPING VIII.3.5(a). klækʔən
Sf

claden   *n* GOOSE-GRASS II.2.5. kleɪdn Do,
kleɪdən Do

clagged up   *adj* STICKY, describing a child's
hands VIII.8.14. klagd ə̃rp Nb, klagd ʊp Nb
Y*[old]*, tlagd ʊp Cu

claggy   *adj* STICKY, describing a child's hands
VIII.8.14. klagɪ Nb Cu Du La Y, tlagɪ We La

Figure 2.5   Page from the *Survey of English Dialects Dictionary and Grammar*, showing entry for **circle** (Upton, Parry and Widdowson, 1994, p. 80).

Figure 2.6   Page from the *SED Dictionary*, showing entry for **halo** (1994, p. 189).

Upton and Oliver Pickering at Leeds University, the Leeds Archive of Vernacular Culture (see: http://library.leeds.ac.uk/special-collections/collection/61/the_leeds_archive_of_vernacular_culture) was developed from 2002 onwards in order to make available online archival material from the SED, including extensive selections from the IM (at: http://library.leeds.ac.uk/special-collections/collection/61/the_leeds_archive_of_vernacular_culture/74/incidental_material_documents_sed).

The *SED Dictionary* is useful to any scholar wanting easy access to the particulars of the countrywide distribution of the lexical items captured by the Survey, as long as one is prepared to forego the finer, precise details of provenance, locality by locality. In the volume as a whole, pages 1–475 are the *Dictionary*, pages 477–504 the *Grammar*. The latter is included in emulation of Joseph Wright's *English Dialect Grammar* of 1905, which was appended to the final volume of the *EDD*, and because the editors 'consider it to be essential to a proper understanding of the functioning of the lexis' (Upton, Parry and Widdowson, 1994, p. v). More on this in section 2.3 below. The *Dictionary* is easy to use, highly organized, and moderately **structuralist** in its approach;

that is to say, following Orton's vision, core entries present complete sets of variants collected for each lexical notion investigated by the Survey, allowing the reader a snapshot of the nationwide system of variation for each notion, though without the statistical information that would point to dominant or recessive forms (or indeed the maps that might contribute to the same end). (There is more on structuralism in Chapters 5 and 6 of the present book.) The *Dictionary* makes available in compact form the lexical riches of the SED. The editors freely acknowledge that it is not 'a general dictionary of English dialects' (p. v) on the scale of the *EDD*.

2.2.3   The *wickishness* of dialect lexicography

In due course, then, despite Harold Orton's initial vision of the SED, the Survey produced a dictionary of English dialects. Furthermore, the lexicography of dialectal English thrived in the post-*EDD* world, in dictionaries, glossaries, and other formats, and a line of descent can be traced from Joseph Wright's achievement to much of this work. It may be the oldest tradition in the study of regional English, but dialect lexicography remains in good health, or *wickish* ('bright, in good health'), to use the Lincolnshire adjective recorded by the *EDD*. The following sections provide a brief guide with examples.

2.2.3.1   More dictionaries

Having said that, descriptors such as *dialectal*, *non-standard*, and *regional* become interestingly thorny, and perhaps even untenable, in relation to many of these newer projects. Here are some examples in chronological order:

- *A Dictionary of Canadianisms on Historical Principles* (Avis et al., 1967; online version by Dollinger et al., 2013).
- *Dictionary of Jamaican English* (Cassidy and Le Page, 1967, 1980), based in part on fieldwork done by Cassidy in 1952 using the work sheets of the Linguistic Atlas of the United States and Canada, which you can read about in my Chapter 5, section 3.1.
- *Macquarie Dictionary* of Australian English (Delbridge and Butler et al., 1981, 1991, 1997, 2005, 2009, 2013; also online since 2003).
- *Dictionary of Newfoundland English* (Story, Kirwin and Widdowson, 1982, 1990; online edition 1999).
- *Dictionary of American Regional English* (*DARE*; Cassidy and Hall, 1985-2013; digital edition, Hall, 2014).
- *The Australian National Dictionary: A Dictionary of Australianisms on Historical Principles* (Ramson, 1988; online since 2008).
- *Dictionary of Caribbean English Usage* (Allsopp and Allsopp, 1996).
- *A Dictionary of South African English on Historical Principles* (Silva et al., 1996; online, 2014).

• *The Dictionary of New Zealand English: A Dictionary of New Zealandisms on Historical Principles* (Orsman, 1997).

The content of these sizeable dictionaries can be described as 'non-standard' in relation to British Standard English and to a quite ill-defined and indistinct entity: International Standard English, which we can think of as a kind of meeting place for the Englishes of the world where their differences get ironed out or smoothed over. Leaving aside *DARE* and the Newfoundland dictionary for a moment, we could say that the subject matter of each of these dictionaries is 'regional' in the sense of arising out of a particular geographic area and being distinctive in relation to these Standards and to other 'regional' Englishes across the world. For these are dictionaries of emerging or emerged national varieties of English (national varieties which have grown out of splendid mixtures of transplanted dialects), and, while they frequently show the influence of Wright's *EDD* (and the *OED*), they also, by listing distinctive national vocabularies, are contributing to the creation of new standard Englishes. This is a nice twist in the story of the dialect dictionary – but such a twist that one begins to wonder whether the name *dialect dictionary* is appropriate (think also of the *DSL* here), even though, from another point of view, 'Dialects are both national and international' (Crystal, 2015, location 23). (The Caribbean dictionary does not quite fit smoothly with this point, as it describes the English usages of nearly 20 territories, including 12 independent nations.) In this way, these dictionaries can be seen as fostering national identity or even contributing to nation-building, like Noah Webster's post-independence *An American Dictionary of the English Language* (1828). As such, they have a role in Phase 4 of Edgar Schneider's five-phase model of the development of **'New Englishes'** (Schneider, 2003), a phase which he calls **endonormative stabilization**, literally 'forming a standard from within'. They also have some connection with the famous and idiosyncratic 900-page *Glossary of Anglo-Indian Colloquial Words and Phrases*, better known as *Hobson-Jobson*, by Colonel Henry Yule and Arthur Coke Burnell, first published in 1886, the central aim of which was to describe and explain words of Indian origin which had entered the English language during British rule in the subcontinent, such as *avatar*, *guru*, *nirvana*, and indeed *Hobson-Jobson* ('A native festal excitement ... an Anglo-Saxon version of the wailings of the Mahommedans as they beat their breasts in the procession of the *Moharram* – "Yā Hasan! Yā Hosain!"'). This dictionary lists a distinctive vocabulary of regional origin, but its standpoint is more imperialist than nationalist. It has fascinated generations of scholars and writers and has hardly ever been out of print, and now also comes in a 2013 Kindle edition.

The *Dictionary of American Regional English* (*DARE*) is an exception in this list above, as it details the regional English lexis of the United States rather than assembles the vocabulary of an individual national variety. As the *DARE* website puts it: 'When the American Dialect Society (ADS) was founded in 1889, one of the major goals of its charter members was to do for the United States what Joseph Wright was doing for England in compiling his *English Dialect Dictionary*' (*DARE* website, accessed 5 January 2016). Throughout the early decades of the twentieth century, the membership of the ADS was energetic in producing lists of dialect words, and Harold Wentworth's *American Dialect Dictionary* (1944) amalgamated these lists into a single volume, including material from Canada and Bermuda. But *DARE* was a project of a different order. *DARE* took longer to complete than the *EDD*: its six volumes were published between 1985 and 2013, with an electronic edition following in 2014. To be fair, however, the project only got going in earnest in 1962, when Frederic Cassidy, Professor of English at the University of Wisconsin-Madison, was appointed its Chief Editor. Cassidy finalized the lengthy *DARE* questionnaire (over 1600 items), with the help of the ADS word lists, and between 1965 and 1970 fieldwork for *DARE* was carried out using methods which by that time were well established in dialect surveys. Over 1000 evenly distributed localities were chosen across the United States, and 80 trained fieldworkers sought informants to interview who were native to each locality. Nearly 3000 informants were interviewed. The informants' responses provided data for the dictionary, along with a massive collection of printed sources. Cassidy was particularly interested in the older regional lexis, and so two-thirds of the informants interviewed were in the 60-plus age-group. He also wanted to assess linguistic change across the generations, and about a quarter of the informants were aged between 40 and 59, and 10 per cent were under 39. Biographical details of informants were collected in order to enable the researchers to identify informant samples from a particular age-group or social class or ethnic group or sex (*DARE* website: 'History of DARE', accessed 5 January 2016).

Like the SED *Dictionary*, *DARE* uses data collected by fieldwork during a limited time period. Also, like the *EDD* and *OED*, it is a citation dictionary, giving quotations from a range of written sources, with the aim of providing a historical overview of the life of each word in the dialects of American English. Like John Ray's pioneering work on English English, *DARE* seeks to distinguish the regional from the general in American English. It is also etymological, endeavouring to explain how each word got into American English in the first place. It is unusual too, in that it is in some measure a linguistic atlas as well as a dialect dictionary. A selection of the *DARE* lexis is also displayed on computer-generated maps using the data collected by fieldwork between 1965 and 1970.

The entry for the noun *chowder* in Figure 2.7 is divided into three sub-entries, and after section 1 there is a stylized map showing occurrences of *chowder* and its associated variants across the United States.

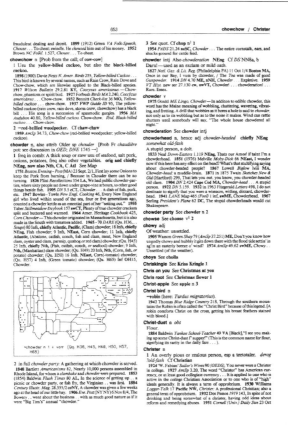

Figure 2.7   Sample page from the *Dictionary of American Regional English*, Volume I (Cassidy, 1985, p. 653).

Taking the conventional dictionary entry first, we have the lexical item in bold followed by its grammatical class and any alternative spellings, plus here the note that it can be used attributively, as in *chowder party*, at section 2 of the entry. The etymological information is next, between square parentheses, and here refers to entries in the *OED* and the *Dictionary of Newfoundland English* (which indicate that the word probably came from French and travelled to the United States via the Breton fishermen who took it to Newfoundland). The first definition follows, then in bold a summary of provenance for this use and a cross-reference to the map below. Before we get to the map, the citations are listed in chronological order, including, at 1965–70, data from *DARE* fieldwork. In the Dictionary, this part of the list frequently gives detailed information on provenance and the informants who provided the instances of the item. Also included is a brief reference to the item number in the *DARE* questionnaire. (Volume V of *DARE* includes its full bibliography.)

The map is intriguing. It is a compact and simple map. Each occurrence of *chowder* across the territory is marked by a black dot denoting each relevant community. The map is computer-generated and the size of the states has been distorted to reflect population density. Hence, for example, New York State is enlarged while Nevada is reduced. This permits a relatively uniform distribution of communities across the map, making it easier to interpret each map, especially when a variant is clustered in a bunch of neighbouring communities. The legend gives the lexical item and cross-refers in detail to the *DARE* questionnaire.

DARE in many ways is a model modern dialect dictionary. All the key characteristics from the tradition of dialect lexicography are present, but honed by a superior systematicity in methods and a greater clarity and comprehensiveness in presentation. Since 2014, *DARE* has been available digitally, by subscription. Many free sample entries and maps are available via its website (http://dare.wisc.edu/), including examples of maps that display the lexical variation by the social variables of community type (rural versus urban), age, sex, race, and education.

The *Dictionary of Newfoundland English* (*DNE*) is another exception in the list of mainly national dictionaries above, as Newfoundland and Labrador is a province of Canada. However, it became a province as recently as 1949, and linguistically the island of Newfoundland and nearby coastal Labrador is quite distinctive compared with the rest of Canada. Newfoundland English is the oldest 'overseas' variety of English, dating back to the very early seventeenth century, and shaped by the speech of immigrants from the west of England, south-eastern Ireland, the Channel Islands, France, and Scotland. The influence of the *EDD* is again in evidence in the *DNE*, for which work began in the 1950s. The *DNE* aims to tell the history of each item of English vocabulary linked especially with Newfoundland, that is, words which entered the language via Newfoundland English or which are peculiar to Newfoundland, using many sources ranging from sixteenth-century documents to twentieth-century audio recordings collected by fieldwork. Figure 2.8 shows the entry for *chowder* from the 1999 online version, which cross-refers to the *OED* for the main sense, before providing information on *chowder beer*.

In summary, then, at the bigger end of the scale, dialect lexicography continues vigorously. In these dialect dictionaries, there is continuity with the older aims, methods, and designs, and there is also change that is in keeping with the global spread of varieties of English and with the possibilities offered by new technology, such as online access, easy searchability, and more. For example, digital dialect dictionaries, like the Innsbruck *EDD* and the planned second edition of the *Dictionary of Canadianisms on Historical Principles*, offer the possibility of creating digitized corpora from their entries (including the

Figure 2.8 Entry for *chowder* from the online edition of the *Dictionary of Newfoundland English* (1999, accessed 28 October 2016).

citations) that provide large, accessible research resources for linguists and historians (see Markus, 2012; and Dollinger, 2006).

2.2.3.2   More glossaries

The story is comparable at the smaller end of the scale. Glossaries of English dialects have continued to be published in substantial numbers in the twentieth and twenty-first centuries. Exact quantification is difficult to gauge because of localized publishing and online enterprises, a point made similarly by Graham Shorrocks (1996) in relation to dialect literature. Shorrocks's short survey makes a useful distinction (p. 386) between *literary dialect*, that is, the representation of non-standard speech in literature that is otherwise written in Standard English, which (literary dialect) has sometimes been used as source material by dialect lexicographers, and *dialect literature*, that is, literary works composed wholly or mostly in a non-standard dialect and aimed mainly at a non-standard-dialect-speaking readership. The latter tradition was exemplified above in Chapter 1 by Tim Bobbin's *A View of the Lancashire Dialect* (1746a) and is closely associated with the glossary tradition. Dialect glossaries also are primarily aimed at the popular end of the market. In light of the preceding section, we can see many of them as mini-versions of the national-identity-promoting dialect dictionaries, albeit the identities being promoted frequently are regional rather than national – though such unambiguous categorizing can sometimes offend the sensibilities of the speaker communities involved. Furthermore, and somewhat conversely, although I have talked above of the *distinctiveness* of the dialects being described (a quality routinely emphasized by the dictionaries and glossaries themselves), the lexicographical works habitually reveal local varieties that are shot through with connections to other varieties and regions. Consider, for example, the *Guide to Pembrokeshire Place-Names and Dialect* (1960, 1974), by Percy Valentine Harris, and *The Shetland Dictionary* (1979, 1984, 1993a, 2009), by John J. Graham. The glossary section of the former illustrates a dialect of Welsh English (a national variety of English much affected by contact with the Welsh language) that is untypical as such because of long-standing English settlement and English-speaking in South Pembrokeshire, leading to many lexical connections between South Pembrokeshire English and the traditional English dialects of south-western England. The latter is a glossary of a dialect of Scots (which one can treat as either a historical dialect of English or as a language of Scotland), but an unusual one which was also shaped by the form of Norse that preceded English by 500 years in the Shetland Isles, known as Norn, coming from Norway. Graham's *Dictionary* records a number of Shetland words of Norn origin surviving into the twentieth century, such as *vaelensi*, 'a violent gale; very stormy weather' (interestingly subsumed under *violency* by the *OED* (accessed 8 January 2016)). In an article called 'The Survival of a Tongue on the Margins of Scots', Graham (1993b, p. 19) refers to the Shetland dialect as his 'mother tongue', and on their excellent website the members of the Shetland ForWirds society describe their aims as 'to foster and promote the use of written and spoken Shetland dialect as a valued and essential element of Shetland's distinctive heritage and culture' (http://www.shetlanddialect.org.uk/about-us, accessed 8 January 2016). The site contains an online version of Graham's *Dictionary*, together with sound files, a dialect map of Shetland, examples of dialect literature, and a guide to resources and publications. It is an exemplary modern environment in which to place a dialect glossary.

You will have noticed that here in this subsection on glossaries I have just been talking about a work that is inconveniently called a *Dictionary* by its author. I will direct you on this point to my loose distinction made near the start of Chapter 1, where I said that the term *dictionary* usually refers to the larger projects, and *glossary* usually to the smaller in scale. This is my approximate summary of the situation, but the naming choices made by individual authors and editors keep presenting exceptions. *The Shetland Dictionary* is comparatively short, and I have put it into this section. *Hobson-Jobson* is much larger, and I have put it into the preceding section on dictionaries, even though it refers to itself as a *Glossary*. However, F. T. Elworthy's *West Somerset Word-Book* is also 900 pages long, and both I (in Chapter 1) and he refer to it as a glossary. I refined my use of the term *glossary* at the start of Chapter 1, section 3, and I will emphasize that fine-tuning further now. Where I have discussed dialect dictionaries I have had in mind the larger projects, not just according to the size of the final publication but also because of the size of the project as a whole and the size of the geographical area investigated, typically national territories. When discussing dialect glossaries, I have had in mind shorter works and smaller regions. This is a workable though not a watertight division, because not all projects fall neatly into one category or the other – reflect on the *DNE*, for example, or, to bring in a nicely complex case, the 400-page *A Concise Ulster Dictionary* (Macafee, 1996). On balance, I would file both of these under *dialect dictionary*.

Two or three more points before we conclude this section.

The Internet, unsurprisingly, has stimulated dialect lexicography. We have already seen that many of the big academic dictionaries have an online presence. There are lots of dialect glossaries online. Lots. They all offer valuable information and observations. Many are purposely humorous, not all are academically (or terminologically) rigorous, but neither of these traits is a completely new phenomenon. In a rapid and less than rigorous experiment, I Googled a number of place names coupled with the keywords *dialect* and *dictionary* or *glossary*, and found quickly on nearly every occasion at least one relevant website for each locale. Here is a brief but wide-ranging list of examples (all accessed 8 January 2016), in alphabetical order:

- *Australian Slang*, at: http://www.koalanet.com.au/australian-slang.html, part of a site designed to promote the town of Noosa in Queensland.
- *Boston to English Dictionary*, at: http://www.celebrateboston.com/culture/dictionary.htm, part of the Celebrate Boston website.
- *The Dialect Dictionary*, at: http://www.thedialectdictionary.com/, a site designed (anonymously) in order to assemble contributions from users.
- *Jamaican Patwah: Patois and Slang Dictionary*, at: http://jamaicanpatwah.com/dictionary, interactive and anonymously managed, a glossary of Jamaican Creole.
- *A Dialect Dictionary of Lumbee English*, by Dannenberg et al., http://www.learnnc.org/lp/editions/nc-american-indians/5760, online version on the Learn NC website of a booklet originally published in 1996, describing the dialect of the Native American Lumbee tribe of North Carolina.
- *Pembrokeshire English*, at: http://www.pembrokeshirecoast.org.uk/?PID=218, part of the Pembrokeshire Coast National Park website.
- *Pittsburghese*, at: http://www.pittsburghese.com/, a site celebrating the Pittsburgh dialect and accent, including a glossary.

- *A Glossary of Quaint Southernisms* (of the United States), at: http://www. alphadictionary.com/articles/southernese.html, part of the extensive 'alpha-Dictionary language resource site' managed by the linguist Robert Beard.
- *Talkin' Texan and Southern Slang: Howdy Get Rowdy*, at: https://truetexan living.wordpress.com/2012/10/25/talkin-texan-and-southern-slang/, a short word list compiled by student (in 2012) and Texan, Tyler Cole Stevens.
- *Tok Pisin/English Dictionary*, at: http://www.tok-pisin.com/sort-tokpisin. php, offering translations from the English-based pidgin/creole of Papua New Guinea into English, part of Tok-Pisin.com.
- *Yorkshire Dictionary*, at: http://www.yorkshire-dialect.org/dictionary.htm, part of a site constructed by Kevin Wilde to promote Yorkshire dialect verse.

The website developed by the BBC as part of its *Voices* project in 2005 still contains links to a number of dialect glossaries of British English, some in the form of contributions from site visitors (such as Nick Stephens of Cornwall, whom I quote at the opening of Chapter 1), which are accessible via: http://www.bbc.co.uk/voices/wil/.

Finally, in Britain there are at present some publishers who have specialized in producing series of dialect glossaries aimed at the general and non-specialist reader, such as Abson Books, Bradwell Books, and Dalesman Books, and there are many dialect and local societies, most notably the Lakeland Dialect Society (founded in 1939), the Lancashire Dialect Society (1951), the Northumbrian Language Society (1983), and obviously the Yorkshire Dialect Society (1897), who continue to contribute to the glossary tradition.

2.2.3.3 More dialect lexicography

In the twentieth century, new genres of research arose in dialect study. I have already indicated the first, that is, the linguistic atlas. Linguistic atlases are the subject of the following three chapters of the present book, which tell the story of the dialect cartography of English and also explore the pioneering, formative late-nineteenth-century European atlas projects. The study of dialectal lexis was a major component in most of the twentieth-century atlases. In addition, modern linguistics became established as a discipline, departments of linguistics were set up in universities, and the sub-discipline of sociolinguistics evolved. All of these developments led to new work on dialectal vocabulary that did not necessarily follow the dictionary/glossary format.

Near the start of my Chapter 1, I said that I would not be dealing here with the lexicography of occupational dialect, and I have stuck to that demarcation, though the frontier between this and the lexicography of regional dialect is sometimes quite porous, as we see, for example, in Bill Griffiths's fine works (2007, 2008; see also 2004, 2005, 2011) that deal with the language of the mining and fishing industries in the context of the regional dialect of north-east England (the miners' dialect is named *pitmatic*), and Stephen Calt's *Barrelhouse Words: A Blues*

Dialect Dictionary (2009), which has regional and African-American Vernacular English dimensions. These two twenty-first-century publications exhibit that drive that runs consistently through the history of the dialect lexicography of English: the drive to record for posterity the words in question, and to bring them more fully into public consciousness, sometimes because of a perception that they are obscure or marginal, and sometimes because of a perception that they are (also) in part or whole threatened with extinction. Additionally, these books are to differing degrees tinged with nostalgia for a seemingly lost or disappearing vocabulary and way of life. Nostalgia is nothing new in this context. Nostalgic loss is hinted at in the comments of *Voices* contributor Nick Stephens that opened Chapter 1: 'Probably could have written a book on this but sadly my grandparents have passed on now.' It is there in more obvious form in two popular 2015 books: David Crystal's *The Disappearing Dictionary: A Treasury of Lost English Dialect Words*, and Robert Macfarlane's *Landmarks*. Crystal's book raids Joseph Wright's *EDD* in order to celebrate 'one of the greatest – yet most neglected – lexicographic achievements of modern times' (location 94), and to inspire new interest in a selection of 900 'old' words 'whose meaning is still relevant today', such as, *all-overish* 'slightly out of sorts, nervous' (north-west, mid, and south England), *arse-verse* 'a spell written on the side of a house to ward off fire and witchcraft' (Scotland, Yorkshire), *betwattled* 'confused, bewildered' (south-west and north England), and *shupernacular* 'superior, excellent' (Shropshire), describing alcoholic liquor, but unfortunately not *maze* or *mazed* 'crazy'. Macfarlane's best-selling book is a kind of romance about the regional lexis used for the landscapes of Britain and Ireland, drawing on a large number of dialect and specialist glossaries, though he does not concur with my characterization of it as nostalgic: 'To celebrate the lexis of landscape is not nostalgic, but urgent' (p. 9). The theme of loss runs through *Landmarks*; the *loss* that inhabits *glossary*, I might say, in tribute to Macfarlane's prose style. I have already mentioned the sense of urgency expressed by many dialect scholars in and about their work, but Macfarlane's view is that this kind of lexicography does not simply record before loss occurs, it actively prevents loss.

2.3   Dialect grammars

Here is a description of a non-standard grammatical feature: 'In Warwickshire, Worcestershire, Pembrokeshire, Gloucestershire, Oxfordshire, Berkshire, Surrey, Hampshire and south-west country the past participle has the prefix [ə].' From this summary, we infer that this is a regional dialectal feature of British English and that it goes under the heading of that part of descriptive grammar known as **morphology**, the study of word structure. The other major part of descriptive grammar is **syntax**, which is concerned with sentence and phrase structure. The term **past participle** is the traditional label for that form of the verb which can be used with another, auxiliary verb to express past actions (*I have written*), and used for passive voice (*the sentence was written*), or used as an adjective (*the written word*). Here is an example of the dialectal feature mentioned above: 'the prefix [ə] before the past participle, as *I've* [*have*] *a-done*'. This type of dialectal feature is known as *A*-**prefixing**, because of the [ə]-sound that is added at the start of the participle. Here are some more examples: *a-broke, a-broked, a-broken, a-drank, a-drink, a-drinked, a-drunk, a-drunked, a-gived, a-made, a-put, a-reached, a-stealed, a-stole, a-stolen, a-took,* and *a-tooked*. This is quite a range, and we see here also a number of non-standard forms of the main part of the participle, like *broke* and *broked*. Here is one more example: *I've a-knowed them there pigs*. The Standard English version of this sentence would be 'I have known those pigs.'

And here are the sources for these descriptions and examples: the first, at the top of the preceding paragraph, is from Joseph Wright's *The English Dialect Grammar* (*EDG*; 1905c, p. 297); the second is a snippet from A. J. Ellis's *On Early English Pronunciation*, Part V (1889, p. 43); the long list of forms is from the *SED Dictionary and Grammar* (Upton, Parry and Widdowson, 1994, p. 491); and the final example is from *The Electronic World Atlas of Varieties of English* (*eWAVE*, accessed 13 January 2016; Kortmann and Lunkenheimer, 2013, http://ewave-atlas.org/valuesets/60345). This gives us a record of this dialectal feature of British English stretching from the mid nineteenth to the early twenty-first century. Three of these sources can be described as dialect grammars, and there is a thread of continuity running between them all.

The *EDG* was published both separately and as part of Volume VI of the *EDD*. It is over 700 pages long, but most of those are taken up by phonology and the index, with only 40 or so pages giving an outline of the non-standard features of British English morphology, dealing with forms of the indefinite and definite article, nouns, adjectives, pronouns, verbs, and adverbs. There is no dedicated coverage of syntax. In its scope and design, Wright's *EDG* exerted an influence over subsequent typological descriptions of dialect grammar (**typology** here meaning 'classification according to type'), but it was not the first work to take up the subject. As we have just seen, there is some discussion of grammar in Alexander Ellis's 1889 volume on the phonology of English dialects, a work which is treated fully in Chapter 5 of the present book. Both William Barnes and Frederic Elworthy published dialect grammars, either within their glossaries (Barnes, 1863, 1886; Elworthy, 1886) or separately (Elworthy, 1877), and there were other dialect lexicographers who took an interest in grammar, such as Georgina Jackson in her *Shropshire Word-Book* (1879). Before the *EDD*, Joseph Wright was best known for his *A Grammar of the Dialect Of Windhill in the West Riding Of Yorkshire* (1892), and the *EDG* follows closely the template of this earlier volume. The focus of all of these grammars was morphology, or *accidence* as it was termed at the time.

All of this work, especially Wright's, informed the content of the SED's *Questionnaire* (Dieth and Orton, 1952, 1962), and, as we saw above in section 2.2.2, an SED grammar was eventually published together with the Survey's dictionary. Its scope follows the *EDG* quite closely, and it lays out the non-standard grammatical features (mostly morphological, a few syntactic) obtained in response to the *Questionnaire*. The list of examples above is the sum of the *A*-prefixed past participles recorded as responses to Dieth-Orton questions. Their geographical provenance is mainly in south-west England, with occasional instances in Herefordshire, Berkshire, Norfolk, Lancashire, and Northumberland.

The SED data, as we know, was obtained by means of fieldwork interviews with local informants. Non-standard grammatical material is harder to elicit under interview conditions than lexical, because informants are more prone to monitor and adjust their grammar than their lexis in an interview situation, and also, as Alva Davis et al. (1969, p. xii) point out in relation to fieldwork in the United States, 'the more complicated the [linguistic] item, the more difficult it is to frame questions to elicit, unequivocally, specific natural responses'. An interview that stimulates more freely flowing conversational exchange or personal narrative (and on occasion this was possible during parts of an SED interview) is more likely to achieve success in eliciting non-standard grammar. There is more discussion of elicitation methods in various parts of the present book, especially in Chapters 4 and 6 (particularly with regard to phonological data in Chapter 6). In the present day, the availability of big electronic corpora of materials provides another sort of resource by means of which dialect scholars can analyse grammar and other kinds of features. The word **corpus**, from Latin, literally means 'body', and a **linguistic corpus** is a body of data, usually comprised of written text or transcriptions of recorded speech. Since the 1980s, increasingly large computerized corpora have been compiled for researchers to use to test their hypotheses and as basic material for their enquiries. For example, there is VARIENG (more fully the Research Unit for the Study of Variation, Contacts and Change in English, at: http://www.helsinki.fi/varieng/), based at the University of Helsinki, which bridges **corpus linguistics** (the study of language by means of large collections of machine-readable text-records of language in use) and the study of language variation and change. VARIENG has compiled a number of corpora in order to provide material for linguistic research, including dialect research, such as historical corpora of English and Scots, and corpora of British English dialects. Other corpora of interest to dialect scholars include the International Corpus of English (ICE; http://ice-corpora.net/ice/), the Salamanca Corpus: Digital Archive of English Dialect Texts (http://www.thesalamancacorpus. com/index.html, which includes a very useful section on glossaries), and the Freiburg English Dialect Corpus (FRED; http://www2.anglistik.uni-freiburg. de/institut/lskortmann/FRED/).

In addition to the SED, many of the other linguistic atlas projects of the twentieth century investigated grammar, particularly morphology. The chief elicitation tool of the Linguistic Atlas of the United States and Canada, the set of 'Work Sheets', included grammatical items. One of the editors of the *SED Dictionary and Grammar*, David Parry, also produced a *Grammar and Glossary* (1999) based on the materials of the survey which he directed in Wales, the Survey of Anglo-Welsh Dialects (SAWD).

The Electronic World Atlas of Varieties of English took a different approach to gathering its material. Between 2008 and 2011, *eWAVE*'s directors, Bernd Kortmann and Kerstin Lunkenheimer (Kortmann is also the director of FRED), enlisted a team of 83 contributors (experts on 76 different varieties of English across the world) and asked them to answer 235 questions, each question dealing with a different morphological or syntactic feature liable to vary across the 50 dialects of English and 26 English-based pidgins and creoles, with a view to assessing the frequency of occurrence of each feature. The resulting open-access online resource enables students and researchers to look at the results by variety and by feature, and includes attested examples and interactive maps. Under the questionnaire item *A-prefixing on elements other than* ing-*forms*, we find the past participle *a*-forms, such as *I've a-knowed them there pigs*, from the south-west of England, where, according to the contributor Susanne Wagner (2013), the feature exists but, in the early twenty-first century, is rare. For English worldwide, *eWAVE* records a 20 per cent attestation for *A-prefixing on elements other than* ing-*forms* (ing-*forms* meaning words like *doing* and *going*), including in a number of creoles. *eWAVE* developed out of a previous project headed by Kortmann, the *Handbook of Varieties of English* (Kortmann et al., 2004, 2008), and it is the present-day counterpart to the nineteenth-century typological grammars by Barnes, Elworthy, Wright, and others. It also exemplifies an area of modern linguistics that has emerged out of work on dialects of English across the world: the study of **World Englishes**, a phrase recorded first from the early 1980s by the *OED*.

In terms of the amount of work done, one can see the study of dialect grammar as something of a poor relation when compared with the study of dialectal lexis and pronunciation, but, on the other hand, there is a substantial body of research out there. As well as the investigations described above, there is work of a more theoretical nature, and I discuss this in Chapter 7. There is plenty of work that uses a sociolinguistic approach (**sociolinguistics** is introduced in Chapter 6), and a good selection of this is provided in a collection called *Real English* (Milroy and Milroy, 1993), which includes details (Cheshire et al., 1993) of the Survey of British Dialect Grammar, carried out in the late 1980s using a questionnaire on morphology and syntax completed by school pupils in mainly urban areas of Britain, mainly England. There is also plenty of work that goes beyond typology, aiming to uncover histories and/or explanations for features of dialectal grammar and their use, such as that by Jan Tillery and Guy Bailey (1998) on *yall* ('you all', literally) in Southern States American English, and the research by the Finnish dialectologist Markku Filppula on Irish English (1999), and that by another Finn, Ossi Ihalainen, on so-called **peri-phrastic *do*-constructions** in Somerset (Ihalainen, 1976), as in sentences like *I do dig the ground*, where the *do* is unstressed, that is, it has no emphasis in the rhythm of the sentence and is simply used a tense marker. Ihalainen's research was followed up by Klemola (1994, 1996, 2002) and Penhallurick (1996), and it builds on that by earlier dialectologists – the example *I do dig the ground* comes from Elworthy (1877). Ihalainen's essay was reprinted in another handy collection of essays on dialectal grammar edited by Peter Trudgill and Jack Chambers (1991), which contains studies on British, American, Newfoundland, Australian, and Irish varieties of English (including one by Walt Wolfram (pp. 229–40, originally published in 1976) on *A*-prefixing on *-ing*-forms in Appalachian English).

2.4   Conclusion

The dialect lexicography of English, then, has a centuries-old history. It is a practice that is still very current, and it is still being expressed prolifically in dictionaries and glossaries, and in other kinds of projects. Some of the practitioners of dialect lexicography have been dialect grammarians too. I talk about grammar in several other sections of this book. Next we move on to a major genre of dialect research already previewed in the chapter above, which I discuss under the heading **dialect cartography**.

2.5   Brief commentary on terms

A number of terms used in this chapter – such as *fieldwork*, *fieldworker*, *informant*, *interview*, and *questionnaire* – are to do with a process and activity crucial to much research on dialect: the collection of the basic data from dialect speakers. We have started to see what this involves, and these terms are illustrated and explained further in the chapters that follow, especially in Chapter 4. I have also used the term *phonology* above, in connection with work by Joseph Wright and A. J. Ellis. The meaning of this term has shifted since the time of Wright and Ellis, and there is specific discussion of this shift at Chapter 5, sections 5.2.1 and 5.3.2, and Chapter 6, section 6.2.

2.6   What you can do

At the ends of five chapters in the present book (specifically this and Chapters 5, 7, 9, and 10), there are short 'What you can do' sections. Each one suggests some ideas for further research, that is, projects that could contribute to one or more of the genres of dialect study described here (lexicography, grammar, phonology, linguistic geography, attitudes and perceptions), drawing on one or more of the approaches discussed (historical, variationist, geolinguistic, and so on). These are not ideas that require applications to funding bodies. They are ideas for small, manageable investigations that might be suitable for dissertations or assignments if you are a student, or for articles, blogs, or just for your own interest and pleasure if you are curious about language variation. They are topic ideas, not detailed designs. This book as a whole provides the context by telling the story of the study of English dialects, and from that you will have a sound basis of knowledge about aims and methods. You can develop that knowledge by exploring the primary works you find inspiring, and by following the guidance given in the further reading sections.

For example, as we have seen in Chapters 1 and 2, compiling a dialect glossary is something that many people have accomplished. It could be a glossary of your village, town, city, or region. You could start by compiling a word list based on your own observations. You can collect material in person or online with the aid of your own questionnaire, utilizing your observations and local knowledge to construct it, taking guidance from existing questionnaires, perhaps even using an existing questionnaire that would enable you to compare your data with the lexis of other areas (see for example the language survey kit used for BBC *Voices*: http://www.open.edu/openlearn/history-the-arts/culture/english-language/download-your-language-survey-kit). You could take an existing glossary as your starting point, whether it be ten years old or 200 years old, and use it to discover changes in your area's vocabulary over time, by comparing with your own survey. Has there been lexical loss or erosion in your area? Has there been lexical innovation? Has contact with other languages affected the local English? You could attempt a short history of local vocabulary if you know or think that it has been investigated before – you might be surprised by what you find in the archives of the local library and press, or in the records of local societies, or online. Once you have compiled your word list, you can examine each item more closely. What is its etymology? Where does it come from? Is it used in other regions? Exactly how 'local' is it? This kind of work can take you on a journey into regional history and culture, as well giving you an excuse to explore marvellous resources like *DARE*, *DSL*, the *EDD*, and the *OED*.

Questionnaires are a less productive means for collecting non-standard grammar than they are for vocabulary: the questions are not so easy to construct and the context tends to inhibit the response more than is the case with lexis and phonology. A more conversational, less controlled interview is better, especially for capturing basic items that you know occur frequently in casual speech. Also, the large corpora mentioned above and below make available a wealth of data to mine for grammatical features. For smaller projects, it is best to focus on a limited number of features, or just one, like Tillery and Bailey (1998) did on *yall* and Ihalainen (1976) on periphrastic *do*-constructions, mentioned above, or like W. E. Jones (1952) on the definite article in Yorkshire. If the feature that you are interested in has a history of documentation and research, this permits a comparative approach. In fact, my brief excursion above on *A-prefixing* (on elements other than *ing*-forms) gives a taste of what can be done by way of a historically orientated, comparative study.

Resources and further reading

Another authoritative overview of lexicography in general is the comprehensive, single-volume *Oxford Handbook of Lexicography* (2015), edited by Philip Durkin, which includes among its many contributions an essay by Clive Upton on 'Regional and Dialect Dictionaries', one by Stefan Dollinger on 'National Dictionaries and Cultural Identity', and another by Julie Coleman on 'Slang Dictionaries', as well as a very useful timeline of lexicography by John Considine. The older and slimmer collection, *Studies in Lexicography* (1987), edited by Robert Burchfield, includes insider accounts of the *Dictionary of American Regional English* and the *Australian National Dictionary* by their editors, Frederic G. Cassidy and W. S. Ramson, respectively. In addition, there is information on the Scottish dictionaries in the chapter by A. J. Aitken, whose collected writings on Scots can be accessed at: http://www.scots language.com/aitken-papers, part of the website of the Scots Language Centre, which provides access to a wide range of fantastic resources. Note also that a *Concise Scots Dictionary* was published in 1985 (editor-in-chief, Mairi Robinson), drawing upon the bigger (that is, great) Scots projects. For a historical perspective on Shetland and Orkney dialect, see Thomas Edmondston's *Etymological Glossary* (1866), downloadable from the Internet Archive. All the websites of the national dictionaries of varieties of English mentioned in the chapter above are fruitful sources of further material, especially those of *DARE*, *DNE*, and *DSL*. Take a look at the websites of the Coal Mining Oral History Project and lexicographer Michael Quinion (*World Wide Words*) for more on *pitmatic*. The former offers a short glossary gleaned from interviews with miners and their families in County Durham, and the latter gives a brief account of *pitmatic* in among its wealth of information on the changing lexis of modern English. See also the excellent website of the Durham and Tyneside Dialect Group (http://www.indigogroup. co.uk/durhamdialect/index.html), which includes an extensive compendium of word lists covering material from the fourteenth to the twenty-first centuries. For an introduction to the occupational dialect of the traditional industries of the United Kingdom, see Peter Wright's *The Language of British Industry* (1974). Wright was one of the fieldworkers for the SED, and is also the author of several popular-style dialect glossaries, such as *Lanky Twang* (1972), *Cumbrian Dialect* (1980), and *The Yorkshireman's Dictionary* (1980). Bernd Kortmann and his teams of collaborators have contributed enormously to the present-day description and analysis of the grammars of varieties of English worldwide, not just with the resources of *eWAVE* (2013) and its interpretative companion *pWAVE* (2012), but with two preceding projects, the *Handbook of Varieties of English* (two-volume hardback 2004, first volume concentrating on grammar; four-volume paperback 2008), and the *Comparative Grammar of British English Dialects* (Kortmann et al., 2005; Hernández et al., 2011), which makes use of the FRED corpus. The short survey by Edwards, Trudgill and Weltens (1984) on research into British English dialect grammar is useful for its inventory of nineteenth- and twentieth-century works up to 1982. A revised version of this, by Edwards and Weltens, is in *Focus On: England and Wales* (1985), edited by Wolfgang Viereck, an interesting collection which contains a number of essays on morphology and syntax. In the same Varieties of English Around the World series is the corpus-based study of *New Zealand English Grammar* (1998) by Marianne Hundt. This used: the British National Corpus (BNC; released: 1994), the Freiburg-Brown Corpus of American English (Frown; first release: 1999), the Freiburg-LOB Corpus of British English (F-LOB; first release: 1999), the Macquarie Australian Corpus of English (ACE; created: 1986), the Wellington Corpus of Spoken New Zealand English (WSC; released: 1998), and the Wellington Corpus of Written New Zealand English (WWC; released: 1993). The second and third of these are updates of the Brown Corpus of American English (first release: 1964) and the Lancaster-Oslo/Bergen Corpus (LOB; first release: 1976) of British English, respectively. A brief description of ACE is at the Australian National Corpus website, which provides access to a suite of other textual, audio, and audio-visual materials. From this list, we get an indication of the mushrooming of electronic corpora (and their acronyms) for dialect researchers to use. The VARIENG website has an invaluable, authoritative Corpus Resource Database (CoRD, of course), cataloguing, describing, and providing hyperlinks to scores of corpora: http://www.helsinki.fi/varieng/CoRD/index.html. Concordancing software – which lists all instances of a given word in its immediate context in a corpus – is another tool that benefits the modern researcher. Laurence Anthony's AntConc and Tom Cobb's Compleat Lexical Tutor are two well-known, recommended freeware corpus-analysis kits. Benedikt Szmrecsanyi is a prolific and thought-provoking researcher in the field of corpus-based work on English dialect grammar. His output also crosses over into *dialectometry* (discussed in Chapters 4 and 5 of the present book) and the *probabilistic variationist* approach to grammar (discussed in Chapter 7). In particular, see his 2013 book *Grammatical Variation in British English Dialects: A Study in Corpus-Based Dialectometry*. In a move that I should emulate, his web-pages (https://sites.google.com/site/bszmrecsanyi/home) include helpful guidance on the pronunciation of his surname. You can download scans of Elworthy (1886), Jackson (1879), and Wright (1892, 1905c) from the Internet Archive. For more on BBC *Voices*, see the **Resources and further reading** section in Chapter 5.

3 Cartography: European beginnings

3.1 Introduction

Here in Figure 3.1 is one of the earliest published maps of English dialect regions, from 1887, made by the gentleman-scholar and one of the first English dialectologists, Alexander J. Ellis (1814–90).

The map shows, bounded by thick lines, six principal dialect 'Divisions' (the northernmost is the 'Lowland', which Ellis continues onto an accompanying map of Scotland) and, bounded by thinner continuous lines, 32 smaller 'Districts' (another ten Districts are on the map of Scotland) and also, in the form of broken lines, the 'Ten Transverse Lines' drawn by Ellis mainly in order to indicate regional boundaries of pronunciation in England. The map and the volume in which it occurs were the outcome of investigations that had occupied Ellis for over 40 years. The linguistic information overlaying the basic geographical information gives a pretty intricate visual effect, and the original colour version, with its vivid red boundary lines, is very striking.

Figure 3.2 is a much more recent example of a map of regional forms of English pronunciation, from the pages of the British Library's *Sounds Familiar?* website.

Figure 3.1   'English Dialect Districts', appended to Ellis (1889).

Online you can click any of the (colour-coded) human-shaped symbols on
the map to hear a speaker from that locality pronounce the vowel sound
that occurs in words like *bath*, a sound which varies appreciably from the
north to the south of England. (The colour-coding on the original interactive
map groups the speakers according to which variant of the vowel they use.)
Beneath the map you can click to listen to examples of regional variation in

Figure 3.2 'Regional Voices: Phonological variation', at: http://www.bl.uk/
learning/langlit/sounds/regional-voices/phonological-variation/ (accessed
28 October 2016).

other pronunciation features, such as **STRUT~FOOT** (in which the vowel in
words like *strut* is different from that found in the *foot* group, as is the case
in most accents of English, apart from that of northern England, where the
vowel /ʊ/ occurs in both word-groups), **definite article reduction** (in which
the has an abbreviated pronunciation), and **rhoticity** (in which the *r* that
occurs after a vowel in words like *far* and *farm* is articulated, rather than being
silent), each of which as it happens is referred to also in 1887 by one or more
of Ellis's transverse lines. For well over a century, dialectologists have grappled
with an assortment of means to represent or symbolize variant pronunciations
on their maps, but the *Sounds Familiar?* interactive map bypasses the issue,
allowing the viewer access to audio recordings, thanks to the capabilities of
the Internet and digital media. The viewer here is also a listener, and this map
exemplifies one of the recurring themes of the present book – the interplay
of dialect study and technological innovation. With ingenious simplicity, this

map in its original colour form also presents a more immediate visual pattern of regional linguistic variation than that of Ellis.

This chapter and the two that follow tell the story of the **dialect map** and **linguistic atlas** from Ellis's Dialect Districts to *Sounds Familiar?* We will explore the reasons why linguistic atlases appeared, and we will consider their purposes, their methods, and their presentation (their final form, how they look); and in the process we will say more about Ellis and *Sounds Familiar?*

The present chapter recounts the beginnings of linguistic cartography in nineteenth-century Europe, which produced the first and highly influential national linguistic atlases. Chapter 4 concentrates on the motivations and impact of these works, and Chapter 5 pursues the story into the twentieth and twenty-first centuries, spotlighting the cartography of regional English.

As with lexicography, **cartography** (the making of maps or charts) is something of a grand tradition in dialect study. Many linguistic atlases have been large or very large or very, VERY LARGE projects, producing large (etc.) and information-packed publications. And there have been many linguistic atlases. In the two-volume *Language and Space* (Auer and Schmidt, 2010; Lameli et al., 2010a and 2010b), a comprehensive survey of language mapping, over 300 linguistic atlases are mentioned, covering all continents of the world except Antarctica, and dating from nineteenth-century philology to twenty-first-century digital linguistics. That is an extensive body of work. In Chapters 3, 4, and 5 we focus on origins, main developments, and selected examples, in order to uncover basic motivations and arrive at an overview of the mapping of English. Here we are concerned with foundations and fundamentals. Elsewhere in the present book, further examples of the mapping tradition are considered. Linguistic cartography is such a prevalent practice in dialect study that discussion of it spills over into most of the other chapters of this book, especially those dealing with perceptual dialectology and geolinguistics (Chapters 9 and 10 respectively).

Prevalent, yes, and yet there have been criticisms. Interested specialists like Ronald Macaulay have felt driven to ask 'What am I getting for my money?' (Macaulay, 1985, p. 172). Macaulay points out that linguistic atlases tend to be expensive to produce and expensive to purchase. What are they for? Who are they for? Aims, methods, approaches, presentation: linguistic atlases, it seems, are prone to attack on all these fronts. For example, here is J. C. Wells reviewing *The Linguistic Atlas of England* in 1978: 'So this atlas reflects a quarter of a century's achievement in English dialectological scholarship. Immense time, labour, and intellectual effort have been expended. Why, then, is one left with such a sense of disappointment?' (http://www.phon.ucl.ac.uk/home/estuary/lae-revw.htm, accessed 28 May 2015, no page numbers). And, 'when I compare it with what has been achieved in the United States (Kurath and McDavid, 1961) or even in Scotland (Catford, 1957), I am ashamed for my country' (Wells, 1979, p. 42). Goodness me. In their way, it seems, linguistic atlases have been controversial. What are we to make of such censure?

It is not uncommon in academia and science for specialists to be in dispute, over theory, method, and results. In principle this is a good thing. In the field of linguistic cartography, the visuals are crucial, and so presentation has also been argued over. As traditional, philological dialectology ebbed in the 1960s and 1970s, for a while the grand lexicographical and cartographical enterprises were particularly vulnerable to criticism from the newer quarters of sociolinguistics and structuralist linguistics. The comments of Macaulay and Wells can be seen in this context, and we shall return to them later in the story, in Chapter 5.

But what of the non-specialist viewer of the linguistic atlas? Do linguistic maps have non-specialist viewers? If the map is freely available online or in a reasonably priced paperback or e-book, then yes, they do, and there are linguistic atlases, such as the *Atlas of English Dialects* (Upton and Widdowson, 1996, 2006), which are designed deliberately to make specialized research accessible to the 'untrained' viewer (Upton, 2010, p. 143). If the map is in an expensive volume the size of a coffee-table, then the viewer will most likely consult it in a library, often a university library. I am sure that not all viewers of these volumes are professional academics. Somewhere in between the 'untrained' viewer and the professional academic is the student learner, and the Internet has brought new ways of tailoring dialect cartography to the needs of students, as exemplified by the resources made available by *Sounds Familiar?* and by the BBC *Voices* project and its offshoots. We shall look at these again in Chapter 5.

However, when it comes to linguistic atlases, the viewing experience, whether specialist, untrained, or in-between, involves a quite specific, personal comparison of the *map* with the *territory*.

3.2   The map *is not* the territory

In *Science and Sanity* (1933, 1994, p. 498), the philosopher Alfred Korzybski says, 'A language is like a map; it *is not* the territory represented, but it may be a good map or a bad map.' Korzybski uses the relationship of a map to the territory it depicts as an analogy for the relationship between language and the 'extensional' world it refers to, the world around us. Robert P. Pula, in the Preface to the fifth edition of *Science and Sanity* (1994, p. xvii), sums up this problem regarding maps:

> the map *is not* the territory; no map represents *all* of 'its' presumed terri-
> tory; maps are self-reflexive, i.e., we can map our maps indefinitely. Also

every map is *at least*, whatever else it may claim to map, a map of the map-maker: her/his assumptions, skills, world-view, etc.

We expect a map to be authoritative, and we easily overlook the fact that a map *is not* the territory, is not the whole story, and so we can be misled by the map into an understanding that is partial. Indeed, from this point of view, maps are inherently misleading. So it is too with language – it gives us a skewed, partial understanding of the world. Korzybski's purpose was to warn us of the persuasive and ideological traits of language, a theme taken up by the General Semantics movement which he founded. However, even though the subject of the present book is language, the subject of the present chapter is maps (albeit maps about language or maps *of* language). Any map is a distortion, a limited depiction of a territory. The distortion can be elementary, as when a large territory is depicted, and the distortion can be easily forgotten. For example, the Mercator projection in maps of the world exaggerates the size of areas far from the equator, but we have become so used to Mercator we tend to forget the distortion.

A linguistic map, on the other hand, can all too easily remind us of its 'distortion'. Why?

If the linguistic map depicts a territory which includes the viewer's home or somewhere familiar to him or her, typically he or she will seek to compare what the map depicts with their own experience – for example, in the *Sounds Familiar?* case above, to evaluate the pronunciation of *bath* assigned to their home area. Consequently, if the pronunciation of *bath* in my home town on the map does not correspond with the pronunciation of *bath* in my mouth then I might be, like J. C. Wells, *disappointed*. (Though probably not enough to be ashamed for my country.) It might be a bad map. Or it might be that I am misreading or misviewing the map, or perhaps expecting too much of it. The map *is not* the territory. In other words, and here is my point, the process of constructing a linguistic atlas is a long process of abstraction. At each stage the data can be in some way sifted or skewed, for legitimate reasons, from collection through to presentation. This does not invalidate the linguistic map any more than the Mercator projection invalidates maps of the world, but it does give us a more fundamental context in which to judge a linguistic atlas. Jerry Brotton, in his *A History of the World in Twelve Maps*, says (2012, p. 438), 'Maps offer a proposal about the world, rather than just a reflection of it, and every proposal emerges from a particular culture's prevailing assumptions and preoccupations.' This thought also informs the discussion of the following chapters. Even a good map is not the same thing as the phenomena it depicts, and this is particularly so when the phenomena, as with large-scale dialect surveys, are voluminous: 'This makes the linguistic-mapping approach exceptionally complicated' (Lameli, 2010, p. 573). Despite this significant tension at the heart of linguistic cartography, the map-making impulse has perpetually been strong in dialectology, and in this chapter and the next two we examine why.

3.3   The origins of linguistic cartography

Map-making is a deep-rooted human activity. What was the first map?

In *Unweaving the Rainbow* (1998, pp. 296–9), Richard Dawkins suggests that our ability to make and comprehend maps goes back over two million years to the very origins of humankind, perhaps even before the dawn of language. He speculates that *Homo habilis* may have developed their ability to interpret the footprints and spoors of the animals they tracked sufficiently to represent terrain and animal movement by using sticks to draw on the dusty ground. A little more cautiously, Charles Bricker (Tooley and Bricker, 1976, p. 9) says that the first maps 'were primitive "notes" men kept as records of the places they visited and the ways there and back', drawn on bark or animal skins, or cut into bone or wood, or even constructed using palm-leaf fibres and shells. The essential aim – an aim which persists up to present-day Sat Nav (satellite navigation) machines using the GPS (Global Positioning System) – was to help travellers find their way. Figure 3.3 is a rather particular surviving early example: painted on an Egyptian sarcophagus about 4000 years old, it is 'a kind of road map for the dead' (Tooley and Bricker, 1976, p. 11) probably modelled on a real map of the Nile Valley.

Approximately 6000 years later, in the nineteenth century, cartography became a major concern in the study of language.

By this time, map-making had advanced considerably, influenced during the Renaissance (roughly AD 1400–1650) by art, by interest in the scientific thought

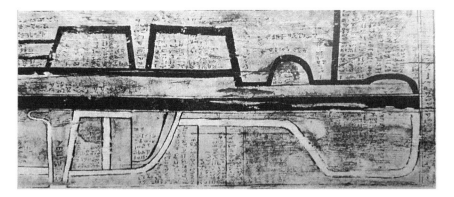

Figure 3.3   Map on a sarcophagus from Egypt's Middle Kingdom (between 2445 and 1580 BC) (from Tooley and Bricker, 1976, p. 11).

of Ancient Greece, and by contemporary scientific and technological advance. It had been facilitated by the printing press (the first printed map was produced in 1472 in Germany) and it had been spurred on by the Age of Exploration (between the fifteenth and seventeenth centuries). In 1569, the Flemish geographer Gerhard Kremer, better known as Gerardus Mercator, introduced his map projection, designed to make maps as effective as the globes that had been in use since the late fifteenth century. In 1791, the British Ordnance Survey was established, which went on to consolidate the use of **contour lines**. The concept of a line on a map joining points of equal value had been in use for some one hundred years, and is, as we shall see, of some relevance to linguistic cartography.

The first flowering of linguistic cartography in the late nineteenth century was inspired in great part by major developments in language studies, which led to the collection of vast amounts of materials from the living dialects of European languages with the aim of improving knowledge of the histories, territories, and internal divisions of these languages, as well as knowledge of processes of linguistic change. Before this, during the eighteenth century, map-makers had already started to add thematic data (such as climate, geology, and trade) onto the topography that their maps depicted: 'a correlative approach that visually combines the terrestrial dimension with specific natural or social phenomena' (Lameli, 2010, p. 569). This is in essence the idea behind the linguistic map: linguistic data placed onto the depiction of territory, clearly intending to display the correlation between the two.

Historically, in cartography, there are two chief types of maps: **general-purpose** or **reference maps**, which are concerned with geography solely, and which dominated cartography until the mid eighteenth century; and **thematic maps** (Chen, 2003, p. 39). A linguistic map is a thematic map. As Chen puts it (p. 39), the intention of a thematic map is to make it easier for the viewer to grasp 'the spatial distribution of phenomena'. The two main components of a thematic map are a geographical base map and a thematic overlay. Chen (p. 40) gives us a handy and simple formula by which we can judge any thematic map, and therefore any linguistic map: 'Thematic maps must be well designed and include only necessary information. Simplicity and clarity are important design features of the thematic overlay.'

Lameli (2010, pp. 569–70) notes that there were some works published before the late nineteenth century showing the regional distribution of language phenomena, for example, by Lambert ten Kate (1723, on European languages), and by Gottfried Hensel (1741, on the world's languages). Lameli describes (pp. 570–4) the key works from 1800 onwards which preceded and influenced the first major atlases of European dialectology.

- *Die Mundarten Bayerns grammatisch dargestellt* ['Bavaria's Dialects presented in terms of grammar'] (1821), by the German Johann Andreas Schmeller;

a lengthy description of the dialects of Bavaria using collected data, which has a single map at its close (reproduced in Lameli et al., 2010b, Map 0801; see Figure 3.4), 'A little map on the geographic Overview of the Bavarian Dialects' [*Kärtchen zur geographischen Übersicht der Mundarten Baierns*]. On the map, groups of dialect characteristics are assigned letters that link with descriptive sections in the book's text.

- *Asia Polyglotta* ['The Many Languages of Asia'] (1823), by the German Julius Klaproth, which has a single map of Asia at the end of the volume, showing the territories of language families by means of coloured boundary lines and shaded areas on a topographical base. The language territories are named after their speakers (for example, 'Indo-Germanen', 'Semiten', 'Georgier'), emphasizing the connection between languages and ethnic groups (reproduced in Lameli et al., 2010b, Map 0001; see Figure 3.5).
- *Atlante Linguistico d'Europa* ['Linguistic Atlas of Europe'] (1841), by the Italian Bernardino Biondelli; a work with maps which use colour shading to portray the territories of the major languages of Europe and language families of the world.
- *Slovanský Zeměvid* ['Survey of Slavic Lands'] (1842), by the Hungarian Pavel Jozef Šafařik; a map which shows the extent of Slavic-speaking territories using coloured boundary lines and shading (reproduced in Lameli et al., 2010b, Map 1501).
- *Sprachkarte von Deutschland* ['Language Map of Germany'] (1844, though drawn in 1843), by the German Karl Bernhardi (reproduced in Lameli et al., 2010b, Map 0802), which uses coloured lines to show the borders of the German language area and its internal regional divisions. Bernhardi's map was primarily ethnographic in its sources rather than linguistic, and had a political aim, that being to give some definition to the concept of a German nation (Scheuringer, 2010, p. 159). It also 'stirred interest in linguistic research on German dialects' (Scheuringer, p. 160).

To this list we can add the German August Fuchs's 1849 map of the extent of Romance languages in Europe (see Swiggers, 2010, Map 1301), which uses coloured boundary lines.

In these initial examples, we have linguistic maps but not linguistic atlases, that is to say, these are either free-standing thematic maps (Šafařik) or thematic maps which complement text elsewhere in a larger work (Schmeller, Klaproth, Biondelli, Bernhardi, Fuchs). Schmeller and, to some extent, Bernhardi deal with dialects, but the remainder are concerned with languages and language families. All are manifestations of the nineteenth-century interest in relationships between languages. Some, especially Šafařik and Bernhardi, indicate nationalistic, even nation-building intent. All help to demonstrate that, by the second half of the nineteenth century, it had been recognized that

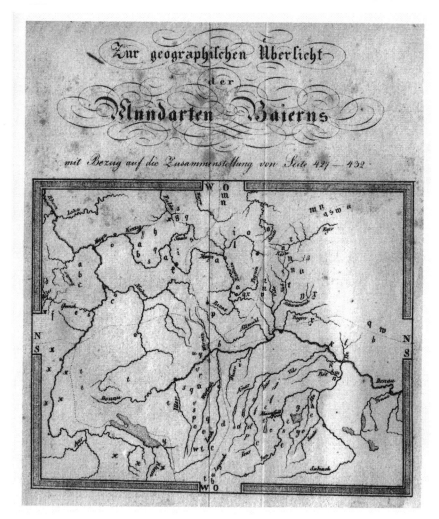

Figure 3.4   Schmeller's (1821) distribution of dialects in Bavaria (reproduced in Lameli et al., 2010b, Map 0801).

a map could be a vehicle for the presentation of linguistic data. In 1844 (p. 573), Johann Andreas Schmeller called for philologists to concentrate on the specific, on the occurrence of individual linguistic features (see Lameli, 2010, p. 574). His is the only map in the list above that refers to linguistic features. In all of this, we see the preconditions not only for linguistic cartography and the great national linguistic atlases and dialect surveys, but also for the notion of the linguistic **corpus** (a body of collected material) and eventually for modern, descriptive linguistics.

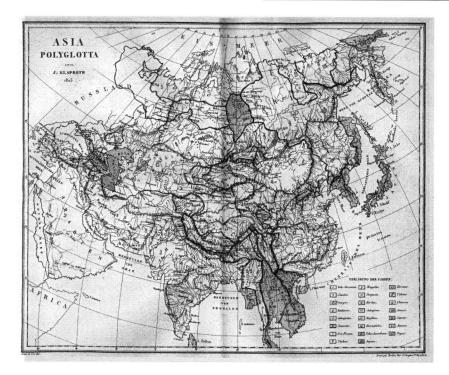

Figure 3.5 Klaproth's (1823) map of language families from *Asia Polyglotta* (reproduced in Lameli et al., 2010b, Map 0001).

In England, significant advances were made in the study of dialects during the last 30 years of the nineteenth century, but the first large-scale linguistic atlases got underway in Germany and France, under the guidance, respectively, of two important pioneers of dialectology, Georg Wenker and Jules Gilliéron.

3.4   Georg Wenker and the linguistic atlas in Germany

In 1876, Georg Wenker (1852–1911), a native of Düsseldorf and a librarian at the University of Marburg, embarked on a remarkable enterprise: the collection of a vast database (as we would now call it – the term *database* came into use only in the second half of the twentieth century) of German dialects in order to produce a linguistic atlas of the nation. Using a question-naire comprised of a set of 42 sentences dealing with everyday matters and written in standard German, Wenker contacted schools by post, asking for his sentences to be translated (by schoolteachers and pupils) into the local dialect. At his disposal was the well-developed German postal system, which was unified with telegraph services in 1876 under the name *Reichs-Post und Telegraphenverwaltung*. At first targeting northern Germany, the questionnaire was revised in 1877 (38 sentences) and again in 1880 (40), until eventually, with the support of the Imperial Chancellor, Otto von Bismarck, material from over 45,000 locations across the whole German Empire was returned to Wenker (Scheuringer, 2010, pp. 160–1). Here are two examples from the final group of *Wenkersätze* ['Wenker-sentences']: sentence 10, *Ich will es auch nicht mehr wieder thun!* ['I won't do it again, (I) promise!']; and sentence 11, *Ich schlage Dich gleich mit dem Kochlöffel um die Ohren, Du Affe!* ['I'll beat your ears with a wooden spoon in a minute, you monkey!'] (for the full collection go to: http://www.diwa.info/Geschichte/Wenkersaetze.aspx?set=0).

Wenker's *Sprach-Karte der Rheinprovinz nördlich der Mosel* ['Linguistic Map of the Rhine province north of the Moselle'] (1877) was thus the first linguistic map using data from a questionnaire-based survey. Over the next ten years, Wenker produced three groundbreaking collections of linguistic maps (1878, 1881, 1885) leading up to his greatest work, the *Sprachatlas des Deutschen Reichs* ['Linguistic Atlas of the German Empire'] (1889–1923), a project which he did not live to see completed, which ultimately comprised over 1600 maps produced by Wenker, Ferdinand Wrede, and Emil Maurmann. This led, in turn, to the 79 maps of the *Deutscher Sprachatlas* ['German Linguistic Atlas'] (*DSA*; Wrede et al., 1927–56), which used Wenker's data as its basis, followed by the 22 volumes of the *Deutscher Wortatlas* ['German Word Atlas'] (*DWA*; Mitzka et al., 1951–80), for which new data on vocabulary was collected using the Wenker postal method. The University of Marburg remains at the centre of German linguistic geography, having between 2001 and 2009 published a digitized online version of the *Sprachatlas des Deutschen Reichs* (*DiWA*, the *Digitaler Wenker-Atlas*, at: http://www.diwa.info/) along with scans of many other German language maps and atlases, dating from Bernhardi (1844) to the close of the twentieth century, and having developed this further from 2009 to 2015 into a 'regional language of Germany' website (http://www.regionalsprache.de/) in collaboration with the Academy of Science and Literature at Mainz, and, perhaps unexpectedly, the Bundeskriminalamt (Federal Office of Criminal Investigation).

Wenker's 1877 map shows similarities with Schmeller's of 1821, with which Wenker was familiar. (He also knew about Bernhardi's map of 1843.) His next work, a collection of 25 maps, the *Sprachatlas der Rheinprovinz* ['Linguistic Atlas of Rheinprovinz'] (1878), however, is a clear departure in its use of **isoglosses**. The term *isogloss* was first used in English in 1925, but comes from German, where it was recorded in 1892 (according to the *Oxford English Dictionary*, accessed 1 June 2015). Literally it means 'equal word'. The isogloss subsequently has become a staple tool of linguistic cartography. It is like a contour line, in that it is indeed a line, but it is rather peculiar for a contour line, because despite its literal meaning it does not connect points of equal value but separates points of different values. In other words, it is a boundary line. Isoglosses enclose areas which share the same usage and separate from one another areas with differing usages. In order to use isoglosses, the linguistic cartographer needs instances of language phenomena (sounds, words, items of grammar) to be collected from well-chosen localities. Put simply, if two adjacent localities return two different variants of the same overall feature (or **variable**, to use the modern term), then an isogloss can be drawn between the two localities. A network of localities and a corpus of material collected from the network thereby enable the cartographer to draw dialect boundaries by using isoglosses. Although it is a boundary line, the isogloss is a quite different beast from the boundary lines of earlier linguistic maps, because it is arrived at by means of harvested instances of linguistic items as they are recorded in a network of localities. The *Sprachatlas der Rheinprovinz*, although never published by Wenker, is 'probably the first linguistic atlas in the world' (Scheuringer, 2010, pp. 160–1), that is, it is a collection of thematic maps displaying linguistic data, and the maps (rather than text) are the primary means of description. There is just the one surviving copy, held at Marburg. Its successor, the *Sprach-Atlas von Nord- und Mitteldeutschland* ['Speech-Atlas of North and Middle Germany'] (1881), also used isoglosses.

Figure 3.6 is a photograph of an original map from Wenker (1881), which consisted of six hand-drawn maps overall, numbered 1, 2, 18, 19, 27 (Figure 3.6), and 28. Each map shows the regional variants of a selection of linguistic features collected via Wenker's set of sentences. Map 27 shows the variants of numbers 223–6 from the list of features contained in the sentence-set, the pronouns *du*, *dir*, *dich*, and *ihr*. Wenker-sentence number 11, mentioned above, elicited the variants of *du* and *dich* shown in this map. Eventually, by the time of the *Sprachatlas des Deutschen Reichs*, this list contained 339 features in total. Other maps in 1881 showed variation in consonant pronunciation, in forms of the verb *sein* ['to be'], and in more pronouns. On the base map, rivers are depicted, larger settlements are named in full, and each village locality is marked with a dot and initials. Over this are drawn the colour-coded isoglosses, and the **key** or **legend** is given in a box at centre-bottom. Each map also has an overlaid grid to enable easy cross-reference to a separate sheet listing the localities' names in full. Figures 3.7 and 3.8 are enlargements of the key and some isoglosses, respectively.

One of the subscribers to Wenker's work was none other than A. J. Ellis. In his 1882 Address to the Philological Society in London, Ellis delivered a revealing review of Wenker's 1881 Atlas (pp. 20–32). Ellis is able to compare it with his own efforts to date, noting that Wenker, like himself, had 'found it necessary to do away with old conceptions' and 'to turn to the speakers

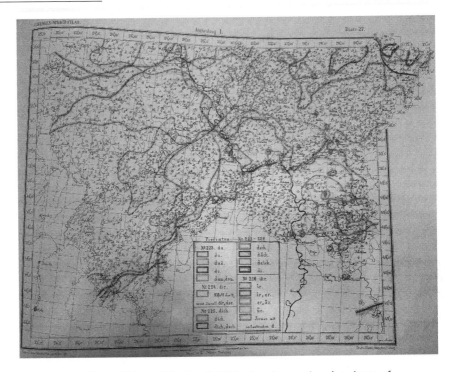

Figure 3.6 Sheet 27 from Wenker (1881), showing regional variants of pronouns 223–6 from Wenker's list of features.

themselves, registering what they said' (p. 25). Here is the desire for renewal and discovery in European philology by investigation of living regional speech. This is a venture that requires new methods and tools. Ellis had aimed at 'the utmost phonetic exactness' (p. 26) when collecting his material in person, because he was interested primarily in pronunciation, but he acknowledges Wenker's postal sentence-set method as more efficient than his own attempts at collecting by post, pointing out (pp. 26–7) that Wenker was aided by a number of factors, these being: support from regional governments (who ordered the schools to answer Wenker's circulars), a more widespread German education structure, the more phonetic spelling system of German, plus the phonic way of teaching used in Germany. Says Ellis (p. 28), 'But how to make this enormous mass of information available was an extremely difficult question, which Dr. Wenker solved in one word – *graphically*.' This indicates how innovative Ellis felt Wenker's linguistic maps to be. Ellis describes (pp. 30–1) the 'coloured lines' drawn 'sharply' between different usages 'marking boundaries, which sometimes unite and form islands' – he is unable, of course, to use the as-yet-uninvented technical term, **isogloss**. Ellis also sums up the pros and cons of Wenker's maps, pretty much in keeping with the Chen formula (2003) mentioned above, which emphasizes clarity and simplicity. Ellis says

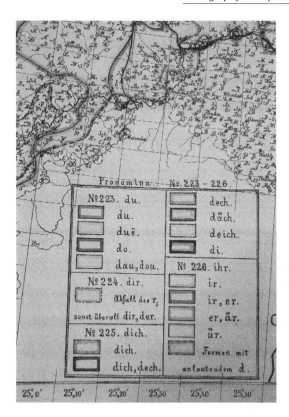

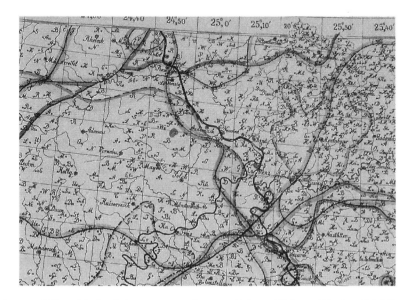

Figures 3.7 and 3.8   Enlargements of parts of Sheet 27 from Wenker (1981).

(p. 30) that two of the maps (18 and 19) are complex visually. On these, the variants, the boundaries/isoglosses, and the number of shades of the same colour are too profuse for immediate clarity. The solution would be to edit out or subsume some of the detail, which is, however, not advocated by Ellis at this point. For these early dialectologists it was imperative that the newly discovered detail of previously neglected regional speech should be displayed as fully as possible, even if that risked compromising visual effect. Ellis (p. 31) also worries that if one wanted to obtain a full overview of the dialect of any one locality, one ultimately would have to consult all of Wenker's maps individually. Nevertheless, he remains convinced (p. 32) that maps are the best way to present the mass of information collected by Wenker. He concludes (p. 32) that the 1881 Atlas is 'the greatest, the best-designed, and the best-executed attempt hitherto made to determine the peculiarities of local speech'.

Ellis calls Wenker's project 'Herculean' (p. 25), finishing his review rather ominously with, 'I sincerely hope that Dr. Wenker will live to complete his gigantic undertaking' (p. 32). German dialectologists grappled with the labour begun by Wenker for the next hundred years. Ellis himself was well placed to appreciate the size of the task, and the history of linguistic atlases is strewn with extraordinary, long-drawn-out projects and formidable, highly determined scholars.

The motivations for the first national dialect surveys have already been hinted at in the present chapter, and are discussed also in the context of lexicography in Chapter 2, but before summing up the reasons for the original linguistic atlases (in Chapter 4), we will introduce the second such project, the *Atlas linguistique de la France* (1902–10), by Jules Gilliéron and Edmond Edmont.

3.5   Jules Gilliéron and the linguistic atlas in France (and beyond)

The first national linguistic atlas project was begun in Germany. The first national linguistic atlas project to be completed was in France. This was the *Atlas linguistique de la France* (*ALF*), published in nine volumes containing a total of 1920 maps between 1902 and 1910. Its editor and cartographer was the Swiss philologist Jules Gilliéron (1854–1926), who had launched the survey upon which the *ALF* was based in 1897. Whereas Wenker's method of data collection was postal (Wenker's work was known to Gilliéron) and relied on the translation of a set of sentences into local dialect by intermediaries, Gilliéron's method was direct, using a questionnaire designed to **elicit** or obtain local words and phrases, and asked *in situ* by a **fieldworker** – whose name was Edmond Edmont (1849–1926).

A shopkeeper and pharmacist from Normandy lacking in general linguistic training, Edmont was gifted at rapid and accurate phonetic transcription. His role was to act as an unprejudiced recording machine, and between 1897 and 1901 he carried out field-interviews in 639 localities (actually, 638, for one village was investigated twice (Swiggers, 2010, p. 283)) in France and neighbouring French-speaking parts. Edmont travelled around on a bicycle, transcribing his **informants'** responses immediately and posting his transcriptions to Gilliéron each evening in order to avoid the temptation to adjust his first impressions (Walter, 1988, 1994, p. 95).

Gilliéron's questionnaire was revised during the fieldwork phase, eventually reaching 1920 items – hence the *ALF*'s 1920 maps. Although the use of a dedicated fieldworker and face-to-face, on-the-spot interviews was a notable departure from Wenker, the questions were (like Wenker's sentences) phrased in terms of the standard dialect: in standard French, Edmont would ask questions such as 'How do you say *head* [or whatever the linguistic notion was] in your dialect?'

It was Edmont who chose the localities, which were all rural villages. In most of the localities he interviewed only one informant. In total, 700 informants were interviewed: 640 male, 60 female; ages ranging from 15 to 85; approximately 500 with little formal education, 200 well educated (Davis, 1983, p. 19).

As systematic dialect study developed, the **informant** became a crucial figure. Prior to the *ALF*, in Britain and continental Europe, dialect research had relied very much on the intermediary, who typically would be an educated person with local knowledge who could report back to the principal investigator about the local dialect. The informant, however, is the actual dialect speaker, the primary source. It is the informant who provides the raw data. How informants are selected (whether they are chosen randomly or in order to fulfil certain criteria, taking into account factors such as age, sex, occupation, education, native to the locality or not, and so on) and how they are interviewed (face-to-face, by post, by telephone, by email, via social networks, and so forth), and whether a less formal elicitation method should be attempted, are all basic issues of methodology that revolve around the informant. Most importantly, the choice of informant type should match the aims of the investigation. We shall come back to this issue in connection with linguistic atlases in Chapters 4 and 5. (In present-day surveys, the term **participant** is sometimes preferred over **informant**.)

Like Wenker, Gilliéron promptly set about transferring his collected data to maps. Wenker proceeded from smaller to larger territories, and, as we have seen, never completed the project himself. Gilliéron, with a smaller atlas of the southern Rhone valley already completed (1880), produced in 1902 the first of 1421 maps covering the whole of France (later *ALF* maps covered southern France only).

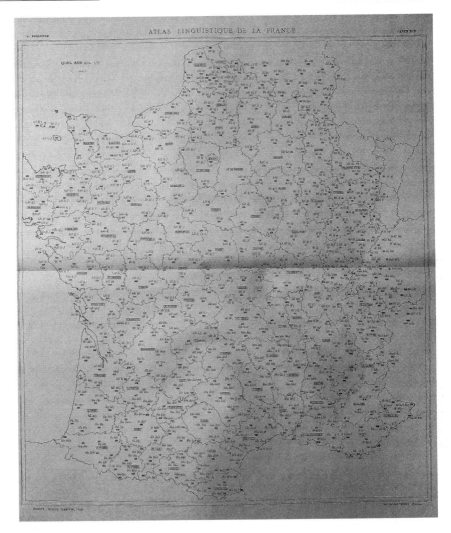

Figure 3.9 Map 9, *quel age (as-tu)?* ['what age have you/how old are you?'],
from Volume 1 of the *Atlas linguistique de la France (ALF)* (1902).

A glance at Figure 3.9, which is a photograph of Map 9 from Volume 1 of
the *ALF*, instantly reveals a different cartographic approach from Wenker's.
There are no isoglosses. Each locality is represented on the map by a number,
and next to each number is the linguistic item – in the case of Map 9, the
local form of the standard French *quel age* ['what age'], given in a close
phonetic transcription (though not strictly following the conventions of
the International Phonetic Alphabet, which was in its infancy at this time).
In their discussion of **dialect geography** (more on this term at the close of
the present chapter, and in Chapter 8), Jack Chambers and Peter Trudgill

(1998, p. 25) divide linguistic maps into two categories: **display maps**, where the harvested responses for linguistic notions/features are simply transferred onto the map; and **interpretive maps**, in which a degree of analysis of the collected data is carried out. Chambers and Trudgill state that display maps are far more common, though interpretation is not entirely absent from two of the display-orientated projects that they mention, that is, the *Linguistic Atlas of New England* (Kurath et al., 1939–43), and the *Phonological Atlas of the Northern Region* (Kolb, 1966). (See Chapter 5.) However, the *ALF* is at the extreme display end of the display-interpretive spectrum. Gilliéron uses its maps purely to document the recorded data. Wenker's work is in the interpretive category, because he uses isoglosses, and the isogloss is intrinsically interpretive. It is 'a very abstract conceptualisation of the way in which dialect regions meet' (Chambers and Trudgill, 1998, p. 104). It emphasizes and brings to light patterns of distribution, presenting stark boundaries which often stream-line the complexities of linguistic diversity. This immediacy, one could argue, is helpful and illuminating for the viewer, and better exploits the visual potential of a map. From another viewpoint, as Lameli points out (2010, p. 577), Gilliéron rigorously pursues the 'documentation principle', exemplified also by a companion guide to the atlas volumes, *Atlas linguistique de la France: Notice servant a l'intelligence des cartes* ['Instructions for the understanding of the maps'] (1902), which provides details of localities and informants, commentary on the informants' responses to the questionnaire, and explanation of methods. As Lameli puts it (2010, p. 578), 'The user thus finds a sound data basis for linguistic analysis'. In 1874 (p. 450), A. J. Ellis, with reference to English dialectology, outlined his judgement of the role that 'word-collectors' should perform: 'Their business is to hand over the materials in a trustworthy form, unadulterated with superficial and superfluous additions, containing what is wanted and *no more*'. This also is the business of Gilliéron and Edmont, that is, to provide the basic data for the scholarly community to analyse. The sifting and skewing that I said earlier was intrinsic to linguistic cartography occurs at a more rudimentary level in the *ALF* (compared with Wenker), in the selection of its localities, informants, and linguistic notions/features – as with all data-based linguistic surveys, the corpus must inevitably be a sample, and sampling requires decisions about whom and what to include.

Subsequent to the *ALF*, France has been well served by linguistic atlas projects, including the remarkable *Nouvel Atlas Linguistique de la France par regions* ['New Linguistic Atlas of France by regions'] (*NALF*), launched by Albert Dauzat in 1939 and still ongoing under the guidance of the Centre National de la Recherche Scientifique, which divided France into 24 regions, to be investigated by small teams of linguists, and which has produced dozens

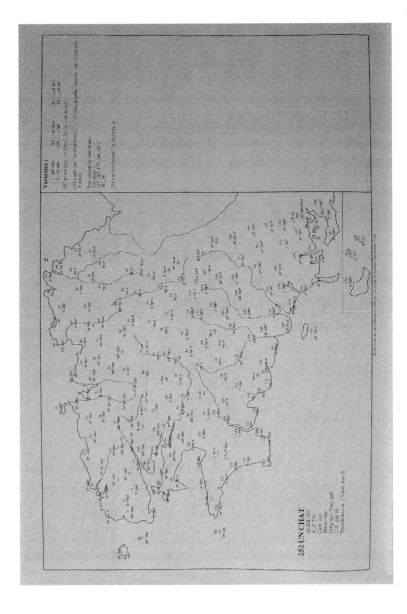

Figure 3.10 Map 252, *a cat*, Breton responses, with cross-references to other atlases and dictionaries at lower left, from the *Nouvel Atlas Linguistique de la Basse-Bretagne*, Volume 1 (Le Dû, 2001).

of volumes containing thousands of maps (Swiggers, 2010, pp. 284–5). The influence of Gilliéron and Edmont persists in French linguistic cartography and beyond. Look, for example, in Figure 3.10, at this map published in 2001, from the *Nouvel Atlas Linguistique de la Basse-Bretagne* ['New Linguistic Atlas of Low Brittany'] (Le Dû, 2001-2), an atlas of Breton.

Gilliéron himself went on to publish a supplement to the *ALF*, on Corsica (1914–15), using material collected by Edmont, and their imprint is particularly noticeable in the *Sprach- und Sachatlas Italiens und der Südschweiz* ['Speech- and Things-atlas of Italy and Southern Switzerland'] (*AIS*) (1928–40, eight volumes, plus an index published in 1960, total of 1705 maps), produced by two Swiss scholars, Karl Jaberg (1877–1959) and Jakob Jud (1882–1952), who both studied under Gilliéron. Territorially the *AIS* covers Italy and southern Switzerland; linguistically it maps dialects of Italian, Sardinian, and Rhaeto-Romance, also known as Ladin. The *AIS* is commonly seen as a rigorous working through and improving of the methodology and aims of the *ALF*. For example, it included urban centres, using more than a single informant in the larger cities (just a quick note at this point that the choice of localities and informants made by some of the philological linguistic atlases was criticized by sociolinguists later in the twentieth century for being under-representative of the territories under investigation); in their lengthy questionnaire (2000 questions for the majority of localities), Jaberg and Jud introduced **indirect** questions, of the type 'What is/do you call this?' (indicating an object), with the aim of getting a more natural response than possible with the **direct** 'translations' prompted by Edmont and Wenker; and more contextual linguistic and ethnographic information is given. Its title, literally 'language- and things-atlas', marks it out as explicitly following the approach that became known as *Wörter und Sachen* ['words and things'], refining an interest that colours the *ALF*, that is, Gilliéron's belief in the primacy (in language study) of individual words and their individual histories. The *Wörter und Sachen* approach stresses the importance of tailoring a methodological and interpretive framework to the particularities of the territory and the culture of the social groups being investigated. Figure 3.11 is an example map from the *AIS*.

In July 1931, Jakob Jud and one of the fieldworkers for the *AIS*, Paul Scheuermeier, visited the United States to assist with final training for the first stage of the Linguistic Atlas of the United States and Canada. Before we turn (in Chapter 5) to the beginnings of linguistic cartography in North America, and to the first dialect maps of British English and American English, we can now summarize (in Chapter 4) the reasons for and the effects of the earliest dialect atlases.

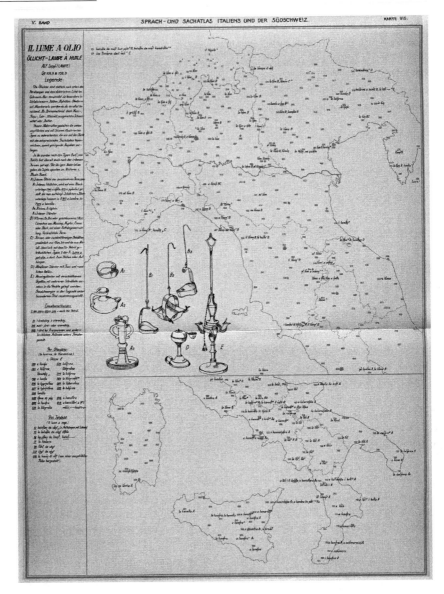

Figure 3.11 Map 915 of the *Sprach- und Sachatlas Italiens und der Südschweiz* (*AIS*; Volume 5, 1934), *il lume a olio* ['oil lamp'] (reproduced in Lameli et al., 2010b, Map 1305).

3.6   Brief commentary on terms

A few times in this chapter I have used the term *dialectology* for the field of enquiry initiated in the late nineteenth century by the work of scholars like

Ellis, Wenker, and Gilliéron. Over time, commentators came to associate the early decades of the discipline with dialect cartography in particular, that is, with *dialect geography* or *linguistic geography*, to use the more frequent terms. It is a bit of a simplification, but the period from the late nineteenth to the mid twentieth century can be seen as a time when dialect study was dominated by this 'traditional' or philological dialectology or linguistic geography. That period drew to a close with the advent of sociolinguistics in the 1960s, and the story of what happened to the terms *dialectology* and *linguistic geography* from the 1960s onwards is told in Chapters 8 to 10 of the present book. In summary, it is a tale of rise and fall, and rise again.

Resources and further reading

The most useful companion to this chapter and the two that follow is the two-volume *Language and Space* set (Auer and Schmidt, 2010; Lameli et al., 2010a, 2010b), which contains in total some 80 essays by leading experts, some of them providing overviews of different approaches and themes (such as Clive Upton on 'Designing Maps for Non-linguists'), some giving outlines of work on different territories and languages (such as Hermann Scheuringer on German, and Pierre Swiggers on the Romance languages of Europe), and some offering handy summaries of genres as a whole (like Alfred Lameli on 'Linguistic Atlases — Traditional and Modern'). The collection reproduces many examples of dialect maps, and Volume 2 includes a full list of linguistic atlases. (A third volume of *Language and Space*, on Dutch, was published in 2013.) For highly readable expositions of the history and significance of cartography in general, try Jerry Brotton's *A History of the World in Twelve Maps* (2012) and Simon Garfield's *On The Map* (2012), and, for a more pictorial experience, *Landmarks of Mapmaking* (1976), by R. V. Tooley and Charles Bricker. There are several excellent web resources that I know of that you can explore for digitized versions of early linguistic cartography: *DiWA* or the *Digitaler Wenker-Atlas*, at: http://www.diwa.info/; the 'Regional Language of Germany' site (REDE), at: http://www.regionalsprache.de/; the Munich Digitization Center (MDZ) of the Bavarian State Library (Bayerische StaatsBibliothek), at: http://www.digitale-sammlungen.de/index.html?c=startseite&projekt=&l=en; *NavigAIS*, the online edition of *AIS*, at: http://www3.pd.istc.cnr.it/navigais/; and Nick Wedd's maproom.org, at: http://www.maproom.org/. In 2010, Joachim Herrgen provided a short guide to using *DiWA*, emphasizing its potential for researchers, integrating as it does the 1653 maps of the *Sprachatlas des Deutschen Reichs* into a geographic information system which permits comparison with other geo-referenced materials.

4 Cartography: Purpose, legacy, and the early linguistic atlases

This chapter includes the following:

- The effect on dialect study of nineteenth-century philological research into linguistic change.
- Guide to aims, methods, and presentation in dialect cartography.
- Overview of acoustic research on dialects of English.
- Overview of the study of discourse in dialects of English.
- Explanation of the 'neogrammarian hypothesis', John Wells's 'lexical sets', and further discussion of the *isogloss*.

4.1 Introduction

In this chapter, we continue the story of dialect cartography by exploring more deeply why the first major linguistic-atlas projects came about. I also outline the reasons for their enduring relevance to the field that they brought into being, and I summarize central methodological issues which are then illustrated further by more detailed study of selected works in Chapter 5, which concentrates on the linguistic cartography of varieties of English. Chapter 4 also contains a section on the study of dialect pronunciation, especially research on regional variation in **intonation** and **prosody**, and on the study of areal diversity in **discourse**.

4.2 Purpose: describing diversity and explaining change

From the outset, linguistic atlases have been associated with an interest in the nation and its character and history. Many linguistic atlases have been national in scope; many have been linked with national pride. In nineteenth-century England, growing interest in the national language, which included a desire to define its character and reveal its early history, fed into an increasing curiosity about its regional forms. Allied with a developing sophistication in **philology** (as language study was called at the time), this led to **lexicography** on an impressive scale. Great dictionary projects were launched, and many glossaries were published (see Chapter 1). In continental Europe, similar conditions preceded the first linguistic atlases. The business of describing and demarcating the German language and its territory contributed to the shaping of the German nation (German unification took place in 1871), while in France and Italy the *ALF* (*Atlas linguistique de la France*) and *AIS* (*Sprach- und Sachatlas Italiens und der Südschweiz*), respectively, were involved in debates about the unity of the nation (Swiggers, 2010, p. 273). There were also purely philological motivations for the early atlases.

Philology as it was practised in nineteenth-century Europe had been inaugurated by an Orientalist from a Welsh family, Sir William Jones (1746–94), in an address made in Calcutta in 1786 (see also Chapter 1 of the present book). Jones drew attention to similarities between a number of languages of Europe, the Middle East, and the Indian subcontinent, postulating that they all derived from a single common source. (Although it produced a landmark moment, Jones's thinking is prefigured by nearly five centuries by the comments of the Indo-Persian scholar and poet Amīr Khusrau in 1318 on similarities between Sanskrit and Arabic (see Franklin, 2006, p. 81).) This hypothetical source language came to be known as **Indo-European**, and eventually **Proto-Indo-European** (PIE). Scholarly interest in language history consequently became channelled towards reconstructing PIE, locating its homeland, and charting its ensuing divergence into numerous branches which spread across Europe and Asia. Philologists wanted to explain how these branches split into sub-branches, and to describe the processes which occurred as these sub-branches broke up into further divisions, until in due course the modern languages of Europe emerged. The theory of a **family tree** of Indo-European was developed by the German philologist August Schleicher (1821–68), and it helps us understand how some philologists pictured the course of this divergence and descent. Philology involved comparison of data from different languages; it was concerned with uncovering the modes of linguistic change; and intrinsically it was concerned with linguistic diversity – how languages diversified into dialects, how dialects diverged to form new languages. It was concerned with the very definition of the difference between *language* and *dialect*. At some point, once a dialect of a language has accumulated sufficient changes or sufficient differences that distance it from the parent language, or from other dialects of that language, it (the dialect in question) could be considered a 'separate' language. It is, albeit, a separation with many residual links and ties. The **wave theory**, put forward in 1872 by the German Johannes Schmidt (1843–1901), helps us imagine how some changes spread like ripples, from a central point of innovation outwards through speech communities and across territories. Ironically, such waves of innovation can increase similarities between previously 'separate' dialects and languages when the waves travel through more than one dialect region or language territory.

Alexander J. Ellis, the man who first used the term *dialectology* in English (in 1874), is again of use to us here, this time summing up why philologists turned to the study of dialect with such intensity. At the conclusion of his final address as President of the Philological Society, in London, May 1882, Ellis talks of 'the dialects of cultivated nations' which are 'unrecorded by the speakers, but which philologists are endeavouring to preserve as part of the material whence a science of language may be constructed' (p. 146). The investigation and description of dialect speech was becoming essential to the development of philology. The apparently rapid transformations brought about by technological advances, population change, and improvements in communication routes and education made the job of investigation seem urgent, but a central reason to record and collect from the living speech of regional speakers was because it was crucial to the philological enterprise.

In an influential piece published in 1878, two German philologists, Karl Brugmann (1849–1919) and Hermann Osthoff (1847–1909), argued in favour of studying living speech rather than relying on old, written documents. They say (online edition, no page numbers):

> The older linguistics, as no one can deny, approached its object of investigation, the Indo-European languages, without first having formed a clear idea of how human speech really lives and develops, which factors are active in speaking, and how these factors working together cause the progression and modification of the substance of speech. Languages were indeed investigated most eagerly, but the man who speaks, much too little....

> Precisely the most recent stages of the newer Indo-European languages, the living dialects, are of great significance for the methodology of comparative linguistics ... In all living dialects the shapes of sounds peculiar to the dialect always appear much more consistently carried out throughout the entire linguistic material and maintained by the members of the linguistic community than one would expect from the study of the older languages accessible merely through the medium of writing ...

(Translation by Judy Haddon)

Linguistic change had been studied before, much had been deduced about Indo-European languages, but here we see evidence of a new approach in which the key materials come from speech in all its diversity. The earliest linguistic atlases were the first large-scale contributions to this new approach.

The piece by Brugmann and Osthoff (a preface to the first edition of a journal they had founded) is best known as a kind of manifesto for one particular group of philologists based in Leipzig, the '**Junggrammatiker**', or

'neogrammarians' (literally 'new grammarians'), containing as it does the group's most famous dictum, that 'every sound change, inasmuch as it occurs mechanically, takes place according to laws that admit no exception'.

The study of historical sound change in Indo-European had already led to two famous 'laws' being formulated by philologists: **Grimm's Law** (1822), put forward by Jacob Grimm (1785–1863), though actually an elaboration of earlier work by others; and **Verner's Law** (1875), a refinement of Grimm's Law, put forward by Karl Verner (1846–96). Grimm and Verner showed the detail of systematic, regular correspondences between certain **fricative** and **plosive** consonants in the Germanic branch of Indo-European compared with other branches. (Consonant sounds are articulated by means of some kind of obstruction temporarily blocking the flow of air through the vocal tract, causing a short spell of friction in the case of fricative consonants (such as *f*) or a sudden release or 'explosion' of air in the case of plosive or *stop* consonants (such as *p*).) To take one example, where a word in (for instance) Sanskrit, Greek, and Latin began with a /p/ sound, the Germanic languages have an /f/ sound, as in Latin *pater* (from the Italic branch) compared with English *father* (the Germanic branch). These correspondences, once discovered, amounted to a whole series of connected changes or a **chain shift**. Grimm's and Verner's laws together are also known as the **First Germanic Consonant Shift**, which is a reconstruction of part of the process that took place as the Germanic dialect of Indo-European diverged from the parent tongue in the first millennium BC in northern Europe, until it became a distinct sub-language. This Proto- or Common Germanic language itself later diverged into sub-branches, leading in time to languages such as Dutch, English, Frisian, German, Swedish, and others – all members of the Germanic family. By the 1870s, some philologists had begun to think of such sound shifts as being entirely regular and exceptionless when they happened, carried out consistently in the applicable words throughout the community in question. It was their aim to arrive at 'laws', that is, descriptions which would be all-encompassing, accounting for all the data. In 1876 (p. xxviii), the oldest of the neogrammarians, August Leskien, in measured style put the case for exceptionless sound laws, arguing that 'exceptions' which themselves occurred 'as a result of specific, recognizable causes' (translation of Leskien by Koerner, 2004, pp. 47–8) are not in the strict sense of the word 'exceptions'. That is, they too are law-governed and are not merely random. He added that conceding the possibility of such random 'arbitrary, accidental deviations' (or 'unmotivated exceptions', as Brugmann and Osthoff refer to them) would lead ultimately to the conclusion 'that the object of investigation, language, was not accessible to scientific insight'. In 1878, Brugmann and Osthoff firmly stated the exceptionless dictum as one of the important principles of the neogrammarian movement.

By looking at Grimm and Verner, we can glimpse how theories advance in philology and linguistics: Grimm refines and adds to descriptions put forward by earlier work; Grimm's Law is shown to have exceptions, which appear as a result to diminish the explanatory power of the law; Verner identifies the further regularities that explain the exceptions and is able to augment and improve Grimm's Law. (I am reminded here of the time, when I was a research assistant at the University of Leeds, that I listened to the eminent literature scholar, Professor Norman Jeffares, giving his explanation of the puzzling idiom 'It's the exception that proves the rule' – Jeffares believed that 'proves' in this case was a shortening of 'improves'.) The ideal practice for a discipline that aims to be scientific is that hypothesis is tested by evidence, hypothesis is refined, then tested further, even if the procedure involves dispute and controversy. The development of an overarching theory of linguistic change has remained a driving force in dialect study since the late nineteenth century, and the neogrammarian hypothesis of exceptionlessness has consistently been a part of the discussion, as we shall see in the later chapters of the present book.

To return to the particulars: once fully and properly formulated, a sound law would describe a process (or set of processes) that applied in all the relevant words in the language or in the dialect (that is, in the speech community) in question, namely, in those words providing the pertinent phonetic environment, or as Brugmann and Osthoff put it: 'all words in which the sound subjected to the change appears in the same relationship are affected by the change without exception'. This was the somewhat controversial stance taken by the neogrammarians, more plainly put here by Brugmann and Osthoff than by Leskien. One can begin to see the relevance of dialect study to the testing of such a hypothesis. For example, if one, after careful historical research, postulated a law that stated that in a particular language all words with a plosive /k/ keep the /k/ sound in northern dialects, but shift to a fricative /x/ sound after vowels and word-finally in southern dialects, then this is a hypothesis that can be tested by a dialect survey. A linguistic atlas would show – if the hypothesis is correct – that the /k/~/x/ isogloss would follow the same path for all of the relevant words, separating two consistently distinct speech communities: one unaffected by the change, and one in which the sound change has occurred without exception in all the relevant words. In fact, this change is one part of the **Second Germanic Consonant Shift**. This set of changes brought about the division of German into a northern dialect, called Low German, and a southern, called High German. The Shift is thought to have been complete in the southern, mountainous area by AD 600, but did not operate in the northern lowlands. Two examples of the words affected are *ik* (northern) compared with *ich* (southern) [the pronoun 'I'], and *maken* (northern) compared with *machen* (southern) ['to make']. Georg Wenker's survey was indeed to throw significant new light on this, as well as more broadly on the Second Germanic Consonant Shift, and on the neogrammarian principle of exceptionless sound laws.

However, while Wenker's work took place in the context of the general philological climate outlined above, it would be risky to see it as prompted specifically by the neogrammarian controversy. It has indeed often been either stated or implied that Wenker embarked on his survey in response to the neogrammarian hypothesis, but this view is now questionable, even 'no longer valid' (Schrambke, 2010, p. 91). It is likely that this view originated in some over-interpretation and mild rewriting of the history of the project by Wenker's assistant and successor, Ferdinand Wrede (1863–1934) (see Koerner, 2004, pp. 43, 45, 50–1), though it also seems as if Wenker himself made no attempt to correct Wrede's assertions, and Kretzschmar (2002, p. 81) shows that Wenker judged some of his findings in the context of the regularity-of-variation issue. Koerner argues (2004, pp. 56–8) that Wenker's emphasis shifted during his career, from at first using dialect data to answer historical-philological questions to later a primarily descriptive approach, with a particular desire to provide a solid evidential basis to enable accurate representation of the dialect boundaries of German, because he believed that their existing representation in the literature was erroneous.

Nevertheless, Wenker's findings contributed significantly to the neogrammarian debate, providing proof in the infancy of dialectology of its value to linguistic theory.

Figures 4.1 and 4.2 are taken from two of the hand-drawn maps in Wenker's *Sprachatlas des Deutschen Reichs* (1889–1923) showing, respectively, the isoglosses for *ich* and *mach(en)* as they run east-west towards the border with the Netherlands.

The two isoglosses run along a nearly identical path through most of the German speech area until they reach the neighbourhood of the River Rhine. Here they become out of sync with each other and also with the neogrammarian maxim. The *mak~mach* isogloss crosses the Rhine just south of Düsseldorf, while the *ek~ech* isogloss heads northwards to cross the Rhine near Ürdingen. This gives us an area between Düsseldorf and Ürdingen in which the change to /x/ has not taken place without exception. (You will notice also from these excerpts that there are two vowel variants at large for *ich* in the High German area. This is also the case in the north, though not visible in Figure 4.1. Wenker-sentence number 10, mentioned in Chapter 3, section 4, elicited the variants of *ich* shown in Figure 4.1, while the *mach(en)* material was obtained by means of sentence number 17, *Geh, sei so gut und sag Deiner Schwester, sie sollte die Kleider für eure Mutter fertig nähen und mit der Bürste rein machen* ['Be a good girl/boy and tell your sister to finish sewing the clothes for your mother and clean them with a brush'].) Figures 4.3 and 4.4 zoom in on the key localities.

This opening out of isoglosses at the Rhine was repeated in Wenker's data for other changes specified in the Second Germanic Consonant Shift, producing

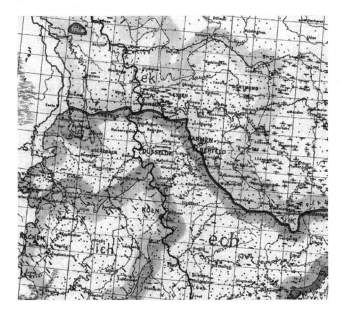

Figure 4.1   Part of Map 143 *ich* from the *Sprachatlas des Deutschen Reichs,* taken from the online reproduction of the hand-drawn original at: http://regionalsprache.de/SprachGis/Map.aspx?shortUrl=Y1vbU283 (accessed 30 December 2016).

an effect – and a puzzle – that became known as the **Rhenish Fan**. It seemed to represent a blow against the neogrammarian principle and in favour of those philologists who, to put it bluntly, believed that language in its living manifestation is just too diverse for such exceptionless laws to apply. Among these was Jules Gilliéron, who is associated with the slogan 'chaque mot a son histoire' or 'each word has its own history' (though Bill Kretzschmar (2002, p. 84) questions whether Gilliéron ever really used the phrase). Gilliéron's approach prioritized individual words and their individual histories, which led him to believe that the diversity that this uncovered was at odds with a strict adherence to the 'laws' which arose from treating words in classes or groups. Gilliéron went so far as to suggest that the notion of a 'dialect' was a 'false linguistic unity' (Gilliéron and Mongin, 1905, p. 24, as cited by Kretzschmar, 2002, p. 84), such was his concentration on single words. In this view, the notion of a coherent or consistent speech community becomes at best a convenient abstraction, one which highlights patterns but smoothes out messiness in the data.

This polarization of viewpoints – one arguing for systematicity in language (coupled with the aspiration that language study be a science with an appropriate object of investigation), and the other arguing in favour of letting the data in all its diversity lead the way (though also pro scientific methodology) – has continued

Figure 4.2   Part of Map 267 *mach(en)* from the *Sprachatlas des Deutschen Reichs,* taken from the online reproduction of the hand-drawn original at: http://regionalsprache.de/SprachGis/Map.aspx?shortUrl=Y1vbU283 (accessed 30 December 2016).

to characterize this discussion and also dialect study and linguistics in general. In a detailed interrogation published in 1981, the leading sociolinguist William Labov (1981a, p. 268) rephrased the neogrammarian controversy thus: 'In the evolution of sound systems, is the basic unit of change the word or the sound?' His answer in 1981 was to try to unravel the dichotomy, arguing that contemporary studies of sound change in progress showed neogrammarian regularity in some respects and ongoing **lexical diffusion** (gradual spread through the word-group) in other respects, and that this necessitated moving away from the old antagonism. On the other hand, Kretzschmar (2002, p. 92) charges Labov with going too far in his pursuit of abstraction and his goal of perpetuating the neogrammarian principle. Kretzschmar (p. 93) argues for describing individual features on their own terms, for observing the speech behaviour of individuals, and only after doing so to strive to 'make generalizations about how such habitual behavior by individuals might best be considered in terms of groups'. As a result

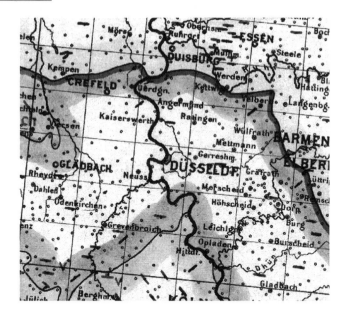

Figure 4.3   Enlargement of *ich* isogloss crossing the Rhine.

of this approach, 'We can recognize that language variation is not a distortion of a linguistic system, neither merely borrowing [of forms from one dialect to another] nor just change in progress, but is itself the normal condition of a language' (p. 93). In practice, strangely enough, progress can be made by means of this conflict and the continual testing of one school of thought by the other. We shall return to this in a minute, but first let us look at the additional probing prompted by the discovery of the Rhenish Fan. (Note that William Labov's engagement with the neogrammarian question, particularly in his research in Philadelphia and on the Northern Cities Chain Shift in American English, is discussed further in Chapters 7 and 10 of the present book.)

In the context of the neogrammarian debate, the Rhenish Fan clearly requires explanation. Clearly change had not advanced uniformly. Further understanding lay in looking beyond the purely linguistic factors. Lehmann (1973, p. 117) points out that the more southern *mak~mach* isogloss corresponds with the extent of the political and cultural influence of the city-state of Cologne (Köln, to the south of Düsseldorf, and in the /x/ area) from the thirteenth century, and the more northern *ek~ech* isogloss with the city's greater influence from the fourteenth to the sixteenth centuries, suggesting that *ek* was affected more strongly than *mak* at the later stage, under the influence of the prestigious Cologne dialect. McMahon (1994, pp. 228–9) says that the isoglosses revealed that the Consonant Shift spread in stages, moving steadily overall from south to north, but affecting different words at different rates, and that this progression was further fractured by change diffusing outwards

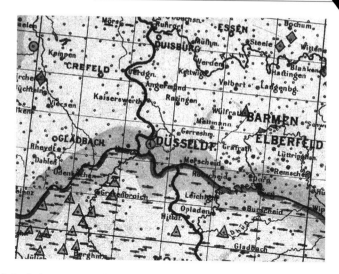

Figure 4.4   Enlargement of *mach(en)* isogloss crossing the Rhine.

from political and cultural centres (like Cologne), which act as a focus for innovation. Change thus affects more isolated **relic areas** to a lesser extent or at a slower rate. She adds that areas with a long settlement history, such as the Rhenish Fan area, may be subject to diffusion or influence from more than one focal point and are in effect **transition areas** between dialect regions. This is corroborated by Chambers and Trudgill (1998, pp. 92–3), who also note that there are in fact, even if on a smaller scale, such transition areas throughout Germany and Holland all along the length of the isoglosses that contribute to the Rhenish Fan. We could say that, on this evidence, the neogrammarians were wrong, but not completely wrong, and that the 'diversity-ists' were right, but not completely right. And vice versa, if you follow. A sound change takes time to spread, and may be affected by a number of sociocultural factors, and therefore at any given moment may not appear to be 'exceptionless'. Nonetheless, reasons for the exceptions can be uncovered. We could also understand the situation in the 'Labovian' terms mentioned above. (There is more on the theme of the geographical diffusion of linguistic innovations in the final chapter of the present book, on modern *geolinguistics*.)

Lawrence M. Davis (1983, p. 94) provides us with another way to encapsulate this state of affairs: 'linguistic behavior is inconsistent but … the inconsistency is, paradoxically, ordered'. According to this view, there is order and pattern at work in linguistic diversity and change, but there are also exceptions or disruptions to the order, and there are explanations waiting to be discovered for those exceptions, and certainly, in a general sense, language is always in flux. Nevertheless, pending such explanations, the data may well appear to display a quite bewildering variety.

la to sum up a later milestone in the quest to explain the
haphazard linguistic variation, that is, the momentous
William Labov from the 1960s onwards which started
quiry into **linguistic change in progress** (discussed in
s 6, 7, 9, and 10 of the present book). But, on a concluding
ber again the measured definition of exceptionlessness by
en in 1876 – it is quite in keeping with the idea that eventually
exceptions' will be explained and will therefore turn out not to be 'exceptions'.

4.3 Legacy: what happened after the first atlases?

To be honest, we have already begun to consider the legacy of the first atlases.
We have already seen that they suggested basic issues of theory and approach
for subsequent generations of dialect scholars to grapple with. The light
that they threw on contemporary questions in philology raised an array of
possible lines of enquiry for the future. In addition, scholars were eager to
learn methodological lessons from these huge data-collecting surveys. In the
short sections below, I summarize their impact on future work, bearing in
mind that we look in more detail at some of the issues, terms, and examples
in other chapters of the present book.

4.3.1 Localities and informants

The early atlases and the surveys upon which they were based had an interest in
history – primarily linguistic history, but also to an extent cultural and national
history. This interest is perpetuated in many of the surveys which followed
in Europe and North America in the twentieth century. Hence there was an
emphasis (though to a lesser degree in America) on collecting data from what
were perceived as the most traditional dialects of living speech, that is, those
dialects with the longest history, or as the eminent Austrian-American dialectologist Hans Kurath (1891–1992) put it, 'the speechways of the folk' (1972, p. 13).

In Europe, following the early work, there was an inclination for atlas surveys
to concentrate on rural villages and the more elderly of their inhabitants. Wenker
and Gilliéron created the principle that a national dialect survey requires a
network of localities: selected locations of human settlement evenly spaced
throughout the territory under investigation. The data-collecting descriptive
linguist is faced with a tough fact of life, which is that language use happens all
over the world all the time. Descriptive linguistics, therefore, requires sampling.
The network of chosen localities is one manifestation of sampling in national
dialect surveys. As more work was done on these 'conservative' or older, rural
dialects, the reach of some of the surveys broadened. For example, in the 1920s
and 1930s the AIS included urban centres (as noted in Chapter 3), and from the
outset in North America both rural and urban communities were investigated.

A major swing occurred with the rise of the sociolinguistic approach in the 1960s, shifting more attention towards urban localities and, for a short while, away from atlases. But *perceptual dialectology* (see Chapter 9), *geolinguistics* (see Chapter 10), and the digital revolution helped reinvigorate linguistic geography, leading to many new works, such as the sociolinguistic *Atlas of North American English* (*ANAE*; Labov, Ash and Boberg, 2006), undertaken at the turn of the twentieth and twenty-first centuries, which used a three-stage sampling process to select city localities for its study of urban dialects.

When it comes to the sampling of informants, there are two main types: **judgement sampling** and **random sampling**, which are discussed further in Chapters 6 and 7.

Briefly for now, in judgement sampling, the investigator seeks informants who meet set criteria formulated by the investigator. In other words, the investigator has judged in advance what type of speaker would best provide the data being sought. It is this method that characterized the *ALF*, and many later atlas surveys followed suit. In its bias towards selecting male rather than female informants, the *ALF* set the tone for some later surveys, such as the Survey of English Dialects (SED), a project which resulted in a number of atlases and whose director Harold Orton advocated choosing male informants in the belief that 'in this country [England] men speak vernacular more frequently, more consistently, and more genuinely than women' (Orton, 1962, p. 15). Orton's co-director of the SED, Eugen Dieth (1951, p. 73), believed that women were more likely to veer towards Standard English in their speech. The proportion of male to female informants in the SED is about two-to-one. In keeping with the interest in history, some later surveys (like the SED) drew their informants from the older age-groups (60-plus in the case of the SED), though the *ALF* was more inclusive, and when North American work got under way in the 1930s, a broader range of age-groups and of social-class groups were looked at there. Following the first atlases, there was also an aim to collect from informants who had been lifelong residents of each locality investigated and, in British surveys, informants who had had minimal education. This is in accord with the aim of collecting material that best represents the most historical local 'speechways', as unaffected as possible by modifications triggered by education or a transient lifestyle (or, indeed, wartime service). Again the *ALF* was more wide-ranging and less focused than this, with just under a third of its informants in the more highly educated category (Petyt, 1980, p. 42), whereas the SED informant sample represented 'a restricted social class most likely to have retained the oldest form of local speech' (Stanley Ellis, 1976, p. 95), that is, older lifelong residents who often had left school at an early age. (A rather different restriction on the audio recording part of the SED fieldwork noted by Stanley Ellis in 1952, before the advent of battery-powered tape recorders, was that interviews were 'limited to those informants who have electricity in their homes' (p. 568).) The first of the American atlases, the *Linguistic Atlas of*

New England (*LANE*; Kurath et al., 1939–43), systematically sought representatives from three social groupings, 'the cultured, the middle class, and the folk' (Kurath, 1972, pp. 13–14), because the remit of the projected and overarching Linguistic Atlas of the United States and Canada was to study the speech of several social levels – that said, representatives of the 'cultured' class were interviewed in only about 20 per cent of *LANE* localities, mainly in the cities.

In random sampling, each member of the speech community must have an equal chance of being selected for interview. Each informant is chosen randomly from some kind of comprehensive list. In practice, a truly random sample is difficult to achieve, and will likely be supplemented by appropriate judgement techniques. Random sampling came to prominence with statistics-based variationist sociolinguistics in the 1960s, and the *ANAE*, for example, selected its 762 informants using a process that aimed to be as random as possible, in order to ensure that the sample was suitably representative of as large a proportion as achievable of the North American urban English-speaking community. But judgement sampling does play a role in the *ANAE* too: over 60 per cent of its informants are female because of the project's interest in linguistic change in progress and its team's view that young urban women are at the forefront of certain sound changes. The selection of informants was slanted towards this group.

At this point, think back for a second to section 2 of Chapter 3, 'The map *is not* the territory'. It is easy to understand how sampling of communities and speakers influences what ends up on a linguistic map. The geographical territory will be there, complete, on the base map, but the data overlaying it will be partial in some way, due to sampling of localities or informants or linguistic features or all of these. Such sampling or selection when done well will be in keeping with the aims and interests of the survey.

4.3.2 Fieldwork

Among the early dialectologists, both Louis-Lucien Bonaparte (discussed in Chapter 5) and A. J. Ellis on occasion gathered material directly from dialect speakers, as did some of their helpers, but the father of all fieldworkers, so to speak, is Edmond Edmont. Edmont did on-the-spot interviews with local informants and was trained in phonetic transcription and fieldwork by Jules Gilliéron. Ever since, the use of fieldworkers in this way has been common in dialect surveys. For example, the SED used 11 trained fieldworkers to collect its data directly from informants during the 1940s, 1950s, and 1960s, and this method is the norm in the linguistic-atlas projects of North America. Georg Wenker, in a sense, did not do fieldwork, using the postal service and intermediaries. This approach was by no means abandoned after the introduction of Edmont and Gilliéron's method, and has been used subsequently in other major surveys. One such is the *Linguistic Geography of Wales* (*LGW*; Thomas,

1973), for which a 750-item questionnaire on lexis was sent out to educated intermediaries who then chose elderly informants in 182 rural localities to answer it, and another is the Linguistic Survey of Scotland (LSS), which sent two mainly lexis-collecting questionnaires in the early 1950s to headteachers (mostly) who passed them on to suitable middle-aged and older informants in Scotland, the far north of England, and the northern parts of Ireland. One could argue that collection by means of telephone (as for the *ANAE* (Labov et al., 2006)) or email or the Internet are modern successors, in that the established postal service is a forerunner to each of these media. In these methods, there is no face-to-face interaction, unless via video-calling – let us say there is no face-to-face-on-the-spot interaction, and the 'fieldworker' is not actually in the field. However, neither is there an intermediary, and in this respect once again technological advance has assisted dialect study by expediting large-scale, inexpensive data collection, as in the online Language Lab/Word Map survey of the BBC *Voices* project between 2005 and 2006.

4.3.3   Elicitation

Edmont asked questions, though like Wenker's posted sentences they involved informants translating from standard forms into their own dialect. The questionnaire has remained a constant presence in dialect atlas surveys, and future researchers refined it in order to avoid over-conditioning informants' responses. The questionnaire/interview method has been much augmented since the early days, especially by elicitation techniques introduced by sociolinguists (like William Labov and Lesley Milroy), even if most of these innovations were originally for surveys with aims other than producing linguistic maps.

The questionnaire appears in a range of guises. As we know, one is the postal questionnaire. The postal questionnaire is most useful for elicitation of lexis and least suitable for matters of pronunciation, though in fact Wenker's interests were mainly phonological and morphological. (To **elicit** is to 'draw forth' something.) It has some practical advantages, such as facilitating a large sampling of the population and being less expensive than fieldwork. The online Language Lab survey done for BBC *Voices* used a newer incarnation of the postal method: a downloadable questionnaire which consisted of a set of lexical 'prompts'. For example, its first section asked participants to 'List your words for how you feel' under the following six notions: *unwell, hot, tired, pleased, cold, annoyed.* In 2005–6, just over 62,500 participants (not intermediaries) responded to this questionnaire and a preliminary selection was used for online maps showing variants of 16 notions across the UK (see: http://www.bbc.co.uk/voices/).

Many other surveys have favoured a questionnaire designed for use *in situ* by the fieldworker in direct interviews with the informant, and using questions which encourage the informant to give their local variants for given notions without the fieldworker naming the notions (and thereby affecting the responses). This can be done in a number of ways, for example, by describing an object or by showing a picture or by providing the informant with an uncomplicated gloss of the notion, as in, 'What do you call a jacket and trousers together when they match?' For this notion, a smartly dressed fieldworker could simply point to their attire and ask, 'What do you call this?' Not that a *whistle and flute* is the best outfit for fieldwork, in terms either of practicality or of helping to create an informal and relaxed ambience – putting 'the newly-formed acquaintance on a friendly footing', as Harold Orton described it (1962, p. 17). A basic issue with questionnaires is that they might be seen as inherently fostering a formality which is counter-productive when collecting everyday conversational speech. This takes us to what William Labov in 1972 labelled **the observer's paradox**, a term which brought into sharper focus the basic predicament facing dialect researchers: 'To obtain the data most important for linguistic theory, we have to observe how people speak when they are not being observed' (Labov, 1972b, p. 113).

On the other hand, a questionnaire enables the investigator to collect data that is directly comparable from locality to locality and speaker to speaker across a territory. This comparability is essential to cartographic projects whether large- or small-scale. In the national surveys that followed the first atlases, the questionnaires tended to be comprehensive and lengthy, such as the 1322-item SED questionnaire devised by Eugen Dieth and Harold Orton (Dieth and Orton, 1962), made up of questions on syntax, morphology, pronunciation, and lexis, which was trialled through six versions between 1947 and 1962 (Fees, 1991a, pp. 36–45). Rather more manageable is the substantially downsized version of the SED questionnaire used by David North and Adam Sharpe to produce the 42 maps of their *Word-Geography of Cornwall* (1980). For the Linguistic Atlas of the United States and Canada, a 750-item work sheet was compiled (shorter versions were often used), each item being a targeted notion, with the fieldworker given the freedom to elicit the variants by guiding the conversation or by framing their own questions.

Data collected in these ways could include detailed, high-quality pronunciation material, either transcribed phonetically by the fieldworker or from the 1950s onwards audio recorded by portable machines. Successive generations of portable audio recorders have revolutionized dialect data collection: reel-to-reel tape recorders in the 1950s, cassette tape recorders in the 1960s, and digital recorders in the 1990s. Other earlier types of audio recording were made by some surveys: for example, on aluminium disc/aluminum disk in the 1930s for *LANE*, or using a wire recorder (developed first in the late nineteenth century in the form of magnetic recording on steel wire), as for the first stage of the *Linguistic Atlas of the Upper Midwest* (*LAUM*) from 1949 (see Allen, 1973–6). Audio recording spares the fieldworker from the tricky chore of transcribing interviews then and there while interviewing, and it allows more data to be collected more quickly. Needless to say, digital recordings are now possible without the need to go into the field – via the Internet.

Whether used during interviews or at a later stage, the **International Phonetic Alphabet** (**IPA**) is an invaluable tool for dialect fieldworkers and all other collectors of spoken language, providing a universally agreed set of symbols for transcribing all possible speech sounds. The International Phonetic Association was founded in 1886, and by 1899 its Alphabet had reached a form that has remained very stable ever since. A. J. Ellis was among those who helped devise the IPA, and Jules Gilliéron was a member of the Association. The full IPA chart is reproduced in the preliminaries of the present book.

In 1982, in his three-volume guide to *Accents of English* worldwide, the linguist and phonetician John C. Wells provided another handy apparatus for dialectologists, one which has since in use become standard practice for descriptions of regional pronunciations, that is, his **standard lexical sets** (Wells, 1982, pp. 119–24, 127–68). These form into a collection of 27 keywords, each keyword standing for 'a large number of words which behave the same way in respect of the incidence [occurrence or manner of occurrence] of vowels in different accents' (p. 120), and which 'enable one to refer concisely to large groups of words which tend to share the same vowel, and to the vowel which they share' (p. xviii). Thus the KIT set stands for all words which have a stressed, short /ɪ/ vowel or variants thereof in them, which Wells then called 'the KIT vowel' or simply 'KIT'. Other lexical sets are, for example, BATH, FLEECE, MOUTH, and so on, the total collection being designed to cover the full range of stressed and unstressed vowel phonemes in English, and equipping scholars with an efficient shorthand for accent descriptions and inventories. The lexical sets have become the standard format in accent studies, and I make use of them occasionally (or refer to other similar keywords used by researchers) in the present book.

4.3.3.1   A short excursion, at this point, on acoustic analysis and intonation

While we are on such matters, I will point out that in the present book there is no one chapter dedicated to the interest in studying regional and social variation in pronunciation or phonology, that is, in studying regional and social accents, because this interest cuts across all the other major themes of the book. From Bonaparte, A. J. Ellis, Joseph Wright, Wenker, and Gilliéron through Kurath, Raven McDavid, and Orton to Labov, Peter Trudgill, and Dennis Preston, the interest in variation in sounds is present, if not always as the primary focus (though there are plenty of works in which it is the primary focus, such as Ellis, 1889; Orton, 1933; Kurath and McDavid, 1961; and Wells, 1982). Work on regional pronunciation figures to a lesser or greater extent in dialect lexicography and cartography, variationist sociolinguistics and dialectology, perceptual dialectology, and geolinguistics, and is touched on or described in many places in this book. A couple of aspects of pronunciation that do not feature greatly – and which are also comparatively under-represented in the history of dialect research as a whole – are regional variation in **intonation**, that is, the pitch or 'melody' patterns that characterize speech, and in **prosody**, that is, intonation plus the loudness, tempo, and rhythm of speech. These are facets of **suprasegmental phonetics and phonology**, the study of sound patterns above or over or across individual segments such as consonants and vowels, which in turn are studied in **segmental phonetics and phonology**. Both segmental and suprasegmental phonetics and phonology also connect with **acoustic phonetics**, the study of the physical properties of speech sound by instrumental (mechanical and electronic) means. Acoustic analysis, in this sense, is different from the kind of analysis done in **articulatory phonetics**, which describes the articulation of speech sounds, and which for the most part has been done by phoneticians using the IPA. In dialect research, segmental phonology has featured much more strongly than suprasegmental study and articulatory analysis much more than acoustic (in other words, most work has been done in the segmental, articulatory mode), though here once again the innovations of digital technology have facilitated and stimulated investigations. Digital audio recordings and freely available software programs such as Praat (Boersma and Weenink, 1992–2016) and its add-on Akustyk (Plichta, 2003–12), WaveSurfer (Sjölander and Beskow, 2005–12), and Audacity (Mazzoni, Dannenberg et al., 1999–2016), or rather costly ones such as Adobe Audition and Magix Samplitude, enable precise acoustic analyses that previously were possible only for researchers with access to expensively equipped phonetics laboratories.

William Labov was involved in pioneering segmental acoustic analysis of vowel sounds in the late 1960s (see Labov, Yaeger and Steiner, 1972), centring on measurement of their **formants**, a **formant** being a concentration of acoustic energy indicating the way in which air from the lungs vibrates in the vocal tract during articulation. Each formant is made up of a band or clustering of frequencies, and for any vowel the air vibrates at many different frequencies simultaneously. Three formants characterize the quality of each vowel sound: F1, F2, and F3, with F1 and F2 receiving most attention from researchers as they correlate with the vowel's height and frontness/backness, respectively. (In articulatory phonetics, vowels are classified according to which part (front, centre, or back) of the tongue is highest during articulation, as well as according to the shape of the lips (rounded or spread).) Different speech sounds have different, characteristic formant patterns. These can be displayed on a chart known as a **sonogram** or sound **spectrogram**, which shows the spectrum of several seconds of sound, displaying onset, transitions, and formant peaks. A spectrogram is a visual representation of an acoustic signal which displays amplitude or loudness (on a light-to-dark scale, in which white = no energy, black = lots of energy), frequency (given in hertz, on the vertical axis of the chart), and time (horizontal axis). See Figure 4.5 for an example. The first system for generating spectrograms was made in the 1930s (and therefore such acoustic analysis was simply not available to the early dialectologists), and by the 1950s the Kay Sonograph (a spectrograph) was a widely used device. Segmental acoustic analysis of vowel formants appears prominently in Labov et al.'s *ANAE* (2006), on the basis that, 'These measurements are considerably more precise and reliable than estimates of tongue position made by ear, that is, by impressionistic phonetics' (Labov, 2012, location 501), although (as Labov acknowledges) acoustic measurements can be prone to error and should be used alongside articulatory phonetics. The *ANAE* acoustic analyses were carried out using the Kay Elemetrics (subsequently KayPentax) Computerized Speech Lab. Figure 4.5 is a spectrogram from the *ANAE* of one southern speaker's pronunciation of the vowel in the word *past*, showing **'breaking'** of the vowel, that is, its articulation is broken up by an interjected [j] sound, giving an [æjə]-like pronunciation which Labov et al. call **Southern breaking**, a feature of the 'Southern drawl' of the English of south and south-eastern United States.

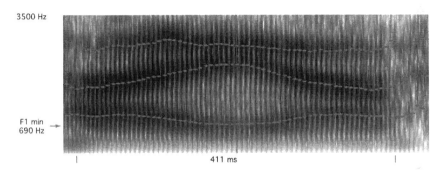

Figure 4.5 Spectrogram including formant trajectories of *past* by a speaker from Birmingham, Alabama, from the *ANAE* (Labov et al., 2006, Figure 13.16).

The spectrogram shows the three formants, with the rising trajectory of the middle one, F2, reflecting the [j]-'break' in articulation. Such analyses inform the map reproduced in Figure 4.6.

The *ANAE* also uses the Plotnik software program designed by Labov (Labov, 2002–11) for showing simultaneously many tokens (instances) of vowel pronunciations for easy comparison, including tokens measured by acoustic analysis. Like Georg Wenker a hundred years before, Labov et al. (2006) were interested in the geographical distribution of speech sounds and in sound change through time, and like Wenker they used isoglosses and symbols to show their results on their maps. Where Wenker used a postal questionnaire and (of necessity) articulatory analysis, Labov et al. used a telephone questionnaire and interview, and acoustic as well as articulatory analysis.

In 1982, J. C. Wells commented that in the matter of the intonation patterns of English dialects 'our ignorance in this area is still very great' (p. 91), and, in

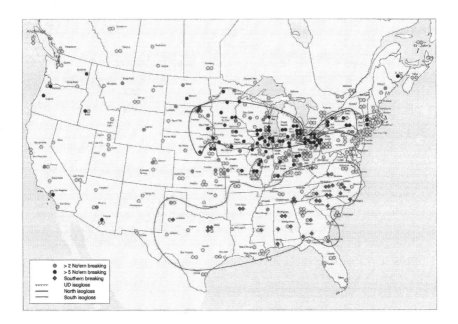

Figure 4.6   Map 13.4 from *ANAE* (Labov et al., 2006), which shows the geographical incidence of Southern breaking as marked by the dark diamond-shaped symbols within the Southern dialect region.

similar style, regarding prosodic features generally, 'we are far from being able to give a coherent account of how these vary from accent to accent' (p. 86). These statements reflected the comparative lack of research on these topics. By 2004, using a successor to Wells's *Accents of English* as evidence, that is, the comprehensive, multi-volume *Handbook of Varieties of English* (Kortmann and Schneider et al., 2004, hardback; and Kortmann and Schneider et al., 2008, paperback), the situation had improved somewhat. The *Handbook* includes descriptions of the phonology and grammar of more than 60 varieties of English worldwide (it is cited also in Chapter 2 of the present book). While many of the contributors mention the shortage of research on prosody, a number provide brief commentaries on the suprasegmental characteristics of their varieties. Those varieties located outside the British Isles and North America are better catered for in this respect in the *Handbook*, but acoustic, suprasegmental studies in general have been on the increase from the 1990s onwards.

For example, the prosody of Welsh English has been investigated by Rod Walters (1999, 2001, 2003a, 2003b), who looked at Rhondda Valleys English in south-east Wales, and by Stefano Quaino (2011), who looked at the English of the north-west and mid-west of Wales. Both researchers worked with limited audio corpora for their suprasegmental work – Walters with extracts from his own fieldwork, and Quaino with excerpts from the digitized-recordings archive of the Survey of Anglo-Welsh Dialects at Swansea University. The focus on limited amounts of data is understandable, as each item typically consists of a few seconds of continuous speech subjected to detailed acoustic analysis. Walters found clear evidence of the influence of the Welsh language in the prosodic patterns of Rhondda Valleys English, including the following strong tendencies: shortening of the stressed vowel of words and lengthening of the succeeding consonant, an emphatic pitch-peak following a stressed syllable, and a high pitch on unstressed syllables (see Walters, 2001, pp. 297–300) – in other words, the so-called sing-song Welsh accent. Quaino found less indication of this in his material (which was less conversational in character than that used by Walters), but he did notice a tendency for his speakers to avoid producing successive weakly stressed syllables and successive strongly stressed syllables, and to prefer a steady 2/4 musical rhythm of alternating weak and strong syllables (Quaino is a musician as well as a linguist). Figure 4.7 is part of Quaino's Praat analysis of the sequence *English and the Welsh word is to say aren't they* (stressed syllables underlined), in which his speaker maintains a 2/4 rhythm despite the occurrence of two successive strong stresses in *Welsh word*. The two stressed syllables are separated to some extent by the lengthening of the intervening -*sh*- [ʃ], as shown in the spectrogram.

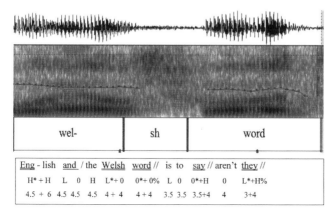

Figure 4.7   Spectrogram extract from Quaino (2011, Example 189, p. 294).

Praat offers a variety of options for doing and displaying acoustic analyses, but Praat spectrograms routinely are made up of two main parts, one showing frequencies (formants, pitch trajectories, intonation), and the other showing the sound waveform, which is a measurement of the variation of sound pressure through time. Figure 4.8 is a Praat spectrogram from Raymond Hickey's website on Dublin English (https://www.uni-due.de/VCDE/), of a sequence by a young female speaker. It shows pitch contour and two versions of the waveform for *I think it's just his style*, which exhibits the so-called **High Rising Terminal** (**HRT**) now found in many anglophone territories. HRT makes a declarative sentence sound like a question, because of the rising tone at the end.

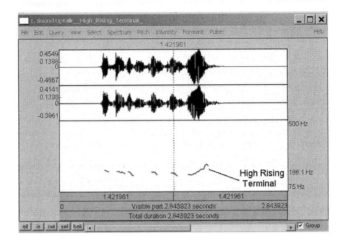

Figure 4.8   Spectrogram from Raymond Hickey's website on variation and change in Dublin English (https://www.uni-due.de/VCDE/index.html, accessed 29 July 2015).

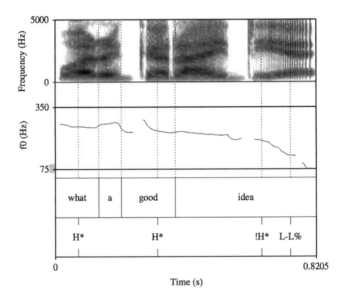

Figure 4.9   Spectrogram and f0 track of the phrase *what a good idea* by a speaker from the Midland dialect region of American English (from Clopper and Smiljanic, 2011, p. 240).

Figure 4.9 is another Praat spectrogram, this time from the article by Clopper and Smiljanic (2011) on the effects of gender and regional dialect on prosody in American English.

This shows the formant patterns at the top, underneath that the pitch contour expressed as f0 or **fundamental frequency** (the lowest frequency of the voice), under that the transcription in ordinary orthography, and at the bottom the transcription using a modified version of the **Tones and Break Indices (ToBI)** system (see Silverman et al., 1992; Beckman and Ayers Elam, 1997; Beckman, Hirschberg and Shattuck-Hufnagel, 2005). ToBI is a notation method first developed in the early 1990s for representing pitch patterns, designed originally for the transcription of standard varieties of English, but here adapted for comparative phonetic analysis of non-standard dialects, with its symbols representing such features as high and low pitch, contours within syllables and phrases, and boundaries between intonational phrases. Clopper and Smiljanic used a corpus of audio recordings of American English assembled with acoustic analyses in mind (the Nationwide Speech Project corpus, as described in Clopper and Pisoni, 2006), and their findings included the observation that male speakers of Southern American English paused more often than each of the other groups in their study (female Southern speakers, female and male Midland speakers), 'which may also contribute to the stereotype that Southern speech is slower than the speech in other regions' (Clopper and Smiljanic, 2011, p. 243). (Stefano Quaino also used a modified version of ToBI, as we can see at the bottom of Figure 4.7.)

Comparative work on British English has also been done between 1997–2008 by the phonetician Esther Grabe and her collaborators for the Intonational Variation in English (IViE) project based at Oxford University, and for its follow-up, the statistical Oxigen project (see, for example, Grabe, 2004; Grabe et al., 2008; and the IViE website at: http://www.phon.ox.ac.uk/files/apps/IViE/). This team also used a specially assembled corpus drawn from nine urban dialects of English in the British Isles and a ToBI transcription system modified so as to aid comparisons between varieties, and they found 'high levels of intonational variation' (Grabe, Kochanski and Coleman, 2008, p. 331) within and across dialects, but also some dialect-specific intonation patterns, that is to say, 'In each dialect, some [intonation] patterns were more popular than others' (p. 331).

And so we can see from these examples alone that progress has been made in answering John Wells's complaints of 1982, sometimes by assembling new corpora and sometimes, as in the study by Quaino, by exploiting an existing corpus in a new way. Incidentally, this suprasegmental work also answers in a tangential way a criticism made by Ronald K. S. Macaulay in 1988 of variationist sociolinguistics, that it had been up until that point 'largely concentrated on decontextualized tokens of phonological variables' (Macaulay, 1988, p. 158). However, Macaulay's argument really was that variationism had neglected investigating the structures of spoken **discourse**, that is, stretches of everyday language larger than a sentence, and this allows me to mention here very briefly that this is another example of an under-explored area in the history of dialect study generally.

4.3.3.2 Dialect and discourse

Macaulay's own work has contributed appreciably to the examination of discourse in English dialect, and in the first and second editions of *The Handbook of Language Variation and Change* (Chambers et al., 2002; Chambers and Schilling, 2013) he delivered two reports on the state of play in discourse variation studies in sociolinguistics as a whole and in ethnography. In 2002 (p. 298), he said, 'the study of discourse variation is still at an elementary stage'. By 2013 (p. 230), he was able to say, 'The sociolinguistic investigation of discourse variation has progressed substantially in recent years'. Once again, the digital revolution is a factor, especially the increasing availability of large computerized corpora and therein the longer stretches of speech (monologues, conversations) required for these analyses. In the still relatively small amount of work related to (and not necessarily principally focused on) the study of discourse in English dialect, there are two strands.

One follows the lead established by William Labov's sustained enquiry from the late 1960s onwards into the structure of oral narratives of personal experience, initiated by Labov and Waletzky (1967) and stimulated by the informant monologues gathered by Labov's innovative elicitation methods (Chapter 6, section 6.4.1 of the present book outlines these methods). The other strand looks at features of discourse organization, or **discourse features** or **markers**, such as the **quotative verbs** *be all* and *be like*, in which a form of the verb *to be* is followed by *all* or *like*, as in *I'm all* '*just come over and see me later on you know after bathing and stuff*' and *he was like* '*oh okay*'. This example comes from Federica Barbieri's study of quotatives in American English (2005, p. 236), which drew on the 2.5-million-word American English conversation component of the Longman Spoken and Written English corpus and the 1.6-million-word spoken component of the TOEFL 2000 Spoken and Written Academic Language (T2KSWAL) corpus. She found that, for example, *be like* forms had the discourse functions of representing the inner speech and emotional states of the speaker, and of quoting or constructing the 'plausible speech' of others (Barbieri, 2005, p. 249). This kind of analysis, then, concentrates on the roles that such **morphosyntactic** forms play in the composition of the larger discourse. There is therefore an overlap here with the study of dialect grammar, **morphosyntax** being the interaction of word structure (**morphology**) with sentence structure (**syntax**). You will find many examples of such forms in *eWAVE* (Kortmann and Lunkenheimer, 2013), the online resource for the study of morphosyntactic variation in English (and a successor to the *Handbook of Varieties of English*), which is discussed in more detail in the sections of Chapter 2 that deal with dialect grammars.

We return now to the main thread of this chapter.

4.3.4   Presentation

The isogloss brings a simple clarity to a linguistic map, unambiguously indicating a boundary with regard to feature use: on one side of the boundary speakers use variant *a*, on the other side speakers use variant *b*. Many would argue, however, that it is also a simplistic clarity, an over-interpretation, an obvious demonstration of the map-is-not-the-territory condition, in that 'on the ground' such absolute boundaries are the exception rather than the rule. The American dialectologist, Craig M. Carver, puts it like this: 'A line isogloss is a convenient fiction existing in an abstract moment in time' (1987, p. 13). Another American linguist, W. Nelson Francis, adds to this (1983, p. 5), saying that while the isogloss is a useful concept, 'it must always be viewed as an abstraction and not a clear line on the land which one might step across from one dialect area into another'. Its abstract and convenient nature is perhaps particularly apparent if one's data is taken from several social groups (for speech varies socially as well as geographically) or if it includes more than one instance of a given feature per informant, as when a survey collects a number of words which test for the 'same' sound – for example, what is the vowel in *brush, come, done, mud, some, sun* and so forth in any given dialect? Informants from different social groups in the same locality may give differing responses, and an individual may switch within their own speech between different vowel and consonant variants on different occasions (conventionally called **stylistic variation**). As Norbert Dittmar (2010, p. 865) notes, this is the principle that the coexistence of multiple variants of each feature in the same locality is the rule, and sole variants are the exception. So linguistic geographers and cartographers have sought to refine their methods of presentation since Wenker pioneered the isogloss. And yet the isogloss remains alive and well, and indeed the history of its use shows that it has been remarkably informative, provoking much research in new directions.

For example, the Rhenish Fan phenomenon showed a complex of variation that came to be seen as characteristic of long-settled regions. The east-west running-together of isoglosses for Second-Consonant-Shift features across the rest of Germany showed the importance of such **isogloss bundles**: the coincidence of a number of isoglosses offers much firmer evidence of linguistic boundaries than can be derived from considering isoglosses individually. But, in addition, the fact that the isoglosses do not run along precisely identical paths pointed up the existence of **transitional areas** between dialect regions. In this view, a dialect region can be understood as having a **focal area** at its centre and transitional areas at its limits. Transitions can also become apparent when examining the data for a single feature from a more statistical point of view. For instance, one could look at all the words containing variants of the same vowel. One might then find that informant *x* uses variant *a* 100 per cent of the time, while informant *y* in a nearby village uses variant *a* 50 per cent of the time and variant *b* 50 per cent of the time, while informant *z* in another nearby village uses variant *b* 100 per cent of the time, and so on. (This kind of scenario is illustrated rather more realistically by Jack Chambers (Chambers and Trudgill, 1998, pp. 106–9) using SED data.) The isoglossic method for showing patterns like this is not efficient or particularly clear, for one would have to produce a different isogloss for each word and then compare all the isoglosses. This weakness was observed by A. J. Ellis in his 1882 review (p. 31) of Wenker's 1881 maps of North and Middle Germany: 'to find the usages for any one particular place, we have to pursue it through all the maps, and note within what limits it exists for every case required'. He adds, 'This is very laborious'. Alternative mapping techniques have therefore been developed in order to cope with statistical analysis of data. Such quantitative work is now frequently referred to under the title **dialectometry** (literally, 'the measuring of dialect'), a term coined (in French originally: *dialectométrie*) by Jean Séguy for a small number of maps at the end of Volume 6 of the *Atlas linguistique et ethnographique de la Gascogne* ['Linguistic and ethnographic atlas of Gascony'] (1973), a contribution to *NALF*. Séguy began to work out a method for calculating and displaying similarities and differences between localities using a statistical approach. The focus on statistical analysis of tokens (that is, individual occurrences) of variants in dialectometry can be seen as descending from Gilliéron's emphasis on individual features and on understanding dialects as convenient abstractions rather than concrete entities, as well as an attempt to improve on the isoglossic method. See Chapter 5, section 4 for more on dialectometry.

Another pattern of isoglosses, in which the lines appear to radiate out like ripples from a centre, led scholars to identify points of origin for innovations which then diffuse outwards, in accordance with Johannes Schmidt's wave theory. Beyond the reach of the ripples one may find **relic areas** unaffected by the innovation, and the centre would be the focal area. The endeavour to profile and measure such processes of diffusion is a core concern of the approach known as **geolinguistics**, which takes into account factors of human geography like population movement and interaction. In its early days, Peter Trudgill (1974b) put forward a tentative **gravity model** in order to measure the strength of influence of one centre of population upon another. Geolinguistics is a renewal of the interest in the interplay of language and space, and it arose in part out of perceived shortcomings in both the original philological and later sociolinguistic modes. It is also quite a tricky term because of the tendency that has developed for it to be used as a replacement for earlier terms such as *dialectology* and *linguistic geography* – that is to say, as an umbrella term for the study of language, society, and geographical space, including reference to work that occurred well before the term itself came to light in the 1960s. (A full discussion of geolinguistics is in Chapter 10 of the present book. It could almost as easily be placed in Chapter 5, which continues the story of cartography, but that is already pretty full. The same is true of another recent strand, **perceptual dialectology** (Chapter 9), which examines folk beliefs about dialect, and which has some relevance to the study of linguistic change and to our understanding of the nature of dialects.)

Further alternatives to the isogloss have been used, and succeeding generations of linguistic cartographers have pursued goals unattempted by the first atlases. Take, for example, the data collected for the SED. As well as having been used for atlases that are primarily isoglossic (such as *A Word Geography of England* (*WGE*; Orton and Wright, 1974) and *The Linguistic Atlas of England* (*LAE*; Orton, Sanderson and Widdowson, 1978)), it has generated atlases which use other presentational methods. These include: the *Atlas of English Sounds* (*AES*; Kolb et al., 1979) with its display maps on which different symbols are assigned to different variants; *The Computer Developed Linguistic Atlas of England* (*CLAE*; Volumes 1 and 2, 1991, 1997, edited by Viereck et al.), made by using computerized SED data, and which also includes dialectometrical contributions; and *A Structural Atlas of the English Dialects* (Anderson, 1987), which attempts a structuralist and statistical analysis in order to produce maps detailing the phoneme-systems of conservative rural English. (We return to the SED project in Chapter 5.)

I should also point out that the term *isogloss* itself is used to refer to two slightly different kinds of boundary line. According to one convention (as described in Chapter 3, section 4), where two adjacent localities have different linguistic variants the isogloss is drawn midway between the two localities. This is the convention used by Wenker in 1881 (though not always with absolute clarity) and, for example, by the *WGE* and *LAE*. The second convention is to draw the isogloss at the limit of the overall territory of a variant. Sometimes the term **heterogloss** is used to refer to this kind of boundary line. For example, Hans Kurath uses the term *isogloss* in this way in his *Word Geography of the Eastern United States* (*WGEUS*; 1949), and later (1972, p. 26) he uses *heterogloss* when referring back to *WGEUS*. Chambers and Trudgill (1998, pp. 89–91) give a more distinct definition of *heterogloss*. According to them, a *heterogloss* is formed by two adjacent lines, each of which connects locations with the same variant (that is to say, line *a* connects localities with variant *a* and line *b* connects localities with variant *b*), and when used at the edges of two adjacent regions they show a kind of no man's land of transition (between the two lines).

Another alternative is the **isopleth**, which connects points which have an equal value, and is thus used like a contour line where statistics are available for usages at each locality in a network (as found in David North's innovative 1985 study of south-east England, which is an effective mix of geolinguistics, statistics, and structuralism). Another presentational technique is the shading or hatching of areas, as used by the *Linguistic Atlas of Scotland* (*LAS*; Mather, Speitel and Leslie, 1975–86; see Figures 4.10 and 4.11), which shows concentrations of particular forms and, by overlaying one form of hatching on another, reveals where different variants are in use in the same area.

Colour shading is now more feasible (and less expensive) because of the possibility of electronic publication of maps. Once again, new technology and dialect study have proved a fertile partnership: online publication of maps, including interactive maps, has had a reinvigorating effect on linguistic cartography.

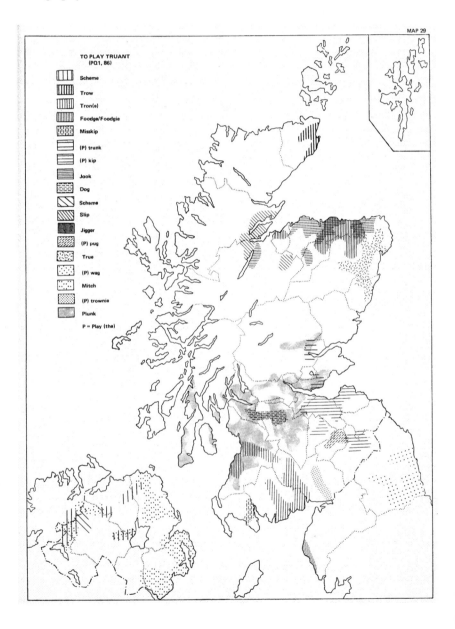

MAP 29

TO PLAY TRUANT
(PQ1, 86)

Scheme
Trow
Tron(e)
Foodge/Foodgie
Misskip
(P) trunk
(P) kip
Jook
Dog
Schame
Slip
Jigger
(P) pug
True
(P) wag
Mitch
(P) trownie
Plunk

P = Play (the)

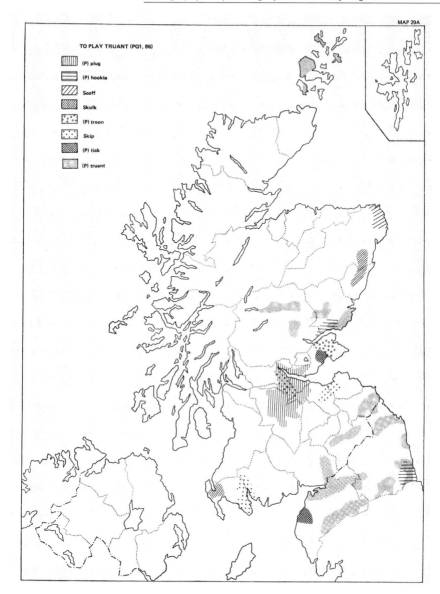

Figures 4.10 and 4.11   Sample maps from the LSS's *Linguistic Atlas of Scotland*: variants of *to play truant* (Maps 29 and 29A, Mather and Speitel, 1975).

4.4 Conclusion

A number of the items mentioned in section 4.3 above are now featured further in Chapter 5, which continues the account of dialect cartography by following the evolution of dialect maps and atlases of English. In summary, for now, we can say that key motivations for the early linguistic atlases (to describe and record living dialects, to study linguistic change, to illuminate cultural and national history) have remained current in dialect cartography and dialect study generally, and that the atlases' achievements and methods were imitated and improved by later scholars. In a 1968 reflection upon American and English atlas projects, Raven I. McDavid, Jr. talks (pp. 27–8) of them as building on principles set up by Gilliéron. Given the pioneering nature and impressive size of the early atlases, it seems unfair to talk of their inadequacies – but as we shall see in the following chapters (and as was indicated at the start of Chapter 3), the big philological projects (earlier and later) were eventually criticized for being naive, limited, and outmoded. A more positive stance is to think of them as agenda-setting in terms of what they discovered, the questions they shed light on, and the questions they raised (but did not or could not answer). Seen from this viewpoint, their influence on subsequent work is pervasive.

4.5 Brief commentary on terms

In this chapter, we have done some looking forward to developments in dialect study that followed the early atlases. As a result, I have been lured into pre-empting the fuller definition and discussion that occurs in later chapters of some terms, specifically with regard to *sociolinguistics* and *variationist sociolinguistics* (Chapters 6 to 8), *phoneme, phonology, structuralist*, and *variant* (Chapters 5 and 6). Read on to those chapters for further information about these terms. I have also avoided using one term, *accent*, in the sense that you will find it being used in studies of prosody, that is, to refer to stress or emphasis in sounds, syllables, and words. So as not to confuse, I use the term *stress* here for that purpose, and retain *accent* solely for the pronunciation features of a dialect.

Resources and further reading

The website of the Linguistics Research Center, University of Texas at Austin, has an excellent and most useful subsection called the Indo-European Documentation Center and, associated with this, a selection of online versions of books edited by Winfred P. Lehmann, including *A Reader in Nineteenth Century Historical Indo-European Linguistics* (originally published in 1967). In this you will find William Jones's *Discourse* of 1786 in full, as well as the celebrated 1878 preface by the neogrammarians Hermann Osthoff and Karl Brugmann. April McMahon's *Understanding Language Change* (1994) is a clear introductory guide to issues in historical linguistics in general. The Department of Linguistics, University of California, Berkeley, has an online Fieldwork Forum which contains advice on doing fieldwork and a list of links to fieldwork resources, including to software sites for Audacity, Praat, and WaveSurfer. Similarly, the Resources web-pages of the Department of Language and Linguistic Science, University of York, give practical information about and links to corpora and databases such as ToBI sound files at Ohio State University and IViE at Oxford University, and to software materials. In dialect research generally, there is much discussion of aims and methods. Any study or survey worth its salt will explain and justify the choices made in its design and execution, and it is always instructive to spend time reading these accounts. And just as sports fans and pundits find endless entertainment in debating tactics and performance, so do linguistic scholars unflaggingly return to talking about, questioning, and even disputing aims and methods. I touch on such deliberations and contests quite a lot in this book, especially in Chapter 8, and each other chapter in its way is concerned with innovation and evolution in methods and aims. Here and now, I will focus my recommendations on a few short, illuminating, and very handy pieces written by eminent, experienced practitioners centred on elicitation, fieldwork, and informant selection. Raven I. McDavid, Jr.'s 'Eliciting: Direct, Indirect, and Oblique' (1985) combines discussion of elicitation methods with a concise historical overview that runs from Wenker through to 1960s sociolinguistics. For the apprentice fieldworker, Lawrence M. Davis gives an even more concise review of work sheets and questionnaires in European and North American linguistic geography in his 'Work sheets and Their Variants' (1971). A little earlier, Frederic G. Cassidy's 'On Collecting American Dialect' (1948) presented some thoughts on designing a questionnaire, choosing informants, and doing interviews for the at-the-time unfulfilled objective of making an American dialect dictionary. Harold Orton and Eugen Dieth's 'The New Survey of Dialectal English' (1951) likewise outlines preparations for the Survey of English Dialects, especially concerning the design of the questionnaire and the nature of the fieldwork. 'Early Work for the Survey of English Dialects' (1968) by Peter Wright and Fritz Rohrer is a brief account of the experience of doing fieldwork for the SED. A digitized version of the article can be downloaded from the University of Leeds Digital Library, and the articles by Cassidy, Davis, and McDavid are available via the online academic digital platform JSTOR, as is Michael D. Linn's 'Informant Selection in Dialectology' (1983), an article which supplied a detailed overview of informant sampling methods at a time when dialect research had shifted towards urban populations and statistical techniques. This bunch of articles not only provides a compact depiction of some fundamental issues in survey design and fieldwork practice, but also offers a good insight into methodology in the days before portable audio and (later) digital technology became the norm. See also Crawford Feagin's 'Entering the Community: Fieldwork' (2013), for a more recent guide. I give further-reading recommendations on modern data-collection methods at the ends of other chapters in this book, particularly Chapter 7. For wide-ranging collections of essays on pronunciation analysis in present-day dialect study, go to *A Reader in Sociophonetics* (2010), edited by Dennis Preston and Nancy Niedzielski, and *Advances in Sociophonetics* (2014), edited by Chiara Celata and Silvia Calamai. Lee Pederson's 'Studies of American Pronunciation Since 1945' (1977) is a comprehensive survey of phonetic and phonological work on American English from the 1940s to the 1970s. Examples of Esther Grabe's work on the pronunciation of varieties of British English can be downloaded from: http://www.phon.ox.ac.uk/files/people/grabe/; and the study by Rod Walters of the pronunciation of Rhondda Valleys English is available at: http://reswin1.isd.glam.ac.uk/rhondda_valleys_english/. The phonologist Jennifer L. Smith maintains a fabulous Phonetics Resources web-page which has links to research, guidance, video, audio, and data on all aspects of present-day segmental and suprasegmental phonetics and phonology, including links to materials by leading experts such as Peter Ladefoged and John Wells, and to resources on accents and dialects of English across the world. The phonetician Rob Hagiwara has a clear and helpful online guide to spectrograms called the Monthly Mystery Spectrogram Webzone (2002–09). When you encounter difficulty in putting IPA symbols into your document, go to Tomasz P. Szynalski's TypeIt website for a simple type-and-copy-and-paste solution. Volume 1 of *Language and Space* (Auer and Schmidt, 2010a) includes a short review by Norbert Dittmar of work on 'Areal Variation and Discourse' which summarizes the situation in the relatively young topic area of regional variation in discourse features. The same volume also has two useful pieces on segmental and suprasegmental phonetics and phonology co-written by Peter Gilles and Beat Siebenhaar. If you want to compare the chronology of dialect survey work with the development of audio recording technology, go to the History of Sound Recording website for information on the latter, at: http://www.recording-history.org/.

5 The cartography of English dialects, and the regeneration of linguistic geography

5.1 Introduction

We have examined what led to the first big dialect atlases in continental Europe, and we have looked forward at their impact on dialect study. In this chapter, we resume the story of dialect cartography by focusing on its development in the English-speaking world, including an introduction to the first linguistic atlases of English. Then we outline what happened to dialect cartography after these big twentieth-century atlas projects reached fruition.

5.2 The first dialect maps of English

By the end of the nineteenth century, large cartographic dialect surveys were underway in Germany and France. Meanwhile, in Britain, there was no sign of a linguistic atlas, but there were some linguistic maps. These maps were the outcomes of innovative and determined work by extraordinary individuals.

5.2.1   The maps by A. J. Ellis: 1876–1889

On Thursday 9 March 1876, A. J. Ellis unveiled his first attempt at a 'large Dialectal Map' of British English in a lecture he delivered at the London Institution (see also Ellis, 1889, p. xix). At that point, his map was incomplete, 'leaving a blank from the Wash to Sussex' (1889, p. xix). His final attempt was in the form of two maps, one of England and Wales, and one of Scotland (prepared with the help of the Scottish dialectologist, lexicographer, and editor of the *Oxford English Dictionary* (*OED*), James Murray), published within pockets at the back of Part V of his *On Early English Pronunciation* in 1889, called *The Existing Phonology of English Dialects* (see Figures 5.1 and 5.2). (A quick note on the term *phonology* at this point: it was introduced into English in the late eighteenth century, but had its origins in Greek, and Ellis used the term to mean 'the science of speech sounds and pronunciation'. With the advent of structuralist linguistics in the early twentieth century, the term developed the more specific sense of 'the study of the contrastive relationships between speech sounds'. I start to discuss this more specific sense in 5.3.2 below, and take it further in Chapter 6, section 6.2.)

These maps show six main dialect regions, which Ellis called Divisions (bounded by thick lines, they are Southern, Western, Eastern, Midland, Northern, and Lowland), which he divides further into 42 Districts (bounded by thinner continuous lines, and numbered with bold figures). Also marked are Ten Transverse Lines (the first isoglosses of British English, indicated by broken lines or small cross-lines and by numbers between parentheses). To the west and to the north, Ellis draws a 'Celtic Border' (CB): he limits himself to English-speaking localities, which he defines as places 'in which the uneducated, or only elementarily educated people speak with each other habitually in English' (1889, p. 12), though he later qualifies this when talking of the CB in Scotland (p. 14, and see section 5.2.3 below). The Transverse Lines (see Ellis, 1889, pp. 15–22) designate the following boundaries:

1. The northern limit of the pronunciation of *some* as /sʌm/, or *sum* as Ellis transcribes it.
2. The southern limit of the pronunciation of *some* as /sʊm/, or *sŏŏm*.
3. The northern limit of **retroflex** [with the tip of the tongue considerably curled back] pronunciation of /r/.
4. The southern limit of the use of [t] or [θ] for the definite article *the*.
5. The northern limit of [ð] initially in *the* in variation with [t] or [θ].
6. The southern limit of the pronunciation of *house* as /huːs/, or *hoose*, and the northern limit of the pronunciation of *house* as /haus/.

7. The northern limit of the use of [t] for the definite article *the*.
8. The southern limit of the pronunciation of *some* as /sʌm/, or *sum*, on travelling from Scotland into England.
9. The northern limit of the pronunciation of *some* as /sʊm/, or sŏŏm.
10. The boundary between what Ellis calls 'Lowland Scotch' and Northern English.

Figure 5.1   'English Dialect Districts' (1887), appended to A. J. Ellis (1889).

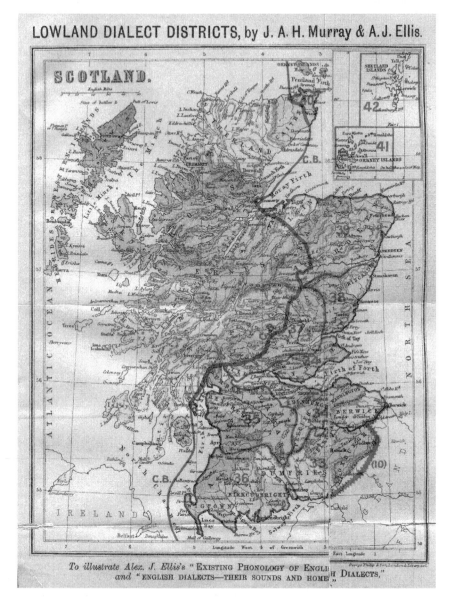

Figure 5.2 'Lowland Dialect Districts', by A. J. Ellis and J. A. H. Murray, appended to Ellis (1889).

As the title of his 1889 volume suggests, Ellis's dialect divisions are based principally on information about pronunciation, but the volume also contains much on grammar and lexis (such as the discussion at p. 43 of *I be*, *I've a-done*, and *I do go* in the western Mid Southern dialect District (District 4 on the map), and the lists of Gower Peninsula words at pp. 35–6). How did he collect this information?

He collected it by means of three elicitation tools. In September 1873, he and James Murray assembled the 'Comparative Specimen', which was a group of 15 short paragraphs containing words and constructions that Ellis required to be translated into the local idiom and pronunciation, much like Wenker's sentence set (but three years ahead of him). Here is his paragraph number (1): *Well, neighbour, you and he may both laugh at this news of mine. Who cares? That is neither here nor there* (Ellis, 1889, p. 7 of the Preliminary Matter). This was supplemented in 1877 by a 'List of Words of which the pronunciation is wanted' or 'classified word list' (Ellis, 1889, p. 16 of the Preliminary Matter), and in 1879 by a truncated set of sentences which Ellis called the 'Dialect Test'. He received material from 1145 localities (Shorrocks, 1991, p. 322). Ellis admits (1889, p. 3) that much the better way to obtain these words as pronounced in the local accent was to go directly to those speakers in whom he was interested, and to whom he gives the label 'the peasantry'. Ellis intends nothing pejorative by this term, or by the phrase 'peasant dialects', which he also uses at times. What he is interested in is the traditional speech of the working class, especially in rural areas. In addition to the logistic difficulties of carrying out such fieldwork on a large scale in the mid nineteenth century, Ellis notes (p. 3) that 'the peasantry throughout the country have usually two different pronunciations, one which they use to one another' and 'the other which they use to the educated', such as himself. Joseph Wright made the same point in the Preface to his *English Dialect Grammar* (1905, p. vii). This phenomenon was elucidated for present-day researchers by the sociolinguist William Labov in the 1960s, who introduced a scale of informality/formality in his elicitation methods, which recognized in stricter terms that speakers have access to a range of **styles** (from casual to formal) in their interactions. Ellis's observation also anticipates **speech accommodation theory**, as developed by Howard Giles in the 1970s (see Giles, 1973), which analyses the ways in which speakers shift their styles according to their perceptions of their interlocutors. Ellis was well aware of the **style-** or **code-shifting** capacities of speakers (not that he used the terms), and of the likelihood that the speech-data could be affected by the mere presence of the investigator (pp. 3–4) – this is the **observer's paradox**, to use Labov's phrase (1972b, p. 113). In the event, Ellis, like Wenker, used the postal method and intermediaries, often clergy, in the belief that they could supply the necessary local knowledge to translate his sentence-sets and word lists. In 1889 (pp. 67–76 of the Preliminary Matter), he records the names of some 900 such helpers, among them William Barnes, F. T. Elworthy, W. W. Skeat, and Joseph Wright. A portion of his material was in fact collected by direct fieldwork interviews (and occasionally, according to A. J. Aitken (1996, p. 16), by 'eavesdropping visits to railway stations'), carried out by Ellis and a few others, including Thomas Hallam, an excellent phonetician (Shorrocks, 1991, p. 323).

A big problem for Ellis was that at the start of his researches no adequate phonetic alphabet was available to suit his needs. In order to 'clothe all these sources of information in a proper garment, which would admit of accurate comparison,' he invented his own 'sufficiently copious phonetic alphabet' (1889, p. 5), which eventually developed into his 'Dialectal Palaeotype' (1889, pp. 76–88 of the Preliminary Matter). He also provided his helpers with a simpler version. As J. K. Local (1983, p. 3) puts it, 'A considerable amount of Ellis's life's work centred on the construction and elaboration of transcription and spelling systems for both linguistic and pedagogical purposes.' In the eyes of a number of later dialectologists, the Dialectal Palaeotype is not the most accessible system, but Local's conclusion is that it is not as difficult as some have claimed and that, 'Many of the practices and principles which Ellis evolved have found their way into present-day transcriptions' (p. 11). Sinclair Eustace (1969) eased the issue by compiling a translation of Ellis's symbols into the International Phonetic Alphabet.

Part V of *On Early English Pronunciation* is a major groundbreaking achievement, the first in-depth survey of English accents and dialects on a national (British) scale, achieving for the description of dialectal pronunciation what Joseph Wright would achieve a decade later for the description of dialectal lexis, in the *English Dialect Dictionary* (*EDD*; 1898–1905). Shorrocks's (1991) appreciation of Ellis argues that he deserves a prominent place in the history of dialectology, as 'the man who produced the very first truly large-scale, phonetic, detailed and systematic survey in dialect geography' (p. 326). There is no doubting the size of Ellis's survey, and one warms to the opening words of the volume: 'After fourteen years' delay ...'.

Nevertheless, Ellis's work suffered criticism over its accuracy and the complexities of its palaeotype from, for example, Joseph Wright (1892) and Eugen Dieth (1946), and it was treated minimally in Sever Pop's (1950) extensive account of dialectology. But Shorrocks (1991) is convinced that the material is reliable and points out that 'Ellis's work was pioneering in its scale, its use of narrow phonetics, its use of the direct [fieldwork] method (in part), and its culmination in a detailed classification of English dialects' (p. 326), as summed up by the two maps. It is ironic that while later dialect-mapping projects of British English (especially the Survey of English Dialects (SED)) were censured for failing to synthesize their data into an overview of dialect regions, Ellis achieved this in 1889, his two maps synthesizing a large quantity of data, an achievement that the SED's Harold Orton would have been aware of. Among the many intriguing artefacts stored in the Harold Orton Research Room at Leeds University (home of the SED) in the early 1980s when I was a research assistant there, were numerous loose-leaf copies of Ellis's maps, plus the map I reproduce here as Figure 5.3.

Figure 5.3   A. J. Ellis's English Dialect Districts interpreted by Harold Orton.

My informed guess at the time, made on the basis of other materials stored with it, was that this was an interpretation by Harold Orton of Ellis's 1887 map, possibly done in the 1950s while SED fieldwork was in progress. (The SED's collection is now part of the searchable Leeds Archive of Vernacular Culture (LAVC). Go to: http://www.leeds.ac.uk/library/spcoll/lavc/index.htm.

An overview of the contents of the LAVC is at: http://library.leeds.ac.uk/ special-collections-explore/409248/leeds_archive_of_vernacular_culture_ survey_of_en.) The purpose of Ellis's maps was to present visually the headline findings of his dialectological work. The data underpinning the maps is given in the 820 pages that precede them. The maps do not amount to a linguistic atlas. (However, since 2012, the dialectologist Warren Maguire has been engaged in an exciting project to produce a series of online maps of the phonological, grammatical, and lexical data from Ellis (1889). The ongoing results of the *Atlas of Ellis* project can be seen at: http://www.lel.ed.ac.uk/EllisAtlas/, a site which includes excellent colour reproductions of Ellis's original maps.) Neither are Ellis's the first published maps of the dialects of England. To whom, then, does the title of First Cartographer of the Dialects of England go? It goes to someone not short of titles.

5.2.2   The maps by Louis-Lucien Bonaparte: 1873–7

One of Ellis's chief helpers was another of dialectology's exceptional individuals, His Imperial Highness Prince Louis-Lucien Bonaparte. Born in 1813 near Worcester, while his family was interned in England, Louis-Lucien was brought up and educated in Italy, returning to live in London in the 1850s. Trained in chemistry, he eventually turned his attention to financing book-printing and to scholarly work on languages. He researched many languages of Europe, but in dialect study he is particularly known for his work on Basque and English. (Collins (1902) shows that the Prince also researched Gaelic, Cornish, Breton, Modern Greek, Italian, Spanish, Portuguese, German, Modern Frisian, Russian, Finnish, Provençal, Gascon, Welsh, Neo-Latin, Slavonic, and Albanian.) By the time of his death in 1891 he had amassed a huge personal library, including many books on English dialects. The *Attempt at a Catalogue of the Library of the late Prince Louis-Lucien Bonaparte* made by Victor Collins in 1894 estimates that the Prince owned nearly 19,000 books and pamphlets. The library is now in the possession of the Newberry Library in Chicago. A. J. Ellis (and Joseph Wright) had access to this collection, and to Bonaparte's own 'database' of English dialects: a series of over 25 dialectal 'translations' (largely focused on pronunciation, but also to a lesser degree on grammar and lexis) gathered by the Prince from local experts in the late 1850s and early 1860s of the biblical *Song of Solomon*, and published between 1858–63 as pamphlets. (A number are available online via Google Books.) A second catalogue by Collins (1902), of publications by Bonaparte, shows that there was also a small number of similar dialect translations of other biblical texts. Figures 5.4 and 5.5 show the first pages of two of the Solomon translations, one in the Cumberland dialect, assembled by John Rayson (1858), the other in the Dorset dialect by

THE SANG O' SOLOMON.

CHAP. I.

THE sang o' sangs, whilk is Solomon's.

2 Let him kiss me wi' the kisses o' his mwouth : for thy luive is far afwore weyne.

3 Becwous o' the savor o' thy guid ointmint thy neame is ointmint teemed out, therfwore dui the meaidens luive thee.

4 Pu' me, we wull rin efter thee: the king hes brong me intui his chammars : we wull be glad an' rejoyce in thee; we wull meind thy luive mair ner weyne: the upreet luive thee.

5 I am black, but bonnie, O ye dowters o' Jerusalem, as the tents o' Kedar, as the cwourtins o' Solomon.

6 Luik nit apon me, becwous I am black, becwous

Figure 5.4 First page of *The Song of Solomon in the Cumberland Dialect*, by John Rayson (1858), commissioned by Louis-Lucien Bonaparte (accessed 12 August 2015, at Google Books).

THE ZONG O' SOLOMON.

CHAP. I.

THE zong o' zongs, that is Solomon's.

2 Let en kiss me wi' the kisses ov his mouth: vor your love is better than wine.

3 Vor the smell o' your sweet-smellèn scents, shed scent is your neäme, an' therevore the maïdens do love you.

4 O draw me on wi' thee, we'll run: the king brought me into his cheämmer: in you we'll be blissom an' glad, we'll meüke mwore o' your love than o' wine, the true-heartèd shall love you.

5 I be zwa'thy, Jerusalem maïdens, but comely, as the black tents of Kedar, as Solomon's hangèns.

Figure 5.5 First page of *The Song of Solomon in the Dorset Dialect*, by William Barnes (1859), commissioned by Louis-Lucien Bonaparte (accessed 12 August 2015, at Google Books).

William Barnes (1859). Each rendition was accompanied by a few pages of commentary on the local forms by the translator. These examples are taken from a compendium of 24 translations published in 1862 (and available at Google Books).

A twenty-first-century equivalent of this approach occurred during the *Evolving English: One Language, Many Voices* exhibition staged by the British Library between November 2010 and April 2011, when members of the public were invited to submit a recording of themselves reading a children's story,

Mr Tickle, by Roger Hargreaves. This was for the BL's *Map Your Voice* project, which garnered nearly 1500 audio recordings from around the world, and which are accessible at: http://www.bl.uk/evolvingenglish/maplisten.html. *The Song of Solomon* is one of the shortest books in the Bible, and relatively free of religious content. The BL's version of *Mr Tickle* (at: http://www.bl.uk/pdf/tickle.pdf) also fits the short-and-innocuous requirement for contemporary users. Note that Bonaparte's procedure is similar to the sentence-set method used well over a decade after him by Ellis and Wenker.

In addition, Bonaparte was interested in mapping English dialect regions, and A. J. Ellis acknowledges (1889, p. 5) that he owed to Louis-Lucien his 'first conceptions of a classification of the English Dialects'. The culmination of this interest was a map by the Prince presented on 7 April 1876 to the Philological Society, as part of a lecture on English Dialects, and published in 1877 (see Figure 5.6).

Bonaparte had produced at least two earlier versions of such a map, in 1873 and 1875. The map of 1873 establishes his method of using main groups and sub-groups of dialects in his analysis (in descending size: branches (3), dialects (11), sub-dialects (26), and varieties (40 and upwards)). This division into bigger regions with sub-regions is already evident to some extent in the titles given to his *Solomon* pamphlets. For example, there are nine 'varieties' (such as Durham and North Yorkshire) which are presented under the heading 'The North of England Dialect'. The map of 1876 seems to have been his final version. It is based partially on his fieldwork (that is, his 'excursions in some of the English counties' (Bonaparte, 1877, p. 570)), partially on the work of other investigators (including Ellis and Murray, and his own intermediaries), and on written sources. The linguistic features that inform the map are mainly grammatical, but also in some measure are drawn from vocabulary and pronunciation (1877, p. 574). It is quite an unusual map. Each red dot (in the original) is a locality, or 'variety' in Bonaparte's terminology, with which he was familiar as a result of his research. The main dialect regions, of which there are 13, are listed in the key at top left, and are marked repeatedly by the same numbers on the map. Red lines connect localities/varieties into 'sub-dialect' groupings or sometimes show one variety 'projecting' into an adjoining county, that is, showing a similarity with the adjoining area. In the *Transactions of the Philological Society* published in 1877, two versions of Bonaparte's map are given, one a black-and-white copy of his 1876 map, the other a very slightly modified colour 1877 version.

Bonaparte's conclusions in 1877 are both tentative and perceptive.

No real exact delimitation of English Dialects is, I think, possible. Arbitrary and imaginary ones may be easily given, but careful and critical investigations in visiting the different parishes and hamlets of England, will soon convince the geographical linguist of the futility of such an attempt. This is owing to the fragmentary state of the present English dialects, which are rather remnants of dialects, imperceptibly shading one into the other, and more or less influenced by standard English, than anything else. At any rate, they are not to be compared with Italian, French, German, or Basque Dialects, whose delimitation, although difficult, is still possible. (pp. 577–8)

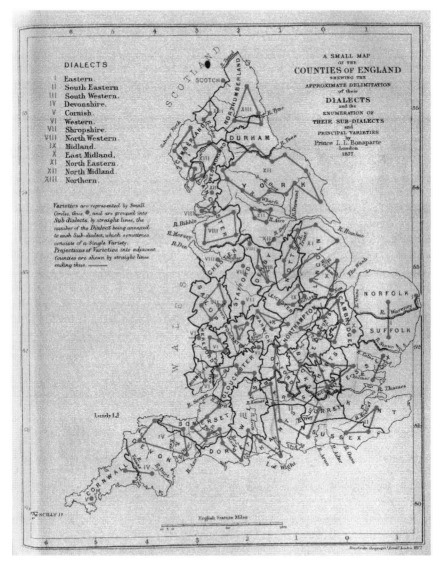

Figure 5.6 'A Small Map of the Counties of England Shewing the Approximate Delimitation of their Dialects and the Enumeration of their Sub-Dialects and Principal Varieties by Prince L. L. Bonaparte, London, 1877' (Bonaparte, 1877, no page number).

He believes that 'the number of varieties is almost infinite' (p. 577) and that his lines uniting the varieties into groups 'possess no power of delimitation either in excluding or including the localities through which they pass or leave at their right and left' (p. 578). In other words, Bonaparte is aware that he is dealing with patterns of similarity and difference based on a limited sample of regional, everyday speech, and that his dialectal divisions are to a degree simplifications of the situation on the ground, especially in England, it seems to him. There is also an intimation of the **bidialectality** of speakers, resulting from the influence of Standard English. One particular challenge for the dialect cartographer is to highlight patterns and at the same time recognize complexity, and this is what Bonaparte tried to do. Remarkably, his map's networks of connecting lines look uncannily like some of the outcomes of modern dialectometric approaches.

Ellis and the Prince gave us the first maps of the dialect areas of England, but none of these is, arguably, the first national-scale dialect map of English in Britain.

5.2.3   The map by James Augustus Henry Murray: 1873

I say 'arguably' for a couple of reasons, but before we get to those let us look at the other contender. In the same year that Bonaparte presented the first version of his map to the Philological Society, the Society also published the map of Scotland which I reproduce here as Figure 5.7.

This map is the frontispiece to a 250-page work called *The Dialect of the Southern Counties of Scotland*, by James Murray (1837–1915), published in 1873 as Part II of the *Transactions of the Philological Society*, 1870–2, and also separately as a book in its own right. It shows the southern limits of Gaelic-speaking at the time (that is, those parts where Gaelic 'is still *spoken by any natives*, regardless of the fact, that English may be spoken by the majority' (Murray, 1873, p. 232)), indicated by the dotted-and-dashed line. To the north and west of this line, the original map is presented mostly in black-and-white, while to the south and east it is shaded in a variety of colours. The various colours are used to represent the main dialects of **Scots** or **Lowland Scotch**, which Murray divides into three main groups, two of which contain subgroups. All of this can be seen more clearly in Jack Aitken's (1996) simplified black-and-white version of Murray's map, given here as Figure 5.8.

For Murray, Scots is the variety (or collection of varieties) of English descended ultimately from the English dialect of Northumbria, which started to spread to southern Scotland in the early seventh century AD (Aitken, 1984, p. 517). A. J. Ellis (1889) had a rather uncluttered way of describing Scots: 'The Lowland Dialects are commonly called Scotch, because they are spoken in a country which has acquired the name of Scotland' (p. 681). These dialects were previously known as *Inglis* in Scotland, but from the end of the fifteenth century as *Scots* or *Scotch*. From this perspective, they can be seen as the

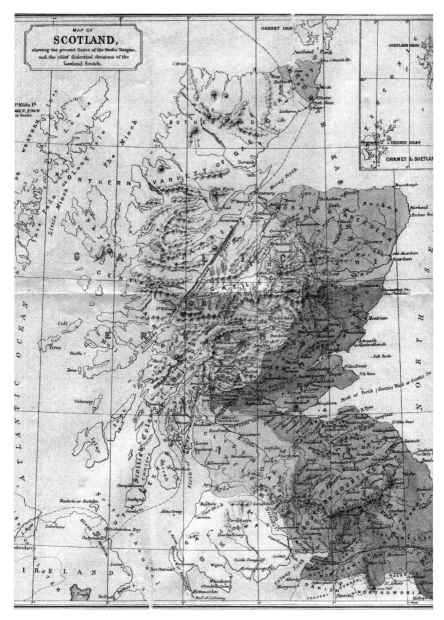

Figure 5.7 'Map of Scotland, shewing the present limits of the Gaelic Tongue, and the chief dialectical divisions of the Lowland Scotch', by James A. H. Murray (1873).

traditional English dialects of Lowland Scotland, marked off from the Gaelic-speaking Highlands by Murray's *Highland Line*, which was renamed in 1889 by Ellis as his northern *Celtic Border*. Ellis also acknowledges that Scots is 'remarkably different' from the English spoken south of his Transverse Line number

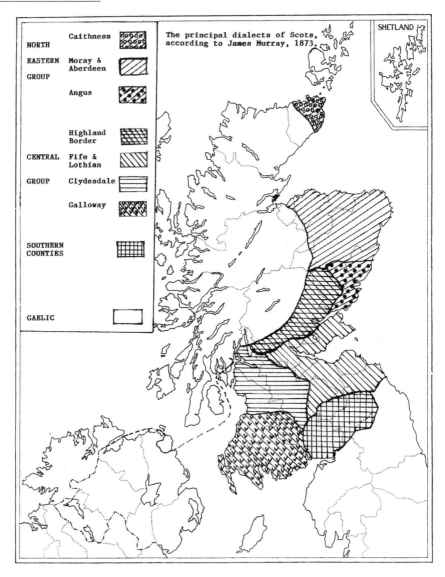

Figure 5.8 A. J. Aitken's simplified replication (1996, p. 23) of J. A. H. Murray's map.

10. It is this difference from English English, plus what Aitken describes (1984, p. 527) as the greater 'dialect-loyalty' of Scottish speakers, plus the 'uniquely copious and distinguished vernacular literature' in Scots (Aitken, 1984, p. 528), that led to the 'dialect' being claimed by its speakers as, indeed, 'Scots', a name which signifies its role as a national *language* of Scotland. This is one reason for my 'arguably', above. By definition, a Scots *language* is not English.

The other reason is simply a matter of timing. Bonaparte's first map was published in 1873 in a pamphlet limited to 250 copies. Murray's map was also published in 1873. However, Murray's book was completed in late 1868 (Aitken, 1996, p. 17), and Bonaparte (1873) acknowledges and uses Murray's classification of Scots. Therefore, if we treat Scots as a descendant dialect of English, Murray's map appears to be the first national-scale (Scotland being the nation) dialect map of English in Britain.

Murray's map is of a broader nature than the later efforts by Bonaparte and Ellis, and contains no isoglosses or variety-connecting lines. Aitken says (1996, p. 26) that 'Murray's dialect boundaries are partly based on existing physical or political boundaries, rather than dialectological ones', though Murray himself says (1873, p. 78) that his dialect divisions, 'being founded solely upon internal characteristics of pronunciation, grammar, and vocabulary, have been found, quite unexpectedly, to correspond with great political and ethnical divisions made known to us by history'. Murray was best acquainted with his own Southern Counties Scots dialect (Aitken, 1996, p. 26) and the core of his book is, as he describes it, an attempt 'to photograph the leading features' (Murray, 1873, p. v) of this dialect based on his knowledge of the speech of Upper Teviotdale, around Hawick, Roxburghshire: 'my native dialect, of which, therefore, I can speak with perfect confidence, and as to which I am a competent witness' (p. 89). His knowledge of the other dialects of Scots was, according to Aitken (1996, p. 26), sketchier, and informed by the expertise of others, such as Alexander Melville Bell (father of Alexander Graham Bell), by historical sources, and by his own fieldwork. It was Melville Bell, a phonetician and inventor of the transcription system called Visible Speech, who introduced Murray to A. J. Ellis in 1868 (Aitken, 1996, p. 16). With the help of local informants, Murray had also transcribed phonetically the first chapter of the biblical Book of Ruth in each of the eight dialect sub-groups he identified (Murray, 1873, p. 239), and a selection of these is appended to his book, transcribed using Ellis's paleotype. The main body of the book is divided into three detailed sections, on the history of Scots, and on its pronunciation, and grammar. Each of these parts created an enduring framework for the study of Scots. The analysis of pronunciation was particularly progressive, for it looked at the vowels not just individually and historically, but as relational sets or systems of sounds.

In 1879, Murray was invited by Oxford University Press to edit the Philological Society's proposed New English Dictionary, which was retitled the *Oxford English Dictionary* in 1933. He worked on the first edition of the *OED* until his death in 1915, regularly putting in 12- or 13-hour working days.

The second half of the nineteenth century was a formative and intensely productive time for the philology and dialectology of English in Britain. Between 1857 and 1859, the Philological Society drew up its plans for a New

English Dictionary, a massive project whose first edition was completed in 1928. The English Dialect Society was founded in 1873, and it embarked on an extensive publishing programme concluded by Joseph Wright's *English Dialect Dictionary* (1898–1905) and *English Dialect Grammar* (1905c). A. J. Ellis, Louis-Lucien Bonaparte, and James Murray individually and as an ensemble were key players in this explosion of activity. They also set in motion the dialect cartography of English, pioneering its methods, producing its first big discoveries, and articulating many significant observations. In the 1870s, the cartography of regional British English was at the forefront of dialect mapping. However, by the early years of the twentieth century, it was lagging behind developments elsewhere.

5.3   The first linguistic atlases of English

The influence of the philological tradition continued in the dialect cartography of British English into the twentieth century – in fact, well into the twentieth century, for it was not until the 1940s that the next national-scale projects began to take shape and not until the 1970s that they reached publication. We look at these in section 5.3.2, below. Before that, we turn to North America, because it was in the United States that the first linguistic atlas of English got underway in 1929, and, curiously, that the next initiative to map dialects of British English happened in 1937. In both subsections, we look at a number of projects, and my narrative dwells a little longer on those with the chronologically earlier beginnings and speeds up rather in dealing with the associated, later projects. In section 5.3 overall, we are dealing with second-phase philological dialect cartography (the earlier European atlases being the zenith of the first phase). By the late 1970s, it was looking like this second phase was also going to be the final phase not just of philological cartography but perhaps of large-scale dialect cartography altogether, for it was receiving some criticism and new approaches were in train. But things did not quite turn out so simply, and in sections 5.3 and 5.4 we also start looking at what happened next.

5.3.1   North America

In the 1920s, among American linguists there was much discussion about the idea of a survey and atlas of American English, and in August 1929 at Yale University a conference attended by 50 scholars took place on the topic of a Linguistic Atlas of the United States and Canada. Immediately following, the American Council of Learned Societies appointed a committee, chaired by the Austrian-born Hans Kurath, whose remit was to submit a plan for such an atlas. In January 1930, the Council endorsed the plan in principle, but requested that as a first step a restricted geographical area be investigated, in order to test methods and requirements. This first step resulted in the substantial, six-volume *Linguistic Atlas of New England* (*LANE*; Kurath et al., 1939–43), a survey conducted from Yale and based on data elicited from over 400 speakers in a seven-state area with an English-speaking history stretching back to the 1620s. *LANE* established a template that has been both followed and modified by a score or more of big American atlas projects, and many smaller-scale ones, since. The most visible present-day manifestation of the Linguistic Atlas of the United States and Canada (LAUSC) is the website of the Linguistic Atlas Project (LAP), administered from the Department of English at the University of Georgia: http://www.lap.uga.edu/. Table 5.1 below summarizes this enormous body of work from 1929 to 2015, and in this section I present its story in concise form, beginning with *LANE*.

One could say that the history of *LANE*, of LAUSC/LAP, and indeed of the dialectology of American English, begins with the founding of the American Dialect Society (ADS) in 1889. The members of the Society were aware of the lexicographical and cartographical achievements of contemporary European dialectology, but they turned their attention primarily to the production of a dialect dictionary of American English. During its existence from 1889 to 1939, the Society's journal, *Dialect Notes*, published lists of thousands of regional words and phrases, but the big dialect dictionary project did not come together until the 1960s. This was the *Dictionary of American Regional English* (*DARE*; Cassidy and Hall, 1985–2014), which is discussed in Chapter 2 of the present book (although it has a relevance here because it makes substantial use of maps). However, from early on there was also some interest in the ADS in mapping dialect areas. In 1894, Georg Hempl, a future president of the ADS, published his postal questionnaire, consisting of over 80 items, and designed to gather lexical, grammatical, and pronunciation material, in order to 'obtain such information as will make it possible to trace, even if but vaguely, the limits of our dialect centers and currents' (p. 155; the questionnaire is also in Hempl, 1896a). Hempl sent the questionnaire to anyone who requested it. In 1896 and 1902, two short articles by Hempl appeared in *Dialect Notes*, each dealing with the variation of a specific feature as revealed by responses to his questionnaire, and each containing one map. Figure 5.9 is the unusual map from the 1896 article, by which time he had received replies from 1600 informants/correspondents.

Based on a preliminary examination of his data, Hempl proposed four main dialect regions for American English: North, South, Midland, and West. These four divisions are shown on the map. Although no topography is shown (that is, there is no base map), the states (or their abbreviations) are placed around the map in approximate geographical formation. Note that four provinces of

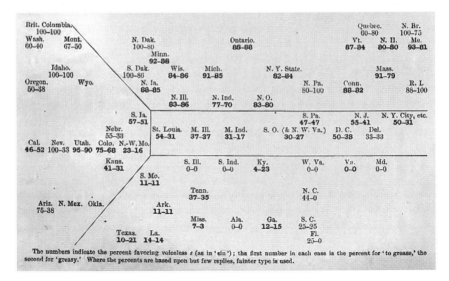

Figure 5.9 George Hempl's 1896 map of the main dialect regions of American English showing percentage scores for use of voiceless /s/ in *to grease* and *greasy* (from Hempl, 1896b, p. 440).

Canada are also included. The divisions are illustrated by an analysis of the pronunciation of the fricative consonant in *to grease* and *greasy*, that is, the variation in these words between voiceless /s/ and voiced /z/ (Hempl's question 45). For each state and province there is a pair of scores, the first number giving the percentage of use of /s/ in *grease*, the second the percentage of use of /s/ in *greasy*. While Hempl acknowledges (1896b, p. 438) that he had received many more responses from the North than from the other regions, his map is nevertheless quantitative, based on statistics. It would be over 70 years before American linguistic cartography returned to a similar statistical approach.

In his second map (see Figure 5.10), from 1902 (by which time he had received several thousand replies), Hempl used a cartographic technique previously employed (along with isoglosses) by Georg Wenker in 1878.

This is a lexical map showing the localities in which *funnel* was found as a variant of *stovepipe* (in response to Hempl's question 59). Dots mark towns in which *funnel* was used, and dots enclosed in a circle mark localities in which it was used exclusively. This kind of symbol-based map would become a common technique in the philological dialect atlases – for example, in Kurath (1949) and Kurath and McDavid (1961).

The variation between *stovepipe* and *funnel* was also investigated by *LANE*, as shown by the visually complex map reproduced here as Figure 5.11 (reminding us somewhat of A. J. Ellis's Transverse Lines), taken from the *Handbook* companion volume to *LANE*. The isogloss for *funnel* is line number 7, and

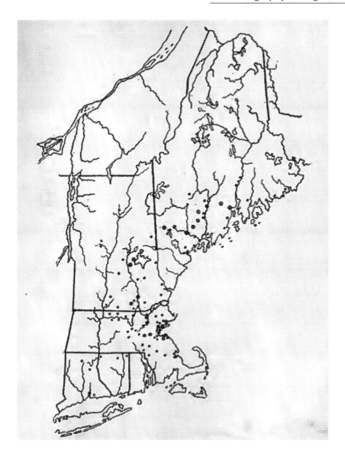

Figure 5.10   George Hempl's symbol map of New England showing the distribution of *funnel* in the sense 'stovepipe' (from Hempl, 1902, p. 253).

stovepipe/funnel is also map number 334 in Volume II of *LANE* (1941), and item number 23.1(b) in the *LANE* Work Sheets. Figure 5.12 is a photograph of *LANE* Map 334, that is, the primary data-display map upon which isogloss 7 in Figure 5.11 is based.

The 'Work Sheets' were the questionnaire for *LANE*; they consisted of 814 words and phrases grouped into 711 numbered items compiled using numerous sources, including: Hempl (most of his questionnaire was incorporated), *Dialect Notes*, and the journal *American Speech*, for the lexical and grammatical features; Kurath's own research for the phonetic items; and Ellis (1889), because Kurath (like Hempl, 1896b) was interested in the British English ancestry of American English forms. The work sheets list all the items for which *LANE*'s fieldworkers were to discover informants' own usages: keywords which informants were to pronounce (phonetic data); notions which they were to name (lexical data,

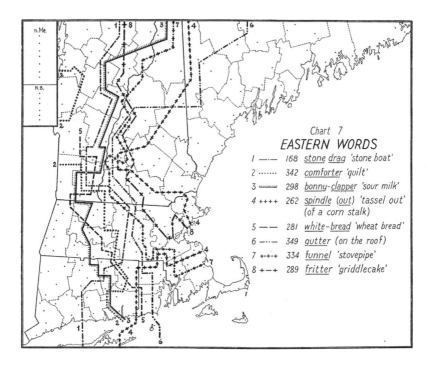

Chart 7
EASTERN WORDS
1 —·—   168   stone drag 'stone boat'
2 ······· 342   comforter 'quilt'
3 ╌╌╌╌ 298   bonny-clapper 'sour milk'
4 ++++ 262   spindle (out) 'tassel out'
              (of a corn stalk)
5 ——   281   white-bread 'wheat bread'
6 —··— 349   gutter (on the roof)
7 +·+·+ 334   funnel 'stovepipe'
8 +—+   289   fritter 'griddlecake'

Figure 5.11   Isogloss map showing western limits of distribution of selected eastern New England words (from Kurath et al., 1939, p. 29).

which was the main focus of interest); and grammatical constructions for which informants' versions were to be elicited (Kurath et al., 1939, pp. 147–8). The work sheets covered everyday topics and concepts, such as the weather and domestic matters, with some sections concentrating on farming terms. The exact wording of the questions used to elicit the usages was left to the survey's nine fieldworkers, who were highly qualified and thoroughly trained (including input from the Europeans Jakob Jud and Paul Scheuermeier in the summer of 1931 at Columbia University, New York City (see Kent, 1931)). Their work was closely monitored and assessed. Fieldwork commenced in September 1931 and was completed by September 1933, the fieldworkers transcribing the inform- ants' responses in a finely detailed phonetic notation based on the then 30-year- old International Phonetic Alphabet. (One of the fieldworkers, Miles L. Hanley, carried out a programme of phonographic audio recording in the *LANE* area in 1933–4, making 657 double-sided 12-inch records in all (Atwood, 1963, p. 13).) The transcription was written in notebooks that followed the order of the work sheets, with responses recorded down the left side of each page and the right side reserved for additional information, a format that would be mirrored

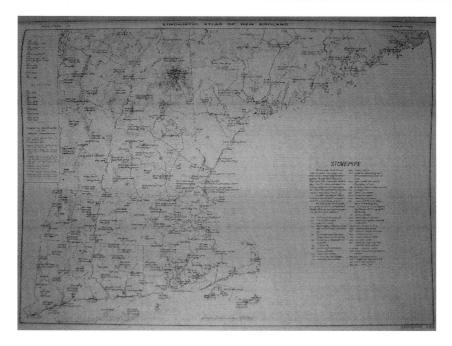

Figure 5.12   Photograph of Map 334 *STOVEPIPE* from *LANE* (Volume II, 1941).

in England by the SED. The total number of informants interviewed was 416. Although the localities (mostly small township communities, plus some cities and smaller parishes) in the network are numbered using a system that runs from 1 to 431, the actual total of investigated communities was, a little confusingly, 213. As I reported in Chapter 4, three types of informants were represented in *LANE*: (i) elderly descendants of old local families, in other words, the type of informant most associated with the philological surveys interested in the oldest living forms of speech; (ii) middle-aged men and women native to the community, with a higher level of education than the first type; and (iii) local people considered more 'cultured', with a college education or the equivalent. In the final list (Kurath et al., 1939, pp. 42–4), informants are also categorized according to their age. This did not mean that all three types were interviewed in every locality. Sometimes only one informant was interviewed, and in one locality, five were interviewed. Type I informants were found in most localities, Type II in about 80 per cent of the communities, and Type III in about 20 per cent, most of these in urbanized southern New England. The actual total numbers for each group presents a slightly different perspective: 148 Type I; 214 Type II; and 51 Type III. In keeping with the principle of providing other and future researchers with the data to enable further analyses, the survey's *Handbook* gives thorough particulars of the informants and communities (pp. 41–4, 159–240), as well as giving a meticulous guide to the transcription system (pp. 122–46), and listing the work sheet items in full (pp. 147–58).

This 'principle of documentation' (Lameli, 2010, p. 577) was also applied to the 733 maps in *LANE*, which adapt the Gilliéron technique of reproducing, in phonetic transcription, the informants' responses next to each locality number. (The *LANE Handbook* does some interpretation of the data in the form of 22 symbol maps and two isoglossic maps (pp. 26–38).) Figures 5.13 and 5.14 show two extracts from Map 132 (Volume I, 1939) for work sheet item 17.6, *frying pan*. Figure 5.13 shows the variants recorded in the Cape Cod and Martha's Vineyard parts of Massachusetts, and Figure 5.14 shows some of the commentary provided with the map.

Each *LANE* map presents the usages (in handwritten black type superimposed on a brown base map) of all the informants on one particular lexical, phonetic, or morphological point. At each locality, a separate response-line is assigned to each informant, and where there is more than one line the order is as follows: Type I informant followed by Type II followed by Type III. Locality numbers that are 'boxed' (for example, 108, 112, 114, 116, 122) indicate communities in which a Type III informant was interviewed. The columns of map commentaries include additional observations by informants, fieldworkers, and the editors. Some commentary is signified in the responses themselves by the use of symbols; for example, by an exclamation mark ! preceding a response, which means 'uttered with signs of amusement', or a superscript dagger †, which means 'characterized by the informant as "old",

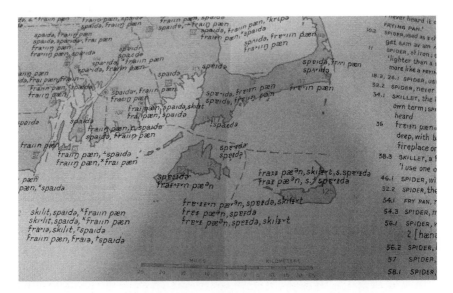

Figure 5.13   Selection from Map 132 *FRYING PAN* (*LANE*, Volume I, 1939), showing the lexical variants *creeper*, *frying pan*, *fry pan*, *skillet*, and *spider*.

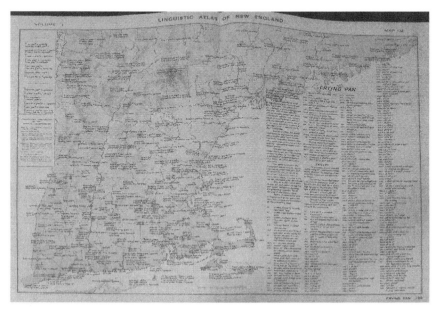

Figure 5.14 Extract from the commentary accompanying Map 132 of *LANE.*

Figure 5.15 *LANE* Map 132 *FRYING PAN.*

out of date, obsolete'. Such amplification is often given where the informant produced more than one response to the question. This profusion of information imposed considerable cartographic demands (as can be seen by Figure 5.15, the full Map 132), but the maps are made easier to read by the ample dimensions of the original atlas volumes at 22-by-15 inches – so that each one is almost literally a coffee-table book.

The costly visual style of the *LANE* maps proved to be the least influential aspect of the survey, and indeed the original print run of the atlas was very small and expensive. It retailed at 180 US dollars, equivalent to over $3000 today. A smaller-sized reprint was published in 1972. But the methods of *LANE*, as described in the more available *Handbook*, had a great influence on subsequent atlas projects in the United States and in Britain.

Kurath himself continued the LAUSC and his work in the eastern states by embarking in 1933 on the Linguistic Atlas of the Middle and South Atlantic States (LAMSAS; originally called the *Linguistic Atlas of the Eastern United States*), which extended the area under investigation south along the Atlantic seaboard as far as northern parts of Florida, and inland to West Virginia. There were two chief fieldworkers, Guy Lowman, Jr., and Raven McDavid, Jr., working between 1933 and 1949 (Lowman died in a car accident in July 1941), with some further fieldwork done by others, including Lee Pederson, between 1964 and 1974, giving a total of 1216 informants, again divided into Types I, II, and III. When computerization of the LAMSAS data began in 1989, it was decided to include some of these in the Linguistic Atlas of the North Central States (LANCS) project instead, giving a final total for LAMSAS of 1162 informants in 484 communities. McDavid became editor-in-chief of the project in 1964, followed by William Kretzschmar, Jr. in 1984. Lee Pederson went on to direct another LAUSC project, the *Linguistic Atlas of the Gulf States* (*LAGS*), and to co-direct, with Kretzschmar, the Linguistic Atlas of the Western States (LAWS). Several versions of the LAUSC work sheets were used by the LAMSAS fieldworkers, each one modified to suit a different stage and region of the survey. (There is a *Handbook* of LAMSAS (Kretzschmar et al., 1993), which gives details of the survey's methods, informants, and localities.) The digitization of the LAMSAS data in the 1990s led to its availability via the LAP websites, including maps that can be generated by user selections. But also, by the early 1960s, the survey had produced three major atlas publications: one on vocabulary (1949), one on morphology (1953), and one on pronunciation (1961). Each of these drew on both *LANE* and LAMSAS data. The cartographic technique preferred in all three volumes was to represent variants on the maps by geometric symbols, such as circles and triangles, with closely related variants sometimes marked by similar-looking symbols. The latter volumes also made occasional use of isoglosses, which featured more strongly in the 164 maps of the first volume, Kurath's *A Word Geography of the Eastern United*

States (Kurath, 1949). In this, isoglosses were used to clarify the boundaries of regionally restricted words, and, by observing where such boundaries tended to 'coalesce to form more or less close-knit strands or bundles' (Kurath, 1949, p. 11), to identify the main dialect areas of the eastern states, as shown in Figure 5.16.

Kurath's North/Midland/South model has been of lasting significance for regional studies of American English, and was seen as groundbreaking, although it does resemble Hempl's less precise set of divisions of 1896. The lexical evidence that underpins the 1949 speech areas was corroborated by the phonological evidence provided in *The Pronunciation of English in the Atlantic*

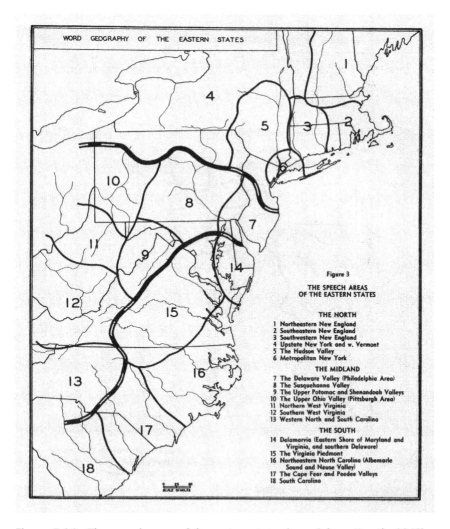

Figure 3

THE SPEECH AREAS
OF THE EASTERN STATES

THE NORTH
1 Northeastern New England
2 Southeastern New England
3 Southwestern New England
4 Upstate New York and w. Vermont
5 The Hudson Valley
6 Metropolitan New York

THE MIDLAND
7 The Delaware Valley (Philadelphia Area)
8 The Susquehanna Valley
9 The Upper Potomac and Shenandoah Valleys
10 The Upper Ohio Valley (Pittsburgh Area)
11 Northern West Virginia
12 Southern West Virginia
13 Western North and South Carolina

THE SOUTH
14 Delamarvia (Eastern Shore of Maryland and
     Virginia, and southern Delaware)
15 The Virginia Piedmont
16 Northeastern North Carolina (Albemarle
     Sound and Neuse Valley)
17 The Cape Fear and Peedee Valleys
18 South Carolina

Figure 5.16   The speech areas of the eastern states (map 3 from Kurath, 1949).

States (*PEAS*; 1961), edited by Kurath and Raven McDavid. In *PEAS*, most of the 180 maps illustrate the accompanying comprehensive structuralist, phonemic analysis of the sound systems of 157 Type III or 'cultured' speakers. (There is a discussion of the structuralist approach in section 5.3.2 below.) The second volume of the trilogy was Elmer Bagby Atwood's *A Survey of Verb Forms in the Eastern United States* (1953), which used data from over 1400 informants to construct 30 maps showing variations in verb inflections and verb phrases.

The Linguistic Atlas of the United States and Canada has continued, even to the present day, though now renamed the Linguistic Atlas Project. The project has proceeded as a series of regional surveys, large and small, united by a central methodology that has nevertheless evolved and varied in keeping with changes of approach in linguistics and advances in the technological aids, and according to differences between the territories themselves. There have been several further large-scale surveys, such as: the *Linguistic Atlas of the North Central States* (*LANCS*), started by Albert H. Marckwardt in 1933; the *Linguistic Atlas of the Upper Midwest* (*LAUM*), initiated in 1947 by Harold B. Allen, who also edited its three volumes of maps and analyses (1973–6), dealing with lexis,

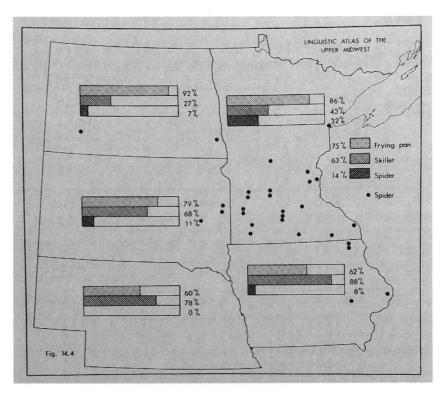

Figure 5.17 Bar graph map for *LAUM*, showing percentage of use for variants of *frying pan* (taken from Allen, 1971, Fig. 15).

grammar, and phonology, respectively; and Pederson's *Linguistic Atlas of the Gulf States (LAGS)*, which shifted the emphasis further towards **'quota sampling'** of informants so as to ensure adequate representation from both sexes, from different racial and age-groups, and from speakers with lower and speakers with higher formal education. Each of these surveys used modified versions of the LAUSC Work Sheets, with *LAUM* adding a supplementary postal-questionnaire component (following the lead of Alva Davis (1949)). Some innovative mapping techniques are found in *LAUM* and *LAGS*. In *LAUM*, in addition to symbol maps and isogloss maps, there are maps in which either bar graphs or pie graphs are simply placed onto the five states under investigation (North Dakota, South Dakota, Nebraska, Minnesota, and Iowa) to show the percentage of occurrence in the (informant) population of each variant, in cases where the mapped notion demonstrates 'dialect merger' in the Upper Midwest between Northern and Midland dialects (Allen, 1971), as in Figure 5.17. The legend at the right of the map gives a statistical overview for the whole region. A more refined (or complex, depending on which way you see it) statistical method was used by *LAGS*. Figure 5.18 is Map 1 from *LAGS* Volume 7.

The content and method of the *LAGS* map require a little unpacking. The base map has the outlines of the seven southern and Gulf of Mexico states of Tennessee, Georgia, Florida, Alabama, Mississippi, Arkansas, and Louisiana,

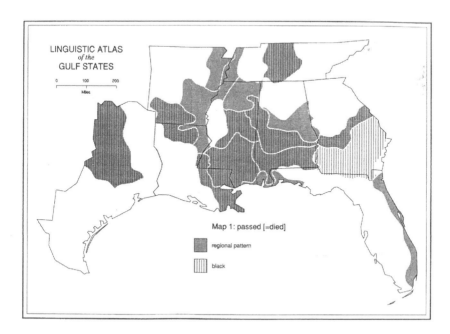

Figure 5.18   Map showing the distribution of *passed*, meaning 'died', by region and for one racial group from *LAGS* Volume 7 (Pederson and McDaniel, 1992, p. 3).

plus eastern Texas. This general area is divided by *LAGS* into 33 subregions, not indicated on the map but given on a transparent overlay included in a pocket inside the volume's back cover. The grey shading on the map shows the regional distribution of the linguistic feature, but this distribution has been measured statistically: for a subregion to be shaded, the usage of the item by that subregion's informants must be greater than or equal to the whole area's average (that is, for all 914 informants of *LAGS*). For *passed*, the average is 13 per cent for the entire territory, and the map is shaded in all the subregions where usage is 13 per cent and above. A map which uses shading (usually differing degrees of shading) and other similar patternings to represent statistical data is called a **choropleth map** (literally 'area + many' map). The aim of Volume 7 of *LAGS* is to superimpose on the general pattern the regional distribution of the variant according to the social variables of race, gender, age, and education, and Figure 5.18, by means of a similar statistical process as that above, adds on the usage data for Black (AAVE) speakers, indicated by vertical lines. As a result, we see the following on the map: a coincidence of general and Black usage over a large part of the south; one part (southern Georgia) where Black usage was high but overall usage low; and a few parts (mostly in Arkansas, Mississippi, Alabama, and coastal Florida) where the percentage or number of Black informants was very low but overall usage was above 13 per cent. On the page facing each map in Volume 7 of *LAGS* is a table of statistics giving a breakdown of scores for each social group in each subregion. This further informs the map, telling us, for example, that all the instances of *passed* in south-east Louisiana occurred in Black speech, and that the shadings in Florida are also exclusively Black usages, though not marked with vertical lines because the percentages there did not reach the average across the whole territory for Black speakers (44 per cent). The maps and tables of *LAGS* Volume 7, therefore, add significant sociolinguistic context to the regional patterns.

As well as such multi-state surveys, smaller surveys investigating single states and city areas have contributed to the LAUSC, and associated with the surveys there is a wealth of university dissertations on regional varieties of American English (see the summaries of Atwood, 1963; Allen, 1977; and Pederson, 1977). Figure 5.19 is a map taken from the most recent LAP website showing the spread of the larger surveys, and Table 5.1 is my summary of the achievements of LAUSC/LAP from 1929 to the present.

The majority of the information in Table 5.1 comes from that available at the LAP website and its previous incarnations (see: http://www.lap.uga.edu/, and http://old.lap.uga.edu/, and http://us.english.uga.edu/cgi-bin/lapsite.fcgi/old/lapw/) as of January 2016. It is modelled on the table in Labov, Ash and Boberg (2006, p. 6). The table begins with *LANE* and then lists the other surveys in clockwise geographical order (see Figure 5.19).

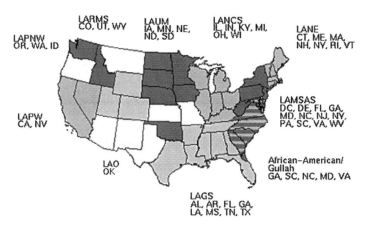

Figure 5.19   Map of the linguistic atlases of the United States (from the LAP website: http://www.lap.uga.edu/Site/Atlas_Projects.html, accessed 31 October 2016).

In the table, the Maps column indicates whether maps feature in the main publications (and/or at the LAP websites), and the Audio column says whether audio recordings were made during fieldwork and whether any have been published (usually on the LAP websites). With the exception of the *DARE* row, 'web' refers to publication on the LAP websites. The references for the publication dates given are, from top to bottom: Kurath et al. (1939–43); Kurath (1949); Kurath and McDavid (1961 – also in the Lowman row); Kretzschmar et al. (2004–6); Pederson et al. (1986–92); E. Bright (1971); C. E. Reed (1957, 1961); Hankey (1960); Allen (1973–6); A. L. Davis (1949, unpublished dissertation); Marckwardt (1957); Shuy (1962); Viereck (1975); Kurath and Lowman (1970); Atwood (1953); Atwood (1962); Cassidy and Hall (1985–2014); *DARE* online at: http://dare.wisc.edu/ (2013–14); Wood (1970, 1971a); Carver (1987); and Labov et al. (2006). A lead name is given for each survey, although this sometimes simplifies the full information. Kretzschmar is the editor-in-chief of LAP.

At the bottom of Table 5.1, I have listed some other notable surveys, some of them closely connected with the LAUSC, and some less so. Informed by cultural geography, Craig M. Carver's *American Regional Dialects* (1987) used the then-available data from LAUSC and *DARE* to produce an in-depth examination of the dialect regions of American English by means of **layers** of composite isoglosses, that is to say, he looked at groups of lexical variants with a noticeably restricted geographical provenance, ascertained the localities with the highest occurrence-scores for each group and then drew the boundary lines to enclose these locality-clusters. He also looked at groups of words that had lower scores in order to identify less-unified, weaker dialect regions

Table 5.1 Summary of linguistic atlas projects in the United States

Acronym	Full title	Field-work begun	Field-work ended	No. of subjects	Lexical pub'n	Phonetic pub'n	Maps	Audio
LANE	Linguistic Atlas of New England (Kurath)	1931	1933	416	1943	1943	Yes	Some
LAMSAS	Linguistic Atlas of the Middle and South Atlantic States (Kretzschmar)	1933	1974	1162 (from an original 1216)	1949 + web	1961 + web	Yes, + web	Yes: web
GDS	Georgia Dialect Survey (Pederson)	1968	1972	288			No	Yes: web
[Roswell]	Roswell Voices, Georgia (Kretzschmar)	2002	On-going	70			No	Yes:2006 + web
ATLSP	Atlanta Survey Project (Kretzschmar)	2003	2003	18			No	Yes: web
[Augusta]	Augusta Survey (M. Miller)	1976	1977	37			No	Yes
AFAM	African-American/Gullah – on the old LAP site (Kretzschmar)	1933	1972	62 inc. 41 from LAMSAS	web	web	Yes: web	Yes
[Gullah]	Gullah (L. Turner)	1933	1933	21	work sheets: web	work sheets: web	No	No
SKNP	St Kitts/Nevis Project (Pederson)	2002	2003	23	transcripts: web		No	Yes: web
DASS	Digital Archive of the Southern Speech (Kretzschmar)	1968	1983	64 selected from LAGS			No	Yes: web
LAGS	Linguistic Atlas of the Gulf States (L. Pederson)	1968	1983	914	1992 + web	1992	Yes	Yes: web
LAO	Linguistic Atlas of Oklahoma (Van Riper)	1959	1963	57			No	Yes: web
LAPW/LAPC	Linguistic Atlas of the Pacific West/Coast (D. W. Reed)	1952	1959	300	1971		No	No

LAPNW	Linguistic Atlas of the Pacific Northwest (C. E. Reed)	1953	1963	51	1957	1961	Yes, + web	Yes
LAWS/LARMS	Linguistic Atlas of the Western States/Rocky Mountain States (Pederson & Kretzschmar)	1988	on-going	280 units/areas	1960 (based on earlier data)		Yes: 1960	Yes: web
LAUM	Linguistic Atlas of the Upper Midwest (H. B. Allen)	1947	1962	208, + 1064 postal	1976	1976	Yes	Yes
LANCS	Linguistic Atlas of the North Central States (A. H. Marckwardt)	1933	1978	564	work sheets: + 1949, 1957, 1962	work sheets: web; + 1957, 1962	Yes: 1949, 1957, 1962	Yes: web
[Southern England]	Southern England (G. Lowman)	1937	1938	59	1975	1961, 1970	Yes	No
	Selected other major projects, in chronological order							
SVFEUS	Survey of Verb Forms in the Eastern United States (E. B. Atwood)	1931	1949	1400: Uses LANE and LAMSAS	1953: morphology		Yes	Yes
RVT	Regional Vocabulary of Texas (Atwood)	1950	1960	468	1962		Yes	No
DARE	Dictionary of American Regional English (Cassidy and Hall)	1965	1970	2777	2014		Yes, + web	Yes: web
DARE online	DARE online survey pilot of Wisconsin (Hall)	2013	2014	245	2014: web		Yes: web	Yes: web
[G. R. Wood]	Regional vocabulary in eight Southern States (Wood)	1958	1959	1000	1970, 1971		Yes	No
ARDWG	American Regional Dialects: A Word Geography (C. M. Carver)	1931	1986	Uses DARE and LAP	1987		Yes	Yes
ANAE	Atlas of North American English (Labov)	1992	1999	768	2006		Yes	Yes: 2006

and transition zones between the core areas. His detailed analyses yielded a reworking of Kurath's North/Midland/South model for American English into a North/South model, with each major category divided into Upper and Lower subregions (Carver, 1987, pp. 245–9). *DARE* itself is discussed in Chapter 2 of the present book. *The Atlas of North American English* (*ANAE*; Labov, Ash and Boberg, 2006) built on LAUSC and determined the dialects of North American urban English by using phonological data, reinstating the North/Midland/ South division in the process. It was also a departure from LAUSC in its innately sociolinguistic methodology, its focus on urban centres, its interest in sound changes in progress, and its use of perception data and computerized acoustic measurement. The *ANAE* is discussed in Chapter 10, section 5 and in various parts of Chapter 4 of the present book. The Atwood volumes (1953, 1962) are offshoots of LAUSC, using versions of the work sheets and, in the case of the eastern survey (1953), data from *LANE* and LAMSAS. Gordon R. Wood's research, like Atwood's (1962), pioneered the use of the computer in storing and processing atlas data (see also Wood, 1971b, and Francis, 1968), though it was clearly with some disappointment that Wood reported in 1977 that, 'The early hope of having academic computers talk with each other over great distances has not been realized for linguistic or literary studies so far as I know' (private communication from Wood mentioned by Allen, 1977, p. 191). Well, to quote Bob Dylan, 'things have changed'. As I remark in a few other places in this book, the advent of the IT and digital era has transformed data collection, analysis, and presentation in dialect study.

Thus the more recent LAUSC surveys have increasingly switched to digital harvesting, storage, and processing of their materials, with the ATLSP and SKNP projects being the first to audio record field interviews digitally and *LAGS* the first survey fully to incorporate computerized preparation of its data. The potential of online publication of data and maps is being realized by LAP, and the preliminary version of *ANAE*, the *Phonological Atlas of North America* (Labov et al., 1997) was published online, at: http://www.ling.upenn. edu/phono_atlas/home.html. It is not only the recent surveys that benefit from the new technology – new life is being given to some of the older data (this will become a familiar theme in the present chapter). GIS (Geographic Information System) software enables the computerized mapping of geographically referenced data to positions on the Earth's surface, and in the 1990s the LAP team developed a GIS plotting system that now enables users to browse and make maps of LAMSAS responses at: http://old.lap.uga.edu/cgi-bin/ lapsite.fcgi/lamsas/. And as I write, the *LANE* work sheets are being digitized at the University of Mississippi, prior to their being incorporated into the LAP website, and some digitized *LANE* material has already been turned into interactive maps using the Google Fusion Tables data management service (private correspondence with Allison Burkette).

As we near the end of this section, one obvious question might come to mind: in the Linguistic Atlas of the United States and Canada, what happened to Canada?

In LAUSC itself so far, Canada does not feature strongly, investigation generally being limited to border communities in connection with some of the northern US surveys (*LAUM*, LANCS, and *LANE*). In *ANAE*, however, Canada received more attention: 41 informants (out of the *ANAE* total of 762) were interviewed in Canada, concentrated in the major cities and the band of territory along the southern border with the United States, where most of the population lives. William Labov and his team identified a relatively homogeneous Canadian English dialect area (based on phonological data) running across this territory from Vancouver to Montreal, and a core Inland Canada region within this larger area, plus a smaller and more diverse Atlantic Provinces dialect region (Quebec, New Brunswick, Nova Scotia, Prince Edward Island, Newfoundland and Labrador) in the east. This breakdown was later refined by Charles Boberg's Phonetics of Canadian English study (Boberg, 2008), which proposed further subdivisions of the *ANAE* Canadian regions. The English speech of the province of Newfoundland and Labrador is well served also by the online, interactive *Dialect Atlas of Newfoundland and Labrador* (Clarke and Hiscock, 2012; http://www.dialectatlas.mun.ca/), based on the field collections directed by Harold Paddock, of the Memorial University of Newfoundland, in the 1970s (grammar and pronunciation, from speakers of traditional dialects) and early 1980s (lexis, again traditional speakers, but quota-sampled to represent both sexes equally and three occupational categories: sea-based, land-based, and trades-based). The first nationwide study was the Survey of Canadian English, directed by Matthew H. Scargill, which, using a postal questionnaire, compared the usages of over 14,000 informants. These were Canadian-born 14- to 15-year-old school pupils and their parents (see Warkentyne, 1971; and Scargill and Warkentyne, 1972). Two further national-scale surveys of regional variation in Canadian English are J. K. Chambers's Dialect Topography Project and Charles Boberg's North American Regional Vocabulary Survey (NARVS), both interested primarily in vocabulary, using statistical analysis and questionnaires requiring written responses (online in their later stages of collection), and both gathering some data also from the United States. In terms of methodology and goals, the Dialect Topography Project was conceived in the early 1990s by Chambers as a sociolinguistic 'alternative' to philological dialect geography (Chambers, 1994, p. 35), aiming to correlate its linguistic variants with the age, sex, and ethnicity of informants. It has an *Atlas of Dialect Topography* website (http://dialect.topography.chass.utoronto.ca/), from which you can download the data to do your own analyses and on which you can construct maps by region, social variable, and questionnaire item and variant. Boberg's NARVS (2005) produced a taxonomy of regional dialects of English-speaking Canada using lexical data that closely matches his later (2008) phonetics-based regions, that is: the West (comprising British Columbia and the Prairies), Ontario, Quebec, the Maritimes, and Newfoundland (I have conflated the two surveys here).

In summary, then, in recent decades the dialect cartography or *linguistic geography* of North American English has become more *sociolinguistic* (a term elucidated in Chapters 6 and 7) and *geolinguistic* (Chapter 10), and more statistical, profiting from information technology. This later work has stood on the shoulders of the American philological atlas projects that were in turn moulded from their European predecessors. The LAUSC project is a grand inquiry into the linguistic and cultural history of anglophone North America. Among its characteristics is not only an interest in the British English correlates of American linguistic features, but also in the surveying of British dialects of English. There was two-way traffic between British and American dialectology in the twentieth century, which included, for example, visits by Harold Orton to Michigan, Kansas, Iowa, and Tennessee (where he even laid plans in 1971 for a dialect survey, co-writing a questionnaire that combined the styles of *LANE* and the SED (Orton, Wright and Jones, 1972)). More surprising is the fact that the first linguistic-atlas fieldwork in Britain was carried out by the principal fieldworker of the opening decade of LAUSC, Guy S. Lowman, Jr. In an attempt to make up for the lack of equivalent British material to compare with the American, Lowman made a dialect survey of the central and southern counties of England in 1937–8, visiting 67 communities, armed with a shortened version of the LAUSC work sheets. (His survey was continued in a further seven localities in 1950 by Henry Collins.) The phonological material that he collected is used in 76 supplementary, comparative maps in *PEAS* (1961), and in Kurath and Lowman (1970). His lexical and grammatical data was later brought to light in a series of pieces by the German dialectologist Wolfgang Viereck (1968, 1975, 1980, 1985b).

By 1937, prompted in part by American interest, the thoughts of concerned scholars in Britain were turning more resolutely towards preliminary planning for a linguistic atlas of British English.

5.3.2 The British Isles

The Survey of English Dialects (SED) – the chief goal of which was to produce a linguistic atlas of England – grew out of the friendship which began in the 1930s between two philologists, the Swiss Eugen Dieth (1893–1956) and the Englishman Harold Orton (1898–1975). In 1927, having just become a professor at the University of Zürich, Dieth was invited to be an editor of the *Schweizerdeutsches Idiotikon* ['Swiss-German Dialect Dictionary']. He published his *Grammar of the Buchan Dialect* in 1932, having previously lectured at Aberdeen University. As a newly appointed lecturer at Armstrong College, Newcastle-upon-Tyne, Orton had set up a survey of Northumberland dialects in 1928 (see Orton, 1930, 1937). He published his study of his home village of Byers Green, *The Phonology of a South Durham Dialect*, based on his undergraduate thesis, in 1933. The two men met sometime around 1932 (Fees, 1991a, p. 14). In 1935, at the Second International Congress of Phonetic Sciences in London, which both men attended, Orton was appointed to a committee charged with preparing a memorandum on the idea of a linguistic atlas of the British Isles. This followed comments by Hans Kurath in a paper delivered at the Congress bemoaning the lack of a British atlas (Kurath, 1936, p. 20), comments which echoed those made by Joseph and Elizabeth Mary Wright in 1923 (J. Wright and E. M. Wright, 1923, pp. 2–3). (Also in 1923, Joseph Wright was one of the examiners of Orton's B.Litt. thesis at Oxford University.) Both Wright and Kurath argued that the history of regional English in Britain and the United States could be illuminated by a linguistic atlas of the traditional British English dialects. Orton and Dieth had in common an interest in English dialects as well as a philological training, and they were in close contact up until August 1939 (Fees, 1991a, p. 14). But any budding thoughts of collaborating on an atlas project were interrupted by World War II. By the time that Orton gave his lecture to the Yorkshire Dialect Society in May 1946, contact between the two men had resumed. In the lecture, Orton talked at length (1947, pp. 6–11) about the recently published *Linguistic Atlas of New England*. He was particularly impressed by the 'most instructive' (p. 6) methods of *LANE*. He also made the point (p. 6) that 'all the linguistic atlases constitute but the beginnings of something much bigger', that is to say: 'They provide raw material for subsequent detailed study.' These comments are prescient, for the findings and materials of the SED have continued to be exploited in a variety of ways ever since its main objective, *The Linguistic Atlas of England* (*LAE*) was published in 1978.

Inspired by *LANE*, Orton and Dieth discussed their blueprint for a national survey in the summer of 1946 (Fees, 1991a, p. 15). It would require a carefully designed questionnaire, administered directly by fieldworkers trained to use the IPA, and it would centre around the vocabulary of farming in order to gather the older, historical speech on a nationwide scale. It was intended that the fieldworker should also spend some time engaging each informant in casual conversation on a subject known well by him or her, and in addition, finances and technology allowing, the survey would make audio recordings of its informants. With support from Leeds University, where Orton had taken up a professorship in 1946, and from the Philological Society, an early version of the Dieth-Orton questionnaire was tested by the project's first fieldworker, John Lloyd Bailes, in Durham in 1947–8. As the venture took shape in these developmental years, it became clear that Orton and Dieth would be responsible for a survey of England, not of the whole of Britain. The historian of the SED, Craig Fees, tells us (1991a, p. 33, and 1991b) that the project's name at this stage was the English Dialect Survey, and that the title Survey of English Dialects was the name given to the publication programme launched in 1962 by the *Basic Material* volumes (Orton et al., 1962–1971; see also Orton, 1962, p. 21). However, the formulation 'Survey of English Dialects' had been used before 1962 (for example, by Dieth in 1946 and 1951), and it has become the generally used name for the whole enterprise. By 1953, the Philological Society had withdrawn from the project, and the Survey was firmly in the hands of Orton and Dieth, and its home was Leeds University.

We already know quite a lot about the subsequent character of the SED from Chapters 2 and 4 of the present book, so here I will take us quickly to the *LAE*, and I will provide a glimpse of the prolific activities hingeing on the Survey from 1950 up to the present.

Between 1947 and 1962, the Dieth-Orton *Questionnaire for a Linguistic Atlas of England* went through six versions, its final one containing over 1300 questions dealing with phonology, morphology, syntax, lexis, and semantics. Figure 2.2 showed us an example page from the final version. The *Questionnaire* was asked in its lengthy entirety once only in each locality, interviews being shared among up to a handful of informants judged by the fieldworker to be representative (elderly) speakers of the traditional (rural) dialect (that is, a **judgement sample** of informants). In his 1963 review of the SED's *Introduction* (Orton, 1962) and first book of *Basic Material* (Orton and Halliday, 1962), Hans Kurath called the Dieth-Orton *Questionnaire* 'quite full' and 'a masterpiece' (Kurath, 1963, p. 126). Fieldwork proper began in 1950 and continued until 1961, by which time a network of 313 localities had been visited, with preference given to 'agricultural communities that had had a fairly stable population of about five hundred inhabitants for a century or so' (Orton, 1962, p. 15). Only a very few large urban areas were included. A list of provisional sites was drawn up in 1949–50 (Fees, 1991a, p. 47), but the final choice of locality was always left to the fieldworker. Figure 5.20 shows the state of play at 1 May 1958 (on a sheet from the Orton Research Room, author unidentified).

The Survey's chief fieldworker, Stanley Ellis, did almost half the localities himself, spending some six years living in a caravan travelling around the country. He later combined an academic career with many media appearances and was a founding figure of forensic phonetics as a discipline. During the 1950s fieldwork years, Leeds University financed the Survey's use of at least

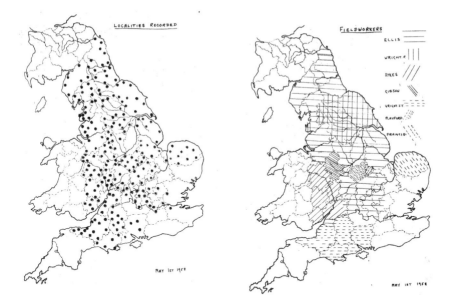

Figure 5.20   Localities in the SED network by 1 May 1958 and areas covered by the fieldworkers.

one motorbike and two 'dialect cars', a Vauxhall 14 and then a Land Rover (as well as the caravan). Craig Fees notes (1991a, p. 79): 'The significance of transport to the conduct of the fieldwork should not be underrated.' Later, the Institute of Dialect and Folk Life Studies (founded in 1964 at Leeds following a proposal by Orton) had its own exceptional technician, Reg Ross, who assisted with all things audio and photographic in the multi-roomed basement of the School of English.

By the summer of 1955, a decision had been made to edit the basic material at Leeds and to prepare phonological maps of the northern counties at Zürich (Fees, 1991a, pp. 34–5), but Dieth did not live to see these tasks achieved, for he died in May 1956. The publication of the fruits of the fieldwork began in 1962 with the first book of *Basic Material* (*BM*), edited by Orton and ex-headmaster and Honorary Editorial Secretary of the Yorkshire Dialect Society, Wilfrid Halliday. Between 1962 and 1971, Orton was joined by three more editors, Barry, Tilling, and Wakelin, and 12 books in total were published, structured into four volumes, each with three parts, presenting in fine phonetics all of the responses to all of the questions in all of the localities. The *BM* is a clear, detailed, meticulous, and substantial database in keeping with Orton's (1947, p. 6) statement about providing raw material for subsequent research. Long sold out and difficult to acquire as a complete set, all the volumes were reprinted in 1998. Figure 2.4 showed us a page from one of the *BM* books. In 1992, a team at the University of Basel, Switzerland, started work on turning the *BM* into a searchable digital database that would preserve the phonetic detail and enable the production of quantitative, statistical maps. For some preliminary examples from this Phonetic Database Project, see Rudin and Elmer (1998), and Elmer (1999). And, as I mentioned in Chapter 2, section 2.2, selections from the 'incidental material' of field-transcriptions (items of interest in informants' speech that occurred during conversation and not as direct responses to questions) were made available in 2005 at the online Leeds Archive of Vernacular Culture pages, at last fulfilling Orton's stated aim (1962, p. 22) to publish this valuable information as a companion to the *BM*.

After the *BM* volumes, two linguistic atlases using the SED data were put out, though neither was the promised *Linguistic Atlas of England*. In 1966, a *Phonological Atlas of the Northern Region* appeared, edited by Dieth's successor at Zürich, Eduard Kolb. In its Preface and Introduction, Kolb makes it clear that from his point of view he was completing the task apportioned to Dieth in 1955 (and in fact the label *Linguistic Atlas of England* is used in the full title of the 1966 work). The northern atlas classifies its mapped sounds according to their historical, Middle English antecedents, and uses a coordinated collection of black, green, and red symbols to represent the variants on the maps. More on this visual style very shortly. In 1974, *A Word Geography of England* (*WGE*) appeared, edited by Orton and Nathalia Wright. As its title denotes, its subject was lexis. The editors decided against using symbols to represent variants ('expensive to insert on a map', and 'may not immediately reveal the distributional areas clearly enough', says Orton in the Introduction (p. 3)), instead opting mostly for 'simple, interpretative' maps (p. 3) using isoglosses and plain monochrome. Etymologies of the variants are also provided in each map's legend. The principles of interpretation, of teasing out the regional patterns, within a historically orientated analytical framework, and of relying on black-and-white isoglossic maps, was carried over into the main atlas, the *LAE*. This had three editors, Stewart Sanderson, John Widdowson, and Orton. Orton died in 1975, three years before publication, and 40 years after an atlas project was first considered.

Because the editors were mindful of the 251 lexical maps already in *WGE*, the bulk of the *LAE*'s maps deal with sounds (300 maps), but morphology (84) and lexis (80) are also well represented. There are also nine maps on syntax. Figure 5.21 is one of the phonological maps in the *LAE*, showing the phonetic variants of the second vowel in **among**.

The map's legend and the discussion of **among** in the *LAE*'s Introduction reveal that the twentieth-century sound variants are analysed in relation to their historical transitions through Old, Middle, and Modern English. The twentieth-century regional distributions are depicted by the isoglosses, each

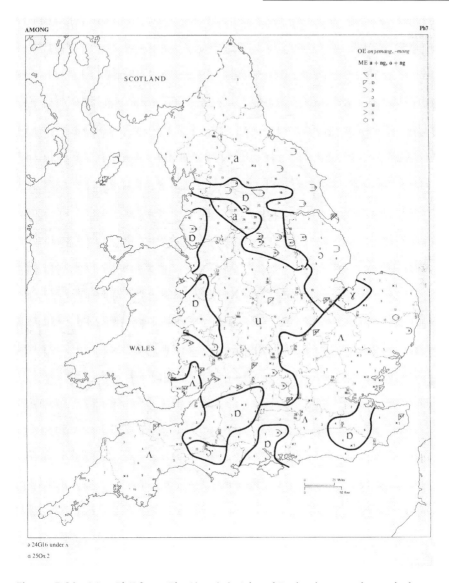

Figure 5.21 Map Ph7 from *The Linguistic Atlas of England*, stressed vowel of **among** (Orton, Sanderson and Widdowson, 1978).

area headed by the appropriate phonetic symbol. The same format is used for the lexical and grammatical maps, but with numbers used to head the areas marked by the isoglosses. Variants which differ from the dominant form in an area are marked at the locality where they occur by an individual geometric symbol. Further unmapped forms are listed beneath the map. These lists are quite extensive for some maps, though not so for **among**.

Figure 5.22 is a working version of Ph7 (supplied to me by Clive Upton, who was a research assistant for the *LAE*), which shows the role played by the geometric symbols in the process of composing an isoglossic map, and Figure 5.23 is the note written by Harold Orton himself outlining to his colleagues the reasons for mapping the stressed vowel of **among**.

Figure 5.22   Working version of *LAE* Ph7 (with thanks to Clive Upton).

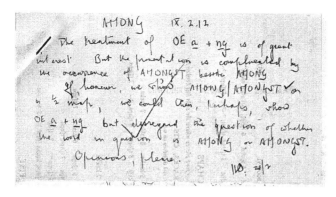

Figure 5.23   Handwritten note by Harold Orton suggesting *LAE* Map Ph7.

Such symbols had a bigger role in the next major atlas based on the SED data. This was the *Atlas of English Sounds* (*AES*; Kolb et al., 1979), the successor to Kolb's northern atlas, again dealing only with phonology, edited by a team headed by Kolb, and following his principle, as articulated in the earlier northern volume, of giving the reader 'the greatest possible freedom in interpretation' (Kolb, 1966, pp. 13–14), thereby abstaining from using isoglosses, but with the one proviso that similar sounds are represented on the maps by similar symbols. Figure 5.24 is an example map from the *AES*, showing its own treatment of **among**. The original uses three colours (black, green, and red) for the symbols, and the monochrome reproduction here renders the variants [a] and [ɒ] hard to distinguish on the map, as they are represented by the same symbol in different colours in the original, ◌ (red) and ◌ (black), respectively!

The split between the Leeds and Swiss productions at this time illustrates quite well the categorization by Chambers and Trudgill (1980, 1998) of linguistic maps into two main types: **interpretive** (*WGE*, *LAE*) and **display** (like the Kolb maps). The Leeds atlases follow the Georg Wenker isoglossic tradition, while the Kolb maps lie somewhere between Wenker and Jules Gilliéron, whose maps in the *Atlas linguistique de la France* are ultra-non-interpretive.

As we saw way back near the start of Chapter 3 of the present book, the *LAE* received hostile reviews from the phonetician John Wells in 1978 and 1979. Wells criticized the *LAE* for its omission of urban information and for the absence of structuralist phonemic analysis. In Chapters 3 to 5, I have charted the historical, philological approach, and it is within this framework that the *LAE* is expressed. Wells's criticisms can be understood in the context of the argument between new and old schools that engulfed dialect study in the 1960s to the 1980s, the story of which is told in Chapter 8. For now, let us note that some other contemporary reviews of the *LAE* ranged from a little warmer (McDavid, 1981) through positive (Macaulay, 1980) to glowing

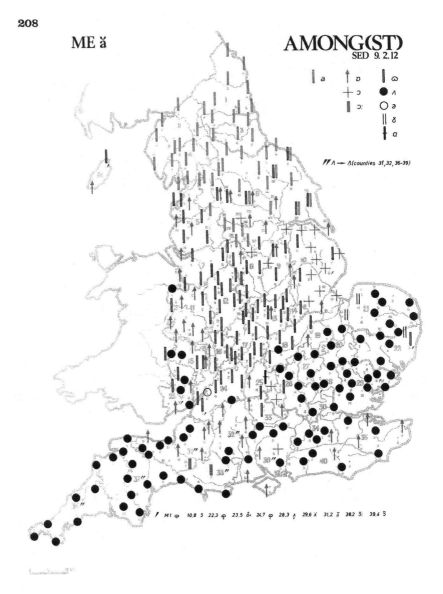

Figure 5.24   Map 208, **among(st)**, from the *Atlas of English Sounds* (Kolb et al., 1979).

(Burgess, 1978). Also, before we move on, I will say just a little more about the remarkable productivity inspired by the SED.

In 1991 (private correspondence quoted by Fees, 1991a, p. 5), the German dialectologist Wolfgang Viereck calculated that there had been more than 150 publications that had used the SED data. His own major collaboration with Heinrich Ramisch and others, *The Computer Developed Linguistic Atlas of England 1* and *2* (*CLAE*; 1991, 1997) added another, one which answered a criticism of the earlier SED atlases concerning the shortage therein of quantitative analysis. Peter Anderson's *A Structural Atlas of the English Dialects* (1987) responds to this criticism too, as well as using a structuralist approach to the SED data and presenting half-a-dozen comparative maps based on A. J. Ellis's material (1889). (Kolb's *AES* also had a number of 'composite maps', each one showing statistically analysed variants in a group of words.) In addition, there have been two SED atlases aimed at the non-specialist viewer, each avoiding technical terminology and the IPA, and each in a smaller, bookshelf-friendly format: *Word Maps* (Upton, Sanderson and Widdowson, 1987), and *An Atlas of English Dialects* (Upton and Widdowson, 1996, 2006). And then there are the audio recordings.

The expense and bulkiness of equipment, the cost of audio tapes, and periods of petrol rationing (for the early tape recorders could not be lugged around without transport) all contributed to difficulties in getting the SED audio recording programme underway. However, it started hesitantly in February 1952, and then in July 1953, thanks to advice and collaboration with the BBC, a Wright and Weare (or Ferrograph) reel-to-reel tape recorder was acquired, and Orton and Dieth made the decision to audio record the casual speech of one informant per locality. Stanley Ellis carried out the majority of the audio recordings, which were still taking place up until 1974. In the end, tape recordings were achieved in nearly 290 of the 313 localities in the SED network. Orton's 1962 publication programme included a plan to put out phonetic transcriptions of the tape recordings, and in the following decades schemes were periodically proposed to issue selections from the audio recordings themselves. By the start of the new millennium, neither aim had been realized. But think back now to Figure 3.2, which showed a phonological map from the British Library's *Sounds Familiar?* website, which was created in 2007 and aimed at non-specialists. Another map at the homepage of *Sounds Familiar?* (http://www.bl.uk/learning/langlit/sounds/) links to what it calls 'modern' and 'older' dialect recordings from the BL's sound archive. The 'older dialect recordings' from England indicated on this homepage map are selections from the SED, because digitized copies of the SED audio recordings are now held at the BL. The BL's online dialect audio archive at *Sounds* (http://sounds.bl.uk/Accents-and-dialects), launched in 2004, makes available a much more extensive selection, for it boasts extracts from each of the localities where recordings were made, together with commentaries on the non-standard features. Furthermore, at Leeds University between 1997 and 1999, the SED audio recordings were indeed transcribed, although not phonetically, as part of a Leverhulme Trust-funded project (see Klemola and Jones, 1999). Plans to publish these transcriptions (800,000 words) and the audio recordings (65 hours) on CD-ROM remain in the pipeline at the time of writing, and below is a short extract from the transcription of a recording made in the village of Coleford, Somerset, in July 1956. 'SE' is the fieldworker, Stanley Ellis, 'JS' is the informant (male, aged 84 at the time, and a retired miner).

<SE Aye.
Did you used to have a village football team when you were a lad? SE>
<JS Uh well uh,
what +...
I were one of [/] one of [\] 'em as [/] as [\] started it,
see,
about here. JS>
<SE Hmm. SE>
<JS We got over in this ground just over here once [/] once [\] or twice,
and uh we did uh +...
Three on us uh s- +...
uh six on us 'd carry a clothes prop. JS>
<SE Hmm. SE>
<JS For to make the [/] the [\] two goals.
We had a ball and that were +...
What were I?
I 'm eighty two now.
What [/] what [\] were I?
Eighteen then,,
wadn't I? JS>

In the transcription, +... indicates utterances left unfinished, [/] [\] enclose unintentional repetitions, and # indicates a pause. Each conversational turn taken by each speaker is enclosed between < > symbols, adjacent to the speaker's initials. Note in particular the construction *For to make* 'in order to make', because we will discover more about such *for to* constructions at the close of the current section. You can hear an audio extract from this same conversation between SE and JS at: http://sounds.bl.uk/Accents-and-dialects/ Survey-of-English-dialects/021M-C0908X0065XX-0400V1.

In each of the other nations of the British Isles, dialect surveys on a coun-trywide scale were started in the mid to late twentieth century, all with the aim of producing linguistic atlases. For the remainder of this section, we take a look at these twentieth-century cartographic projects in Scotland, Ireland, and Wales.

The early decades of the twentieth century saw much activity in dialect lexicography in Scotland. In a lecture to the English Association given in his home city of Dundee in 1907 (see Aitken, 1967/2015, p. 8/p. 2), the co-editor of the *OED*, William Craigie, called for work to be done on Scots. Following soon upon this, the Scottish branch of the English Association set up a Scottish Dialects Committee with William Grant as its convenor. In 1909, Grant published a pamphlet entitled *What Still Remains to be Done for the Scottish Dialects*, which highlighted the Committee's interest in vocabulary and its pronunciation. The initial outcomes of this impetus included Alexander Warrack's *Scots Dialect Dictionary* (1911) – which included an adapted version of A. J. Ellis's Lowland Dialect Districts map and an Introduction by Grant – and four volumes of the *Transactions of the Scottish Dialects Committee* (1913–21). The latter amounted to a preliminary to *The Scottish National Dictionary* (Grant and Murison, 1931–76), which started appearing in 1931, as did the *Dictionary of the Older Scottish Tongue* (Aitken et al. 1931–2002). The idea of a linguistic atlas of Scotland was rather put on hold in these decades. It was revived in 1935 as part of a prospective British survey by the committee of the Second International Phonetic Congress that included Harold Orton as a member, and in Scotland in 1936 by a Memorandum prepared by John Orr of Edinburgh University for the Scottish Archive for Ethnological, Folkloristic and Linguistic Studies (Mather, Speitel and Leslie, 1975, pp. 5–6). In truth, the Memorandum, which took Jaberg and Jud's *AIS* as the best model for Scotland, came about in no small part owing to the advocacy of a young scholar called John Cunnison Catford. In July 1937, Catford gave a paper on 'Scottish Dialects and the Proposed Linguistic Atlas of Scotland' at an international ethnology and folklore conference in Edinburgh (as reported in the journal *Man*, 1937). The proposed atlas thus led something of a double life up to 1953, developing in principle as part of a larger British project, coordinated by the Philological Society from 1946 on, but in practice as a comprehensive Scottish project with a different approach and methodology from the English survey based in Leeds. In 1948, the Linguistic Survey of Scotland (LSS) was started at the University of Edinburgh by the heads of the three interested departments: Angus McIntosh (English Language and Linguistics), David Abercrombie (Phonetics), and Myles Dillon (Celtic). Dillon left Edinburgh in 1949, to be replaced by Kenneth Jackson. John Orr was a great supporter of the LSS, and J. C. Catford was a fieldworking member of its team in 1949 and the 1950s. His work in phonological theory (for example, Catford, 1957) had a formative influence on the Survey. In 1952, McIntosh published a short book previewing some of the Survey's findings and plotting the way ahead. In January 1953, the Dialect Survey Planning Committee of the Philological Society acknowledged in its final report that the SED and the LSS were being run from and financed by the Universities of Leeds and Edinburgh, respectively, as separate surveys, and the Society's role in the projects was ended (Brough and Scott, 1955, pp. 206–7).

Although there is a line of inheritance that runs from Murray, A. J. Ellis, Wenker, Gilliéron, Jaberg and Jud through to the LSS, the Scottish Survey made some departures from its predecessors, and in a number of ways it was notably different from the SED.

The LSS investigated regional variation in two languages of Scotland, Gaelic and Scots, but the Survey was not confined to Scotland. Its area comprised the whole of Scotland including Orkney and Shetland, the two northern counties of England bordering on Scotland (Cumberland and Northumberland), the Isle of Man, and the six counties of Northern Ireland and some neighbouring parts of the Republic – in other words, it covered Scotland and nearby territories with which Scotland has historical linguistic (Scots, English, Celtic) connections. The LSS focused on lexis and phonology, in the speech of mostly middle-aged or older natives, or, in McIntosh's terms (1952, p. 85), the speech of locals 'resistant' to outside linguistic influences. The three volumes of *The Linguistic Atlas of Scotland* (*LAS*; Mather, Speitel and Leslie, 1975, 1977, 1986) dealt with Scots only. Volumes 1 and 2 concentrated on lexis, Volume 3 on phonology. As well as maps, each volume contained comprehensive data lists (or 'basic material'). A decade after the LSS was wound up, the Gaelic data was published in tabular form over five volumes under the title of *Survey of the Gaelic Dialects of Scotland* (*SGDS*; Ó Dochartaigh, 1994–7). These are the main publications of the LSS.

As I reported in Chapter 4, section 3.2, the LSS used two postal questionnaires to collect its lexical data. These were sent out in 1951 (for Volume 1, responses from 1774 informants) and 1953 (Volume 2, 832 informants), totalling nearly 420 questions, some of them multi-part. From 1955 onwards, a phonological questionnaire (over 900 items, plus 75 morphological questions) was also used in 250 localities to the south and east of the Highland Line and in Northern Ireland in interviews carried out by trained fieldworkers. Usually one informant per locality was interviewed and tape-recorded. We can already see that the LSS had similarities with (for example, informant type, and a judgement sample) and differences from (use of postal questionnaire) the SED, and we get an indication that the Scottish team was willing to use a mix of methods according to the needs of the task (for example, postal for lexis, interviews for phonology), but it was in the presentation of its maps and in the treatment of sounds that the LSS broke new ground.

Figures 4.10 and 4.11 showed us two examples of maps from Volume 1 of the *LAS* in which different shadings (made using Letraset patterns) mark the provenance of different variants. The process of constructing these maps consisted of three stages: the familiar plotting of variants in individual localities followed by the drawing of isoglosses, and then a third stage in which isogloss-enclosures were replaced by shadings, thus allowing the overlaying of one pattern on another where different variants are used in the same area. This style was tried out as early as 1952, in McIntosh's short preliminary book, from which Figure 5.25 is taken.

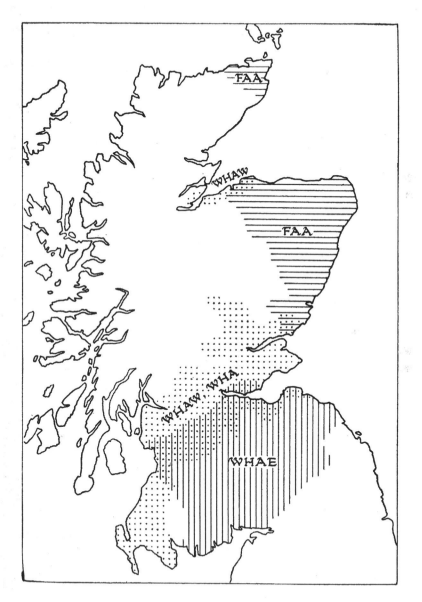

Figure 5.25   Preliminary LSS map of Scots forms for interrogative *who* from McIntosh (1952, p. 117).

It is a simple and clever technique, though visually complex when three or more shadings/variants co-occur. The *LAS* also used simple symbol maps, in Volume 1, for example, for some phonetic material, and maps combining symbols and shadings, in Volume 2. In Volume 3, symbol maps were used for phonological material of a different kind. As its editors said: 'This, we believe, is the first large-scale presentation of a phonological survey on *functional lines*, that is, by means of the technique of contrasts and oppositions of the stressed vowels of the recorded speech-sounds' (italics in original; Mather, Speitel and Leslie, 1986, p. xi). What does this mean?

What it means in general terms is that, although following in certain ways the philological tradition, the LSS in the third volume of its atlas was connecting very firmly and clearly with twentieth-century structuralist linguistics. The work of the Swiss scholar Ferdinand de Saussure in the early years of the twentieth century is usually seen as the beginning of structuralist linguistics, and with it came a new definition in language study of the object of analysis. Here is a statement by the dialectologist and sociolinguist Uriel Weinreich which sums up this definition: 'Regardless of all its heterogeneity, structural linguistics defines a language as an organized system' (Weinreich, 1954, p. 388). Weinreich continued: 'It was one of the liberating effects of structural linguistics that it made possible the treatment of a language as a unique and closed system whose members are defined by opposition to each other and by their functions with respect to each other, not by anything outside of the system.' I shall illustrate and explain what this view entails for dialect study very shortly, and then we shall return to Volume 3 of the *LAS*, but first a couple of other points.

The shift in language study from the historically orientated philological approach to system-orientated structuralist thinking is a transition that I touch on every so often in the present book because it had particular effects in dialect study, and especially in dialect cartography. Put briefly, the second-phase philological dialect cartography that lived on into the 1970s was often out of sync with the switch to structuralism that had occurred elsewhere in language study (Kurath's and McDavid's structuralist *PEAS* being one exception to this tendency). Hence, in part, John Wells's criticism of the *LAE* (see above). This disconnection was also a factor in the late-twentieth-century debate within dialect study that I describe in Chapter 8.

Present-day dialect study is fully cognizant of the structuralist way of thinking, but structuralism was not wholly embraced by most of the older work we have looked at so far in this chapter, and the structuralist view as characterized by Weinreich does present a predicament for the dialect scholar who knows better than most that a language is indeed heterogeneous, and therefore conceivably a disorganized system, except that that is an oxymoron. Uriel Weinreich was one of a number of scholars in the 1950s and 1960s who grappled with incorporating narrow structuralism into dialect study (others were G. R. Cochrane (1959), William G. Moulton (1960, 1962, 1968), and Ernst Pulgram (1964)). Weinreich's 1954 article was the starting point for much subsequent debate. In it he makes two moves away from the 'narrow' structuralist view of language given above. First, he points out (p. 389) that any given language is not so much a single system but an 'aggregate' of various systems, or subsystems, ordinarily called *dialects*. Second, he postulates (p. 390) a new kind of dialectology whose business it would be to compare the similarities and differences between dialects treated as subsystems of a language. This comparison would then be termed a **diasystem**. To illustrate this briefly, I will return to a trait of British English that we have already encountered.

A few of A. J. Ellis's Transverse Lines refer to the geographical provenance of different pronunciations of the vowel in *some* and words like *some*, that is, they refer to the pronunciation /sʊm/ (Line number 2) in traditional accents of northern England, and to the pronunciation /sʌm/ (Line 1) in southern England. Ellis's interest was in identifying the regional extent of each vowel sound, and he also knew that historically speaking the southern sound is an innovation (Ellis, 1889, pp. 15–17). The innovation dates from the seventeenth century and is known (after Wells, 1982) as the **FOOT-STRUT split**. In the Middle English period of the language (AD 1150–1500), these two groups of words (the FOOT group and the STRUT group) had the same vowel sound, but then in southern England the STRUT group split from the main group, resulting in two **phonemes** where there used to be one. The fact that there are two phonemes can be demonstrated by a **minimal-pair test**, in this case by **minimal pairs** like *could–cud*, *look–luck*, *put–putt*, and *stood–stud*. A minimal pair is a pair of words that are distinct in meaning but phonically identical except for one sound. The two different sounds function to distinguish the two words, and are accordingly termed **phonemes**. Once we start to consider the functions of sounds in this way we are entering into the structuralist view of language, and therefore into the structuralist understanding of the term **phonology**. In southern English English (and in Received Pronunciation), pairs such as *could–cud* are distinguished by the /ʊ/ vowel in the first word contrasting with the /ʌ/ vowel in the second. The minimal-pair test tells us that /ʊ/ and /ʌ/ are therefore two phonemes of southern English English (and RP). This structuralist procedure is concerned with the contrastive **phonological** or **phonemic** functions of the sounds. If we apply this particular minimal-pair test to a speaker of traditional northern English English, we would find no such distinction at work, for *could–cud*, *put–putt*, and so on, would each be a pair of **homophones** (same pronunciation but different meaning) in this accent, both words in the pair retaining the older, pre-split /ʊ/ phoneme. The structuralist is interested in this organizational difference between the two accents: where in its vowel system northern English has one phoneme, southern English has two. Using Weinreich's idea of diasystems, we could demonstrate this structural difference as follows:

$$\frac{\text{NE} \quad \upsilon}{\text{SE} \quad \upsilon \sim \Lambda}$$

A full phonological diasystem for northern and southern English would lay out in such manner all the vowel and consonant phonemic correspondences. Weinreich also suggested that lexical and grammatical diasystems could be constructed in this approach, according to which dialectological research would be 'the study of diasystems' (p. 390). Volume 3 of the *LAS* was the first major dialect atlas to put such structuralist thinking into practice.

The result is a work which unites the structuralist notion of a language being a single system with the intricacies of on-the-ground variation across a sizeable territory. In order to achieve this, the LSS team developed a new concept, the **polyphoneme**. Each polyphoneme is a grouping of phonemes that share certain phonetic characteristics and that are historically related. Using data elicited by the minimal-pair-based LSS phonological questionnaire, which collected pronunciations of stressed vowels in an extensive set of phonetic environments (that is, before different types of consonant sounds), *LAS* 3 includes **systemic maps** showing total numbers of phonemes and numbers of phonemes per polyphoneme in each locality, and **word maps** showing the lexical distribution of the polyphonemes. For example, Figure 5.26 is word map number 17, showing the vowel polyphonemes that occur across the Scots territory in **nut** (questionnaire item 057).

In all, across the territory, four polyphonemes are found in **nut**, each one encompassing a number of phonemes. The polyphoneme \W\, for example, refers to /ʌ/-type vowels, and \Y\ to a group of vowels with higher and more fronted articulation.

The LSS was a survey which placed the features of Scots in both a historical and a systemic context; it is both philological and structuralist. In 1965, the LSS became a fully fledged department of the University of Edinburgh, heartening those scholars who believe that such research 'is not a once-for-all business, but a continuing project' (Petyt, 1980, p. 94). Such straightforward sentiments, however, are no match for the recurrent upheavals of university management structures, and in the mid 1980s the LSS was disbanded as a separate department. But, like the SED, it has had a productive afterlife. For example, its audio recordings are available at Edinburgh's School of Scottish Studies Sound Archive, and, under the leadership of Angus McIntosh, the tools, aims, and methods of the large-scale dialect survey were adapted to what has become a major series of linguistic atlases of earlier periods in the history of English, including two linguistic atlases of Middle English (McIntosh et al., 1986, and Laing, 2013) and one of Older Scots (Williamson, 2008–13),

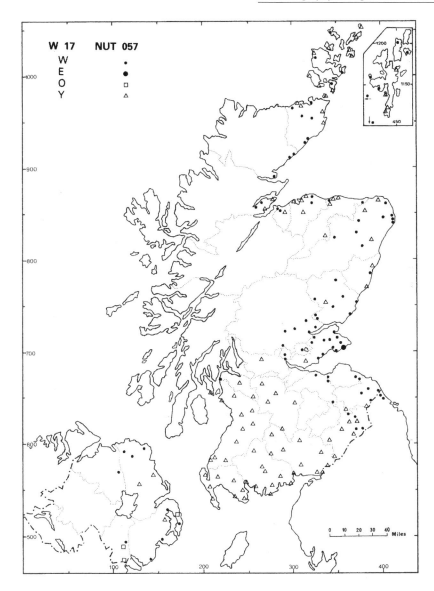

Figure 5.26   Symbol map of polyphonemes occurring in **NUT** (from Mather, Speitel and Leslie, 1986, p. 295).

all of which are currently based at Edinburgh's Angus McIntosh Centre for Historical Linguistics (http://www.amc.lel.ed.ac.uk/).

The fieldwork for the LSS in Northern Ireland was done with the help of the Folklore and Dialect Section of the Belfast Naturalists' Field Club, which, under the leadership of G. Brendan Adams and Richard Hayward, started a dialect survey of English in 1951 in the area encompassing the old nine-county province of Ulster and the neighbouring Counties of Leitrim and Louth to the south. (Since 1920, Ireland has been divided into two territories: Northern Ireland, comprising six of the counties of Ulster; and the Republic of Ireland, or Éire.) The Ulster Dialect Archive of the Ulster Folk Museum was established in 1960 as the home for this material (see: https://nmni.com/uftm/Collections/Library/Dialect-archive), and the 1964 collection of essays edited by Adams was the first published outcome of this arrangement. The collection included a detailed structuralist phonological study by Robert J. Gregg, who completed his doctoral dissertation on Ulster dialects in 1963, using elderly informants (see also Gregg, 1972), and a historically orien-tated lexical study by Patrick Leo Henry, dealing with the whole of Ireland but based on a small selection of display maps using data collected for the author's Linguistic Survey of Ireland. Henry had published a Preliminary Report on this survey in 1958, which despite its name was a good 150 pages in length, describing phonological, grammatical, and lexical data (including two lexical display maps) collected in the field using a questionnaire (first drafted in 1953, and supplemented by a postal lexical questionnaire) at 31 rural local-ities across the island of Ireland from a 'consciously old-fashioned stratum of society' (Henry, 1958, p. 101). In the 1990s, Caroline Macafee used the materials of the Ulster Dialect Archive for *A Concise Ulster Dictionary* (1996). There is no shortage of published work on the English dialects of Ireland (see also, for example, Filppula, 1999; Hickey, 2007; Corrigan, 2010; and Kallen, 2013), nor of terms for the language and its varieties on the island. Henry's preference is for *Anglo-Irish* (his survey's name became the Linguistic Survey of Anglo-Irish (LSAI)), while in more recent work the terms *Hiberno-English* (Filppula) and *Irish English* (Corrigan, Kallen) are popular, and in addition there are competing terms for the English dialect of the north-east corner – that is, *Scotch-Irish* (Gregg) or *Ulster Scots* (Adams, Hickey) – with its origins in the immigration of Scots speakers in the seventeenth century. In 1941, in a memorandum on the *Necessity of an Irish Linguistic Survey*, addressed to the Dublin Institute for Advanced Studies and to the Taoiseach of Ireland, the Norwegian linguist Alf Sommerfelt had argued that a linguistic survey and atlas of the Irish language in the philological mould was 'an urgent neces-sity' (Baumgarten and Sommerfelt, 1974, p. 130). He proposed that the survey should also explore the vocabulary of 'Anglo-Irish' (or Irish English). This aspiration was realized for the Irish language by Heinrich Wagner's four-volume *Linguistic Atlas and Survey of Irish Dialects*, published between 1958 and 1969, which opted for Gilliéron-style display maps. However, when we are looking at the execution and completion of national dialect surveys of English, as we are, then the record in Ireland is patchier than that for England, Scotland, and Wales.

P. L. Henry provided a further glimpse into his LSAI lexical research in 1985, including two symbol maps, but the survey was not concluded. There was a promising development in March 1972, when a working party was formed at a Colloquium on Hiberno-English held at the New University of Ulster whose members subsequently became the directors of the Tape-recorded Survey of Hiberno-English Speech (TRS), a project aimed first at the northern counties of Ireland but with ambitions of whole-island coverage. One of the directors was G. B. Adams. The other two were Michael V. Barry and Philip M. Tilling, both co-editors with Harold Orton of SED *Basic Material* volumes, and the purpose of the survey was 'to provide a picture of the English speech of Ireland which would complement that provided for England by the SED and for Scotland by the LSS' (Adams, Barry and Tilling, 1985, p. 67). The TRS was thus shaped by the earlier surveys, especially the SED, though more restricted in one way, in that it was limited to phonology, and wider in range in another, in that it sampled informants in rural areas from three age-groups: 9–12 years, 35–45 years, and 65–75 years. A 379-item phonological questionnaire was composed (Adams, Barry and Tilling, 1976) for use by a handful of interviewers in the field, taking 61 of its questions directly from the SED questionnaire, but with input also from the LSS, Henry (1958), and Gregg (1972). In the 1980s, some initial findings were published (for example, Barry, 1980, 1981, and Adams, Barry and Tilling, 1985), focusing on the path of the linguistic boundary running east-west across the island (approximately in keeping with the political boundary) between northern Scots-influenced Hiberno-English (or Irish English) and southern Hiberno-English (or Irish English), the latter historically stemming from the mid east of Ireland and influenced originally by western and south-western English English. The eight maps in Adams, Barry and Tilling (1985) each show isoglosses that run differently for each age-group, suggesting a temporal difference as well as a spatial transition between the northern and southern varieties. However, by the end of the 1980s, the TRS had been discontinued.

And yet, as with the SED and LSS, the TRS has had a life beyond its ending. Tape recordings from the TRS were given by Michael Barry to Raymond Hickey in 1984. By the time the TRS ended, recordings from 193 localities throughout Ireland had been made. Hickey digitized a sample of the recordings and used them for his audio tour of varieties of Irish English called *A Sound Atlas of Irish English*, published in 2004. Details of Hickey's TRS – Digital project are also provided in his information-packed Irish English Resource Centre website, at: https://www.uni-due.de/IERC/index.html.

Finally in this section we look at Wales, where in October 1968 the Survey of Anglo-Welsh Dialects (SAWD) was begun at Swansea University, conceived by its founder, David R. Parry, as an inquiry into the English speech of Wales in the philological tradition, and inspired by Parry's experience as a postgraduate student under Harold Orton between 1959 and 1961, and as a fieldworker for the SED in Monmouthshire in 1960. Parry's choice of the label *Anglo-Welsh* rather than *Welsh English* for his Survey reflects the customary use of the term in Wales as, for example, a descriptor in 'Anglo-Welsh literature' and as a name for the English-speaking community of Wales. The aims and methods of SAWD mirrored those of the SED, with the intention being 'to provide material for Wales that is directly comparable with that obtained in England' (Parry, 1999, p. 1), a comparison that would include the construction of composite maps from SAWD and SED data. The SAWD questionnaire (Chesters, Upton and Parry, 1968) was for the most part the Dieth-Orton SED questionnaire, with around 35 of the original questions edited out and about 25 new ones added. Up to 1982, postgraduate and undergraduate student fieldworkers comprehensively trained by Parry travelled to all parts of rural Wales to interview and audio record speakers of Welsh English, until a network of 90 SAWD localities was chosen out the nearly 120 investigated. The SED's judgement sample of informants was followed: a small number of speakers per locality in the 60-plus age-group with minimal education were sought, who had spent little or no time living away from their village. To date there has been no SAWD atlas, but rather the big SAWD publications have included isoglossic atlas sections alongside exhaustive phonological accounts and dialect grammars and glossaries of the network. The first three volumes dealt with south-east, south-west, and north Wales, in that order (Parry, 1977, 1979, and Penhallurick, 1991, respectively). In 1985, in a chapter by Parry in the collection of essays on linguistic geography edited by Kirk, Sanderson and Widdowson, the first composite maps of England and Wales appeared, six in all. Another 50 were published (along with 90 maps of Wales only) in Parry (1999), which was a detailed overview of all the rural SAWD data. For the first time, a cartographic view of the patterns of regional continuity and difference in features of the traditional Welsh English and English English dialects was available. Figure 5.27 is a hitherto unpublished draft composite map by Parry, dating from 1984, of the distribution of the phrase *for to* meaning 'in order to'.

The dispersal of the form in south England and south Wales looks haphazard but makes more sense when one discovers that Joseph Wright's *EDD* records it in this sense in west Somerset and Cornwall, that it is found a dozen times in the (unpublished) Klemola and Jones transcriptions of the SED audio recordings for Somerset, plus 17 times in Devon, twice in Cornwall and once in Gloucestershire, and that it is also recorded in Irish English (see, for example, *eWAVE* item 202, 'Unsplit *for to* in infinitival purpose clauses'). Accordingly, we can interpret this as a historical dialectal feature (one of many) connecting south-west England with long-standing English-speaking enclaves in south-west Wales and south-east Ireland. The *EDD* information compared with the Parry map leads us to speculate that the form's geographical spread is receding by the 1970s, but this

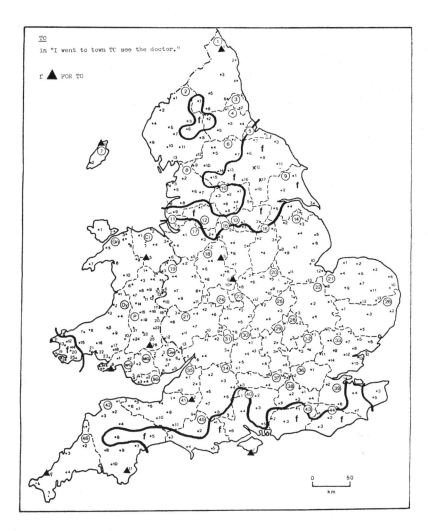

Figure 5.27   Unpublished draft map by David Parry of SAWD and SED data showing distribution of *for to*, 'in order to', in the sentence 'I came ... see the doctor', SAWD/SED question IX.5.9.

is countered somewhat by the additional evidence of the 1950s-to-1960s SED audio, which in turn might be taken as an indication of the more casual style of informants' speech in these less scripted conversations compared with the questionnaire sessions, leading to their increased use of non-standard features.

A second phase of SAWD was begun in 1985 using a more sociolinguistic methodology to collect material from a number of age-groups in urban areas of Wales. This data was used in Heli Paulasto's book (2006) on the syntax of Welsh English. The materials of SAWD are now stored in the Archive of Welsh English (see: http://www.swansea.ac.uk/riah/researchgroups/lrc/awe/), and the digitized audio recordings are also held at the British Library, where they can be accessed on site via the BL's catalogue (see: http://www.bl.uk/reshelp/findhelpsubject/socsci/socioling/soundrec/sociolingsound.html). In his retirement years, David Parry has completed an as yet unpublished fuller edition of his 1999 volume which includes a thorough phonemic analysis of the rural SAWD data.

5.4   Conclusion: the regeneration of linguistic cartography

Many words ago, at the start of this lengthy tale of dialect cartography, I quoted Ronald Macaulay's rather direct question about the purposes of linguistic atlases: 'What am I getting for my money?' The question was posed in 1985 (p. 172), a good century into the history of dialect mapping and linguistic atlases, but less than 20 years after the first digital audio recorder, just 14 years after Gordon R. Wood boldly claimed that 'computers open the way to new kinds of dialectology' (Wood, 1971b, p. 41), and a few years before the terms *Internet* and *World Wide Web* started to seep into public consciousness. Macaulay mulled over the expense, visual styles, and relevance of the philological atlases, but I suggest that his critique is no longer applicable: information technology has put dialect cartography into a new context.

Since the days of Georg Wenker and Jules Gilliéron, dialect cartography has been re-theorized by structuralism and fortified by sociolinguistics, and both of these developments have added to the need that has always been present: for the capability to collect and handle large amounts of data, that is, the need for quantitative, statistical analysis. The IT revolution has provided that capability. (Generative linguistics has also had some impact on dialect study (see Chapter 7), although its principal aim of developing a characterization of humans' innate mental capacity to acquire and process language is fundamentally different from the aims of most dialect study, and generativism has made a relatively small impression on dialect cartography.)

Dialect mapping and linguistic atlases have always dealt in large quantities of data. In the narrow social-scientific-research sense of the word, dialect cartography now has at its disposal the tools enabling it to be fully *quantitative*. Maps can be based much more readily on calculations using many tokens of many features gathered from many informants. The data can be collected more speedily too. In addition, maps can be published online comparatively quickly and inexpensively, and the reader/user can be actively involved in tailoring the display to their interests and enquiries.

The umbrella term regularly used for this modern quantitative linguistic geography is **dialectometry**, coined by Jean Séguy (1914–73) in the early 1970s. As 'the measuring of dialect', dialectometry is all about numbers – about numerical classification applied to geographical space – and it has been made possible by computers, which can manipulate the data once it is in machine-readable form. Since the early 1980s, dialectometrical techniques have been applied to old resources, such as the *ALF* and *AIS* (see Goebl, 2010), LAMSAS (Kretzschmar and Schneider, 1996), and the SED (Viereck, 1985b; Viereck and Ramisch, 1997), and centres of dialectometrical output have developed at the universities of Regensburg, Germany (Hans Goebl and others), Salzburg, Austria (also Goebl), Groningen, Netherlands (Wilbert Heeringa and others), and Athens, Georgia, USA (William Kretzschmar and others). Using computer-enabled statistical measurement and choropleth presentation, a dialectometrical map can show dialectal similarities and differences between localities and regions based on a mass of data (a **similarity** or **difference map**) rather than on an individual linguistic variable. Dialectometry can correlate the linguistic similarities between localities in a network covering a large territory with the geographical proximities between localities in order to produce maps that show more clearly dialectal similarities that might be due to more local interactions (a **correlation map**). Dialectometry can show the linguistic landscape from the point of view of one locality, with darker-shaded areas on the map indicating localities that are more linguistically similar to the original reference point (a **reference point map**). In an **MDS map** (**multidimensional scaling**), all linguistic

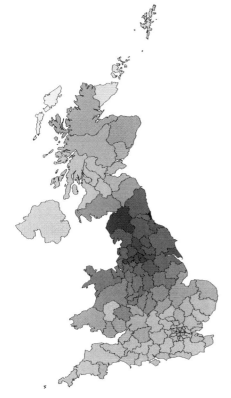

Figure 5.28 MDS map of dialect regions of British English by Martijn Wieling using BBC *Voices* data from 2004–5, from http://www.gabmap.nl/voices/ (accessed 3 March 2016).

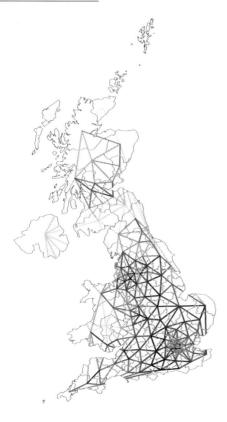

Figure 5.29   Difference map with lines connecting neighbouring postcode areas, by Martijn Wieling using BBC *Voices* data, from http://www.gabmap.nl/voices/ (accessed 3 March 2016).

differences (in the data) between all localities are visualized simultaneously by giving similar colours to linguistically similar areas. In his 2010 summary, Hans Goebl defines *dialectometry* as 'the *quantitative* arm of classical, atlas-based and *quality*-oriented linguistic geography' (p. 453), arguing that dialectometrical techniques demonstrate the 'discovery that underlying deep structures of the linguistic management of space by humans show well-formed spatial patterns' (p. 436) which are 'the spatial counterpart' to the neogrammarian sound laws.

This view transports us neatly back to the first linguistic atlases, and I will end this chapter by inviting you to compare two examples of dialectometrical maps of British English with two early maps. The dialectometrical maps are both from the research of Martijn Wieling and his collaborators at the University of Groningen, using data collected in 2004–5 by the BBC *Voices* project, and accessible at: http://www.gabmap.nl/voices/. (See also Wieling, 2013.) Figure 5.28 is an MDS map of the complete *Voices* data set. The original downloadable map is in colour, on which similar colours are used to indicate linguistically similar postcode areas. We can get some idea of the main dialect regions in this monochrome reproduction by the degrees of grey shading. You can compare this map with those of A. J. Ellis from 1887 and 1889 (Figures 5.1 and 5.2). Figure 5.29

is a difference map by Wieling in which lines connect neighbouring post-code areas. The darker the connecting lines, the more linguistically similar are the areas. You will surely want to compare this with the 1877 map by Louis-Lucien Bonaparte (Figure 5.6).

5.5   Brief commentary on terms

In this chapter, I have allowed myself some leeway to slip between the neutral label *dialect cartography* and the more loaded but more usual *linguistic* or *dialect geography*, as I have also started to slip into more discussion of the controversy about the philological approach in dialect study, the story of which is continued in Chapter 8. In addition, I have started to explain some of the relevant terminology of structuralism, but have also sneaked in occasional use of a key term from the sociolinguistic approach without yet explaining it fully, that is, *variable*, which is described in the next chapter.

5.6   What you can do

Over the last three chapters, we have looked at many examples of linguistic cartography, including a lot of big examples – national and international surveys producing maps and atlases of extensive territories. You probably think at this point that such endeavours are beyond the scope of these 'What you can do' sections, which suggest ideas for small, manageable projects that make a contribution to dialect study. And you are right. However, some of the work mentioned in the last three chapters is on a more moderate scale. For example, for their *Word-Geography of Cornwall* (1980), North and Sharpe used existing SED data, collected more data themselves in 17 localities in the spring and summer of 1979 by means of a reduced form of the SED questionnaire, and produced 42 maps of a relatively small geographical area (Cornwall), completing the project in September of the same year. In the first 'What you can do' section in Chapter 2, I mentioned the piece by W. E. Jones (1952) on the definite article in Yorkshire. This was a summary of Jones's MA dissertation, submitted in 1950, the field data being collected in 1949-50. Jones (1952) presented two hand-drawn maps, each showing the geographical spread of the variant phonetic forms of the definite article as recorded in Yorkshire, first by A. J. Ellis (Map A) in 1889 and then by Jones (Map B) in 1949–50. This is a splendid example of what can be achieved by small-scale linguistic geography: as with North and Sharpe, the territory is modest in size; one variable only is considered; and yet the findings tell us something significant about the spatial and temporal variation of a feature with a prominent regional social value.

The bigger surveys offer opportunities as well when their data is available for further and comparative use. For example, the SED's *Basic Material* has been used over and over, as Orton hoped; the ongoing digitization of LAUSC data (and its online availability together with interactive map-making software) makes accessible more corpora; and Wieling's website at Groningen was developed so that 'dialectological analyses using the *Voices* data can be readily conducted' (Wieling, 2013, p. 208).

As for doing an elementary phonological analysis (see Chapter 4.3.3), here are your essentials: a target speech community, John Wells's standard lexical sets, a minimal-pairs-based elicitation tool (for examples see Labov, 1966/2006, pp. 416–18, and Houck, 1968, pp. 120–4), and a digital audio recorder. Decide on your informant-sampling procedure (see Chapters 4, 6, and 7), get recording, and you will be able to collect the data needed to work out a simple phonemic system of your community. The free software *Express Scribe* (http://www.nch.com.au/scribe/) will help you with your transcription. If you collect some extended speech from your informants you can do an acoustic analysis on your computer using a program such as Praat. The more training in linguistic analysis you have, the better, but the basic tools are easily available. The increasing access to valuable audio data, like that at the British Library and the Australian National Corpus, also improves the potential for studies of dialectal variation in discourse features. See also my comments below on Melchers (1996).

Resources and further reading

The three websites of the Linguistic Atlas Project (2011, and the two older sites: 1998, 2005) are the best places to start exploring the linguistic atlases of North America further. If one digs just a little, one can find numerous progress reports and reviews of the projects of the Linguistic Atlas of the United States and Canada by participants such as Hans Kurath, William Kretzschmar, and Raven McDavid, and I would recommend four overviews in particular, in chronological order: Raven and Virginia McDavid's 'Regional Linguistic Atlases in the United States' (1956); Elmer Bagby Atwood's 'The Methods of American Dialectology' (1963); Harold B. Allen's 'Regional Dialects, 1945–1974' (1977); and McDavid et al.'s 'Inside a Linguistic Atlas' (1986). It is also worth doing the occasional online search for used copies of some of the primary texts, such as volumes of *LAGS* or the reprint of *WGEUS*, as they can be obtained at surprisingly reasonable prices. In 1969, a convenient

Compilation of the Work Sheets of the LAUSC was published, edited by Alva Davis, Raven McDavid and Virginia McDavid. For book-length appraisals of work on regional variety in Canada see *Focus on Canada* (1993), edited by Sandra Clarke, *The English Language in Canada* (2010) by Charles Boberg, and *Canadian English: A Sociolinguistic Perspective* (2015) by James A. Walker. For summaries of mid-twentieth-century linguistic geography in the Caribbean (an area neglected in the chapter above) see Frederic Cassidy's 'English Language Studies in the Caribbean' (1959) and David DeCamp's 'The Field of Creole Language Studies' (1968). And *American Voices* (2006), edited by Walt Wolfram and Ben Ward, is a collection of accessible, succinct essays by specialists, originally published in *Language Magazine*, giving a wide-ranging overview of the diversity of English dialects in North America. Regarding the large twentieth-century surveys of English in the British Isles, the website of the Leeds Archive of Vernacular Culture gives you access to audio, incidental material, and photographs from the Survey of English Dialects, and the website of the Angus McIntosh Centre for Historical Linguistics, University of Edinburgh, provides a wealth of tremendous material on English and Scots from the great historical linguistic atlas projects that followed the LSS. Craig Fees's (1991a) invaluable account of the SED can be downloaded from the author's website, at: http://craigfees.com/documents/1991-imperilled_ inheritance.pdf. Via linguistlist.org you can see videos of eight lectures given by J. C. Catford about his academic life on the occasion of his retirement from the University of Michigan Linguistics Department in 1985: http://linguistlist. org/issues/19/19-492.html. The sixth lecture (28 March 1985) focuses on his work for the LSS. Raymond Hickey's Irish English Resource Centre website has information on the history, linguistic geography, and sociolinguistics of Irish English, as well as audio samples and a summary of Hickey's restoration of the TRS. There are also extracts from *A Sound Atlas of Irish English* and a link to a companion website on Hickey's *Variation and Change in Dublin English* project. See also his *A Source Book for Irish English* (2002). The website of the Archive of Welsh English contains a bibliography of works on Welsh English, as well as a history of the Survey of Anglo-Welsh Dialects written by its director, David Parry, at: http://www.swansea.ac.uk/riah/researchgroups/lrc/awe/storyof sawd/. See also Parry (1985, 1999) and Penhallurick (2012) for more on SAWD and English in Wales. *Studies in Linguistic Geography* (1985), edited by John Kirk, Stewart Sanderson and John Widdowson, is a very useful collection of ten essays reviewing the state of play in late-twentieth-century British linguistic geography, including contributions on dialectometry (Wolfgang Viereck) and generativist phonological maps (Beat Glauser). The generative approach is also discussed in an essay by Sjef Barbiers in Volume 1 of the compendious *Language and Space* series (Auer and Schmidt, 2010), which in addition has a piece on 'Traditional Dialect Geography' by Renate Schrambke. Volume 2 of the same series (Lameli et al., 2010a, 2010b) includes essays on mapping British English (Heinrich Ramisch) and American English (Tom Wikle and Guy Bailey), and a summary of dialectometry by Hans Goebl (dialectometry also features in the essay by Ramisch). For more information on BBC *Voices* and its offshoots, go to the original *Voices* website, and see the 2013 collection edited by Clive Upton and Bethan Davies, *Analysing 21st Century British English*, and its companion website. An English Dialects App, developed by a team led by Adrian Leemann, has produced some interesting maps comparing data collected via the app in 2016 with SED data: https://www.cam.ac.uk/research/ news/cambridge-app-maps-decline-in-regional-diversity-of-english-dialects. In 2017, a project at Leeds University was announced aiming to put the SED archive more fully online and to carry out a real-time follow-up survey to the SED: https://www.leeds.ac.uk/news/article/4120/updating_the_most_compre hensive_dialect_survey_ever. *An Index to Dialect Maps of Great Britain* (1991) by Andreas Fischer and Daniel Amman is a helpful reference guide. In 1996, Gunnel Melchers published an essay summarizing her doctoral work on the SED audio recordings and looking at their potential for acoustic and discourse analysis. Her transcriptions were included in the Helsinki Corpus of British English Dialects: http://www.helsinki.fi/varieng/CoRD/corpora/Dialects/ index.html. Part V of A. J. Ellis's *On Early English Pronunciation* can be down- loaded from the Internet Archive, and Robert Sanders compiled an exhaustive bibliography of Ellis's writings which is available from the Memorial University Digital Archives Initiative, at: http://collections.mun.ca/index.php. The orig- inal was published in three parts in *Regional Language Studies (Newfoundland)*, Numbers 13–15 (1991–4). Finally, we bring together the nineteenth-century starting point and twenty-first-century end point of the chapter above: as part of the Spoken English in Early Dialects and *EDD Online* projects at the University of Innsbruck, Christoph Praxmarer (2010a, 2010b) produced some dialectometrical, reference point maps of English dialect regions using data from Joseph Wright's *English Dialect Dictionary*.

6 Sociolinguistics

6.1 Introduction

In November 1962, a 35-year-old man, college educated, a native of New Jersey, United States, dressed in middle class style, with jacket, white shirt and tie, entered a department store in New York City and said to a sales assistant, 'Excuse me, where are the women's shoes?' The assistant replied, 'Fourth floor.' The man leaned forward and said, 'Excuse me?' The assistant reiterated, but this time more carefully and emphatically, *'Fourth floor.'* There was nothing exceptionally unusual in this behaviour, nor perhaps in the fact that the man repeated his two questions about a fourth-floor department in another two New York City stores. What was really bizarre was that in these three stores the man asked these questions a total of 264 times. Why did he do this? Chiefly because he believed that *'if any two sub-groups of New York City speakers are ranked on a scale of social stratification, then they will be ranked in the same order by their differential use of (r)'.*

The man was William Labov (born 1927, in Rutherford, New Jersey), the most influential and best-known figure of sociolinguistics, who in 1962 was a research student at Columbia University, NYC (the details above come from Labov, 1966/2006, pp. 41, 45–6, 100). He had no especial interest in women's shoes. And before asking his questions he knew perfectly well that the women's shoes section was on the fourth floor. Truth be told, he was not interested in any of the departments on any of the fourth floors. His intention was to get the assistant to say the phrase *fourth floor* twice: first of all casually and then carefully. Hence his first question could be modified so as to refer to any section which Labov knew was on the fourth floor.

The phrase *fourth floor* contains two potential instances of the **variable** (r): one word-medially, post-vocalically (that is, after a vowel) and pre-consonantally in *fourth*; and one word-finally, post-vocalically in *floor*. A variable, put simply, is something which varies in its execution, and (r) is a **linguistic variable**, or to be even more precise, a **phonological variable**, which is a unit of sound that is realized ('made real' or performed or executed) in potentially a variety of forms. The concept of the linguistic variable was introduced by Labov in the mid 1960s (Labov, 1966/2006, p. xi), and the formal notation for a linguistic variable is to place it between rounded parentheses ( ). The linguistic variable has been a key concept in dialect study ever since. The variation in question here is between the presence or absence of (r) in the pronuncia-tion of these two words, that is, between its articulation or non-articulation (execution or non-execution). Labov believed that the phonetic environment could affect (r), so that (r) could vary differently in *fourth* and in *floor* because in each word it occurs in a different phonetic context (medially, finally, and so on). He also believed that (r) could be affected by the **style** of articulation used by the speaker, that is, **casual style** (in response to the first question) or more **formal style** (in response to the second question). Although such variation was generally appreciated before this study, this close codifying of **stylistic stratification** was another innovation introduced by Labov. His chief hypothesis, however, was that variation of (r) could be correlated with the **social stratification** of speakers.

What this means is that Labov believed that in the English speech of New York City **post-vocalic (r)** before a consonant or word-finally was a prestige feature, that is, its presence/use was linked with speakers from the higher social classes, or, to put it another way, in the perceptions of NYC-English-speakers presence of post-vocalic (r) (as opposed to its absence) was considered more formal and more standard (as opposed to non-standard), and indicated the higher class background of the speaker. Post-vocalic (r) before a consonant or word finally is also known as **rhoticity**, and those accents which possess it are described as **rhotic**. British Received Pronunciation (RP) is non-rhotic, and in British English rhoticity is not prestigious, and is associated with non-standard accents. In his department store study, Labov wanted to show that rhoticity in NYC English was prestigious and correlated with social stratification. How did he achieve this?

Spoken instances of the phrase *fourth floor* constituted Labov's data. Posing as an unexceptional customer asking two questions was his elicitation method, neatly sidestepping the **observer's paradox**, a term coined by Labov in 1972 (1972b, p. 113) to label the well-known snag for investigators seeking to observe and collect naturally occurring speech: the very presence of the investigator by default affects the speech situation. What Labov needed was a representative sample of speakers/informants from a range of social classes. As his survey was a small pilot study, his data collection had to be achieved simply and quickly. Furthermore, in addition to his other hypotheses, Labov wanted to demonstrate that with respect to the differential use of (r) in English, New York City functioned as a single **speech community**. One of the fundamental tenets in his work is that 'the language of individuals cannot be understood without knowledge of the community of which they are members' (Labov, 1966/2006, p. 5), that is, that variations in their speech can be explained with reference to shared communal behaviours. He chose to interview one occupational group only: department-store sales assistants. He selected three department stores: Saks Fifth Avenue, Macy's, and S. Klein. Crucially, each store occupied a different position on a scale of social stratification, in terms of its location, prices, and fashion prestige. Saks was the high-end store, Macy's the middle-ranking, and Klein was at the lower, cost-cutting level. Labov argued that the differing working conditions in the three stores, plus the differing social evaluations of the sales jobs when compared between the three stores, served to stratify socially the sales assistants themselves. By restricting his sample in this way to one occupational group subtly stratified, he aimed to show that structured (r) variation pervaded New York City English generally. He predicted (1966/2006, pp. 41–2) that his data would show: '*sales people in the highest ranked store will have the highest values* [that is, scores for articulation] *of (r); those in the middle ranked store will have intermediate values of (r); and those in the lowest ranked store will show the lowest values*' (italics in the original). Figure 6.1, from Labov's results (1966/2006, p. 47), corroborates this hypothesis.

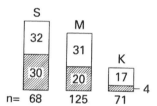

Figure 6.1   Overall stratification of (r) by store, from Labov (1966; 2nd edn of 2006, p. 47).

In Figure 6.1: S = Saks, M = Macy's, and K = S. Klein; the shaded areas = those informants who always articulated (r); and unshaded areas = those who sometimes articulated (r). Other results showed that (r) did indeed vary according to phonetic environment and style. Of most interest was the narrowing of the difference between Saks and Macy's scores in emphatic *floor*, owing to a large increase in Macy's score for emphatic final (r). Labov explains this (1966/2006, pp. 47–8) as being due to *r*-pronunciation being treated as a norm to be aimed at: Saks employees routinely use it more often; Macy's employees use it less so, but when carefully monitoring their own speech they use it more often in the position (word-finally) where they are more aware of it.

Following each surreptitious 'interview', Labov made a note of the 'informant's' responses, as well as brief biographical details. Consequently he was able also to analyse his data according to the non-linguistic variables of race, sex, and age (see Labov, 1966/2006, pp. 49–54).

William Labov's New York City department store study is one of the earliest and most famous works of sociolinguistics. It effectively encapsulates for us the continuities and breaks in sociolinguistic dialect studies with the dialectological tradition. This chapter is an introduction to the sociolinguistic approach to the study of dialect.

Like those who preceded him in dialectology, Labov was concerned with the correlation of place and speech. Although not apparent from our discussion so far, he was also interested in linguistic change. But he was starting to investigate in depth other correlations – of speech with social class, age-group, gender, and style, for example – which dialectology had paid attention to only in passing or intermittently. His methods were startlingly different: a concentration on a very few aspects of phonology allied with many comparatively short, easily executed interviews, which permitted an attempt at a **quantitative** or **statistical** analysis, because many tokens of each variable could be collected, the whole process greatly facilitated by the use of a portable tape recorder. The shift in dialect study towards urban speech exemplified by Labov came hand in hand with quantitative analysis. His terminology at this time was also crystallizing hitherto hazier concepts (for example, *linguistic variable*, the *prestige* of variants, *stylistic stratification*). And in the background, informing the whole project, was twentieth-century structuralist linguistics.

The NYC department store survey was, as mentioned above, a pilot study. It was a preliminary to Labov's doctoral research and was first published in 1966 as part of a slightly modified version of his eventual dissertation. A revised, longer version of the store survey appeared in 1972 (1972a, pp. 43–69). In the present book, I refer to the revised, second edition of Labov's doctoral dissertation published in 2006 (see pp. 40–57 for the department store survey), which includes additional reflective commentary by the author from the perspective of 40 years after the original research. We shall concentrate on the larger project presently, after a very short history of the origins of sociolinguistics.

6.2   The etymologies of *dialectology* and *sociolinguistics*

As David Byrne put it, 'Names make all the difference in the world' (Talking Heads, 'Give Me Back My Name', 1985 [*Little Creatures*]). The names in question here are of the two academic disciplines particularly associated with the study of dialect since the advent of systematic language research from the nineteenth century onwards: *dialectology* and *sociolinguistics* are the two main modern approaches, and these names carry a good deal of significance and connotation. Moreover, and interestingly, for a while dialectologists and sociolinguists fought like cat and dog over the best way to study dialect. Why? And why is it no longer so easy to tell them apart? The present chapter and the next two explain and answer these questions. A brief summary of the etymologies of the two names will help to clarify the main issues here.

According to the *Oxford English Dictionary* (*OED*; accessed 14 October 2015), the word *dialectology* (which joins *dialect*, from the Greek δάλεκτος 'discourse, conversation, way of speaking, language of a country or district', with – *ology*, also from Greek, giving the sense 'the study or science of') was first used in English in 1820 in the translation of the title of a scholarly article on 'Arabic dialectology', and then in English proper in 1879 by the editor of the *OED* himself, J. A. H. Murray. However, the *Transactions of the Philological Society* show that Alexander J. Ellis used the term in his Presidential Address of 1874, in the sentence, 'But in dialectology, above all branches of philology, the study of sound is supreme' (p. 449). He went on, 'It is only by serious study of phonology that we can raise dialectology to the rank of philology. When we know the words, then we can go really to work on meaning, descent [that is, etymology], idiom, grammar, thought' (p. 449). Philology, as we know from the preceding chapters, was the approach to language study that came to prominence during the nineteenth century in Europe. The theory that many of the languages of Europe were related to each other as well as to other languages in Asia, originating from a common source, led to a great deal of interest in the histories of European languages, and to increasingly sophisticated hypotheses about the processes of linguistic change. By the end of the nineteenth century, philologists had started in earnest to mine the living, traditional dialects of Europe for the data they believed they needed to develop the discipline. Great dialect atlas and dictionary projects got underway. Dialectology began as a sub-discipline of philology (as the quotations above from A. J. Ellis illustrate), imbued with philological values, interests, and methods. (The quotations also illustrate Ellis's preoccupation with the pronunciation of English, or its phonology, as he calls it.)

The early dialectologists' interest in history was manifested in accounts of words, sounds, and grammatical constructions treated as entities in themselves (though we should remember that the neogrammarians considered sound-sets in groups of words) rather than as contrastive elements in structured systems (as found in the structuralist approach). As dialectology proceeded in Europe and North America, its ways and means were adapted and modified, but its philological core endured through to the 1970s.

By that time, however, philology was no longer the dominant approach to language study. Its place had been taken by *linguistics*, which from the early decades of the twentieth century broadened the scope of language study, in the process de-emphasizing the interest in history. And a new sub-discipline of linguistics had emerged: *sociolinguistics*.

According to the *OED* (accessed 14 October 2015), the term *sociolinguistics* (from Latin *socio-*, derived from *socius* 'companion, associate', joined with *linguistics* 'the science of languages' – the compound is modelled on forms such as *sociology*, and means 'the linguistics of society', that is, the study of the social aspects of language) was coined in 1939 by T. C. Hodson in the title of an article for the journal *Man in India*, 'Socio-linguistics in India'. In this article, Hodson 'discusses language as a social instrument, terms of address, context as an integral element of language, and the languages of tribal peoples, among other topics' (Hymes, 1979, p. 141). Three other early uses of the term are by Haver Currie (1952), who claimed to have invented it (Paulston and Tucker, 2003b, p. 1), Einar Haugen (1951), and Eugene Nida (1949). Nida uses the term in his book on **morphology** (the grammatical analysis of words), in the phrases 'sociolinguistic environment' and 'socio-linguistic setting' in a passage (1949, p. 152) about speech in its social and cultural context. Haugen, in a rather confusing passage (1951, p. 213), seems to be suggesting *socio-linguistics* as an alternative term for *semantics*. Currie uses the term in his article 'A projection of socio-linguistics: The relationship of speech to social status' (1952), which deals with the variation of speech according to social register (Koerner, 1991, p. 65). Apparently Currie had used the word at a conference in 1949 (Hymes, 1979, p. 141; Joseph, 2002, p. 109). By the mid 1960s, the term was starting to become the favoured name for a new branch of linguistics. Its scope was wider than that of dialectology, and its aims, thinking, methods, and even terminology differed in significant ways from dialectology.

For example, to a sociolinguist the term **phonology** means something quite different from what it meant to A. J. Ellis. To Ellis, the term referred to the study of sounds in a language or dialect, in particular their history and the accurate description of their articulation. To a sociolinguist the term refers generally to the functions that sounds have and the place that they occupy in the relational sound system of a language or dialect (a rather more abstract viewpoint), whereas the description of their production and acoustic perception belongs to **phonetics**. Sociolinguistics belongs to modern structuralist linguistics, in which there is an emphasis on investigating the function and place of linguistic features in the context of the (structural) networks or systems which they form, so that the account of, for example, a given sound-feature is concerned with its function considered alongside (the functions of) other sound-features in a dialect or language. To use a simple illustration, the sounds represented by the letters *b* and *p* in the English words *bit* and *pit* are phonetically very similar, but the small phonetic contrast between them ([b] is voiced, [p] is not) is used **phonologically** in English to distinguish words and meanings, as evidenced by *bit* and *pit*, giving two structural units or **phonemes**, /b/ and /p/. The Finnish language, alternatively, has no phonological distinction based on the phonetic difference between [b] and [p]. Different languages and different dialects of the same language can make use of the array of possible consonant and vowel sounds to create different **phonological** or **phonemic** systems. Conventionally in notation a phoneme is enclosed between forward slashes, for example, /b/ and /p/, and /r/, and so on. Actual **phonetic realizations** or performances of sounds in utterances are transcribed between square brackets, for example, [r], meaning a 'rolled' or 'trilled' articulation of /r/, distinguished from an approximant [ɹ] or retroflex [ʈ] or flapped [ɾ] articulation of /r/, and so forth. (For a rolled articulation the tip of the tongue taps the upper teeth-ridge several times quickly; for a flapped articulation it does so once; for an approximant the tip of the tongue is curled back slightly but does not touch the roof of the mouth; for a retroflex articulation it is curled back much more.) Each of these in the English language is a phonetic variant of the /r/ phoneme. Each of these variants is different in sound, but the sound-differences do not distinguish word meaning. They do not perform that phonological function. We use these phonetic transcriptions for the actual sounds of speech, but we use the phonemic symbols for the functional elements of sound systems, that is, the elements whose contrasts affect meaning. (And we use the term *phonological variable* for any feature in a phonological system which is subject to variation.)

The structuralist is interested in describing structured linguistic systems (in pronunciation, vocabulary, grammar) and how they work. Rajend Mesthrie illustrates this (2000, p. 61) by suggesting that modern linguists would prefer dialect maps 'drawn on the basis of isoglosses for vowel *systems*' (my italics) rather than the maps charting individual vowels that are found in the 'atomistic' philological approach. (Though we already know from Chapter 5 of some examples of structuralist maps based on Linguistic Survey of Scotland

and Survey of English Dialects data (in Mather, Speitel and Leslie, 1986, and Anderson, 1987, respectively).) In reality, full-blown, thoroughgoing, large-scale structuralist dialect surveys (such as a comprehensive structuralist survey of dialects on a national scale) are difficult and comparatively rare – though this does not reduce the importance of structuralist theory, which underpins all sociolinguistic dialect study (including the large-scale *Atlas of North American English* (Labov, Ash and Boberg, 2006)). Structuralism in relation to dialect cartography is considered in Chapter 5 of the present book, and all the new work that we look at in Chapters 7, 9, and 10 is founded in the structuralist view of language. My purpose here is to emphasize that the fundamental mindset of sociolinguistics is structuralist, while the philological approach of dialectology pre-dates structuralism. That said, and to qualify the foregoing a certain amount, Martyn Wakelin pointed out in 1977 (p. 59) that 'even before the advent of structuralism dialectologists were aware of the importance of linguistic systems' and that 'the concept of system is inherent in traditional approaches', for example, in accounts tracing the developments of sounds from previous stages which postulated earlier, historical phonemic systems in the language or dialect under consideration. It remains true, nevertheless, that the structuralist intervention of the early twentieth century radically altered the directions and emphases of language study.

While urban dialects had not been completely ignored in European dialectology and had featured firmly in American dialectology, from the early 1950s we see the start of a number of determined attempts to tackle the dialects of single urban areas, beginning with the Norwegian Eva Sivertsen's survey of *Cockney Phonology*, which was started before 1951 and published in 1960. Yet it was also becoming apparent that the established sampling methods were inadequate for the much larger, more mixed, more transient populations of urban localities, and the old philological (non-structuralist) approach was also increasingly seen as outmoded. Sivertsen's survey in fact utilized a contemporary phonemic analysis, but she had a mere four main informants, all elderly women from Bethnal Green. Interestingly, a 1962 review of it by the Survey of English Dialects' chief fieldworker, Stanley Ellis, criticized Sivertsen's 'interesting experiment' for neglecting historical factors (S. Ellis, 1962, p. 324). In the 1960s, sociolinguistics entered the arena. It was grounded in structuralism, infused with a different approach to sampling, dedicated to a statistical approach reliant on collecting many tokens of variables, and attentive to urban populations. By the 1970s it seemed as if the name *dialectology* signified a discipline that had had its day.

But what was the range of the new discipline of sociolinguistics? Exactly where had it come from? And what was its full impact on dialect study?

6.3   Where did sociolinguistics come from and what is its scope?

When it emerged in the 1960s, sociolinguistics was a new expression of an old interest. The old interest lies in the recognition – an obvious recognition, one would think – that language is a social entity, and that there exists an intimate relationship between the characteristic configurations of language and of society. This is recognized as early as the linguist and philosopher Wilhelm von Humboldt's 1811 essay on the grammars of native languages of the Americas (see the online *Stanford Encylopedia of Philosophy*, at: http://plato.stanford.edu/entries/wilhelm-humboldt/#Wor).   In   narratives that trace the origins of sociolinguistics, some importance is given to the philologist Antoine Meillet's statement in a lecture delivered at the Collège de France in 1906 that 'language is a social institution' and therefore 'it follows that linguistics is a social science' (Meillet, 1921, p. 17; see also Davis, 1983, p. 85, and Labov, 1966/2006, p. 11). Meillet was familiar with the work of the early linguistic geographers (Koerner, 1991, p. 60), and was also a pupil of Ferdinand de Saussure, whose 1916 *Cours de linguistique générale* (*Course in General Linguistics*) is often seen as the dawn of structuralist linguistics. One of the influences on Saussure's thought was the work of the American philologist William Dwight Whitney, whose view it was that language is essentially societal and communal in nature (Whitney, 1867, p. 404, cited in Koerner, 1991, p. 59). The pre-history of sociolinguistics is marked in this way by a web of subject-area and personal connections criss-crossing between Europe and North America.

For example, and furthermore, Max Weinreich, known for his work on Yiddish and to whom the slogan 'A language is a dialect with an army and a navy' is frequently attributed, did his doctoral dissertation (on Yiddish, 1923) under the supervision of Georg Wenker's successor at the University of Marburg, Ferdinand Wrede. Max's son Uriel Weinreich studied under Jakob Jud in Zürich in 1948–9, and then under André Martinet at Columbia University in New York City. Martinet himself had studied under Antoine Meillet. Uriel Weinreich's doctoral dissertation (1951) with Martinet led to his book *Languages in Contact* (1953), a noteworthy precursor to sociolinguistics, whose title came from a series of lectures given by Martinet. In 1954, the younger Weinreich published the influential essay 'Is a Structural Dialectology Possible?'. He was also later the supervisor of a doctoral dissertation submitted in 1964 at Columbia University, and, yes, the author was William Labov, and the dissertation was published in 1966 as *The Social Stratification of English in New York City*. (See Koerner, 1991; Paulston and Tucker, 2003b; and Labov, 1966/2006, for more on this little mesh of details.)

dissertation was the larger project for which the department store
had been a pilot, and it is the most seminal work of sociolinguistics.
It is very much concerned with the interrelationship of speech and community, and is structuralist in its phonological analysis. But Labov rejects another
line of linguistics that came out of Saussurean thought, that is, the study
of the psychological foundations of language by methods divorced from the
description of language use and linguistic diversity in society, and which in
the work of Noam Chomsky from the 1950s onwards explicitly treated the
living heterogeneity of language as of minor significance. For Chomsky, true
linguistics is about how the mind processes language and it is therefore a
natural science not a social science. This school of thought became known
as **generative linguistics**, and it dominated linguistic theorizing through the
1960s to the 1980s. Although studying language without recourse to extensive data from the speech community is anathema to Labov, he was willing to
make use of generative ideas about the phonological and grammatical forms
that might underpin speakers' performance of linguistic variants, as we shall
see in Chapter 7 of the present book.

Viewed from the wider perspective, sociolinguistics was inspired by interests, ideas, and methods from three subject areas: dialectology (or linguistic
geography), anthropology, and sociology.

Up to a point, sociolinguistics was a development of earlier work in
dialectology. Both disciplines investigated the variation of speech in relation
to locale. In other words, both were interested in regional dialects. However,
in the early years of sociolinguistics there was no production of large-scale
dictionaries and atlases. Rather the focus was on the phonology and (to a
lesser degree) the grammar of individual urban localities, particularly the
statistical correlation of phonological variation with the age, class, ethnicity,
and sex of speakers. Sociolinguistics concentrated on social variation in particular locations. From the outset, sociolinguistics also had a broader scope than
dialectology, and is concerned with a range of topics, such as language and
gender, pidgin and creole varieties of language, bilingualism and multilingualism, and language planning and educational policy. It connects with
other sub-disciplines of modern linguistics, such as **pragmatics** (the study
of language in use generally) and **discourse analysis** (the study of extended
stretches of language), and from the beginning there were strands of sociolinguistics that were more allied with anthropology and with sociology than was
the type of sociolinguistics pioneered by Labov in 1966. It is this Labovian
strand that is most relevant to dialect study and therefore to the present book.
It is referred to by an assortment of names in the literature, with *social dialectology, urban dialectology, variationist sociolinguistics* or *variationist theory* or
variationism, and *Labovian sociolinguistics* among the most prominent.

For good reasons, early dialectology had been mainly interested in the older, traditional regional dialects. But by the 1950s this was beginning to look like a preoccupation which neglected the speech of the young and middle-aged, of women, of urban dwellers, indeed of everyone apart from elderly, rural working-class males, and which disregarded other important factors in the explanation of the linguistic behaviour of dialect speakers, such as their ability to shift between *styles* and thereby use different variants of the same variable under differing conditions. Yet the early dialectologists were not entirely unmindful of these questions. For example: in Chapter 5 we saw that in 1889 A. J. Ellis was conscious of what we would now call *style-* or *code-shifting*; both Wenker and Gilliéron commented in their work on variation according to age-group (see Lameli, 2010, p. 578, citing an 1889 map by Wenker, and the commentaries in Gilliéron and Edmont, 1902, p. 21); Jaberg and Jud included some urban centres in their *Sprach- und Sachatlas Italiens und der Südschweiz* (*AIS*; 1928–40); and following the lead of Hans Kurath and the *Linguistic Atlas of New England* (*LANE*; Kurath et al., 1939–43), from the start in American linguistic geography there was an awareness that age, education, and occupation should play a systematic part in the selection of informants, as well as attention being given to urban centres. A striking forerunner of Labovian sociolinguistics is the 1948 article by another of the eminent linguistic geographers of American English, Raven I. McDavid, Jr. The article is titled 'Post-vocalic /r/ in South Carolina: A Social Analysis', and in it McDavid identifies the cause of *r*-present and *r*-absent speech in South Carolina. The distribution is complicated and perplexing if considered purely geographically (McDavid, 1948, pp. 197–8), but McDavid finds that the cause is a social-class phenomenon, that is, the spread of *r*-lessness from the prestige and historically British-inclined accent of upper-class Charleston. But the most exceptional antecedent to variationist sociolinguistics is Louis Gauchat's 'L'unité phonétique dans le patois d'une commune' ['Phonetic unity in the dialect of a single village'], a study into the French dialect of the Swiss village of Charmey begun in 1898 and published in 1905 (and in an English translation by Sarah Cummins in 2008). Gauchat was born in 1866 near Neuchâtel, Switzerland, and was a contemporary of two other distinguished Swiss linguists, Jules Gilliéron and Ferdinand de Saussure. Although carried out in the earliest phase of European dialectology, Gauchat's survey of Charmey correlated linguistic data with age-groups and showed an awareness of social factors and speech style. In other words, 'his predilection for the social uses of language led him to anticipate most aspects of what was to become [60 years later] variationist linguistics' (Chambers, 2008, p. 219). William Labov references him at the start of his 1966 dissertation (1966/2006, p. 12).

Labov's work in New York City is also anticipated by his own smaller study in 1963 of Martha's Vineyard, an island off the coast of New England, and by

John L. Fischer's 1958 study of the use of present participial –*in* versus –*ing* (for example, *playin'* or *playing*) among children in a New England village. Fischer concluded (p. 485) that the variation could be revealingly correlated with the gender, personality, mood, and class of the speaker, with the formality of the social context, as well as with the perceived standardness of the individual verb. Uriel Weinreich had some input into the piece. Fischer was interested in the mechanisms of linguistic change, and recognized that he was breaking with traditional dialectology, proposing to call studies like his own 'comparative idiolectology' (p. 487).

Although Labov acknowledged in 1966 (2nd edn 2006, pp. 15–16) the influence of the work of anthropologists on socially significant linguistic variables, anthropological (or ethnological) sociolinguistics has different foci from the sociolinguistics pioneered in Labov's NYC study. A leading figure in this strand was the American Dell Hymes, who was influenced by the anthropologists Franz Boas and Edward Sapir, and who is best known for developing an approach known as the 'ethnography of speaking', the aim of which was to describe the linguistic and cultural conventions that underpin spoken discourse. In terms of subject matter, there is an obvious affinity between language study and anthropology. One can argue, in fact, that language study is one sub-branch of anthropology. Nevertheless, there has certainly been at some points in the history of modern linguistics a desire to establish it as an autonomous discipline in its own right. It is against this background that Roger M. Shuy made the statement, in his outline history of American sociolinguistics (1990; extracts reprinted in Paulston and Tucker, 2003a, pp. 4–16), 'sociolinguistics constitutes something of a return to anthropology' (p. 5). (It is fair to say that dialectology – whose course for most of the twentieth century ran somewhat outside of modern linguistics – did not lose sight of the interconnection of language and culture.)

Sociology, too, as the study of human society in general, obviously is concerned in part with language. In the 1960s, at the borders of sociology and linguistics a brand of investigation called the 'sociology of language' developed, an approach where we find sociologists engaging with language issues and using some tools from linguistics, as in the work of Basil Bernstein and Joshua Fishman. A rather overlooked pioneer in this area is Monsignor Paul Hanly Furfey, who taught what seems to have been the first ever full course on the sociology of language in 1943 (including among its topics dialect geography, and speech and social class), at the Catholic University of America in Washington, D.C. (see Joseph, 2002, pp. 112–13). In the early 1950s, two of Furfey's research students, George N. Putnam and Edna M. O'Hern, carried out a study of a ghetto dialect of Washington, D.C. (Putnam and O'Hern, 1955). This included analysis of prosody (rhythm and intonation) and grammar, and evaluation of recordings of speakers by another 70 listeners, who were asked to rank the speakers' social status on the basis of the recordings (Joseph, 2002, pp. 121–2). Social evaluation of speech and linguistic variables was to be an essential part of Labov's research and of a strand of sociolinguistic work on attitudes to accents and dialects which fed into the growth of **perceptual dialectology** from the 1980s onwards (discussed further in Chapter 9). The wider scope of Labovian sociolinguistics compared with dialectology (that is, its concern with the wider social context for regional speech) owed much to the influence of sociology. A major contribution also came from the methods of data collection and sampling used in sociology. We see this illustrated in the following explanatory account of Labov's 1966 study of NYC English.

6.4   Sociolinguistics and dialect study: the first major work

In the remainder of this chapter we become familiar with William Labov's *The Social Stratification of English in New York City* (1966/2006), looking at its aims, methods, and findings, and highlighting the innovations that changed the course of dialect study. This will prepare us for Chapters 7 and 8, which look at the repercussions of the sociolinguistic upheaval.

In 1966, William Labov showed in detail that the correlation of linguistic data with a range of social variables could elucidate hitherto inadequately explained aspects of regional language variation.

A language such as English varies according to its geography. At the same time, it will vary according to social class – not all speakers from the same locality will speak the same dialect of English uniformly if those speakers vary in social class. The speech of the locality as a whole can vary along a non-standard to standard continuum that correlates largely with social stratification. Similarly, the local speech may vary in regular patterns that become apparent when the linguistic data is matched with information about the age, sex, and ethnicity of speakers. What is more, each individual dialect speaker will tend to vary his or her own speech according to the social situation, in relation to such factors as the perceived informality/formality of the context and the social class of the other interlocutors. We each may pronounce any given word differently not only in comparison to other speakers but also according to whether we are speaking to friends or to strangers, whether we are in a bar or at home or in work or in a classroom, and so on. If the investigator of dialect ignores such social and stylistic correlations, then it is likely that the data will appear to contain what looks like quite random or 'free' variation. But when the sociolinguistic correlations are made, this random variation might assume regular patterning, and its causes are revealed. The variation then appears not random but structured. What we see is 'orderly' or 'structured heterogeneity', to use the terms first developed by Weinreich,

Labov and Herzog (1968) in a paper given at a conference at the University of Texas in 1966. For as long as dialectologists focused on the speech of one class (rural working class) and one age-group (elderly), it was to some extent defensible to neglect these correlations. However, when the focus expanded it was time for the methods, aims, and general approach to evolve in new directions. The notion of structured heterogeneity is central to the sociolinguistic way of doing dialect study, as Weinreich, Labov and Herzog stated in 1966: 'The key to a rational conception of language change – indeed, of language itself – is the possibility of describing orderly differentiation in a language serving a community' (1968, no page number, online version). (In the process some aspects of the older dialectological approach became newly neglected, for a while at least. As noted above, the sociolinguistic approach in its early days was less concerned with vocabulary, with dictionaries and atlases and national-scale projects, and with history.)

6.4.1   NYC 1966: Labov's variables and contextual styles

We have seen how Labov broke with tradition in his New York City department store study. His innovations are played out much more fully in the larger survey. In this he increased the number of phonological variables to five:

1. (r), as before, that is, presence or absence of /r/.
2. (æh), by which he refers to variation in the **height** of the vowel in words like *ask, bad, bag, cash, dance, pass* – one of the ways in which vowel sounds are classified is according to their height, that is, the relative height of the tongue during articulation; the lower variants in these words in NYC are associated with prestige.
3. (oh), that is, variation in the height of the vowel in words like *all, awed, caught, dog, lost, off, talk*; the lower variants are associated with prestige, though less consistently than in (æh) in NYC.
4. (th), that is, articulation of *th-* as in *thing* varying between fricative [θ] and plosive [t], the former being the prestige form, and the latter having less prestige.
5. (dh), that is, articulation of *th-* as in *then* varying between fricative [ð] and plosive [d], the former being the prestige form, the latter having less prestige.

Labov selected these phonological variables because they are high in frequency and are amenable to statistical analysis on a linear scale, and they 'have a certain *immunity from conscious suppression*' (1966/2006, p. 32; italics in original), that is to say, speakers are less conscious of their prestige-value than they would be with grammatical and lexical variables.

Labov also refined his investigation of stylistic variation by setting up four contextual styles, some with subcategories (1966/2006, pp. 58–74), each associated with a different elicitation technique:

A. Casual speech, falling outside the formal interview (such as interruptions, speech with a third person), or in response to questions about childhood rhymes and customs, and to the question 'Have you ever been in a situation where you thought there was a serious danger of your being killed? That you thought to yourself, "This is it"?'
B. Careful speech, occurring as part of the interview, which took 30 to 45 minutes.
C. Reading style, in which the informant read aloud two short specially designed texts, occurring after the question-and-answer interview session.
D. Formal style, occurring when the informant read word lists, the last and most formal of these, D', being a list of minimal pairs – a **minimal pair** consists of two words that may vary only in one element of their pronunciation which serves to differentiate their meaning, such as *sauce* and *source*: in a rhotic accent /r/ differentiates the two, in a non-rhotic accent they are homonyms. Minimal-pair tests provide information about the phonemic oppositions or contrasts between sounds that the phonological systems of dialects are built on.

Labov's fundamental hypothesis remained the same: that NYC speech varied in tandem with social stratification. He had his list of required linguistic items, and he had his elicitation methodology sorted. What he also needed were his informants, and the nature of his survey dictated that his sample should be representative of the whole population of New York City, which in the 1960s was approaching 8 million people. This necessitated a sampling method that had to be of a quite different character from those used by the earlier dialectologists in rural localities.

6.4.2   NYC 1966: Labov's informant sample

The earlier method was **judgement sampling**; Labov's was a form of **random sampling** (a method occasionally also called **probability sampling**). The notion of **representativeness** is key to population sampling: in order for findings to have validity, the data must be obtained from sources that are representative of the population whose speech is under investigation.

Even in a rural village of 500 inhabitants it would be highly ambitious to aim to interview all the inhabitants. The apparatus that the earlier dialectologists developed with progressive rigour was to work out in advance what would be the characteristics of their ideal informant and then in each locality to interview a relatively small number of people who fitted this profile. The basic idea in this **judgement** method is that the informants are representative because they are typical of the group under investigation, the researcher having already decided in advance what constitutes such a representative informant. **Quota sampling** is a version of judgement sampling in which the investigator (using his or her existing knowledge) divides the population into groupings according to factors like class, age, and sex, and then decides how many representatives of each grouping should be sought and interviewed. Quota sampling in rudimentary form was used for the *Linguistic Atlas of New England* (*LANE*; Kurath et al., 1939–43), which sought one informant from each of three groups: elderly working class; middle-aged middle class; and 'cultured'. Informants from the first two groupings were sought in all 213 localities of *LANE*, but from the third group only in the larger cities. An advantage of judgement sampling is its practicability. A basic criticism of it is that judgements about the social composition of a community in relation to the variation of its speech should follow rather than precede a survey.

In an urban locality, whether it is New York City or, say, Norwich, UK (population approximately 160,000 in the late 1960s), it is clearly totally unrealistic to interview the whole population. In addition, a full Labovian survey requires a representative sample of the population as a whole: all classes, age-groups, ethnic groups, and both sexes, in principle sampled without any bias built into the process. This is a different kind of representativeness: each member of the population must have an equal chance of being selected for interview by a sampling method that is truly **random**, along the lines of methods used by sociologists, geographers, and opinion pollsters. And, 'A true random sample is dependent upon a selection process that is independent of human interference' (Linn, 1983, p. 232), with numbers or names being selected from a list by lottery or computer, for example. In practice, a truly random sample in a linguistic survey is extraordinarily difficult to achieve, to such an extent that, in the view of the dialectologist Lawrence M. Davis (1990, p. 5), 'no major linguistic study to date has used one [a random sample] in the strictest sense of the word [random]'. Here, briefly, is what Labov did in 1966 (his fieldwork actually began in July 1963 (Labov, 1966/2006, p. 100)).

He restricted the area under investigation to the Lower East Side of NYC, in the borough of Manhattan. In fact, he restricted it to the eastern part of the Lower East Side. The area chosen had a population of 107,000 in 1960 (Labov, 1966/2006, p. 105). Labov argued (pp. 97–8) that it was sufficiently representative of NYC as a whole in terms of its constituent social classes and ethnic groups. In selecting his informants, Labov was able to piggyback on a comprehensive sociological survey that had been carried out recently (1961) in this area of the Lower East Side. This was a survey designed by the New York School of Social Work, Columbia University, as part of the Mobilization for Youth Program (MFY) (see MFY, 1962). The MFY survey took four months to map its survey area, giving each dwelling a serial number; the resulting list of 33,932 units was divided into 250 equal intervals, from each of which five households were selected randomly; 40 interviewers were trained, and from each household one adult over 20 was randomly selected for interview, with determined efforts made to interview even the most reluctant interviewee (Labov, 1966/2006, pp. 99–102), for random samples become less random each time the survey fails to interview a randomly selected informant. In summary, the MFY survey 'had been carried out with every precaution against bias and inaccuracy which is available to survey methodology' (p. 100), and 'it was apparent that I [Labov] could not hope to approach the precision of the MFY sampling technique by my own efforts' (p. 99).

The MFY survey ultimately had 988 informants, still far too many for Labov's mostly one-man band to handle (he had one co-fieldworker, Michael Kae). He refined the list further by including only native English speakers, by excluding informants who had subsequently moved, and by adjusting his coverage of some ethnic groups (pp. 107–17). This left him with 195 individuals from the MFY survey who were to be interviewed between July and September 1963 for Labov's American Linguistic Survey (ALS), as he called it. Of these, 122 were successfully interviewed; 68 of their children also participated; and some linguistic information was eventually obtained from a further 33 'non-respondents'. The main body of informants were the 122 adults in the ALS. This number was further reduced for the central analysis by eliminating those English speakers in the group who had come to the United States after the age of five, and also any informants who had come to NYC after the age of eight (p. 119). Three new, non-MFY informants were added to the small upper middle class group, the highest of the socio-economic classes in the study (p. 119). This gave a final figure of 81 ALS informants (p. 120).

At this point one comes to the trickiest question: is data elicited from 81 speakers representative of a speech community of 8 million? A linguistic geographer of the philological bent, smarting from criticism that his or her own judgement-sampling methods led to unrepresentative results, might respond to this question with a negative. They might add that Labov was unusually lucky to have his sample largely arranged in advance, and that even this rigorous 'random' sample includes of necessity some stages that are judgement in type. Labov's view, as expressed 40 years later, is that 'from 60 to 100 speakers are needed to register social stratification by age, gender, and social class of a given city' (1966/2006, pp. 400–1). Samples under 60 'often fail to show statistical significance' (p. 401). (Labov does call his method in 1966 random sampling, but he also calls it, more precisely, *stratified random sampling*, a term which will be explained shortly.)

It is commonly accepted in statistics that random sampling is required if one is to make statistical claims about a sampled population. (The type of representativeness present in judgement samples is not conducive to statistical assertions about whole populations, because it is based on investigator-choice, which would somehow have to be factored into the statistical analysis. This is not to say that judgements are absent in random sampling, as we have already seen.) Thus we find L. M. Davis arguing (1983, pp. 69–84) that random sampling requires statistical rigour and an elementary knowledge of statistics, which by no means all dialect researchers have possessed. Such knowledge, which Davis helpfully provides an outline of, enables us, for example, to calculate the **mean** (arithmetic average) and **standard deviation** of a **frequency distribution** (the average deviation of the elements in a list of scores from the mean), and once we can do this it sets us on the path to calculating whether differences exhibited between two or more sets of scores are statistically significant. Putting this very simply (so that even I can begin to grasp it), frequency scores from one group in our sample may produce a mean of 50 per cent, while the frequency scores from another group give us a mean of 75 per cent. On the face of it, this looks like a significant difference in usage between the two groups. But it may be that the sample comprising one group is smaller than the sample comprising the other. A data set gathered from a small sample is more open to being affected statistically by exceptionally high or low scores from (say) just one or two members of the sample, which may skew the results and render the mean, well, meaningless. Calculating the standard deviation of the scores in each group/sample and then comparing the standard deviations highlights discrepancies between the groups/samples, and reveals the statistical validity of the comparison. One formulaic calculation for evaluating the reliability of the difference between the means of samples when the samples are small is called a *t-test* (see Davis, 1982, pp. 84–5; Davis, 1983, pp. 75–6; and Davis, 1990, pp. 14–16, 30–9). Scepticism about the soundness of the statistics in the new approach was also voiced at the time, as we see from the comments of Joan Baratz at the 1969 Round Table Meeting on Linguistics and Language Studies at Georgetown University, who worried about sociolinguists borrowing 'a sophisticated terminology of social stratification' (in Shuy, 1969, p. 186) from other disciplines while having 'neglected to take the necessary procedures for analyzing the numerical data which result from such classifications' (p. 187).

Davis (1983, pp. 94–101) subjects some of Labov's 1966 findings to statistical tests and is unhappy that Labov does not in certain of his graphs provide the actual data scores from which he calculates the various percentages, thus preventing his reader from working out standard deviation. (The information needed to work out standard deviation here is: the number of informants in the group/sample; the token/frequency score obtained from each informant; and the mean for the sample. The percentages derived from the scores are insufficient in themselves.) Take, for example, the graph in Figure 6.2 (from Labov, 1966/2006, p. 152), which we will examine further in a moment for the reason that it shows an interesting and very suggestive crossover pattern. Although Labov provides in another section (p. 121) numbers of informants in each socio-economic class (SECs are numbered 0 to 9 in the graph; see also Labov's table at his p. 139) and also some scores (p. 140) for phonological variants by class, the numbers of informants are small. Because Labov does not provide all (r) scores for each individual informant, then at best, argues Davis (1983, p. 100), the graph shows only 'certain trends'. He says (p. 100), 'if a few informants exhibited a large number of a certain variable, it would look as though the whole class were acting that way'. Davis does not believe that Labov's general conclusions are invalid, 'but it would be helpful to know just how to interpret some of the findings which are quantitatively expressed' (p. 100). In his commentary 40 years on, Labov, perhaps mindful of such criticisms, points out that this crossover pattern, recognized first in 1966, has subsequently appeared many times in studies (Labov, 1966/2006, pp. 151–2). Hence the successful repetition of results is used to defend non-use of formal statistics to test the quantitative process. (A lesson here for those of us less than well equipped to negotiate the labyrinths of statistics when presenting our quantitative findings is to be transparent, that is, present the raw data as well. Not that I imply that William Labov was thusly less than well equipped.)

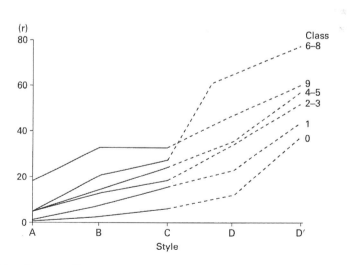

Figure 6.2   Class stratification of (r): six class groups (from Labov, 1966; 2nd edn of 2006, p. 152).

Davis admits that 'there is no clear prescription for sample size' (1983, p. 70), and Labov makes the telling point (1966/2006, p. 401), 'Size is almost secondary to design.' A well-designed and well-executed sampling method permits the linguistic researcher to interview fewer informants than is usual in the social sciences. Linguists, after all, do not just collect simple items of information about their sample; they also analyse in detail the communication medium (speech) of their informants, and this is traditionally a very time-consuming business. This is another reason for the focus in early sociolinguistics on far fewer variables than in the older dialectology – the expansion of social and stylistic analysis, and the requirements of a quantitative approach to the speech of urban populations entailed a greater measure of practicability elsewhere in survey design. Davis (1990, p. 6) comments on the tensions in this way, 'Statisticians unfamiliar with real-life problems ... would sneeringly look down their noses at such [judgement-determined 'random'] samples, label them *convenience samples*, and point out that we simply cannot use any statistical tests on such samples.' Let us remember also that quantitative analysis is fundamental in the philosophy of surveys such as Labov's. These surveys are built on the belief that speakers use different variants of the same variable at different times, in patterned ways, and description of phonological variation, therefore, depends on the collection of many tokens of the variable (unlike in the earlier dialectological surveys).

The point remains that an apparently obvious way to improve the representativeness of the random sample is to increase its size, but as Michael Linn says (1983, p. 233) in his discussion of informant selection, this must be within viable limits. (It is also true that a badly designed survey with a large sample is still a badly designed survey.) A relevant case here, with regard to viability, is the radical, carefully designed, but arguably over-ambitious sociolinguistic Tyneside Linguistic Survey (TLS) formulated in the mid-to-late 1960s at the University of Newcastle-upon-Tyne, UK. Here the plan was to gather exhaustive data relating to a large set of phonological, lexical, and grammatical features from over 400 informants, with social and linguistic groupings to be determined progressively as the survey proceeded, but in 1985 Val Jones reported that 'Limitations of funding and person-power ... meant that the original goals have only been partially fulfilled, and that for no more than a small fraction of the original sample' (Jones, 1985, p. 164). Although the TLS produced numerous publications, the website of the Newcastle Electronic Corpus of Tyneside English, which incorporated and preserved the surviving TLS data, gave an impression of a survey that eventually faltered (http://research.ncl.ac.uk/necte/basecorpora.htm, accessed 7 April 2015), an impression confirmed by one of the Survey's leaders, John Pellowe (1991, p. x), who blames 'errors in administration and management' for the project's failure. Linn advocates **stratified sampling** and **replicated**

subsampling (or **replicated sampling**) as refinements of random sampling which increase statistical reliability. These are ways of dividing up the population into smaller groupings and then applying random procedures to these. Stratified sampling in particular also involves a judgement procedure, in which the population is divided into strata in advance according to criteria such as social class, age, ethnic group, and sex. Labov's method in NYC was stratified random sampling. The TLS procedure (according to Pellowe et al., 1972, and Val Jones, 1978) was a sophisticated three-stage design, involving an intricate mix of judgement, random, and stratified sampling intended to ensure reliability. The second stage was a random sample which acted as a check on the first-stage sample which combined judgement and random procedures. Phase three was a stratified sample. One could debate whether the meticulousness that characterized the planning and execution of the TLS also contributed to its problems. The TLS did not do things the easy way. It was innovative in its philosophy and methodology, aiming to produce a comprehensive understanding of Tyneside English, using not only an all-embracing sampling process but also a pioneering computer-based analysis.

Interviewing by telephone and via the Internet can reduce the financial and time costs of data collection, and automatization and digitization of data collection and analysis make possible larger samples, but the design of the sampling procedure remains of paramount importance.

6.4.2.1   Short interlude: a top ten of informant-to-population ratios

Many surveys are described in the present book. In light of the foregoing discussion, and bearing fully in mind that survey design is paramount, it nevertheless occurred to me that it might be interesting to calculate one simple statistic for comparison for a number of surveys: the ratio of number of informants interviewed to total population of the area surveyed. This at least might tell us something about the range of sample sizes and will illuminate the general discussion about sampling, which continues in Chapters 7 and 8. In the event, the calculation was not always that simple to make, and my workings out are detailed below the list. Here then are ten surveys selected for illustrative purposes by me in order to compare the ratio of informants interviewed to total population of area surveyed. Also included is a very brief description of the informant sampling procedure used in each survey. The chapter references are to the present book. The final ratios are approximate. The order runs from lowest to highest ratio.

1. Aaron J. Dinkin's 2013 geolinguistic survey of the Northern Cities Shift in eastern New York State (see Chapter 10.5), using an 'availability' sample (like Labov's department store study) followed by a stratified random sample: 1 informant to every 2330 speakers in the total population.

2. Peter Trudgill's 1968 Labovian survey (published in 1974) of the social differentiation of English in Norwich (see Chapter 7.2.3.1 and Chapter 9.3), using a stratified random sample or 'quasi-random sample' as he calls it (1974a, p. 21): 1 informant to every 2670 speakers in the total population.

3. Kerswill et al.'s 2008 geolinguistic survey of diphthong shift in the London boroughs of Hackney and Havering (Chapter 10.5), using what seems to be a judgement sample: 1 to 3850. (If the survey is treated as looking at London as a whole, this becomes 1 to 65,765.)

4. Malcolm Petyt's 1971 Labovian survey (published in 1985) of industrial West Yorkshire (Chapter 7.2.3.1 and Chapter 8.2), using a mainly random sample with some stratifying adjustments: 1 to 5600.

5. Orton et al.'s Survey of English Dialects (Chapter 2.2-3 and Chapter 5.3), fieldwork done mainly in the 1950s, judgement sample: 1 to 8500.

6. Kurath et al.'s *Linguistic Atlas of New England* (1939–43; see Chapter 5.3), judgement/quota sample: 1 to 19,630.

7. Alexander J. Ellis's 1889 survey of English dialectal pronunciation (Chapter 5.2) – I am slightly shifting the goalposts here, as Ellis mostly used intermediaries rather than interviewing informants directly: 1 helper to every 30,000 speakers.

8. Barbara and Ronald Horvath's 2001 geolinguistic study of urban centres in Australia and New Zealand (Chapter 10.4), an 'availability' sample: 1 to 37,470.

9. Gilliéron and Edmont's *Atlas linguistique de la France* (1902–10; see Chapter 3.5), judgement sample: 1 to 39,000. (This is for the rural population of France in 1891. For the population as a whole, it would be 1 to 54,300.)

10 Labov's 1966 survey of NYC, using a stratified random sample of a repre-sentative district: 1 to 99,000 speakers. (This using the details given in the present chapter, and for the total population of NYC in the mid 1960s. For the eastern part of the Lower East Side only the ratio would be 1 to 1320, putting it at the top of this list.)

(Information on my workings out is as follows. *1*. Dinkin (2013, p. 9) gives his number of interviews as 98, and the 2010 census total population of the communities in his data set as 228,063. *2*. Trudgill's informant sample was 60, and the approximate population of Norwich in the mid 1960s was 160,000. *3*. Total number of speakers sampled by Kerswill et al. (2008) was 111, and the Greater London Authority's DataStore web-pages give combined populations of Hackney and Havering in 2001 as 427,072. The population of London in 2001 was 7.3 million. See http://data.london.gov.uk/dataset/census-2001-key-statistics-01-population. *4*. Petyt's informants numbered 106. The total population of Bradford, Halifax, and Huddersfield in 1971 was

594,500, according to the populstat website. See http://www.populstat.info/.
5. Total number of informants in the SED was 989 (my thanks to Clive Upton
for this number). According to the Office for National Statistics web-pages, the
population of England in 1950 was just over 40 million (Jefferies, 2005, p. 3).
But Brown (2009) tells us that the rural population of the United Kingdom as
a percentage of the total population was 21 per cent in 1950. This would give
an approximate rural population of England in 1950 as 8.4 million. 6. The
total number of informants for *LANE* was 416. The total population of New
England in 1930 was 8,166,341 (this from the United States Census Bureau
web-pages: https://www.census.gov/population/censusdata/urpop0090.txt).
7. Ellis had 900 helpers. According to populstat, the population of England in
1874 was 27,111,500. 8. The Horvaths' informants numbered 312. The populstat website gives the combined total population of the nine centres surveyed
as 11,689,700. 9. *ALF* informants numbered 700, and the rural population of
France in 1891 was 27,439,000 (Grigg, 1980, p. 203). 10. Enough said above.)

6.4.3   NYC 1966: studying linguistic change

We return now to Figure 6.2, in order to consider another of the main themes
of Labov's work, and an interest that connects him with the philological
founders of dialectology: the explanation of linguistic change.

In addition to analysing the variables in relation to social class (using a scale
set up by MFY, based on occupation, education, and income), in 1966 Labov
looked at the distribution of the variables in **apparent time** (1966/2006, pp.
199– 240), that is, across successive age levels. This is the method he uses in
order to identify **linguistic change in progress**. He introduces two concepts:
linguistic **change from above**, by which he means change over time resulting
from 'overt social pressures' (p. 206) to adopt a prestige feature or to drop a
stigmatized feature, that is, the change occurs 'above' the level of conscious
awareness of speakers; and linguistic **change from below**, that is, change over
time 'accomplished without public attention' (p. 207) until a late stage – it
occurs 'below' the level of conscious awareness of speakers, and the new feature
being adopted sometimes has **covert** rather than **overt prestige**. The term
covert prestige refers to features which are attractive to speakers not because
of their openly acknowledged, public associations (as is the case with standard
features) but because of their local, communal, in-group associations, such as
non-standard features which connote solidarity or friendliness or informality.
According to the apparent-time method, the distribution of a given feature
across the age levels of a population sample will be different according to
whether that feature is involved in a change in progress or whether the situation is static. For example, the crossover pattern in Figure 6.2, where the
use of the prestige /r/ phoneme by the lower middle class (6–8) jumps to

exceed the upper middle class (9) in the most formal styles is **hypercorrection** (an 'over-compensation' by the lower status group), and suggests a change from above in progress. When Labov analyses the scores for the (r) variable by age (pp. 217–26) as well as by class and style, the pattern that emerges matches his concept of change from above in progress: a prestige feature associated with the highest-ranking social group is being adopted by lower-ranking groups. The apparent-time distributions suggest not only that middle-aged members of the middle-ranking group are adopting /r/, but also that the prestige of /r/ is affecting the behaviour of other groups. In the most formal styles, the younger and the older speakers from classes 0–8 show a trend of increased /r/-use compared with the casual styles, though the scores for the elderly group are lower than for the younger and middle-aged speakers. The scores of the middle-aged speakers in these formal styles are more in accord with the younger speakers of class 9 than with the much lower scores of the older speakers of class 9. Labov says (p. 219): 'In this age level [young speakers], the upper middle class [class 9] does seem to represent the maximum use of (r-1) [r-presence] at which all other groups are aiming in formal styles.'

In a case of change from below, on the other hand, we see a gradual spread of change from one social group to others, expressed as a shift in behaviour of successive generations, as in the adoption of slang terms or, as Labov tentatively proposes (1966/2006, pp. 226–33), in the movement towards higher vowels in NYC (with some suggestive variation across ethnic groups) in (æh) and (oh). For Labov, change from below 'is a form of self-identification, of group membership, which establishes the speaker as an authentic representative of a sub-group within the community' (p. 231). Such change, provoked by the covert prestige of a feature, can induce a counter reaction from above linked to the overt prestige of another variant.

One example of a static situation, where there is no evidence of a change in progress in the social significance of a variable, would be indicated by a pattern in which a socially stigmatized variant is not used at all by the higher social groups, but is used frequently by the lower social groups, with the middle-ranking groups using it less as they grow older and come into contact with prestige forms (as indicated by the apparent-time age-group analysis). In this scenario, this pattern for this variable would be duplicated without change as time goes by. It would be a static pattern (see Labov, 1966/2006, p. 204).

There is another evident way to investigate linguistic change, and that is to study it **diachronically** or in **real time**, by revisiting the same locality at different points in time and re-sampling the population (a **trend survey**), or even by re-interviewing the same informants over a period of years (a **panel survey**). As the data resources accumulated by systematic dialect study grow and grow, real-time surveys become increasingly feasible. (One example, discussed in Chapter 7, section 2.3.1, is Trudgill (1988).) That said, the apparent-time method was another enabling and productive innovation by Labov.

6.4.3.1   NYC 1966: prestige and perceptions

As you will have noticed, an important concept in Labov's investigation of linguistic change is **prestige**. A linguistic feature only possesses prestige when the members of a speech community perceive the feature to have it. There is nothing intrinsic in the prestige of linguistic variants. It depends entirely on social, communal perceptions and associations. All of this applies also to stigmatized features. It follows, therefore, that the Labovian line of inquiry into linguistic change entails the study of perceptions of linguistic variation, and of speakers' evaluations of and attitudes towards the speech of others and themselves. The evolution of folk beliefs about different varieties of English is a considerable topic. In Chapter 1 we touched on the role that cultural attitudes played in the very gradual development of the dichotomy between dialectal English and Standard English, and in Chapter 9 I give an account of the type of study known as **perceptual dialectology**, a form of linguistic geography in which non-specialists' perceptions of regional dialects are measured and mapped. In fact, we could say that perceptual dialectology is founded in the view that everyone is an expert on dialects – in other words, societal beliefs can tell us much about the nature of language variation. What Labov wanted to do in 1966 was to achieve a quantitative measurement of his informants' opinions about NYC English and about their own performance of it. The former he termed **subjective evaluation**, and the latter **self-evaluation**. In order to collect data on subjective evaluation, he devised a **subjective reaction test** (**SR test**; see Labov, 1966/2006, pp. 266–72, 419), and for self-evaluation a **self-evaluation test** (**SV test**; pp. 300–2, 419), a type more usually now called a **self-report test**. He thought that the tests would reveal that New Yorkers have an awareness of the relative social prestige of different variants, and that this would corroborate his findings about New Yorkers' usages (the **production data**, as opposed to the **perception data**). Believing direct questioning would reveal little specific, detailed information about his five variables (listed above), he designed his tests to uncover evaluative behaviour which was 'more systematic, more completely internalized than any reply we might elicit by the overt discussion of speech' (p. 266).

In the SR test, he used recordings of NYC speakers made during his fieldwork. He chose recordings from five informants. He excerpted from these recordings the same sentences from the same passage read by each speaker. Each variable was concentrated in a different sentence, with one sentence (the *zero sentence*) containing none of the variables under study, and which functioned as a kind of control element in the test. So he ended up with the same selection of sentences performed by each speaker, and each sentence in

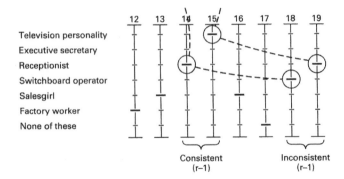

Figure 6.3   Structure of subjective evaluation form for (r) in New York City (part of Figure 11.4 from Labov, 1966/2006, p. 284).

each speaker's set elicited performance of a different variable (except for the zero sentence). The speakers were selected for their differing treatments of the variables. The speakers' sentences were then played on a tape in mixed order to most of his NYC informants, who were asked to rate each sentence as if they were a personnel manager judging the speaker's suitability for a range of different jobs, from factory worker to television personality. These ratings were marked by the listeners or **respondents** on a tabular grid, which gave Labov his required index scores. Figure 6.3 is a selection from one of these tables.

In Figure 6.3, the vertical scale of jobs is on the left. The numbers along the top represent different sentences in the compilation tape played to respondents, and each circled bar is a verdict given by a respondent. Sentences 14 and 18 were performed by the same speaker, and 15 and 19 were by a second speaker. In sentences 14 and 15, the two speakers were using /r/ more consistently than in sentences 18 and 19. We can see in this one example that the respondent rates consistent use of /r/ more highly in terms of job type than inconsistent use of /r/ (even though the same speakers were involved), and this response is in keeping with Labov's hypothesis that /r/-presence is perceived as a prestigious variant of the (r) variable in NYC.

In the SV test, Labov's respondents listened to a small number of keywords containing his variables being pronounced using a range of variants. The respondents were asked to circle on a form which variant (or variants) they thought that they habitually used themselves. These perception scores were then compared with the production scores of the same informants, the comparison also being broken down according to criteria such as class, sex, ethnic group, age, and (production) style of speech. Overall, NYC speakers over-reported their use of the prestigious variants. For example, in his analysis of self-evaluation for (r) (pp. 302–9), Labov says, 'It appears that there is little relation between the amount of (r) which New Yorkers use, and their impressions of their own speech' (p. 304). New Yorkers claim that they use post-vocalic /r/ more than they actually do. What this shows, argues Labov, is the NYC speakers' awareness of /r/-presence as a prestige norm. In the more detailed analysis of (r), the following is revealed: among the non-users of /r/, only the very oldest respondents/informants show 'immunity' (p. 308) to the influence of /r/ in perception data (no over-reporting); the middle-aged speakers over-report /r/-use, and show the most tendency to acquire /r/ in their careful speech; the younger speakers show 'strong (r)-positive tendencies in the SV test' (p. 307) in terms of over-reporting; over-reporting occurs in all socio-economic classes, but is highest in SECs 0–2 and 6–8.

In summary, and sticking with the (r) variable as our example, we see the lower middle class hypercorrecting in the most formal styles, especially the middle-aged in this class, and the perception tests indicating a communal awareness that /r/-use is felt to be a correct form (which is associated with the usages of the youngest speakers of the highest social class), plus only the oldest speakers showing a degree of resistance to the new norm. This then is consistent evidence of a change from above in progress and of the community moving towards use of a new norm feature. Labov suggests (p. 296) two possible triggers for the shift from earlier r-lessness to new prestige r-presence: the decline after World War II in the global prestige of British English RP (a non-rhotic accent), and the association of r-lessness with low-prestige African-American Vernacular English.

The fact that New Yorkers tend to hear themselves in accordance with their perceived norms rather than as they actually sound, allied with the hypercorrection of the lower middle class in perception and production tests, indicates to Labov 'a profound linguistic insecurity' (p. 318) at work in NYC. He links linguistic insecurity in general with the 'doctrine of correctness' (p. 318) that emerged with regard to British English in the seventeenth and eighteenth centuries, that is, the societal belief that certain linguistic variants were correct while others were faulty or deviant. We charted this process in Chapter 1 of the present book, for it is intimately bound up with the division of English into standard and non-standard dialectal varieties, and also with the advent of dictionaries and manuals of grammar. But this doctrine also motivates linguistic change in communities, because acquisition of the overtly prestigious norms becomes an integral part of upward social mobility. In 1966, Labov added another task to his battery of tests: a **linguistic insecurity test** (1966/2006, pp. 319, 421), where speakers were asked to choose which of two variant pronunciations was correct, and then to check whether that was their own habitual pronunciation. The test aimed to measure the extent to which respondents/informants considered their own pronunciation incorrect. Tellingly, when one considers later conclusions from Labov's decades-long inquiry into linguistic change, he found that NY women scored 50 per cent higher than men on linguistic insecurity (pp. 320–1). This linguistic insecurity or 'special concern of women for conformation to prestige norms', says Labov (1966/2006, p. 322), 'takes on a more positive aspect when viewed as a concomitant of social mobility'. It stimulates and drives the spread of linguistic change. For more on this, and Labov's subsequent work, read on to Chapters 7, 9, and 10.

6.5   Conclusion

In the final pages of the final chapter of his 1966 study, Labov talks of the 'targets' that inspire linguistic change. By this he means the norms that speakers aim at, norms which can possess either overt or covert prestige. On the evidence that he has presented, Labov argues (1966/2006, p. 378) that 'linguistic behavior is highly normative, or goal directed'. Furthermore, 'In aiming at such targets, it is only natural that the speaker will go beyond them' (p. 378). The pressure to conform in one way or another (to either overt or covert norms) can mean that pressures in favour of ongoing change 'can be exerted on individual words; or upon entire phonemes; or most likely, series or orders of phonemes', therefore perhaps causing knock-on effects in the community's sound system as a whole. Reading these conclusions, one is jolted into thinking that they seem to be phrased in such a way as to suggest a resolution of an old and familiar issue: the neogrammarian controversy.

Methodologically, Labov's early work changed dialect study greatly. But in his aims and interests there is a continuity with the philologists who invented dialectology. Part of his achievement was to quantify and bring into focus known concerns. His NYC study has proved extraordinarily influential, though not everyone has been convinced by its sampling and statistics, and some old-school linguistic geographers and new-school geolinguists (see Chapter 10) have criticized Labovian variationist sociolinguists for neglecting in their urban studies the interplay of speakers with geographical space. The research in the variationist strand that has followed Labov has supported his early findings. Like that of the preceding mighty figures of dialect study, Labov's body of work is a gigantic contribution to the field. In addition to the present chapter, it features strongly in those that follow.

6.6   Brief commentary on terms

Just to re-emphasize some points from the chapter above. William Labov is a major, perhaps *the* major pioneer of sociolinguistics, but his work on dialects/

varieties and linguistic change is just one (rather important) strand of socio-linguistics in general. Throughout most of its history, scholars have struggled somewhat to agree on a universally acceptable name for this strand. I mentioned a few in section 6.3 above. In the Introduction to the first British Labovian survey, Peter Trudgill (1974a, pp. 1–3) settled on *sociological urban dialectology* as the name for this kind of work. Some time later, Clive Upton (2000, pp. 66–8) advocated *social dialectology* for the Labovian work, contrasting it with *sociolinguistic dialectology*, which he uses for the 'interface' (p. 68) between sociolinguistics generally and dialectology. However, later still, David Britain (2010b, p. 74) called the Labovian strand *sociolinguistic dialectology*. And so on. Sometimes even the shorthand labels *modern dialectology* or *urban dialectology* have been used, contrasting with the *traditional dialectology* of the early *linguistic geographers* (or the *linguistic geography* of the *traditional dialectologists*). One textbook alone cannot solve this issue. However, in this volume, especially from this point on, I have tended to have in mind the (I hope) unambiguous title *Labovian variationist sociolinguistics* as the full descriptor for this strand.

Resources and further reading

Consulting Labov's groundbreaking 1966 study of NYC English was made much easier in 2006 when Cambridge University Press published its edition. My advice is either buy it, borrow it, or at least read the parts that are available via Google Books. There are many introductory books on sociolinguistics, and all of them refer to the work of Labov. Two widely ranging and concisely packaged general guides are *Introducing Sociolinguistics* (2009, 2nd edn), written by Rajend Mesthrie, Joan Swann, Ana Deumert and William L. Leap, and *An Introduction to Sociolinguistics* (2015, 7th edn), by Ronald Wardhaugh and Janet M. Fuller. For a book-length and accessible account of Labov's contribution to language study, see *Labov: A Guide for the Perplexed* (2013) by Matthew J. Gordon. Konrad Koerner's 'Toward a History of Modern Sociolinguistics' (1991) is a brief but clear and effective exposition of the antecedents that led to sociolinguistics. Two very good collections of classic pieces are *Sociolinguistics: The Essential Readings* (2003a), edited by Christine Bratt Paulston and G. Richard Tucker, and *The New Sociolinguistics Reader* (2009), edited by Nikolas Coupland and Adam Jaworski. There is only a small amount of duplication in the volumes' selections; each volume offers an excellent choice of articles; and taken together they provide extensive coverage. It is also worth one's while to take a look at the early collection edited by William Bright of *Proceedings of the UCLA Sociolinguistics Conference, 1964* (published in 1966), which includes an essay by Labov that introduces the notion of *covert prestige* as well as conveying his emerging thinking on *hypercorrection, change from above* and *below*, and the *apparent-time method*. Seek out, too, Labov's highly influential collaboration with Uriel Weinreich and Marvin Herzog, 'Empirical Foundations for a Theory of Language Change' (1968), which can be accessed in the online edition of the volume it first appeared in, at: https://liberalarts.utexas.edu/lrc/resources/books/directions/5-weinreich.php. For unusually comprehensible elucidation of statistics in dialect study, see the 1982 and 1986 articles by Lawrence M. Davis, the third chapter of his *English Dialectology: An Introduction* (1983, pp. 69–84), and especially his short book *Statistics in Dialectology* (1990). An interesting sequel to Labov's department store survey was published in 2012 in the *Journal of English Linguistics*. This was 'The Social Stratification of /r/ in New York City: Labov's Department Store Study Revisited', by Patrick-André Mather, who in 2009 replicated the methods of the Labov original and found a continued increase in rhoticity, plus evidence of greater integration of African American speakers into the shift towards *r*-fullness. Finally for this section, I recommend Graham Shorrocks's article 'Further Thoughts on the Labovian Interview' (1985) as an astute critique that highlighted weaknesses and strengths in both the Labovian approach and that of prior dialectology, as well as recognizing the need for further developments – we see many such developments in the remaining chapters of the present book.

7 After sociolinguistics: Variationist dialect study

This chapter includes the following:

- Overview of the Detroit Dialect Study, 1966–8.
- Introduction to work on African-American Vernacular English (AAVE).
- Guide to *variable-rule analysis*.
- Summary of Peter Trudgill's research into Norwich English, 1968–88.
- Explanation of *principal components analysis* and *social network theory*.

7.1 Introduction

We could read a fair bit into the simple statement: 'Sociolinguistics came after dialectology'. We can understand this to be a straightforward description of chronology. Sociolinguistics came about later in time than dialectology; it followed dialectology, in which case we can understand dialectology to be the most pioneering form of systematic dialect study. But because the sociolinguistic approach came after dialectology, because it is more recent, we could consider it to be an improvement on dialectology, a mark of progress in dialect study. We could also understand the statement 'sociolinguistics came after dialectology' as saying that the former aggressively hunted down the latter, perhaps with a view to eliminating it. Well, all of these readings inform this chapter and the next, which are also about what happened 'after sociolinguistics'. First, in this chapter, I look at the work that followed William Labov's survey of New York City English in 1966, and then, in Chapter 8, I narrate the story of the conflict between dialectologists and variationist sociolinguists that occurred in the second half of the twentieth century, a story which provides another perspective on what happened 'after sociolinguistics'.

Chapters 9 and 10 continue down this path by describing two major 'post-sociolinguistic' trends, *perceptual dialectology* (Chapter 9) and *geolinguistics* (Chapter 10). (You will have noticed immediately the interesting revival of the term *dialectology* in the first trend, made all the more interesting when we consider that the term *geolinguistics* was in the 1980s proposed as a new name for dialect study in its post-sociolinguistics form.)

7.2   The research that followed Labov's New York City study

In Chapter 6, I described Labov's 1966 study of NYC English as the most seminal work of sociolinguistics. Labov's early work helped found sociolinguistics in general. More particularly, it created a productive strand of research within sociolinguistics, which we can call *Labovian variationist sociolinguistics*. After 1966, many researchers followed Labov's lead, using and adapting his methods, interests, and aims in their own work. When reviewing this body of work in 2006, Labov himself characterized it as investigating language change and the structure of language by the study of linguistic variables in spontaneous speech, using a representative sample of speakers from the speech community to provide the data (Labov, 1966/2006, p. 380). In his overview of this strand, the sociolinguist Robert Bayley (2013, p. 85) says that its central ideas are that 'an understanding of language requires an understanding of variable as well as categorical [universal, invariable] processes and that variation seen at all levels of language is not random'. Chapters 9 and 10 of the present book look more widely at kinds of dialect study that developed out of the variationist sociolinguistic approach, and in this chapter I give an overview of the surveys inspired by the *Social Stratification of English in New York City* (*SSENYC*), dwelling for a while on one or two that took place at key moments or that represent particularly noteworthy developments, including developments in the theory of the linguistic variable.

7.2.1   The Detroit Dialect Study (DDS), 1966–68

The first of these surveys, which was almost contemporary with *SSENYC*, was the Detroit Dialect Study (DDS), for which Labov was a consultant. Fieldwork for this survey was carried out from Michigan State University in the summer of 1966 by a team of 12 linguists under the direction of Roger W. Shuy (detailed in Shuy et al., 1968b), and its *Final Report* was released in April 1968 (Shuy et al., 1968a; available at http://eric.ed.gov/?id=ED022187). Funding from the US Office of Education enabled a comparatively large team to be put together and a large number of fieldwork interviews to be carried out. Training of the fieldworkers began as early as 1964 (Wolfram and Schilling-Estes, 2008, p. 14). The influence of *SSENYC* is evident in the design and methods of the DDS. A stratified random sample of 702 informants from three age-groups was assembled. (The population of Detroit in 1960 was nearly 1.7 million, giving an informant-to-total-population ratio of 1 to approximately 2420.) The 'Base Sample' was put together via 20 elementary schools in ten areas within the city limits of Detroit: names were selected randomly from each school and families were then approached with interview requests. The three age-groups were schoolchildren, their parents (one parent from each family), and sometimes a grandparent (occasionally also a great grandparent) from the selected family. An 'Ethnic Sample' was also added, from a further 11 schools. This was 'a judgement sample based on information about sociologically interesting areas of Detroit that were not included in the Base Sample' (Shuy et al., 1968b, p. 9), such as the west Detroit Polish area and some African American neighbourhoods, with informant families once again approached through schools located at the centres of the areas in question. Although the total number of informants was over seven times that in the final *SSENYC* sample, the DDS sample was not as rigorously tailored towards selecting lifelong and native residents as Labov's NYC pool had been. The fieldwork interviews were taped using high-end reel-to-reel Uher recorders. Each interview using the DDS questionnaire took about an hour to complete. The questionnaire consisted of four relatively informal discursive sections with an emphasis also on elicitation of lexis, followed by a 'Short Response' section with an emphasis on one-word answers, and a reading passage and word lists. Like Labov's NYC study, the aim was to elicit a range of speech styles, though these were not so precisely defined. After the interviews, the fieldworkers transcribed phonetically the Short Response data, and then the transcriptions were coded by two research assistants into alpha-numeric symbols which could be retrieved by a computer program in such a way as to enable statistical analysis of phonology and lexis. The discursive sections from a selection of interviews were also typed up in everyday orthography. As well as grouping the informants according to age, ethnicity, and sex, social stratification was done using American census data and taking into account three scales: type of residence (measured according to factors like number of rooms, whether the residence was 'sound and had all plumbing facilities' (Shuy et al., 1968b, p. 13)), level of education, and type of occupation.

   Although a prolific researcher in dialect studies and sociolinguistics, Roger Shuy's interests in later years moved more towards forensic linguistics, and the data collected by the DDS was not mined as much as was originally intended. In reality, the project as such seems to have been wound up by the end of the 1960s. On his retirement from teaching, the entire DDS collection of audio recordings was donated by Shuy to the Georgetown University Lauinger

Library archives, where the tapes are now stored in the Special Collections Department. However, two significant outputs followed close on completion of DDS fieldwork: the *Final Report* (1968), and Walt Wolfram's 1969 book on Detroit African-American speech.

The *Final Report* was made to the sponsoring agency. Following so soon upon completion of the fieldwork, the tone and content of the Report is preliminary and tentative, but one also gets the sense from our present perspective that it was opening some pathways for future research. It contains several of what it calls 'pilot studies' which correlate performance of variables with social categories, but these pilots are done with a much-reduced informant sample: no more than 36 interviews per study. As well as a small number of phonological variables (presence/absence of nasalization of vowels in the environment of a following nasal consonant, realization of the nasal consonant in -*ing* as either [n] or [ŋ] (as in Fischer, 1958)), a few grammatical variables are considered. For example, by means of the graphs that are one of the presentational hallmarks of Labovian surveys, scores for the use of **multiple negation** are matched with social status, age, sex, and ethnicity (Shuy et al., 1968a, Part III: pp. 7–23). In Standard English the usual convention is that in a negative sentence the negative element occurs only once. Thus *He can't write anything* and *He can write nothing* are both acceptable negative sentences in Standard English, but **He can't write nothing* is not. In the last example there is a double negative, and the negative sense of the sentence is cancelled. It is considered ungrammatical (in Standard English). Its meaning would be along the lines of 'He can write something'. In non-standard varieties of English, however, double and even multiple negatives can occur without affecting the overall negation of the sentence. In such cases, the negation is understood to be reinforced rather than cancelled out. Multiple negation used to be routine in all varieties of English, before becoming socially unacceptable in the emerging standard dialect in Britain between the sixteenth and eighteenth centuries. Accordingly, multiple negation has non-standard connotations, and the hypothesis explored in the DDS *Final Report* is that the feature is an index of social stratification. What the team did was calculate for each of the informants in the pilot study the percentage of actual occurrences of multiple negation in their interview performance in relation to the number of total potential occurrences in certain types of sentences (specifically, where a negative co-occurred with an indefinite pronoun such as *anybody* or *anything* – multiple negation would turn these into *nobody* and *nothing*). They found a patterned correlation with each of the social variables. The lower-class informants were more likely to use multiple negation than those higher up the social scale; adults were more likely to use it than children, except in social class III (informants were grouped in four social classes for this pilot, I being the highest and IV the lowest); men used it more than women; and African

Americans used it more than white Americans. The social-class gradation also applied consistently across the gender and ethnicity differences. These findings suggest that, to an extent, multiple negation in Detroit was associated with lower-class speech, masculinity, and African-American speech.

Part IV of the *Final Report* is titled 'Some Sociolinguistic Implications for the Teaching of English', which argues that 'the long cherished notion of the mutually exclusive tasks of linguist and educator is in serious question' (Part IV: p. 17), and which provides a good deal of frank advice for teachers of English in the United States, including, for example, the following in connection with the **bidialectalism** or **biloquialism** of speakers:

> The English teaching profession has been handicapped by a monolithic view of its task and an inadequate analysis of its problem. Its responsibility is not to eradicate the social dialects which are inappropriate in the classroom. ... It has seldom occurred to English teachers that their customers may want or need to switch from schoolroom English to playground English as well [as] from playground to schoolroom. Identification of appropriate variants may be the best identifiers [*sic*] of the substance of good teaching.
>
> (p. 23)

In 1968, sociolinguistics was new, as was the term *bidialectalism* (which has survived in preference to *biloquialism*), which refers to a speaker's capacity to switch between two regional or social dialects of a language, a capacity that was in the process of being elucidated by sociolinguists. Also new was sociolinguists' view that educators needed to be convinced that they (sociolinguists) had a valid contribution to make to educational policy and practice, because of what they were discovering about language use and variation. Studies on language and education became a major theme in sociolinguistics generally. The point being made here by the DDS *Final Report* is that sociolinguists were detecting what were the variants that speakers used appropriately in different social contexts, and that this should inform classroom teaching. What was needed was a better understanding on the part of educators of the grammars, phonologies, and vocabularies of non-standard speech, and of the relationship between non-standard and standard speech. In future years, sociolinguists continued to advocate the position that both non-standard and standard dialects should be supported in education, as well as students' abilities to code-switch between dialects. See, for example, William Labov's interventions in the so-called Black English trial in Ann Arbor, Michigan, in 1979 (Labov, 1982b) and in the 'Ebonics' controversy that began in California in the late 1990s (Labov, 1997; Labov et al., 2008). Labov's work in Harlem between 1965 and 1968 on the speech of African Americans places him also in the vanguard of this campaign by sociolinguists. (Labov (1967a, 1967b, 1968),

Labov and Cohen (1967a, 1967b), Labov and Robins (1969), and Labov et al. (1965) were the opening outcomes of the Harlem project. More on this work below and in Chapter 9.)

7.2.1.1   The DDS and AAVE, 1969

This brings us to the work on African-American Vernacular English (AAVE) that came out of the DDS. (The *OED*'s first citation for the term *African-American Vernacular English* is Rickford et al. (1991), which was a published version of a paper first delivered in 1988; other terms were current before *AAVE*.)

Soon I will provide a short summary of Wolfram (1969). Before that, a quick mention for a follow-up survey to the DDS done by Roger Shuy after he moved to Georgetown University, Washington, D.C., in 1967 (see Shuy, 1969; Shuy et al., 1969). This plugged a gap in the original survey by carrying out a subjective reaction (SR) test modelled on that done in NYC by Labov (1966/2006). Short audio recordings of about 20 adult male speakers from the original DDS corpus were played to 620 Detroit residents. This large group included samples of young and adult respondents, African Americans and white Americans, male and female respondents, and selections representing a range of social classes. The respondents were asked to rate the voices in the recordings on a series of descriptive scales, each one lying between two polar adjectives, such as *awkward* to *graceful*, *thin* to *thick*, and *correct* to *incorrect*. A table in Shuy (1969, p. 180) shows the mean scores for each sub-group of respondents for the *correct* to *incorrect* scale, with the stimulus audio recordings speakers split into social classes, and into African American and white groups. In the table, the highest incorrectness scores are given to working class and to African American speakers. Furthermore, Shuy (1969, p. 182) reports that 'From these data [in the SR survey as a whole], it seems relatively clear that Detroiters of all ages do extremely well in identifying the race of the speaker.' To give this statement some context, at the time there was controversy over whether such a variety as AAVE could be said to exist. Shuy's conclusion was that 'there is a clear polarization in Detroit (and probably elsewhere) which enables residents there to think accurately along the lines of race with respect to the speech of their city' (p. 182). (See Chapter 9 for more discussion of perceptions of dialects.)

Walt Wolfram's doctoral dissertation, published in revised form in 1969, was one of the first steps in the identification of AAVE as a distinct variety of English. Contrast this with Labov's comment, some four decades later, that 'it is often said that AAVE is the most closely studied nonstandard dialect in the world' (Labov, 2012, location 637). Wolfram is one of those who said so, in a 2008 interview with Natalie Schilling-Estes (p. 361), adding that 'little was known in the 1960s about what the features of this variety were, or what the features of these varieties were' (his final point here being that AAVE is not a monolithic, homogeneous dialect). We can see, therefore, that it was a pretty significant ball that Wolfram and the DDS helped set rolling in the late 1960s. Using data from 48 African American speakers in the DDS corpus, evenly distributed among four social classes, three age-groups, and both sexes, Wolfram's book examines their performance of four phonological variables and four grammatical variables, particularly in relation to social status. The volume is much referenced in the wealth of literature on AAVE that followed, and so it is surprising to see the negative reaction to it in a contemporary review by R. K. S. Macaulay in the journal *Language* (Macaulay, 1970). (In 1973, Macaulay completed his own Labovian survey of Glasgow, UK, with G. D. Trevelyan.) But it is the DDS rather than Wolfram's book that Macaulay criticizes. He says Wolfram's analysis is 'often penetrating' (p. 773). William Labov (1969, p. 761) was more generous, calling it 'meticulous'), but also that the DDS data is flawed because of a lack of rigour in informant sampling compared with Labov's NYC study, a point that echoes some of the discussion in Chapter 6 of the present book: when it comes to the informant sample, design is more important than size. (For his Glasgow survey, Macaulay used a refined version of the DDS's informant sampling procedure: a quota sample giving an equal representation of both sexes from three age-groups in four social-class categories, accessed via schools, and emphasizing residence in Glasgow from early childhood as a criterion for selection (Macaulay and Trevelyan, 1977, pp. 18–19).)

An accessible outline of AAVE and subsequent research on it is given by Labov in his 2012 book on American dialects. Bearing in mind the rider that 'there is wide variation in the use of English across the African American community' (Labov, 2012, location 2130), the book's Appendix (which is in my Bibliography as Labov et al., 2008) reports on some of the main features of AAVE in general. A number of these were identified in Wolfram's variables in 1969, including multiple negation, 'zero' forms of auxiliary *be* (as in *he going* and *we coming*, or indeed *somebody knocking on my door*), *r*-less pronunciations, and simplification of consonant clusters (so that *desks* and *tests* are pronounced as *des'* and *tes'* or *desses* and *tesses*, for example). The view of Natalie Schilling-Estes in 2008 was that Wolfram's 1969 book was 'extremely important foundational work' for AAVE (Wolfram and Schilling-Estes, 2008, p. 361), to which her interviewee (Wolfram) replied, 'I think we've helped establish the primary descriptive base of the variety.'

Starting in July 1965, the Cooperative Research Program of the United States Office of Education sponsored a project led by Labov into the non-standard African-American speech of a number of northern American cities, especially that of the Harlem neighbourhood of Manhattan, New York City. Mention of this fits into our narrative here in two ways: the research is another example of foundational work on AAVE; and it very much follows on from Labov's

1966 study, adapting *SSENYC* methods to surveying AAVE communities. The numerous early publications of the project were mentioned above, and it resulted in Labov's book *Language in the Inner City* (1972c). The main, two-volume report on the project was produced by Labov and his collaborators in 1968. This report elaborates the notion of the linguistic variable as a useful concept for understanding variation and change in a speech community, and it marks the beginning of an attempt by Labov to combine the data-driven variationist approach with the theory-driven mindset of **generative linguistics**.

7.2.2   Variable-rule analysis, 1968 onwards

The basic goal of generative linguistics is to describe a **universal grammar** (UG). This UG, the theory proposes, exists in the minds of human beings. It is the most fundamental template that enables us to understand and use language. It is envisaged as an innate aspect of human biology, a linguistic organ of the body. The earliest major work of generative linguistics was Noam Chomsky's *Syntactic Structures* (1957). Chomsky became the most prominent linguist of the twentieth century, and the generative linguistics that he spearheaded became a dominant force in language research. Since 1957, Chomskyan generative linguistics has sprouted quite a few offshoots and has undergone several overhauls and rethinkings, but the central aim has remained constant: to explain as minimally as possible how a native speaker of a language is able to recognize as grammatical or ungrammatical any linguistic sequence in that language which he or she encounters or produces. 'Grammatical' in this sense does not refer to the rules that are taught in schools, but to our ability to identify a sequence as being recognizably linguistic and acceptable (in a most general sense) as an instance of the language in question. Speakers can do this thanks to the internalized, mental linguistic device that they possess, for it is by means of this device that grammatical sentences are *generated* (according to the theory). This **generative grammar** of a language thus depends on the mental linguistic device or **faculty of language** (FL), as it is known (the name *language acquisition device* is also used by some), and the description of FL would be the universal grammar. I say 'minimally', because, as Chomsky (2000, p. 13) put it, 'languages must somehow be extremely simple and very much like one another; otherwise, you couldn't acquire any of them', his conviction being that exposure, experience, mimicry, and learning are not sufficient in themselves to explain how we acquire language so rapidly and easily as infants. We must, he argues, have an innate predisposition to be linguistic. It follows then that the accurate description of FL, when arrived at, would itself be simple and elegant.

In the generative view, linguistic diversity and dialects are superficial phenomena. In a move that develops from Ferdinand de Saussure's (1916) division of language into *langue* (underlying structure) and *parole* (the execution or performance of language), generative theory sets aside the abundant diversity of language (*parole*) in order to isolate its core template. This was called the 'axiom of categoricity' by the sociolinguist Jack Chambers in 1995 (pp. 26–8), on the basis that the FL is conceived of as an absolute entity devoid of the kind of variability present in the executive part of language. Generative theory tends to proceed along rationalist lines rather than empiricist lines. The former approach prioritizes reason rather than sense-data as the basis of scientific enquiry, and Chomsky considers his linguistics to be a natural science. Generative theory is concerned with the essential nature of language, with the underlying template that powers all linguistic performance. In contrast, empiricism prioritizes directly observable sense-data, such as the corpora gleaned in sociolinguistics from speakers' linguistic performances, and this kind of linguistics tends to be considered a social science. Sociolinguistics and dialect study generally are primarily concerned with the investigation of speech and what it tells us about the workings of language. One can see pretty quickly how the generativist view of language sits uneasily alongside the variationist perspective. However, what William Labov began to flesh out in 1968 was a universalist programme that depended on the discovery of **variable rules**. Nevertheless, this sociolinguistics was a *probabilistic* rather than a categorical enterprise, aiming to reveal the patterns, causes, frequencies, and underlying configurations of competing variants.

Variable rules are arrived at by finding out the **constraints** that limit or condition the ways in which linguistic variables can vary. Constraints can be *internal* or *external*. **Internal** or **linguistic constraints** are those which occur in the linguistic environment of a variable. Take, for example, the vocalization of the velar (ł) variable among AAVE speakers. (A velar *l*, which is given the phonetic notation [ł], is articulated at the back of the vocal tract, with the back of the tongue raised towards the soft palate. Typically in English it occurs after vowels, while a fronted, alveolar [l] occurs before vowels. *Vocalization* means that the /l/ becomes a vowel.) When this vocalization occurs in the auxiliary verb *will* along with contraction of the word, it can lead to the frequent 'disappearance' of the auxiliary, as when Standard English *I will be here* has the AAVE equivalent *I be here* (Labov et al., 1968a, p. 113). Labov et al. (1968a, pp. 114–17) found that there were several internal constraints on the vocalization of velar (ł) among AAVE speakers. For example, vocalization occurred much more often in the environment of a following /w/ or /j/ or /r/, as in *always, million,* and *already,* respectively, but less often before a following vowel. An internal constraint will tend to act independently of other internal constraints, that is, it will have about the same impact on a variable regardless of other internal constraints in the linguistic environment (Fasold, 1991, p. 4). But an internal constraint will correlate variably with **external** or **social**

constraints, which are the social and stylistic factors that were discussed in Chapter 6 of the present book. For example, in the Harlem study, zero forms of (ł) occurred significantly more often in group interactions between informants (group style) than in individual interviews (single style) (Labov et al., 1968a, p. 117). Once data on all the constraints acting on a variable in a speech community are assembled, then a more complete picture of the regular patterns of variation (for that variable) can be presented. And ordered rules describing the variation can be proposed, rules which have the potential progressively to reveal underlying forms. That is to say, and put simply, if a certain internal constraint is shown to promote the occurrence of a certain variant feature, then it can be claimed that that constraint 'pre-exists' the variant under consideration. That constraint itself could also be a variant affected by other 'pre-existing' constraints, and so on. In such a way, a kind of family tree of dependencies can be traced to more basic underlying forms. In an innovative article published in 1969 based on the Harlem data, Labov outlined his aim of using variable rules to describe the order in which certain processes act on variability. As well as supporting the view of language use as possessing inherent variability and structured heterogeneity, this type of analysis provides a fuller description of the systematic ways in which dialects differ from one another, such as AAVE from Standard English. For example, regarding zero *be* forms (that is, *be* as main or **copula** verb and as auxiliary) in AAVE, by means of a detailed constraints analysis that compared environments in which *is* forms of the verb *be* occurred and environments in which forms were 'deleted' (= zero), and using notation adapted from generative phonology, Labov proposed (1969, p. 736) that deletion of *is* forms in AAVE occurs after contraction of the form. In other words, contraction is a constraint that favours deletion (and at an underlying level these *be* forms are present in AAVE). Other parts of the analysis considered phonological factors that affect contraction and deletion. For instance, returning to the example of auxiliary *will* above, in the 17 phonological rules for AAVE that Labov arrives at (p. 748), we find seven that affect *will*, including the following four, in the following order: loss of initial glide consonant *w*; vocalization of *l* in word-final position; contraction of *will* to vocalized, word-final *l*; and loss of vocalized, word-final *l*, giving a zero form of *will* (p. 755). This then is an ordered set of rules delving deep into phonological and grammatical processes, based on variation data subjected to a comprehensive analysis of environmental factors. Or, as the informatician John Paolillo puts it (2001, p. 7): 'The variable rule thus became a theoretical model of linguistic patterns with an explicit probabilistic component.'

As well as enhancing and deepening the description of variability, and demonstrating that AAVE had as much legitimacy as a dialect as did Standard English, variable-rule analysis provided Labov with what he saw as a necessary corrective to the usual research method of generative linguistics at the time:

The data that we need cannot be collected from the closet [that is, from the native-speaker intuitions of the researcher], or from any library, public or private; fortunately for us, there is no shortage of native speakers of most languages, if we care to listen to them speak. Without such empirical data, we are now in the process of producing a great many well-formed theories with nothing to stand on: beautiful constructions with ugly feet. ... We [that is, Labov, in this article] combined the techniques of generative grammar with quantitative analysis of systematic variation in NNE [*Non-standard Negro English* was the term used in 1969] to arrive at this result [contraction, then deletion of a single consonant as the variable rule underlying zero *is*], and in so doing necessarily enlarged the concept of 'rule of grammar'.

(Labov, 1969, pp. 759–60)

He argues (p. 761) that his analysis corroborates generative ideas (as they existed at the time) rather than undermines them, but he also rejects the generativists' own rejection of speech corpora elicited from speakers. Such corpora were seen in the generative school of thought as providing limited and unhelpful coverage of linguistic forms. Labov, on the other hand, has always believed that linguistic theory must be grounded in empirical data obtained from the speech community.

What happened to variable-rule analysis subsequently?

On the one hand, there have been criticisms of it as a descriptive technique. David Sankoff and Labov (1979) and Fasold (1991, pp. 8–9) noted some early ones which were about statistical procedure, and Wardhaugh (2006, p. 187) pointed out that in practice variable rules can be prone either to over-generalization or over-complexity, while in 2012 one of its practitioners, Sali Tagliamonte (p. 129), acknowledged continuing criticism of statistical methods and the variationist approach in general. On the other hand, variable-rule analysis has also been of enduring use. Tagliamonte takes it as a given that a twenty-first-century practitioner in the Labovian tradition is interested in 'the variable but rule-governed behavior typical of all natural speech varieties' (2012, p. 2), and that 'Variationist Sociolinguistics views the behavior of the dependent variable as it distributes across a series of cross-cutting factors, whether external (social) or internal (grammatical)' (p. 13). As we see, the term *constraint* has been superseded by the more encompassing **factor**, or **factor group**. Tagliamonte is one of the authors (along with David Sankoff and Eric Smith) of one of the computer software programs used for carrying out variable-rule analysis, Goldvarb (available from http://individual. utoronto.ca/tagliamonte/goldvarb.html). Other programs are also used, such as the Statistical Package for the Social Sciences (SPSS), R-Varb, Rbrul, and R. Although by no means a simple tool to use, Goldvarb facilitates the calculations required to correlate occurrences of the (binary) linguistic variable under investigation (which in the terminology of statistics is called the *dependent* or *response variable*, technically a different use of the term *variable*) with the constraints/factors that influence the linguistic variable (which in statistics are known as the *independent variables* or *predictors*). In the discourse of statistics this type of calculation is known as a **multivariate analysis**, because it takes into account many intersecting factors that apply simultaneously to the dependent variable. The type of multivariate analysis used in Goldvarb is known, with much less transparency, as *logistic regression*. If it helps, I can say (with assistance from Paolillo, 2001, pp. 14–15) that in logistic regression the statistical model that is the outcome of the number calculations is then transformed into probabilities using the *logistic function* of the procedure, which is the inverse of the *link* or *logit function* which transformed the original data into numbers in the first place: hence the name *logistic regression*. Put more plainly, logistic regression is a statistical technique which uses quantitative data 'to make reasonable guesses about the possible relationships among different phenomena that a researcher investigates' (Paolillo, 2001, p. 3). The outcome is a statistical and theoretical model of 'how things are in the world' (p. 3), but unlike other types of theoretical models, 'all statistical models recognize a component of chance as an integral part of the model' (p. 3). For this reason, once again, the descriptor *probabilistic* is used.

Earlier versions of the Goldvarb program went under the name Varbrul, which was first developed from work in the early 1960s by the Canadian mathematician, bio-informatician, and computer scientist David Sankoff. As well as being all of these people, Sankoff is a linguist, who along with Henrietta Cedergren (co-author of Varbrul; see Cedergren and Sankoff, 1974) and Gillian Sankoff carried out a Labovian survey of French speakers in Montreal in 1971, doing a stratified sample of the total population of francophones in the city, and subjecting the computerized corpus to the first extensive logistic regression analysis in variationist sociolinguistics. In 1984 and 1995, follow-up real-time panel surveys of the Montreal informants were performed, as well as a real-time trend survey in 1984. The original survey was directed by Cedergren and Gillian Sankoff, and it was designed to examine grammar, phonology, and lexis. (See Sankoff and Sankoff, 1973; Kemp, 1981; and G. Sankoff and Blondeau, 2007.) Cedergren is the author of another of the first wave of Labovian surveys, this time on Spanish in Panama (1973), which pioneered Varbrul, and which was followed by a return trend survey in 1983 (Cedergren, 1984).

7.2.2.1 The Sydney Dialect Survey and principal components analysis, 1977–87

David Sankoff also collaborated with Barbara Horvath in a project (1987) that evolved out of the former's mathematical and linguistic interests and the latter's sociolinguistic dialect survey of English in Sydney, Australia, a further example of the Labovian strand. Fieldwork for the Sydney survey was done in two batches, the first 117 interviews in 1977, and a further 60 in 1980, using stratified sampling. The main publication was Horvath (1985). In their 1987 article, Horvath and Sankoff explain their use of another multivariate statistical technique known as **principal components analysis** (**PCA**), which is available in many statistics packages. This type of analysis is undertaken on the basis that the researcher suspects that some variables (in the statistical sense of the term) in their data might be interrelated in some simpler ways within the context of the overall environment. Principal components analysis, true to its name, identifies in successive and hierarchical fashion the principal components of the variation. Using the full set of variables and variants under consideration, the software does a calculation of the maximum extent of variation first (principal component 1), followed by the second-greatest degree of variation (principal component 2), and so on. The data can then be expressed in a type of graph known as a *scattergram* or *scatter graph* or *scatter plot*, on which the data-points are plotted according to their values on the two axes, each of which is a principal component. Patterns or clusters often emerge, as in Figure 7.1, from Horvath and Sankoff (1987, p. 190), in which the data-points are speakers, measured in relation to principal components 1 and 2 as identified by the analysis.

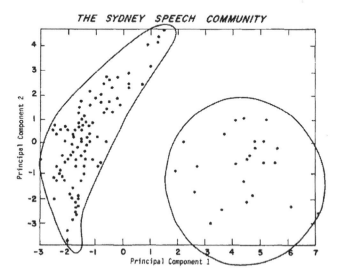

Figure 7.1   The Sydney speech community: speakers plotted against principal components 1 and 2 (from Horvath and Sankoff, 1987, p. 190).

The 1987 article followed on from Horvath's 1985 book, which also made use of PCA. The decision to employ this technique arose out of the nature of the Sydney speech community, which since World War II had received migrants from many parts of the world, especially from Greece and Italy. Unlike Labov in NYC, Horvath wanted to include in her informant sample residents who were non-native speakers of the variety, as well as children (who might be bilingual) from migrant families, as she believed that the factor of ethnicity could be having a significant impact on Sydney English, including on processes of linguistic change. Her original sample was therefore constructed with a view to coverage of the major ethnic groups, as well as status groups, and geographical areas. The 1987 article used only data from the Anglo and Italian speakers. Horvath and Sankoff did not want to carry out their analysis by first organizing their speakers into social groupings (according to socio-economic factors, or age, education, ethnicity, gender, location), in the belief that such groupings are rather blunt instruments to use as a basis for analysis on a small sample drawn from a complex, multi-ethnic community, and that structuring the analysis in this way 'might obscure the real basis of linguistic differentiation within the speech community' (p. 183). Instead they wanted to begin their analysis by grouping their speakers according to their linguistic behaviour only, and once that was done, to interpret the patterns that emerged with the help of the social and biographical information. Principal components analysis enabled this approach. The input to the PCA consisted of the number of occurrences for each speaker of each variant of each of the four vowel variables under consideration (p. 188). The output was four principal components (pp. 188–9, 197–201), and the speakers' scores were plotted onto a series of scatter graphs (pp. 190–200) in each of which the two axes were different permutations of the principal components. Figure 7.1 shows the two main accent divisions in the Sydney English speech community, between the Italian adults in the full-moon-shaped cluster, and the Anglo adults and Anglo and Italian teenagers in the crescent-shaped cluster. We can see that this division is mainly associated with principal component 1, but also that the vertical axis of principal component 2 offers the possibility of subdivisions within each of the main groups, and Horvath and Sankoff explore this further in their article. Using a modified version of the traditional categorization of Australian English accents into Broad, General, and Cultivated varieties, their findings for Sydney English are that: there is a Cultivated variety spoken mostly by upper-working-class and middle class female Anglos; there is a General variety used by most Anglo teenagers, nearly all Italian teenagers, and by upper-working-class Anglo adults; there is a Broad I variety spoken mainly by lower-working-class male Anglo adults; and there are two further varieties used exclusively by Italian adults, these being Broad II and (Italian) Accented (p. 203). They also suggest tentatively (p. 201) that the Italian teenagers may be leading a change towards greater use of the General variety.

Another follow-up study on increasing use of the **High Rising Terminal** or **Tone** in the intonation of Sydney English (HRT, which makes statements sound like questions, is reported in other varieties too, such as New Zealand English, American English, and British English, although it has also been called **Australian Questioning Intonation**), was published in 1986 (Guy et al.), and there is more discussion of Barbara Horvath's innovative work in Chapter 10 of the present book.

7.2.2.2 Summing up variable-rule analysis

You might have noticed that, although I have continued to summarize events in the history of Labovian variationist sociolinguistics, I have digressed from the overview of variable-rule analysis. In conclusion, then, with regard to its use as a descriptive and investigative tool, it continues in common though not obligatory use. In the view of Robert Bayley (2013), quantitative variable-rule-based analysis has proved the systematic nature of linguistic variation and has revealed beyond doubt that non-standard and socially stigmatized dialects 'are orderly, complex, and complete linguistic systems' (p. 102). In a highly methodical but also quite intricate chapter of her 2012 textbook on language variation and change (pp. 120–61), Sali Tagliamonte shows how Goldvarb and other alternative statistical programs can handle the dozen or more factors affecting the tricky case of presence versus absence of *that* in sentences such as *She suddenly decided* [zero] *she'd go to town* versus *She decided that she'd have a new house* (p. 125). As indicated above, Goldvarb can handle binary dependent variables, and presence versus absence gives us a binary variable. Using nearly 2000 data tokens from her corpus of York (UK) English, the findings of the analyses are that six internal constraints or factor groups (p. 127) have statistically significant effects on the variable, and that age of speaker is also particularly significant (p. 155), suggesting a change in usage and social meaning of the variable since World War II. Tagliamonte's chapter is designed to give a practical review of the potential of competing software programs and of modern variable-rule analysis in general, from the standpoint of a practitioner. She concludes that the approach has much to offer, that the range of programs available presents both greater versatility overall and complex choices for investigators, and that it remains the researcher (rather than the program) who asks the most telling questions, and who provides the interpretations and explanations (p. 157). Bayley believes (2013, p. 101) that SPSS and R have more to offer the variationist than Goldvarb.

But what of variable-rule analysis as linguistic theory? What of variable-rule analysis and generative linguistics? This part of the story since 1968 is rather more chequered. Somewhat inconveniently, Chomskyan generative linguistics went on to produce a disorientating series of modifications and embranchments. As I have said, the central notion of the faculty of language remained, and became orthodoxy in linguistic theory (though there are questioning and alternative viewpoints, such as those of the linguist and philosopher Ray Jackendoff, and of the neurobiologist Terrence Deacon). But the *standard theory* of mid 1960s generative linguistics was revised into the *extended standard theory* by the mid 1970s, incorporating *X-bar theory*. In 1981, Chomsky introduced the *principles and parameters* framework (P&P), which became the *Minimalist Program* (MP) by the early 1990s. In other words, the form of generative thinking which provided the context for Labov's late-1960s variable rules underwent extensive revision and was supplanted by later versions. (The Welsh dialectologist Alan R. Thomas was another variationist researcher who grappled with early generative phonological theory, publishing a forward-looking article in 1967.) Concerns were also raised, including from within sociolinguistics (for example, Romaine, 1981), that, as Martin Durrell (2004, p. 198) put it, 'variable rules are essentially incompatible with a generative grammar and that probabilistic rules or quantificational data cannot be part of the linguistic competence of an individual'. The use of the term **competence** in this way is from Chomsky's (1965, p. 4) reworking of Saussure's *langue* notion, later refined again by Chomsky (1986, pp. 22–3) and renamed **I-language**, which is the mastery or knowledge of language that a human is genetically endowed with. One could say that Chomsky and Labov were engaged separately in incompatible quests because they were hunting quite different animals, to use an unsophisticated metaphor. Chomsky's view of the relevance of linguistic variation to his work is indicated by this response he made, in an interview given in 1983, to a question about the relative importance of heredity and environment in language acquisition:

> The language organ [FL] interacts with early experience and matures into the grammar of the language that the child speaks. If a human being with this fixed endowment grows up in Philadelphia, as I did, his brain will encode knowledge of the Philadelphia dialect of English. If that brain had grown up in Tokyo, it would have encoded the Tokyo dialect of Japanese. The brain's different linguistic experience – English versus Japanese – would modify the language organ's structure.
> (Chomsky and Gliedman, 1983: http://www.chomsky.info/ interviews/198311--.htm, accessed 23 January 2015)

Chomsky is primarily interested in the language organ's structure before it is affected by linguistic experience. He is concerned with 'this fixed endowment', rather than with the FL's 'linguistic experience'. In the strict Chomskyan view, 'Linguistic theory is concerned with an ideal speaker-listener, in a completely homogeneous speech-community, who knows its language perfectly' (Chomsky, 1965, p. 3), because Chomsky's quest is for a description of competence or I-language. This is the so-called axiom of categoricity. 'Observed use of language', he says (1965, p. 4), 'may provide evidence as to the nature of this mental reality, but surely cannot constitute the actual subject matter of linguistics'. From this point of view, language use and linguistic diversity are external to the main inquiry. In contrast, Labov's argument would be that there are no basic principles of linguistic behaviour that can be isolated totally from the effects of environment and linguistic experience (Labov, 1994, p. 116), and from this point of view the study of linguistic diversity must be built into any attempt to develop a theory of language.

It is maybe not so surprising, therefore, to read the syntax and sociolinguistics expert Ralph Fasold saying in 1991 (p. 18), 'We should not mourn the quiet demise of the original variable rule. It now seems evident that it was never any more than a display device, anyway.' Having read that, however, it *is* surprising to see him saying in 2013 (p. 185), 'I am going to explore what it would take to adapt some version of Minimalist Program syntactic theory to include linguistic variation', syntax (or grammar) being the centre of attention for generativists. Fasold opens his 2013 essay by asking, 'Does variation analysis even need a syntactic theory?' He adds tellingly, 'think about how annoyed we [variationists] are that practitioners of formal syntax [for example, Chomsky] are quite comfortable ignoring variation analysis', and, 'variationists could perhaps not be blamed for wanting to return the favor'. This makes me think of any number of sporting scenarios where one team perceives themselves as perpetually in the shadow of another, and wants both to beat and be like the dominant team, while also being aggrieved at how little attention the bigger team pays to them. Or maybe it is like a certain sort of sibling rivalry. It is clear, however, that a good many linguists continue to feel that there is a need to combine insights from both kinds of language study, and it should also be said that not all on the generative/formal syntax side have ignored linguistic variation. See, for example, the work of David W. Lightfoot, and Ian G. Roberts. Fasold's (2013) exploration revives the idea of combining a Varbrul analysis with generative theory (p. 197), and makes use of research by Sjef Barbiers on Dutch dialects which appeared in 2005 in a collection of essays called *Syntax and Variation: Reconciling the Biological and the Social* (Cornips and Corrigan, 2005a). Although the marriage of Labov's (social) variable-rule analysis with Chomsky's (biological) generative enterprise did not prove particularly fruitful, variationists have continued to attempt to engage with Chomskyan analysis (for example, the Cornips and Corrigan collection (2005a) includes chapters that use the P&P and MP rubrics), and with other kinds of generative or syntactic theory (see Durrell, 2004; and Fasold, 2013). Two unconventional proposals, made some two decades apart, and well received by some linguists, tackled the matter by sidestepping the problem of reconciling the Chomskyan and Labovian views.

The first is to be found in the work of Charles-James Nice Bailey (1973, 1982, 1987, 1996), which divides language into two sides: the *sociocommunicational*, comprised of the societal factors that shape language as a result of its use; and the *neurobiological*, comprised of the factors of human physiology and biology that interact with language in use (see Fasold, 1991, pp. 17–18). Bailey also sought to integrate more fully a historical or **diachronic** (literally 'through time') perspective into linguistic theory (the *dynamic paradigm*, as he called it (1973, p. 21), sometimes also known as the *developmentalist framework*), and for his purposes he recommended replacing the term *dialect* with *lect*, which he defined as: 'a completely non-commital term for any bundling together of linguistic phenomena' (1973, p. 11), arguing that his *lectology* should both be at the centre of theoretical linguistics and replace dialectology (p. 98). In this framework, linguistic variation is seen as a continuum of differences expressed in the performances of individuals (rather than as the orderly heterogeneity revealed in Labovian groups or speech communities), with this **synchronic** (meaning, 'at one point in time') variation being a reflection of differing stages in processes of diachronic change.

The second proposal is the *modular* approach outlined in a contribution to the Cornips and Corrigan (2005a) collection by Pieter Muysken (2005). The term *modular* is used because the approach 'assumes that the human linguistic capacities do not form a single monolithic whole, but fall into several groups or clusters' (Muysken, 2005, p. 35), including syntax, semiotics (referring to the use of symbols and other signs), interaction, and cognition. Muysken employs each of these categories in his explanation of the variation found in the forms and uses of the *gerund* (that is, a verb form that can act like a noun) in Ecuadorian Spanish.

(There is more discussion of grammar in dialect study in Chapter 2 of the present book. In that chapter, we look at grammar in a wider sense of the term, not confining it to the generative meaning.)

Before I move on to the closing parts of this chapter, a few words more here on Labov's work. Between 1973 and 1977, he was involved in another large sociolinguistic survey in Philadelphia which was designed to identify which social group was leading the many changes in the city's vowel system. The findings of this project on Linguistic Change and Variation (LCV) are discussed in Chapter 9, section 3. The project also fed into Labov's colossal three-volume *Principles of Linguistic Change* (1994, 2001, 2010). Volume 3 deals with cognitive, cultural, and historical aspects of linguistic change; Volume 2 concentrates on the social factors; and Volume 1 focuses on the internal, structural, linguistic processes, giving us also an insight into how Labov's relationship with universalism had developed by 1994.

He says (Labov, 1994, p. 115): 'There is no contradiction between the goals of the universalistic approach and the empirical program that is projected here. The aims are the same: to find the most general principles that govern language structure and language change.' Phrasing counts for a lot, and one can judge the phrase 'the most general principles' as being in keeping with, say, Chomsky's goals, or on the other hand as being a subtle, probabilistic revision of those goals. Compare Labov's statement with the following description given by Chomsky in 1996 of his own project from the 1950s onwards: 'I and others were involved in an effort to construct explicit grammars, that is, explicit theories of a language which would describe systems of rules and principles which would characterize exactly the form and meaning of the sentences of a language' (Chomsky, 1996, no page numbers). Chomsky adds that 'the task is just to separate out these [external, environmental] factors to see what are the [linguistic] principles which are rooted in our nature and therefore will establish the form, the basic form of any human language and to what extent variation is tolerable in [the] system'. This, I think, is not a project that is the same as Labov's, but one can see also why some linguists continue to believe that neither is it inevitably in conflict with it.

In 1994, Labov also had another, older universalist theory on his mind. This was the late-nineteenth-century neogrammarian theory of the absolute regularity of sound 'laws' describing certain types of linguistic change. We came across this theory in Chapter 4, section 2 of the present book. Labov's work on principles of linguistic change follows on from the neogrammarian-inspired debate that surrounded late-nineteenth-century dialectology. His purpose is to search for the 'simplest principles' (1994, p. 600) that underlie the complexity of 'linguistic reality'. In 1994 (pp. 600–5), he proposed 12 general principles of sound change, which he said were 'of varying degrees of strength and certainty' (p. 600), with some principles modifying others or, in neogrammarian terms, dealing with exceptions to earlier principles. Two are presented explicitly as a resolution of the neogrammarian controversy over the **exceptionlessness of sound laws**, that is, the dispute between the (neogrammarian) view that a given sound change will operate in all the applicable, relevant words in the speech community in question, and the view that it spreads gradually and apparently irregularly through the group of words without necessarily affecting the whole set (**lexical diffusion**). Labov decides (pp. 542–3) that regular sound change is characteristic of the initial stages of a **change from below** the level of communal consciousness, and consists typically of phenomena like the vocalization of /l/ and /r/, the deletion of unstressed vowels, and changes in the place of articulation of vowels and in the manner of articulation of consonants. But in addition, lexical diffusion also happens, though normally at a later stage in the process when, for example, the change has accumulated a high degree of social awareness, and has become a **change from above** the level of public consciousness. This latter pattern consists typically of such modifications as deletion of fricative and plosive consonants, and changes in the phonetic length of segments and in the place of articulation of consonants. This formulation, then, does away with the opposition between regularity and diffusion, and presents them instead as two facets or stages of the one process.

In summary, what Labov is engaged in here is an attempt to form a bridge between the pinnacle of nineteenth-century philological theorizing (the neogrammarian hypothesis) and the most prominent theory of twentieth-century linguistics (generativism), by means of quantitative, probabilistic, variationist dialect study. This is a remarkably ambitious undertaking.

With just a short pause for breath, we return again now to my overview of surveys that followed Labov's 1966 NYC study, in order to finish it in just a few more paragraphs.

7.2.3   Early variationist surveys of British English, 1965–92

Many projects on many urban varieties of many languages across the world were carried out in the 1970s to 1990s, as Labov himself notes (Labov, 1966/2006, pp. 380–97). Among these were more on English in North America, including in Philadelphia (Cofer, 1972; this a doctoral dissertation supervised by Labov), in Anniston, Alabama (Feagin, 1979), Ottawa (Woods, 1979), and in Memphis, Tennessee (Fridland, 1999). Variationist sociolinguistic surveys have been done on English in South Africa (for example, Kay McCormick's 1980s–90s work on code-switching between English and Afrikaans in Cape Town's District Six (McCormick, 1989, 2003)), in New Zealand (from the large Wellington Social Dialect Survey or Porirua Project (Holmes et al., 1991) to Scott Allan's small study (1990) of HRT intonation in the Maori and *Pakeha* communities, a topic later pursued by the geolinguist David Britain in a number of articles), and in the British Isles. Variationist studies, large and not so large, have multiplied, as evidenced by the contents of Martin J. Ball's *Handbook of Sociolinguistics Around the World* (2010), a volume centred around the variationist approach containing contributions on work in Africa, the Americas, Asia, Australasia, Europe, and the Middle East. Subsequent to the advent of sociolinguistics in the 1960s, a number of prominent academic journals have been established that publish variationist work, these being, in chronological order, *Language in Society* (started in 1972), *English World-Wide* (from 1980), and *Language Variation and Change* (1989), the last two in particular having a variationist emphasis. The field continues to be highly productive.

But we shall conclude this overview by returning to the early, formative variationist surveys, this time those in Britain.

7.2.3.1   Norwich, 1968–88

The first Labovian survey of British English was carried out by Peter Trudgill for his doctoral research at Edinburgh University, on three consonant and 13 vowel variables in Norwich, East Anglia, his home city. The fieldwork was done in 1968, and Trudgill gained his doctorate in 1971. His dissertation was published in revised form in 1974.

The population of the Norwich urban area in 1968 was just under 600,000, with just over 118,000 living within the city boundary. Trudgill used a 'quasi-random' procedure (Trudgill, 1974a, p. 21) to obtain his informant sample. His informants were to be selected using the register of electors for the whole city, but the sample was drawn from four of the city's 16 electoral wards only, plus from one of the suburban parishes outside the city boundary. This restriction was due to time constraints, but Trudgill argued (1974a, pp. 22–3) that it gave appropriate geographical, social, and economic coverage of the city as a whole. An initial random selection of 25 informants from each of the five areas was made, giving Trudgill 125 names and addresses. Again owing to time constraints, Trudgill decided that he could interview ten informants (randomly selected) from each group of 25, with the further restriction of not interviewing anyone who had moved to Norwich from outside the East Anglia area within the preceding ten years. Because the electoral register did not include inhabitants under the age of 21, a further group of ten randomly selected (from class lists) secondary-school pupils was added, giving a final sample of 60 informants. Trudgill encountered some problems in securing his interviews, such as refusals, or individuals having moved or died since the compilation of the electoral register, but 60 tape-recorded interviews were eventually carried out in July 1968, 50 of them done by Trudgill, and ten by a helper, Adrian Hannah, who was also from Norwich. Like Labov in NYC, Trudgill wanted to collect a range of speech styles, from informal to formal, and he wanted to correlate his data with social class. The more formal speech styles were elicited by several short questionnaire sections in each interview, as well as by word lists to be read aloud, a minimal pairs list, and a reading passage. One very brief section asked for local vocabulary. Casual speech was obtained from interchanges or contributions outside the immediate context of the question and reading sections (the kind of data called 'Incidental Material' or IM, in the Survey of English Dialects), and in storytelling responses to the question (adopted from Houck, 1968, p. 127), 'Have you ever been in a situation, recently or some time ago, where you had a good laugh, or something funny or humorous happened to you, or you saw it happen to someone else?' The informant sample was divided into social-class groupings using index scores calculated for each individual, based on six factors that were felt to be appropriate social-status indicators in 1960s urban England: occupation, income, education, housing, locality, and father's occupation (Trudgill, 1974a, pp. 36–41). Trudgill arrived at five social classes: I, middle middle-class (MMC); II, lower middle-class (LMC); III, upper working-class (UWC); IV, middle working-class (MWC); and V, lower working-class (LWC). He did this by correlating the social-class index scores with the performance by his informants of one grammatical feature (the variable absence of the third-person singular (s) ending in verbs, for example, *he loves* versus *he love*), a procedure that the fellow Labovian, K. M. Petyt (1980, p. 159), criticized as 'circular' (that is, using linguistic criteria to help set up social classes in a survey aiming to investigate possible correlations between linguistic and social data), and Val Jones, of the Tyneside Linguistic Survey, described as 'not necessarily' valid (that is, using the distribution of a grammatical feature to help divide the 'social continuum with which to correlate the distributions of phonological variables' (Jones, 1978, p. 17).) The actual numbers of informants in each social-class grouping turned out to be uneven, ranging from six in MMC to 22 in MWC (Trudgill, 1974a, p. 60). The informants were also arranged in seven age-groups, again with an uneven spread of numbers per group, from age 10 to 19, 20 to 29, and so forth, up to 70-plus (p. 28); and into female and male groups, but with unequal numbers of females and males in most of the age-groups (p. 44).

Trudgill found regular social stratification in most of his variables, including for the increasingly studied realization of the nasal consonant in -*ing* as either [n] or [ŋ] (as in Fischer, 1958, and Shuy et al., 1968a). The highest scores for use of the [n] variant were found in the LWC, casual style, and in male speakers (Trudgill, 1974a, pp. 91–5; though watch out for the confusion of variants and scores at bottom of page 91). The data suggested also that a number of the vowel variables were involved in change in progress led by working-class males (Trudgill, 1974a, pp. 104–12). Trudgill's interviews included questions on attitudes to Norwich speech and his versions of Labov's self-evaluation and linguistic insecurity tests, some of the material from which he used in an article originally published in 1972, and discussed in Chapter 9, section 9.3 of the present book. In addition, the 1974 main volume has a bold and elaborate engagement with a brand of generative phonology derived from a particularly abstract model found in the work of Erik C. Fudge (1967, 1969), and presented under the chapter title 'The Norwich diasystem' (Trudgill, 1974a, pp. 133–93), although the term *diasystem* is a structuralist one, coined by Uriel Weinreich (1954, p. 270). This experiment in searching for internalized, underlying features did not prove as productive for subsequent work as Labov's variable-rule analysis did, and received mixed reviews, ranging from the very critical (Bickerton, 1975) to the simply critical (Petyt, 1980, pp. 160–1) to the friendly (Macaulay, 1976).

In 1983, Trudgill returned to Norwich to supervise a follow-up, real-time trend survey, in which a further 17 informants were selected, conforming to the social-class profile of the 1968 sample. This new group was aged between ten and 25 in 1983, and therefore was the youngest age-group of the combined 1968 and 1983 sample. The results of this return visit were summarized in an article published in 1988, in which Trudgill made a number of interesting points about apparent- and real-time methodology, and about linguistic change in progress. For example, the new group showed a dramatic increase in the use of a labio-dental approximant pronunciation of the /r/ phoneme, which has the phonetic symbol [ʋ]. In this pronunciation, the lower lip edges near to the upper teeth, and in 1968 Trudgill had treated it as idiosyncratic and a speech defect in the small number of speakers who used it. By 1983, however, 'to an astonishing degree' (Trudgill, 1988, p. 40) the younger speakers were using [ʋ], and Trudgill noted (pp. 40–1) that the pronunciation was increasing in other dialects of southern English English also. Another change was the switch of the /θ/ phoneme to /f/, so that *thing* sounds like *fing*, and of the /ð/ phoneme to /v/, so that *with* sounds like *wiv* (this latter switch does not occur in word-initial position). This change had not been recorded at all in 1968, while 70 per cent of the new group showed evidence of it (p. 43). Trudgill noted that there were reports that these fricative mergers were 'spreading very rapidly indeed out from London in all directions' (p. 43). This interest in the **geographical diffusion** of linguistic changes had already resulted in Trudgill producing in 1974 one of the earliest pieces of research in the strand of dialect study subsequently known as *geolinguistics* (see Chapter 10, section 10.3 of the present book for more on this article (Trudgill, 1974b)). His real-time study of 1988, as well as finding some rapid changes in the speech of Norwich youngsters, also found some consolidation of existing trends, leading him to conclude that the apparent-time methodology was 'an excellent sociolinguistic tool', but that real-time study was 'in many ways an even more informative experience' (Trudgill, 1988, p. 48). He did, nevertheless, reflect on one unavoidable way in which the 1968 and 1983 data sets were not strictly comparable (p. 45), that is, that the 1983 informants were more at ease with portable audio (cassette) recorders than the 1968 informants, a fact that conceivably could have led to the greater use of non-standard variants in the later fieldwork interviews. At other points in the present book I mention the facilitating and motivating effects on dialect study of technological change, but here we glimpse the potential of technological change, or rather our adapting to it, to affect individuals' speech patterns in certain circumstances.

In the wake of Trudgill's 1968 work, other British Labovian surveys followed in West Yorkshire (published as Petyt, 1985), Glasgow (Macaulay and

Trevelyan, 1973, 1977), Belfast (see L. Milroy, 1980), and Reading (Cheshire, 1982), with the fieldwork for all of these surveys being done in the 1970s. The Tyneside Linguistic Survey (TLS; also discussed in Chapter 6, section 6.4.2 of the present book), which investigated the English speech of Gateshead and Newcastle, pre-dates Trudgill's survey, as it was planned and piloted before Trudgill carried out his fieldwork (see Strang, 1968, and Pellowe, 1967), and it proceeded as an alternative to the Labovian model in variationist socio-linguistics. The plan for the TLS (see Pellowe et al., 1972; Val Jones, 1978; Jones-Sargent, 1983; and Pellowe, 1991), was that its groupings of speakers would be determined entirely empirically as examination of the extensive linguistic and social data was carried out, using advanced mathematical concepts, 1970s computer technology, and a multivariate technique called **cluster analysis**. The idea was that this would uncover natural sociolinguistic groupings within the sample and generate hypotheses about the interactions between the linguistic and social variables (Jones, 1978, p. 32–3). The doctoral thesis of Val Jones (1978, also Jones-Sargent, 1983) pursued this plan and produced a number of findings that provide food for thought for followers of the Labovian model, such as the lack of a neat fit between the linguistic variety clusters and the social clusters (Jones, 1978, p. 291), and the conclu-sion that the considerable linguistic variability exhibited within groups and even by single informants did not match straightforwardly with simple social or stylistic categories (pp. 289–90).

And finally in this chapter, we look at the work of James Milroy and Lesley Milroy and their team in 1970s Belfast, especially their introducing and devel-oping of **social network theory** in variationist research.

7.2.3.2 Belfast and social network theory, 1975–92

Facebook, as is well known, is an Internet-based social network, launched in February 2004, by means of which you can share information about your every waking and sleeping moment with friends, family, and absolutely anybody else you care to involve in your virtual life. However, Facebook has *nothing* to do with the ideas about social networks that the Milroys imported into soci-olinguistic research, other than its being a particularly twenty-first-century manifestation of the ways in which we link and interact with other individ-uals. The *OED Online* (accessed 22 December 2016) defines a social network as 'a system of social interactions and relationships; a group of people who are socially connected to one another', and gives first use of the phrase as long ago as 1845. The academic study of such social networks, in the fields of sociology, social psychology, and anthropology, can be traced back to the late nine-teenth century. The Milroys were most influenced by work in late-twentieth-century sociology, especially, with regard to their view of linguistic change, by a famous article by the American sociologist, Mark Granovetter, entitled 'The

Strength of Weak Ties' (1973). The concepts from social network theory that most interest us, and which the Milroys used to explain their Belfast data in a series of publications from 1978 onwards are: *close-knit networks*, which are *dense* and *multiplex* in character; *loose-knit networks*, which are not dense or multiplex; *strong ties*, and *weak ties*. I will now explain these terms generally and with reference to the Belfast survey, which was begun in 1975–6 in three well-defined communities in inner-city Belfast: Ballymacarrett, a Protestant area in east Belfast; the Hammer, a Protestant area in west Belfast along the Shankill Road; and the Clonard, a Catholic area in west Belfast, just to the south of the Hammer. Data from these areas was later supplemented by material from the outer-city communities of Andersonstown and Braniel, and from the town of Lurgan, 17 miles south-west of Belfast, but we concentrate here on the inner-city areas.

Let's say that you live in a community where your extended family lives too, and where you know many of your neighbours well, and, if you are in employment, your workmates are drawn from your neighbourhood, and your friends are drawn from your workmates and neighbours and old school friends, and where many of the people in your network also know each other well. This means that you belong to a *close-knit social network*, and because many of the people that you know are also linked to each other the network is said to be relatively *dense*. If in this network individuals are linked to one another in more than one capacity – for example, your workmate is also your neighbour and a family member – then the network is characterized by *multiplexity*. (In contrast, a *uniplex* relationship is where an individual is connected to another in one capacity only.) The *ties* between individuals in close-knit networks are by default *strong*, the *strength of an interpersonal tie* being measured by a 'combination of the amount of time, the emotional intensity, the intimacy (mutual confiding), and the reciprocal services' (Granovetter, 1973, p. 1361) which characterize it. Each of these attributes – close-knittedness, high density, multiplexity, strong ties – adds to the social-norm-enforcing powers of a social network. As the Milroys have pointed out in their work (see, for example, L. Milroy, 1980; J. Milroy, 1992; Milroy and Milroy, 1978, 1985, 1992), in British and American society close-knit, territorially based networks are located most obviously in the lowest classes, but upper class networks have a structural similarity, and the continual reiteration of interactions reinforces established behaviours and social norms in such networks, producing conservativism and solidarity within the networks and fragmentation in the wider structure of society. Obviously, communication and language use is actively involved in this norm-enforcing, but more than that, the language of the close-knit community is itself subject to conservatism and maintenance. In other words, the dialect of a close-knit, dense, multiplex social network will be resistant to linguistic change. This provides us with an alternative or additional explanation for the persistent vitality of non-standard dialects in 'vernacular communities' (Milroy and Milroy, 1992, p. 3), that is, alternative and additional to Labov's notion of covert prestige. And although the Milroys' quantitative, apparent-time survey in Belfast was much influenced by Labov's work, its basis in the inquiry into the language of social networks also provides an alternative form of variationist dialect study to the social-class based Labovian model.

In their research, the Milroys were initially interested in the rise of urban vernacular speech in relatively young industrial cities (Milroy and Milroy, 1978, p. 19), and Belfast presented them with a pertinent location, having expanded greatly since the mid nineteenth century, with many of its older residents in the 1970s having been born in rural areas of Ulster. The segregated working class inner-city areas that they investigated had populations that reflected immigration into Belfast from two quite distinct dialect areas, most of the Protestant immigrants originating from north and east Ulster, and most of the Catholics from central, south, and west Ulster. The sharply segregated nature and historical background of the Belfast communities not only made a social-network-based study very appropriate, but also offered a setting that was exceptionally suited to assessing the effects of urbanization (which engenders *loose-knit social networks*, characterized by many *weak interpersonal ties*) on close-knit networks. The project also implicitly questioned the postulation, as put forward by Labov for NYC, that a large urban population functions as a single speech community. (The core city population of Belfast in the 1970s was somewhere above 300,000.) Therefore, as well as recording two age-groups (40–55 years old and 18–25 years old) and equal numbers of men and women in the three inner-city communities, giving a total of 46 speakers (L. Milroy, 1980, pp. 204–5), the Milroys also rated the informants according to their network scores, which were calculated using a *network strength scale* comprised of a set of five indicators of density and multiplexity, such as membership of a high-density, territorially based cluster, and working at the same place as at least two others from the same area (L. Milroy, 1980, pp. 141–2). Eight phonological variables were studied (pp. 119–120), chosen because of their potential relevance to local, vernacular norms rather than to overtly prestigious norms (remember, the informants were not drawn from a range of social classes), and two speech styles were considered (pp. 62–9): interview (that is, comparatively formal) and spontaneous (comparatively casual, such as conversations between or narratives by informants). The main aim was to look at the interplay of social network and linguistic stability, examining, on the one hand, the capacity of the close-knit working class communities to maintain vernacular norms, and, on the other, the capacity of urbanization to disperse the networks, leading to linguistic change. The variables were considered in relation to the older country dialects that had been brought into Belfast, as well as in relation to the age and sex of the informants, to the three different inner-city areas, to speech style, and to strength of network membership.

There was evidence from some variables of a close relationship between high use of local vernacular variants and high network scores (L. Milroy, 1980, p. 154). When the sex of the speaker was considered, it was apparent that in general in the three communities men used the local vernacular pronunciations more than women (pp. 163–4), though 'women are capable of sometimes using variables particularly associated with men to symbolize their integration into local networks' (p. 164), such as deletion of intervocalic (th) or [ð] in words like *brother* and *mother*, a local feature which shows a comparatively close correlation in female usage with female personal network scores. Although generally women had lower network scores and lower vernacular scores than men (p. 156), only in east Belfast Ballymacarett was there a 'sharp contrast between male and female network scores, with the men scoring very much higher than the women' (p. 159), and it was also in Ballymacarett that the 'sharpest and most consistent patterns of sex differentiation in language' (p. 159) were often found. Lesley Milroy's interpretation of this was that 'Sex-based linguistic norms in Ballymacarett appear to be more or less co-extensive with norms based on network: in other words, the same underlying sets of vernacular norms are likely to be most observable in the speech of men (because they use vernacular variants at a high level) and in the speech of those who are most firmly integrated into the community' (1980, p. 159). Or, to put this another way, 'a dense, multiplex personal network structure predicts relative closeness to vernacular norms' (p. 160). The difference between men and women on the network-strength scale was not as clear or consistent in the west Belfast Hammer and Clonard areas, 'where traditional network patterns are disturbed' (p.163), owing to male unemployment caused by the loss of local industry. Disturbance and dispersal of traditional close-knit networks by such developments disrupts language maintenance and stability (p. 185), opening the door to linguistic change, perhaps in the direction of standardization or in the shape of the importing of forms from outside the area. In 1980 (p. 187), Lesley Milroy speculated that, as the older rural networks migrated to and reformed into the urban networks, a subtle change happened in the use of a well-known Irish variant pronunciation of the vowel in words like *bud*, *cup*, and *hut*, making them sound like *bod*, *cop*, and *hot*; that is, that this variant shifted from being a marker of network loyalty to being a marker of sex, because the correlation between high use of this variant and high network scores applied only in the older age-group in inner-city Belfast, while in the younger age-group it correlated more closely with sex differentiation. Another indication of a linguistic change shows up in a graph presented in Lesley Milroy's 1980 book (p. 124), and also in a

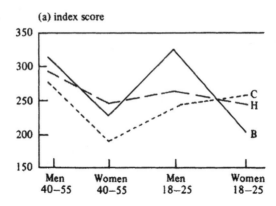

Figure 7.2 Backing of /a/ in Ballymacarett, the Clonard, and the Hammer in Belfast (from Milroy and Milroy, 1985, p. 371).

number of other publications by the Milroys (for example, J. Milroy, 1992, p. 186; Milroy and Milroy, 1978, p. 28; Milroy and Milroy, 1985, p. 371), during which they develop an explanation for it by using Granovetter's *weak tie theory*. The graph is shown here as Figure 7.2.

The graph shows scores for a backed and raised variant of the /a/ vowel in words like *fast* and *man*, producing pronunciations such as [fɔˑəst] 'fo-ast' and [mɔˑən] 'mo-an'. In 1978 (p. 27), the Milroys reported the trend towards this backing of /a/ as a change in progress. Of particular interest is the crossover pattern shown at the right of the graph, a pattern which tends to be associated with a change in progress, because it reverses the generally expected 'stable norm' pattern. Each line represents one of the inner-city communities, and the horizontal axis plots the age- and sex-groups. Referring to the graph in 1978 (p. 28), the Milroys talked of /a/-backing as 'a characteristically Ballymacarett and characteristically male feature, strongest in the Protestant east, weakest in the Catholic west', adding that the Clonard young women 'appear to be introducing an innovation borrowed directly or indirectly from a higher-ranked [in the context of 1970s Belfast] community'. In this group, the general female movement away from /a/-backing is reversed, to the extent that it is also higher than the score for the Clonard young men. By 1985, the Milroys were using Granovetter's work on weak ties to explain how this trend travelled across the segregation divide between Ballymacarett and the Clonard. Granovetter (1973) was interested in how information and influence flows between separate close-knit networks, arguing that communicational 'bridges' between such networks cannot by definition happen between individuals who are strongly tied to one another, and that therefore 'all bridges are weak ties' (p. 1364). The Milroys surmised that, if it were to be found that the Clonard young women were involved in frequent weak-tie encounters with individuals marginal to or from outside the Clonard, then these relationships might act as conduits along which /a/-backing could be transported, leading to the young women outscoring the Clonard young men in its use. While weak ties and loose-knit networks are inherently difficult to study quantitatively, the Milroys noticed (1985, p. 372) that, unlike their male counterparts, the Clonard young women were all in full employment, outside the community at 'the same rather poor city-centre store', in 'a shopping area on the sectarian interface which served both protestants and catholics'. They argued that the Clonard young women working in the shop 'would be extremely well placed to adopt innovations transmitted by persons on the edge of their network who in turn provided weak links with other communities' (p. 373), adding that it was likely, in the context of service encounters in the shop, 'that weak-tie encounters with back [a] users who transmit the innovation will greatly exceed in number strong-tie encounters with non-back [a] users'. In this situation, the large number of innovation-bearing weak ties could compete with and overcome the innovation-resisting strong ties.

The Milroys were eager to develop a structural picture of the relationships involved in transmitting linguistic innovations from close-knit network to close-knit network. In doing so, they describe the Clonard young women as *early adopters*, rather than *innovators*, because the young women actually had high scores on the network-strength scale, that is, they were highly involved in their close-knit network. The innovators were individuals who were marginal to the group, with weak ties to it and to other networks. For the innovation to be successfully transmitted and adopted by the Clonard young women, their encounters with the 'innovators' would have to be numerous, sustained, and frequent. Once the early adopters increase their use of the innovation, it is more likely to be picked up over time by others in the close-knit network to which they belong.

The Milroys' output using social networks proved influential, having a bearing on much variationist research, including, for example, Penelope Eckert's **community of practice** approach in Detroit in the 1980s (discussed in Chapter 10, section 10.5.2 of the present book), and Labov's work in Philadelphia (see Chapter 9, section 9.3), although Labov's 'leaders of linguistic change' are in the Milroys' model 'early adopters' (Milroy and Milroy, 1985, p. 369). The Milroys also think that the peripheral individuals that Labov noticed in the course of his work on Harlem, and who in the local AAVE were called *lames* (see Labov, 1973), are in their model 'innovators'.

7.3   Conclusion

This chapter has been an account of the type of dialect study inspired by the 1960s sociolinguistics of William Labov. This prolific field has focused on the interaction between linguistic variation and linguistic change, on the basis that 'considerable insight can be gained into the structure of language by the study of linguistic variables', and that 'language is located in the speech community, not the individual' (Labov, 1966/2006, p. 380). Chapters 9 and 10 continue this narrative by looking at the further developments in dialect study that occurred once variationist sociolinguistics had become firmly established. Before that, Chapter 8 adds another perspective to the story of dialect study after sociolinguistics: how did the 'traditionalists' react to the Labovians, and vice versa?

7.4   Very brief commentary on terms

Continuing the discussion on terms from the end of Chapter 6, I will here remark briefly on one or two more for what I have been calling in the chapter above *Labovian variationist sociolinguistics*. In order to include this field within the scope of his introduction to dialectology (1980), Malcolm Petyt called it *social and urban dialectology*; and in order to distinguish it from *regional dialectology*, Rajend Mesthrie (2000) called it *social dialectology* (as well as *variationist sociolinguistics*). Robert Bayley, in his contribution to the second edition of the *Handbook of Language Variation and Change* (Chambers and Schilling, 2013), simply called it *the quantitative paradigm*. Often such labels owe much to the context in which they occur.

7.5   What you can do

By this stage, we have encountered quite a battery of methods and tools by means of which we can extend the range of small projects available to us, especially projects focused on phonological variables. Elicitation tools have become more varied, enabling organized collection of different speech styles, from casual to formal. The aim of systematically comparing different social groups (according to class, ethnicity, age, gender) has become established, in order better to understand the nature of linguistic variation and change. The apparent-time method enables provisional conclusions to be drawn about your locality and the temporal variation of its usages; real-time comparisons with earlier surveys have become more feasible as the data collected by systematic studies has accumulated. You can apply the sociolinguistic methods encountered in the last two chapters to the ideas about lexicographical, grammatical, and linguistic-geographical work that I suggested in the 'What you can do' sections in Chapters 2 and 5. With the help of the Goldvarb program, Bayley (2013), Paolillo (2001), Tagliamonte (2006, 2012), and the Goldvarb Online Manual (http://albuquerque.bioinformatics.uottawa.ca/goldVarb/

GoldManual.dir/index.html, Rand and Sankoff, 1990), you can begin to take on practical variable-rule analysis. Among the free resources downloadable from the website accompanying Tagliamonte (2006) is an Interview Schedule that provides a comprehensive list of suggestions for questions that gather relevant biographical details about informants, including some that are useful if you want to build in a social-network viewpoint to your investigation. The innovations discussed in the last two chapters encourage a wider perspective on the processes of variation. For example, for my MA dissertation, a long time ago, using an SED-derived questionnaire, I compared a number of pronunciation variables in elderly speakers in two adjacent rural localities which were historically divergent, owing to differing degrees of contact between the English and Welsh languages in each community (see Penhallurick, 1982). Recently, one of my students revisited the same area to re-examine some of the same variables (Davies, 2016). Some changes were evident. It then seemed to us that a fuller explanation of the changes required a new apparent-time survey, plus the real-time comparison with the original survey, together with collection of social-network information on the new informants in order to gauge the changing nature of the area's communities.

Resources and further reading

As with the other chapters of this book, always include looking at the primary works in your plans for further reading. This is made easier if you have access to the paper and electronic resources of a university library, but there are other possibilities too. For example, used copies of Peter Trudgill's *Social Differentiation of English in Norwich* (1974a) can be picked up at reasonable prices from online retailers and selections from it are on Google Books. It is sensible to keep an eye on such options. The website of the Education Resources Information Center (ERIC) of the US Office of Education is a very useful gateway to open-access full-text resources, including important works by William Labov, Roger Shuy, Walt Wolfram and other American sociolinguists. The web-pages of these three scholars also offer information and free materials, as do the websites of David Sankoff and Gillian Sankoff. Time spent browsing Sali Tagliamonte's web-pages will be particularly fruitful. There you will find current versions of the Goldvarb program, reports on projects on varieties of Canadian English, downloads of publications, and links to resources. Tagliamonte's excellent practical guide to doing variationist research, including doing variable-rule analysis, *Analysing Sociolinguistic Variation* (2006), has a companion website which provides some data-collection resources and advice free of charge. Go to: http://www.cambridge.org/ca/academic/subjects/languages-linguistics/discourse-analysis/analysing-sociolinguistic-variation?format=PB#contentsTabAnchor.

The same author's *Variationist Sociolinguistics: Change, Observation, Interpretation* (2012), *Roots of English: Exploring the History of Dialects* (2013), and *Making Waves: The Story of Variationist Sociolinguistics* (2016) are also highly recommended. Go to this page in Tagliamonte's website for links to associated YouTube videos: http://individual.utoronto.ca/tagliamonte/books.html. The last of these titles has a companion website which features audio clips from the interviews with over 40 leading variationists that form the basis of the book. Tagliamonte is one of the contributors to another fine practical guide to the collection, analysis, and evaluation of data, *Research Methods in Language Variation and Change* (2013), edited by Manfred Krug and Julia Schlüter, which possesses a generous companion website, at: https://www.uni-bamberg.de/eng-ling/research-methods. For more overview of and insight into research on AAVE, see the following essay collections: *Sociocultural and Historical Contexts of African American English* (2001), edited by Sonja L. Lanehart, and *Diversity and Diachrony* (1986), edited by David Sankoff. As a first step in exploring the work of the biolinguists David W. Lightfoot and Ian G. Roberts on language variability, go to their respective home-pages, and for an approachable, brief introduction to the ideas of Noam Chomsky you could do worse than go to Chapter 17 of my textbook *Studying the English Language* (2010b). Follow this by watching Chomsky's lecture, 'What is Language and Why Does It Matter', to the 2013 Linguistic Society of America Summer Institute at the University of Michigan: https://www.youtube.com/watch?v=-72JNZZBoVw. To begin discovering more about the sociolinguistic perspective on other varieties of English across the world, investigate the following collections (and see also the works mentioned at the start of section 7.2.3): *Focus on South Africa* (1996), edited by Vivian de Klerk; *New Zealand Ways of Speaking English* (1990), edited by Allan Bell and Janet Holmes; *New Zealand English* (2000), edited by Alan Bell and Koenraad Kuiper; and *English in Australia* (2001), edited by David Blair and Peter Collins. As for the Tyneside Linguistic Survey, its surviving audio recordings are now part of the Diachronic Electronic Corpus of Tyneside English (DECTE), which combines these with data collected for subsequent projects from the 1990s to the present. For further information and details of how to acquire and use the corpus, go to: http://research.ncl.ac.uk/decte/index.htm. Two key researchers for the original TLS, John Pellowe and Val Jones, contributed an innovative analysis of 'Intonational Variability in Tyneside Speech' (of relevance to Chapter 4 of the present book as well) to the valuable early collection of British variationism, *Sociolinguistic Patterns in British English* (1978), edited by Peter Trudgill, which also includes one of the first essays by James Milroy and Lesley Milroy on social networks. Over three decades later, Lesley Milroy and Carmen Llamas review the extensive body of work in the social-network-analysis framework in an essay in the comprehensive overview of variationist research, *The Handbook of Language Variation and Change* (2013,

2nd edn), edited by J. K. Chambers and Natalie Schilling. A good single-author survey of variationism is Chambers's own *Sociolinguistic Theory* (2009, 3rd edn). John Paolillo's *Analyzing Linguistic Variation: Statistical Models and Methods* (2001) is a handy rarity: a book-length guide to statistical analysis aimed at variationists with no prior familiarity with statistics. It was written particularly with Varbrul in mind. David Sankoff provides a short exposition of variable-rule analysis in Volume 2 of the encyclopedic, three-volume *Sociolinguistics: An International Handbook of the Science of Language and Society* (2005, 2nd edn), edited by Ulrich Ammon et al. And William Labov's 'Building on Empirical Foundations' (1982a), a review of progress in developing a theory of linguistic change and a sequel to his key 1968 piece with Uriel Weinreich and Marvin Herzog, can be found in *Perspectives on Historical Linguistics*, edited by Winfred Lehmann and Yakov Malkiel.

8 The great argument in dialect study

This chapter includes the following:

- The story of the clash between dialectologists and sociolinguistics in the 1970s and 1980s.
- What happened after the conflict subsided.

8.1 Introduction

In 1982, a collection of essays entitled *Linguistic Controversies* was published, edited by David Crystal, and one of the essays was called 'Who is really doing dialectology?' (pp. 192– 208), written by K. M. Petyt. From the titles alone we learn that there was an ongoing dispute at this time about how best to study dialect. In fact, the dispute was fierce, and the title of the Petyt piece implies that he thought that the century-old discipline of dialectology was in need of redefinition. The dispute had started in the 1950s. It prepared the ground for the new variationist sociolinguistics of the 1960s. Through the 1970s and 1980s, old-style dialectologists and new-style variationist sociolinguists were at odds with each other. By the turn of the new millennium, dialectology had been transformed. We have looked at a variety of work from this period in Chapters 2, 5, 6, and 7 especially, but in this section I offer an overview of the Great Argument in Dialect Study of the late twentieth century, giving a flavour of what was said and by whom.

8.2 The big fight: edited highlights

In 1956, the American sociologist Glenna Ruth Pickford launched a broadside in the journal *Word*, with an article called 'American Linguistic Geography: A Sociological Appraisal'. Here are its opening sentences:

Long-term research projects cannot escape the risk of becoming anti-
quated in design before their completion. Some linguistic atlases are
notorious examples.

(Pickford, 1956, p. 211)

Pickford says that the scale of data collection for Georg Wenker's German
atlas 'practically ruled out publication' (p. 211), and she suggests that the
linguistic atlas projects of the United States and Canada 'originated as a somewhat mechanical imitation of European approaches' (p. 212), with the result
that they 'expended vast energies in order to supply answers to unimportant,
if not to nonexistent, questions'. Among the numerous memorable points
made by Pickford is her re-reporting of the tale (from Alexander, 1940, p. 42)
that the American atlas questionnaire could be so formidably long that 'one
informant became deaf during the interview and one died' (Pickford, 1956,
p. 214). (Alexander (1940, p. 42) makes it clear that these interviews took place
in a number of instalments over several days. By the time Petyt (1980, p. 115)
retells the story it has developed a little: 'in the course of this interrogation two
informants went deaf and one died (we are not told how many went mad)'.)
It is American linguistic geography that is Pickford's main target, while she
praises the Europeans for having 'helped to supply answers to important questions of human geography' (p. 211), and she quotes some of them favourably
in support of her argument. The Americans, however, in her view, had been so
preoccupied by geography that they neglected more important (in the American
context) social aspects of linguistic diversity such as 'the political structure of
American society, differences and interrelationships between rural and urban
communities, changes in the size and organization of the family, linguistic
snobbery, and a wealth of other aspects of American social life' (p. 212). One can
tell that this is the perspective of a sociologist rather than a philologist. Pickford
mentions (as a criticism) the pre-structuralist character of the American atlas
projects, but her main concerns are sampling and elicitation methods, in which
'existing American linguistic geography falls short of the standards of social-
science inquiry' (p 212). One could say that in this respect Pickford (slightly at
loggerheads with her own argument) criticizes the Americans for being too ambitious as well as too naive – for expanding their remit to urban areas and higher
social classes but without using the necessary modern methods. She strongly
advocates random sampling, hitherto untried in dialect study, and insists that
the linguistic geographers should take heed of advances made in sociology in
survey design, and should also as a matter of routine enlist assistance from
statisticians and mathematicians. In a paragraph echoed by Labov (1966/2006,
pp. 400–1), Pickford says, 'The important specification in a sample survey, to
insure reliability, is not how many, but how, informants are selected' (p. 218).

Pickford's criticisms resonated through the following half-century of dialect
study. Her 20-page article outlined a programme of action that was taken up in

sociolinguistics and geolinguistics from the 1960s onwards. Part of her point was that one cannot understand fully the nature of regional variation unless one also considers social and stylistic variation, group affiliations, and factors of human geography such as the complexities of the changing relationship between the urban and the rural. She says (p. 225), 'By using techniques developed for some of the most stable peasantries of Europe, American linguistic geographers have come to confusion in the country and chaos in the city.' This is something of a simplification of the issues that faced the early European dialectologists, and Pickford's appreciation of the dialectological history that preceded the American atlas projects is limited to casting them in a poor light when compared to the European projects (much as the review by John Wells quoted near the start of Chapter 3 of the present book compared the *Linguistic Atlas of England* very unfavourably with the American work). Pickford displays little awareness of the reasons why philological dialectology originated and developed in the way it did, and is too dismissive of the value of the traditional fieldwork interview. She also encouraged what turned out to be an enduring and unfair assumption that the philological pioneers of dialectology were simply unaware of the complexities of variation beyond the purely regional and rural. In another dimension of the multiverse, the transition from philology to linguistics and from dialectology to variationist sociolinguistics was no doubt smooth and straightforward, without even the necessity to use these different terms. But in ours, a schism came about.

Pickford was cited in 1976 by the linguist Gary N. Underwood in another oft-mentioned contribution to the debate which itself pulls no punches:

> Linguistic atlas methodology does not need to be modified; it needs to be abandoned and replaced by a new one if we are seriously interested in a realistic, accurate account of regional and social variation in American English. ... For a time I was preoccupied with modifying traditional methodology to overcome valid criticisms. I have since concluded that if we objectively examine the linguistic atlas methodology, the only reasonable conclusion is that the methodology is not salvageable.
>
> (p. 20)

Underwood is more aware than Pickford of the history and antecedents of North American linguistic geography, but like her he wishes to see its range expanded. Underwood wanted American dialectology to include investigation of a comprehensive stylistic range and many social variables, with more emphasis on grammar and on speaker evaluations of variation. Elicitation and sampling methods must be reformulated with this in mind, in Underwood's vision of the way forward, and random sampling should supplant the judgement approach.

By 1976, the first major American and British sociolinguistic surveys of single urban areas had already taken place, providing Underwood and dialect study in general with a new template. What Underwood advocates is extending this type of 'social dialect research' (p. 35) beyond individual urban localities to larger geographical areas. He also uses an indicative new label for the old linguistic geography – 'traditional, mainstream dialectology' (p. 35) – and argues that his predecessors had failed to acknowledge their own theoretical biases or even to recognize that such a thing as 'theory' exists in dialect study.

Applying sociolinguistic, quantitative methods to larger regional and national territories is a challenging pursuit, but a sizeable body of quite diverse work has subsequently been produced, as illustrated by the *Atlas of North American English* (*ANAE*; Labov, Ash and Boberg, 2006; discussed in Chapter 10, section 5 of the present book), by the marrying of numerical dialectometry with socio-linguistic surveys of regions of the Alps (see Dell'Aquila, 2010), by the Syntactic Atlas of Welsh Dialects project conducted under the Edisyn (European Dialect Syntax) umbrella (see http://www.dialectsyntax.org/wiki/About_Edisyn, plus http://lion.ling.cam.ac.uk/david/sawd/index.html and other pages of the website of David Willis), and by the computer-based treatment done by Kretzschmar and others of the 1930s data of the Linguistic Atlas of the Middle and South Atlantic States (LAMSAS; see Kretzschmar, 1996). All of these examples in their different ways answer the call to action made by Underwood in 1976.

Underwood's point about the lack of theory in dialect study refers to the not uncommon belief in 'traditional' dialectology that its practitioners were engaged purely in collecting and presenting data in a manner untrammelled by prior (or consequent) postulation, a belief perfectly summarized early on by A. J. Ellis, who said about dialectology in 1874 that 'word-collectors are not generally philosophic linguists', adding, 'Their business is to hand over the materials in a trustworthy form, unadulterated with superficial and super-fluous additions, containing what is wanted and *no more*, to those who *are* philosophic linguists' (Ellis, 1874, p. 450). This belief has not totally disap-peared. Neither is it totally absent from other forms of descriptive linguis-tics. It is also in itself a theorized viewpoint, one which chooses to overlook the transformations that occur in the process that turns naturally occurring speech into a survey's data (a process described many times in the present book). It is idealistic to suppose that 'the materials' can simply be handed over 'unadulterated' by the collecting and presenting process. But setting that to one side, the sociolinguistic revolution certainly provoked an intense debate about aims and methods, and about the nature of linguistic diversity, as well as a renewal of theorizing about linguistic change. These developments were accompanied also by attempts to bring into dialect research thinking and frameworks from structuralist and generative linguistic theory.

However, by the mid 1980s, the 'traditional dialectologists' were feeling beleaguered. In the published version of the first major British Labovian survey, Peter Trudgill had censured the 'rural dialectologists' (as he called them) for neglecting 'current speech forms' and 'the heterogeneity that is present even in rural speech communities' (Trudgill, 1974a, p. 4). Although he recognized the legitimacy of their interest in older dialect forms, Trudgill said that all the work of rural dialectology 'has left the linguist singularly ignorant about the way in which most of the people in Britain speak' (p. 4). In his view, the future lay with 'sociological urban dialectology' (pp. 3–5). In 1980, Trudgill and another leading sociolinguist, Jack Chambers, had the first edition of their textbook *Dialectology* published, which included two impressively durable and (to some) vexing expressions which were critical of the traditionalists: one is the authors' acronym for what they saw as the 'narrow choice' (Chambers and Trudgill, 1980, p. 35) of informant type in dialect geography, 'NORMs', that is, 'nonmobile, older, rural males' (p. 33); and the other is 'linguistic archaeology', in the sentence, 'Readers and researchers have questioned the relevance of what seems to be a kind of linguistic archaeology' (p. 35). These look like carefully chosen descriptions, but are rather unfair to traditional dialect geography, as well as to older rural males and archaeology. Further negative comments by Malcolm Petyt and John Wells contributed to the sense many 'traditionalists' had that they were up against a chorus of criticism. (See also Edwards, Trudgill and Weltens (1984), who made remarks about the 'theoretical weaknesses' (p. 9) and 'unrepresentative' (p. 10) data of the national surveys of British English dialects.) As we saw in Chapters 3 and 5, John Wells, in his reviews (1978, 1979) of the *Linguistic Atlas of England*, was forthright in condemning this chief publication of the Survey of English Dialects for being inadequate in its interpretation of data and behind the times in relation to contemporary linguistics. Petyt more subtly cast himself in the role of reporter on rather than participant in a controversy. He calls the *LAE* and *The Linguistic Atlas of Scotland* 'splendid' (1982, p. 192), and is not uncritical of Labov and Trudgill, questioning (1982, pp. 204–7) whether an urban population can be as easily comprehended as a single speech community as was claimed for NYC and Norwich, respectively, and using his own mid 1970s sociolinguistic survey of urban West Yorkshire (published in 1985) to underline his argument. However, in both his 1982 and his 1980 critiques, Petyt characterizes traditional dialectology as being fixated on 'genuine dialect', a label which he places between quotation marks, implying that it is a misguided concept, and around which he portrays the older work as restricted and outdated. He says (1982, p. 197), 'Such "traditional" dialectologists have searched for speakers of "genuine" dialect, but they have ended up by presenting a picture heavily biased towards a very small minority among the population', and which is therefore 'barely relevant' to the general linguistic situation. It is true that one can find in the literature instances of philological dialectologists rejecting informants or localities for being tainted by the effects of education and social change, but Petyt's characterization (like the 'NORMs' acronym) reduces and over-simplifies their work and their own understanding of it.

Increasingly, those who felt that they belonged in the 'traditional' camp responded. In 1972 (pp. 169–72), Hans Kurath had given a cool reception to Labov's 1966 NYC study, regarding his sampling methods as dubious, arguing that other areas of NYC had very different social structures from the Lower East Side, and suggesting that for the nearly half of the final set of informants who 'seem to be bilingual' (Kurath, 1972, p. 171) /r/-use might be affected by influence from Yiddish or Italian, which are rhotic languages (that is, /r/ can be articulated in all phonetic environments). In an article called 'Sociolinguistics and Linguistic Geography', published in 1973, Raven McDavid, Jr. and Raymond O'Cain make a plea for future collaboration between the two approaches but also defend American linguistic geography against its sociolinguistic critics, arguing that the non-random, non-statistical sampling was appropriate because the aims of the atlases required inform-ants who were 'strongly identified with their communities' (p. 144). (One can read Petyt's 'genuine dialect' expression into statements like this.) They also tackle what they believe to be some misconceptions by Pickford (1956), their case again resting on a belief that methods were in keeping with aims: 'it was not the aim of the Linguistic Atlas [of the United States and Canada] to break ground in the theory of social stratification but to record the usage of unequivocal social types in relatively stable communities in order to recon-struct as nearly as possible the regional patterns of American speech of a slightly earlier time' (p. 142). In 1977, the director of the Linguistic Atlas of the Upper Midwest, Harold B. Allen, called Pickford's article 'an attention-getting attack' (p. 228), adding (p. 229), 'To attack Atlas research because it is not directed at urban groups is something like finding fault with an electric toaster because it cannot fry potatoes.'

These sentiments – that traditional dialectology and linguistic geography had been misunderstood and misrepresented by sociolinguists, and that the aims and methods of the earlier approach were well matched and justifiable – were widely felt in 'traditional' quarters in the 1980s and 1990s, not just in North America but also in Britain. There was also a widespread view that the early work had paved the way and provided a context for the sociolin-guistic work. As McDavid and O'Cain (p. 147) put it: 'The nature of science is cumulative; like others, sociolinguists build on what has previously been learned.' In 1985, the two surviving editors of the *LAE*, Stewart Sanderson and John Widdowson, stated that the Survey of English Dialects (SED) had 'fulfilled its primary objectives', which were, firstly, 'to establish a linguis-tically comprehensive database for the speech of one particular stratum of society at an especially critical period of social and technological change';

secondly, to make that data available; and finally, 'to enable new comparative studies to be undertaken' (Sanderson and Widdowson, 1985, p. 39). Rather like McDavid and O'Cain, they called for a 'rapprochement between "traditional" dialectologists and sociolinguists, leading to an exchange of ideas and methods' (Sanderson and Widdowson, 1985, p. 46). In 2000, the dialectologist, linguist, and philologist Graham Shorrocks restated the achievements of linguistic geography, adding that 'it produced data that are of interest in other disciplines such as anthropology, history, sociology, folklore, industrial archaeology and material culture – indeed, the history of civilization generally' (p. 89). He also argued (p. 91) that the claim that sociolinguistic studies were more 'complete' than the earlier work (thanks to new sampling methods, a more statistical methodology, and informants drawn from a wider range of social groups) was suspect, because of a narrow focus in variationist work on small numbers of phonological variables.

The most basic conviction in this fightback by the 'traditionalists' was that the earlier work had been misconstrued. However, by naming their researches in such apparently definitive fashion, the linguistic geographers had unwittingly given a series of hostages to fortune: the national atlas projects and dialect surveys too easily gave the impression that they were more comprehensive and more complete than they aimed to be. For example, Harold Orton's project is called the 'Survey of English Dialects' and not the 'Survey of Traditional Rural English Dialects'. Judged as a national survey of all English dialects the SED looks limited. Judged as a national survey of the older rural dialects it looks enormous.

I will give the final word in this section to Yakov Malkiel (1914–98), a prolific and eminent Russian-born philologist who spent most of his working life in the United States. Malkiel turned his 1984 review of Petyt's *The Study of Dialect* (1980) and Chambers and Trudgill's *Dialectology* (1980) into a lengthy historical essay on dialect study and his reviewees' interpretations of it. He says that the techniques of the earliest European dialect geographers were necessary to 'the grand strategy' of amassing a great collection of data 'that could eventually be used for a lexis-based cultural history' (p. 42), and, while conceding tentatively that the SED might not have lived up to its promise (pp. 44–5, 59), he concludes that his reviewees are guilty of distorting the history of philological dialectology, especially its mid twentieth century stage (pp. 44, 59). Finally, he says that the sociolinguistic approach of 'urban dialectology' is *'one desirable line of inquiry'* (p. 59; italics in original), but one that it is not wide enough in scope to fulfil all interests.

In the second half of the twentieth century, then, the study of English dialects was riven into two camps. What happened next? Collaboration? Rapprochement? Or more dispute?

8.3   Whatever happened to dialectology?

Here is a little taste of the way things went. One of the successors of the SED was the Tape-recorded Survey of Hiberno-English Speech (TRS), a study in linguistic geography first set up in 1972 in Coleraine, Northern Ireland. In an essay published in 1985, its three directors, G. Brendan Adams, Michael V. Barry and Philip M. Tilling (the latter two had worked on the SED) pointed out that, because of practical limitations, 'A nationwide survey cannot do more than collect a limited amount of data from a limited number of informants' (p. 72). They say this in a passage which discusses the sociolinguistic criticisms made of the traditional linguistic geographers, adding pointedly, 'and in any case none of the sociolinguists has done a nationwide survey'. More dispute, then, by the look of it. But they also say (p. 72), 'The directors of TRS are well aware of the views of sociolinguists and have attempted, in some way, to reconcile their views with the "traditional" dialect survey method.' This they did by taking a judgement sample of one informant each from three different age-groups in rural localities (that is, three informants per locality) across the northern counties of Ireland, in order to produce a type of apparent-time but non-statistical overview of the regional distribution of features. Similarly, in Swansea, Wales, in the mid 1980s, the hitherto-philological Survey of Anglo-Welsh Dialects (SAWD) began fresh developments which were informed by the newer linguistics: fieldwork for an urban and more sociolinguistic (but non-statistical) phase of SAWD began in 1985 (I was the fieldworker; see Paulasto (2006) and Penhallurick (2012, 2013) for discussion of some of the data), and SAWD's director, David Parry, embarked upon a structuralist phonemic analysis of rural Welsh English dialects which was eventually published in 1999 (pp. 8–104, covering all 90 localities in the final SAWD rural network). Like the directors of the TRS, Parry felt that the criticisms of the linguistic atlases had been unjust in some ways, but he also recognized that there were other, newer lines of inquiry to follow.

Actually this trend had begun quietly in the 1960s. We have seen in Chapter 6 how William Labov's 1966 study of New York City was seen as the sociolinguistic breakthrough in dialect study. Much less well known is the sociolinguistic, quantitative survey of the small town of Cannock, Staffordshire, England by Christopher Heath published in 1980. In a beautifully clear and concise account, Heath carries out separate social and phonological analyses of his informants before rigorously comparing his two independently obtained sets of results statistically, in order to uncover significant correlations, such as the fact that men predominate in the 'broadest' linguistic class, that is, the most local and least RP-like pronunciation style. His informants were selected by means of a two-stage probability sample (Heath, 1980, pp. 9–12). First, on a map Cannock was divided into numbered 0.25-square-kilometre grids. Some of the squares were then adjusted in order to take account of uninhabited and low-population areas. This first stage constructed a valid population from which to select a random sample, and the second stage selected randomly one informant from each square. This was done as follows: a computer churned out numbers entirely randomly; it was calculated that the population for each square would not be more than 1200 adult individuals; a random number less than 1200 was assigned to each square; an alphabetical list of streets for each square was compiled and then cross-referenced to a list of inhabitants from the electoral roll, until the inhabitant with the randomly chosen number was reached. What is surprising here is that Heath's study was completed in 1971, in the form of a doctoral thesis submitted at the University of Leeds, home of the SED. The thesis had been supervised by Stanley Ellis, chief fieldworker for the SED. Furthermore, Heath's two-stage probability sample was carried out in 1967 (Heath, 1980, p. 10). It was based on a design used by the American dialectologist Charles L. Houck for a proposed sociolinguistic survey of the city of Leeds, and Houck took his procedure from that developed by the statistical geographer Christine Leigh at Leeds University in the early 1960s for her doctorate, that is to say, just to emphasize the point, it was contemporary with the MFY survey in New York City. Houck's design was published in 1968 in an edition of the journal *Leeds Studies in English* in honour of Harold Orton's seventieth birthday, and several essays in the collection provide signs that at the time the Leeds school was moving towards urban, sociolinguistic work. One essay in the collection by Raven McDavid, Jr. shows a positive face towards the 'new attention to urban problems', giving a list of American studies in which he liberally mixes sociolinguistic with older work (McDavid, 1968, pp. 43–5), a gesture which can be interpreted as indicating a desire to bring together the two approaches in some way. In this essay, McDavid wants to emphasize how the newer work builds on the older (a line of thought also evident in his 1973 essay with Raymond O'Cain). Also emerging from the Leeds school in the 1980s were structuralist studies, such as Peter Anderson's atlas of English dialects (1987), and some of David North's excursions into linguistic geography in Cornwall and the south-east of England (1982a, 1983, 1985). Let us also not forget Lee Pederson et al.'s *Linguistic Atlas of the Gulf States*, which began in 1968, in which the linguistic geography of the Linguistic Atlas of the United States and Canada was adapted to sociolinguistic concerns.

Thus while the dispute rolled on, some kind of fusion was also taking place. This is why we find the Welsh dialectologist Alan R. Thomas, in his Preface to the *Proceedings* of the 1987 Methods in Dialectology conference, saying: 'these Proceedings mirror the wide range of interests which characterise the practice of Dialectology as a research discipline, and well illustrate the dilemma of the pedant who seeks an inviolate line of demarkation between "dialectology" and "sociolinguistics"' (Thomas, 1988, p. v). These big international Methods conferences increasingly have become a showcase for the diversity of variationist approaches, and they also demonstrate amply in their content that one cannot now do dialectology without taking account of the interests, methods, and findings of the sociolinguistic revolution. Dialectology has expanded.

In the second edition of their *Dialectology* (1998), Chambers and Trudgill observed that 'Recently there has been a rapprochement' between dialectology and mainstream linguistics, which they ascribed with some bravado to 'the rise of sociolinguistics' which 'provided dialectologists with natural allies and broadened the constituency studying language variation' (p. 15). Once one has recovered from the phrase 'natural allies' (with allies like these who needs etc.), one begins to see the substance in this statement. Dialectology expanded by incorporating modes of research from structuralism and sociolinguistics, and this moved it back towards the centre of language study. By the end of the twentieth century, sociolinguistics was beginning to achieve a greater prominence in relation to the abstract linguistics of the Chomskyan, generative approach with which it had both locked horns and engaged since the early 1960s, and this also had the effect of hauling dialectology back towards the mainstream on the coat-tails of variationism. The massive advances of the late twentieth and early twenty-first centuries in information technology have reinvigorated descriptive linguistics generally, because of the hugely increased capacity for handling data, and handling it speedily too. Corpus linguistics, dialectology, and sociolinguistics are among the disciplines which are now simply more feasible as a result of the digital revolution.

But one might ask: is dialectology now subsumed into sociolinguistics? Have the two disciplines merged? One cannot really answer with a plain 'yes' (or 'no') to either of these questions. It is true that one occasionally comes across a general summary which refers to dialectology as a branch of sociolinguistics, but that is to ignore the long and still-relevant history of dialectology – a history that begins about a century before sociolinguistics came about. The name *dialectology* persists, as illustrated by the continuing Methods in Dialectology conferences which take place every three years, where one sees a vibrant field of study fuelled by modern technology engaging with all kinds of issues in regional, historical, and social language variation. In 2000, in a message from a quite other scholarly place (an essay entitled 'Dialectology and Deconstruction'), the literary theorist Nicholas Royle wrote: 'Far from seeing dialectology as an outmoded or dying discipline, one might see it as on the eve of another beginning, a quite different articulation and elaboration' (Royle, 2000, p. 113). With its 'love of memory and the archive', and its 'respect for the strangeness of remains, margins and the idiomatic' (p. 114), plus, I will add, the energy provided by its interest in the effects of progress on language and its embracing of the methodological benefits of technology, dialectology is rejuvenated. It can be distinguished from sociolinguistics up to a point, insofar as the remit of sociolinguistics generally continues to be broader than that of dialectology. If one considers the sociolinguistic equivalent of the Methods conferences, the Sociolinguistics Symposium, held every two years, one tends to find the dialect-study strand enclosed within a 'language variation and change' category, which sits alongside other themes such as language planning, language and gender, bi- and multilingualism, language and the workplace, discourse analysis, language and education, and more. That said, dialect study certainly leaks into these areas and others in sociolinguistics, such as language and class. It is particularly difficult to come up with definitions which clearly and firmly separate dialectology from the Labovian or variationist strand of sociolinguistics. Many have attempted this, including Alan Thomas in 1988 (p. v), despite his own warning against doing so. I will try a different tack. Picture the situation like this: imagine dialectology and variationist sociolinguistics as two countries, side by side on a map. The old country of Dialectology, with its long history, has after a difficult period eventually welcomed many immigrants from the neighbouring newer land of Sociolinguistics, to the extent that Dialectology has changed and one can no longer tell a Dialectologist from a Sociolinguist in the land of Dialectology. Furthermore, the border between the lands has been totally opened up and one can no longer be sure when one has crossed between the two. However, the further one travels into the territory of Sociolinguistics, the more one becomes aware of a growing difference in the terrain and people compared with Dialectology. I will halt the metaphor there before it gets out of hand, but I hope you follow my point. Put more straightforwardly and briefly, Alan Thomas was right in 1988: there is no longer an inviolate line of demarcation between the two areas.

Without wishing to complicate my metaphor or this summary any further, there is another point to make, which is that over time sociolinguists have softened their attitude towards the older dialectology, have used the materials from the older surveys in their books and projects, and have reconnected in new and intriguing ways with linguistic geography, particularly in the strands discussed in the final chapters of this book: **geolinguistics** and **perceptual dialectology**.

8.4   Brief commentary on terms

You will remember that in Chapter 6, section 2, I said that the names *dialectology* and *sociolinguistics* carry much significance and connotation in dialect study. Chapters 7 and 8 have continued to explain why this is the case.

In the earlier chapters of this book, I tried to avoid liberal use of the two terms, partly because some of the work discussed pre-dates both disciplines, and partly because I wished to avoid to some extent describing that work from a perspective inhabited by an awareness of the later split between the two approaches. Hence my use of the more neutral, thematic labels *lexicography* and *cartography* for Chapters 1 to 5.

Resources and further reading

The narrative that I have presented in the chapter above is informed by my memory of the academic environment that I found myself in as a novice in dialect study in the 1970s and 1980s, but it is mainly constructed from my reading of sources. Thus, and on the basis that you are already acquainted with the kind of works described in Chapters 1–5 of the present book, my further reading recommendations at this point are quite simple. Go to the primary sources, in the following order:

1. 'American Linguistic Geography: A Sociological Appraisal' (1956), by Glenna Ruth Pickford.
2. 'The Study of Language in its Social Context', that is, Chapter 1 of Labov (1966/2006, pp. 3–17).
3. 'Stratification on the Lower East Side of Manhattan', that is, the appraisal by Hans Kurath (1972, pp. 169–72) of Labov's NYC study.
4. 'Sociolinguistics and Linguistic Geography' (1973), by Raven McDavid, Jr. and Raymond O'Cain.
5. 'Introduction' to Trudgill (1974a, pp. 1–5).
6. 'American English Dialectology: Alternatives for the Southwest' (1976), by Gary N. Underwood.
7. Reviews (1978, 1979) by J. C. Wells of *The Linguistic Atlas of England*.
8. 'Dialect Geography', that is, Chapter 2 of the first edition (1980, pp. 15–36) of Chambers and Trudgill.
9. 'Who Is Really Doing Dialectology?' (1982) by K. M. Petyt.
10. 'Revisionist Dialectology and Mainstream Linguistics' (1984), by Yakov Malkiel.
11. 'Linguistic Geography in England: Progress and Prospects' (1985), by Stewart Sanderson and J. D. A. Widdowson.
12. 'Quantitative Areal Analysis of Dialect Features' (1996), by William A. Kretzschmar, Jr..
13. 'Purpose, Theory and Method in English Dialectology: Towards a More Objective History of the Discipline' (2000), by Graham Shorrocks.

Then read the chapter above again.

9 Perceptual dialectology

9.1 Introduction

How do we describe a dialect? How do we describe an accent? Well, the whole of this book is about how and why scholars have described dialects and accents – about the data they have collected and the methods they have used in order to analyse the vocabularies, grammars, and sounds of regional speech. But that is not what I am getting at right now. What I am asking is this: what adjectives do people use to describe regional dialects and accents? For example, do they on occasion describe them as *strong*?

> I'm Steph McGovern, I present the business news on BBC *Breakfast* and, yes, I have a strong northern accent. That last bit might not sound important, but every day, without fail, someone will comment on my voice. ... there are quite a few people out there who are nasty about the way I talk.
>
> You would think that after nearly two years in the job, people would be used to my Teesside tones. To be fair most are, but there are still some viewers who can't accept that someone with my accent can have a brain.
>
> (McGovern, 2013, p. 9)

This is from a short article subtitled 'I may be northern – but I'm not stupid', written by the journalist Stephanie McGovern for the UK television listings magazine *Radio Times* in July 2013. By describing her north-east English English accent as *strong* she is indicating that it is perceived as being markedly different from the standard accent of British English, **Received Pronunciation** or **RP**. The adjective *broad* is often used in the same way. The article also clearly implies that such a *strong* accent connotes a lack of intelligence in the speaker, that is, the accent is associated with stupidity, to put it bluntly. But surely it is the case that Stephanie McGovern is indeed not stupid?

> Stephanie McGovern is patently *very* clever, an excellent journalist and a thoroughly nice woman. But every time she appears I have to mute my television. Oh, Steph, that Teesside accent! It's dissonant music to my ears! … Strong regional accents on a national broadcaster are distracting, but a regional accent as marked as Stephanie McGovern's is overwhelming. It drowns out everything a reporter says.
>
> (Graham, 2013, p. 51)

This was the response to McGovern's piece a week later in the *Radio Times* by the journalist Alison Graham, from which we see that a regional accent can be described as *dissonant, distracting, marked,* and *overwhelming,* as well as *strong.* Graham tells us how she also once had a Middlesborough accent like McGovern's, but had then 'sloughed it off' after moving to London, 'because I wanted to be understood and was fed up with people asking me where I was from and treating me like some kind of sweet thing who'd done awfully well for herself' (Graham, 2013, p. 51). Coincidentally, earlier in 2013 the headmistress of the Sacred Heart Primary School in Middlesborough, Carol Walker, had made a similar point by instructing her pupils to avoid using certain local phrases, words, and pronunciations (see 'Language plea by Sacred Heart School, Middlesbrough', at: http://www.bbc.co.uk/news/uk-england-tees-21340029, 5 February 2013; accessed 17 November 2014). In a letter to parents which began, 'Many of our pupils have got into the habit of saying certain phrases incorrectly', Mrs Walker listed 11 linguistic features which she considered were adversely affecting her young students' ability to acquire **Standard English** (the standard dialect of British English), thereby damaging their future prospects. Her list indiscriminately lumped dialectal items (such as the second person pronoun *yous*) with simple writing errors (such as confusing *your* with *you're*). From Mrs Walker's letter we gather that a regional dialect or accent can also be described as *incorrect*. (Other schools in England made the news in 2013 after employing this approach, such as Colley Lane Primary School in Halesowen, West Midlands. See 'Colley Lane school in Halesowen bans Black Country dialect', 14 November 2013, at: http://www.bbc.co.uk/ news/uk-england-birmingham-24941692.)

In addition, accents can be *weird* and apparently measured and compared according to their degree of weirdness, as an online poll for the business and technology news website *Business Insider* demonstrated in August 2013. Using SurveyMonkey's Audience feature, *Business Insider* asked 1603 respondents in the United States to rate the 50 states of America according to a number of characteristics such as drunkest state, most arrogant state, state with the best and worst food, best and worst scenery, and so on. For each question each respondent had to reply naming a state other than their own, and the results were then shown in a number of online maps, in which the state with the highest number of votes was shaded most darkly, while states receiving almost no votes were shown in white.

"The map entitled 'Which state has the weirdest accent?' can be found at http://uk.businessinsider.com/poll-how-americans-feel-about-the-states-2013-8?r=US&IR=T, along with the other maps and commentary by Walter Hickey, dated 20 August 2013, in a piece called 'Politics: MAPS: A Poll Asked America Which States Were The Drunkest, The Hottest [that is, which had most attractive residents] And Which Had The Silliest Accents'. The states with the darkest shading in the 'weirdest accent' map are Massachusetts, New York, and New Jersey in the north-east, Minnesota in the north bordering Canada, and Louisiana and Alabama in the south. Texas, Arkansas, Mississippi, Tennessee, Kentucky, Georgia, West Virginia, and Maine also have some moderate shading. Alaska and California have some very light shading, but most of the western and midland states are very much at the whiter end of the spectrum. In other words, it is the southern and north-eastern states, plus some of the northern states around the Great Lakes, that Americans generally (as represented by the 1603 respondents) judge to have the weirdest English accents. Interestingly, one of the highest-scoring states, Texas, is also the clear winner/loser in the 'Which state is your least favourite?' map. The article does not give information on the geographical spread of the respondents, though it does make the point that SurveyMonkey 'was more accurate predicting the 2012 election than numerous traditional pollsters'."

A small number of the remaining 21 maps in the article have regional patterns fairly similar to the weirdest-accent map, especially the maps charting which state has the best food and which state is the craziest.

Other accents of English, including national accents, can be described as *weird* too, as evidenced by the contributor to answers.yahoo.com who asked 'Do you like the Australian accent?' while saying that it sounded 'weird' and 'a bit strange' (Melissa, 2007; accessed 17 November 2014). A few people responded to the question with descriptions of their own, such as *whiney as hell, sexy, awesome,* and *totally bogan – bogan* being a term in Australian and New Zealand English for 'An unfashionable, uncouth, or unsophisticated person, especially regarded as being of low social status' (*OED Online,* accessed 17 October 2013). And accents can be called *thick,* as the Glaswegian comedian Kevin Bridges points out:

> When you travel with a Scottish accent, it's kind of hard, nobody understands anything you're saying. ... No matter how hard you try and enunciate and use proper English there's still somebody from Leamington Spa ... [puts on posh English accent] 'We saw you on the television, I didn't quite understand everything you were saying ... you've got a really thick Scotch accent.' Whilst to someone in Scotland they'll say, 'We seen you on telly talking like a fuckin' bender ... Care to explain yerself?'

> (*The Story So Far ...,* DVD, 2010)

Okay, point made. From *strong* to *talking like a fuckin' bender,* there are lots of ways to describe regional accents and dialects, and the illustrations above merely make up a small sample. What do we make of this phenomenon?

9.2   A very, very (very) short history of attitudes towards regional accents and dialects of English

We could say that most of the views above are subjective evaluations, especially when compared with the scholarly analyses mentioned in the rest of the present book. Some, like *dissonant* and *distracting,* or *weird* and *sexy* seem to be individual and aesthetic judgements. Some comment on the intelligibility of the accent from the perspective of the outside listener, that is, from the viewpoint of those who do not speak the accent under consideration. This perspective is influenced also by an awareness that a *thick* or *broad* or *strong* or *strange* accent is one which is by a distance different from a standard accent such as RP. But these evaluations are also all outcomes of a deeply ingrained cultural knowledge of the social connotations of accents and dialects, a knowledge connected to the historical segregation of non-standard from Standard

English. Such evaluations might also be expressions of communal or political rivalries. They might not be judgements of the given accent or dialect pure and simple. For example, the maps in the *Business Insider* survey show a good number of negative results for Texas, suggesting that its fairly high score on the weirdest-accent map is just one aspect of a bigger image question (though it does score well on the best-food map). The first recorded evaluation of a regional form of English can be seen in the context of regional and political rivalry. This was in a historical chronicle written in the early twelfth century by the monk William of Malmesbury (*Deeds of the English Pontiffs*). William described the speech of the north-east of England, 'most particularly at York', as 'uncouth and strident' to the extent that 'we southerners can understand none of it' (William of Malmesbury, 1125, edition of 1870, p. 209; translation from the Latin by Willmott, from Penhallurick and Willmott, 2000, p. 27). A north/south rivalry is pretty evident in this. Less obvious is the connection to the political rivalry of William's time between the Christian sees of York and Canterbury. William's allegiance was to the see of Canterbury (Penhallurick and Willmott, 2000, pp. 28, 35). This twelfth-century opinion on northern dialect gives us an idea of just how deep-rooted the social connotations of regional speech are. Figure 9.1 shows this short passage by William as translated into English in 1387 by John of Trevisa, here over two pages from a 1527 manuscript.

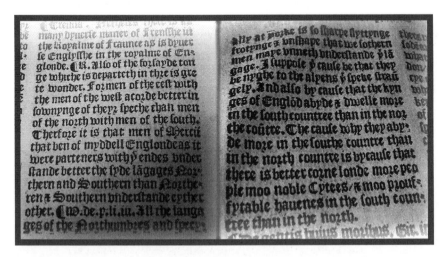

Figure 9.1   William of Malmesbury's early-twelfth-century comments on north-eastern English, as translated by John of Trevisa, from a 1527 manuscript of the latter's English version of the *Polychronicon*.

I mention William of Malmesbury's remarks in Chapter 1 of the present book, where I also chart the role that lexicographers of dialect played from the sixteenth to the nineteenth centuries in the gradual distinguishing of a Standard English from regional Englishes. That slow segregation was an unregulated and unrelenting process in which class prejudice and communal rivalries had a say. Slowly but surely, a prestigious variety of English was set up and identified, a variety associated with the higher social classes of south-east England, with formal writing and speaking, and with a good education. I also mention Edmund Coote in Chapter 1. He was a contributor to the process and belongs to the same line of commentators represented more recently by headmistress Carol Walker from Middlesborough. Coote was headmaster of a grammar school in Bury St Edmunds, East Anglia, at the end of the sixteenth century. In 1596, he published a spelling manual, *The English Schoole-Master*, in which he warned against the detrimental effects that local pronunciations could have on his students' writing. He gave an extended and mixed list of linguistic items, which included some dialectal forms, under the sub-heading 'Corrupt pronunciation and writing' (1596, pp. 30–1). See Figure 9.2, from which we see that *barbarous* is (historically) another adjective used to describe regional dialect.

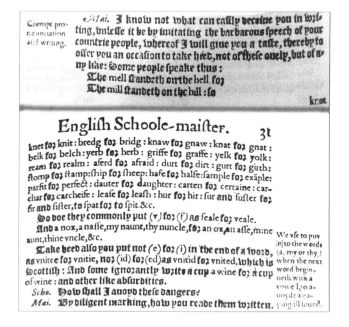

Figure 9.2   Edmund Coote's list of 'Corrupt pronunciations' from *The English Schoole-Master* (1596, pp. 30–1).

By the start of the twentieth century, Standard English was the recognized prestige dialect of English, particularly in Britain, and a prestige accent had also emerged, named **Received Pronunciation (RP)** by the phonetician Daniel Jones in 1926, although A. J. Ellis had talked of 'the theoretically received pronunciation of literary English' as early as 1869 (p. 13). As Raymond Hickey states in his editor's Preface to *Standards of English* (2012, p. xxi), speakers of English around the world now have a notion of Standard English, an understanding albeit informed by their local Englishes and by emerging local standards. He says (p. xxi), 'The reality across the anglophone world is that there is a plurality of standard varieties of English' (and Hickey's volume explores these standards in detail). Once again, dialect lexicography is a major factor in the recognition of these standard varieties, as manifested in the production of national dictionaries of, for example, American English, Australian English, Canadian English, New Zealand English, and South African English (see Chapter 2, section 2.2.3). This centuries-long process of standard(s)-creation in English, then, confers prestige upon the selected variety, and in 1966, in William Labov's study of the English of New York City, prestige was implicated in that old quest in dialectology, the pursuit of a theory of linguistic change.

9.3   Finding covert prestige

On the subject of prestige and linguistic change, Labov has made some striking, intriguing statements, such as: 'We must assume that people in New York City want to talk as they do, yet this fact is not at all obvious in any overt response that you can draw from interview subjects' (Labov, 1966b, p. 108); and, 'Evaluations of language are usually not available to conscious elicitation, but are readily and consistently expressed in terms of personality judgments about different speakers' (Labov, 1972a, p. 310); and, 'Subjective evaluations of social dialects are remarkably uniform throughout the speech community' (Labov, 1972a, p. 310). From such statements, we infer that Labov believes that individuals are motivated to use and acquire linguistic features which at some psychological level they find desirable, and that at any given point in time there is a homogeneous communal understanding of what such features are. This is a communal understanding which individuals might not be fully and consciously aware of (though they might have explicit opinions about the speakers using the features, and about speakers who do not use them), but its existence could potentially be proved by means of carefully designed elicitation tests, such as the subjective reaction and self-evaluation tests he used in his 1966 New York City study (see Chapter 6, section 4). These desirable linguistic features have social prestige. The **prestige** can be **overt** and publicly acknowledged, as is the case with standard features, which are associated with speakers of higher social class and of advanced education. To be sure, members of the community do have some conscious awareness of overtly prestigious features. Or the prestige can be **covert** and unproclaimed, as might be the case with non-standard features, which can connote commonality and friendliness. Following Rajend Mesthrie's summary (2009, p. 89), we can say that overtly prestigious features are associated with social status and covertly prestigious features with social solidarity. The term **covert prestige** was first used by Labov at one of the earliest sociolinguistics conferences, held at the University of California, Los Angeles, in May 1964, the proceedings of which were published as Bright (1966). Responding to a question following his paper, Labov notes that in the case of the English language 'the socio-economic structure confers prestige on the middle class pattern associated with the more formal styles'. He continues:

> One can't avoid the implication that in New York City we must have an equal and opposing prestige for informal, working class speech – a covert prestige reinforcing this speech pattern. ... I think that we can tap the more covert subjective responses by different types of subjective response tests by using various ingenious devices. We can, for example, investigate the possibility that a social value of masculinity is attributed to the casual style of working class speech in New York City.

> (Labov, 1966b, p. 108)

Prestigious linguistic features, both overt and covert, are potentially desirable to speakers in their performance of language for a range of reasons, from professional advancement to in-group membership. In Labov's thinking, prestige is a force which can stimulate linguistic change, as groups of speakers move towards prestigious variants. They can also, as a corollary of this, move away from un-prestigious or stigmatized forms. What Labov required were subtle methodological techniques (or 'ingenious devices') which would objectively show the influence and effects of prestige, believing as he did that simple direct questioning of his informants would be only minimally informative. Note once again his comment which I quoted in Chapter 6: 'The type of evaluative behavior which we wish to measure is more systematic, more completely internalized than any reply we might elicit by the overt discussion of speech' (Labov, 1966/2006, p. 266). After a further 35 years' work on linguistic change, Labov still held this view: 'direct questions are the weakest way of determining underlying attitudes towards a language or dialect' (Labov, 2001, p. 221). Such methodological techniques would be particularly useful in the attempt to reveal covert prestige, which by definition is prestige that is hidden.

Labov's postulation of the existence of covert prestige is akin to the way that physicists postulate the existence of dark matter, which is a hidden, invisible force whose presence is assumed because of effects that can be observed. Covert norms, if they exist, might represent 'adherence and loyalty to local norms and values', or they might be 'symbolic of masculinity or toughness', or 'expressing a warmer, more personal, more human, or more friendly approach to life' (Labov, 2001, pp. 115–16). But as Labov himself put it (private correspondence, 2008b), 'It's very easy to assert that it [covert prestige] exists, but it's another thing to prove that it's there.' Things become simpler when covert prestige goes overground, as in the name of the baked goods and coffee chain *Dunkin' Donuts*, which 'asserts with the apostrophe that *dunkin' donuts* taste better than *dunking doughnuts*' (Labov, 2008b), or in the multi-million-pound 'Every little helps' tele-ad campaign run in the UK by the supermarket chain Tesco, which has used voice-overs from an array of celebrities, many of whom either (i) have or (ii) are known for having or (iii) are known for playing characters who have a non-standard, regional British English accent. Both of these examples are public affirmations of the allure and (in some contexts) superiority of non-standard forms. On the other hand, what terminology do you use to distinguish covert from overt prestige once the former is openly acknowledged? Perhaps by talking of 'opposing values' (Mesthrie, 2009, p. 89) or 'competing value systems' (Labov, 2008b).

In NYC in 1966, although Labov believed that covert norms exerted a significant influence, his evaluation tests did not reveal the proof he sought. Another project that Labov was involved in between 1965 and 1968, in the Harlem neighbourhood of Manhattan, NYC, turned up some evidence of covert norms (see Labov et al., 1968b). Here, the lower working class respondents (unlike the middle and upper working class respondents) did not rate middle class speech as friendly, suggesting a covert norm in operation on the 'friendship' scale (see also Labov, 1972a, p. 250). It was Peter Trudgill, in his 1968 research on Norwich City, who claimed to have found conclusive evidence of covert prestige at work: 'we now have some objective data which actually demonstrates that for male speakers WC [working class] nonstandard speech is in a very real sense highly valued and prestigious' (Trudgill, [1972/]1983, p. 172). In his production data, Trudgill observed male speakers using a non-standard variant, such as a final [n] in *walking* (rather than standard [ŋ], that is, *walkin'* rather than *walking*), more than female speakers (1983, p. 171). This pattern was repeated in most of the other 19 variables considered for this study by Trudgill in Norwich (p. 172), showing a correlation of nonstandard pronunciations with male speech. Using an adapted form of Labov's self-evaluation test, Trudgill examined informants' reactions to a handful of variants. Whereas in NYC Labov had found speakers over-reporting their use of overtly prestigious variants, in Norwich Trudgill found male speakers tending to under-report, that is, they claimed to use a less (overtly) prestigious variant than the one they actually used (Trudgill, 1983, p. 176). Most female speakers in Norwich tended to over-report their use of overtly prestigious variants (pp. 176–7). Trudgill describes this as 'the objective evidence which demonstrates that male speakers, at least in Norwich, are at a subconscious or perhaps simply private level very favourably disposed towards non-standard speech forms' (p. 177). He argues (p. 178) that this shows that many Norwich males are aiming at covert norms associated with non-standard working class speech, and he suggests that this might be connected to a greater sense of class consciousness and a comparative lack of acceptance of middle class models in 1960s British society than in American. The Norwich data also displayed some evidence of covert prestige affecting younger female speakers (pp. 182–3).

Although the concept of covert prestige or 'competing value systems' remained important in Labov's developing research on linguistic change, especially his research on the type of change he called change from below the level of conscious awareness of speakers, he became doubtful that subjective reaction tests and self-evaluation tests could in themselves provide enough proof of the existence of covert norms (Labov, 2001, pp. 220, 512). The general, conscious consensus of communities' attitudes 'is that language should not change, and that any changes that have occurred are bad' (Labov, 2001, p. 222). And yet change occurs and continues to occur, and furthermore it does not always move in the direction of overt norms. 'We infer', reiterates Labov in 2001 (p. 222), 'that there must be hidden or covert values that motivate change.' He continues, 'But so far, it must be admitted that the evidence for those underlying values is weak.' This is Labov speaking in part two of his commanding three-volume, 1700-page *Principles of Linguistic Change*, published between 1994 and 2010. In this grand work on sound change, Labov draws on the combined findings of the field of variationist sociolinguistics that he helped to found in the 1960s, including the results of the Project on Linguistic Change and Variation (LCV) in Philadelphia, which he led in the 1970s, and the *Atlas of North American English*, based on another major survey led by Labov, this time in the 1990s. The LCV sought to discover exactly which group of speakers were the leaders of linguistic change in the Philadelphia speech community. By targeting the sound changes that research had identified, once again correlating the linguistic data with social structure, and then focusing in detail on the speakers surveyed, on their social positions in their local neighbourhoods, as well as on their social interactions, and by using a modified form of the **social network theory** developed by the sociolinguists James Milroy and Lesley Milroy from the 1970s onwards (see Chapter 7, section 7.2.3.2 above), Labov identifies 'upwardly mobile female nonconforming speakers' (2001, p. 518) as leading change from below in Philadelphia. These speakers are 'those women who have the highest degree of social interaction on their local blocks, and the greatest proportion of their friends and contacts outside the block' (2001, p. 501), and who also are individuals who in their youth 'adopted the linguistic symbols of nonconformity' (p. 501), picking up (in Labov's view) variants from outside their immediate community, and maintaining and developing these 'in their upward path later in life' (p. 501). At first such a variant is perceived as characteristic of youthful and 'emphatic, less monitored speech' (p. 517), then later the female adopters spread the use of the variant through their own speech community. They adopt the new variant because of their network ties outside the block and because they have a nonconforming attitude, and they lead change within the block because of their many social interactions there and because they are followed by other upwardly mobile nonconforming speakers. These women are from the second and third generations of newly arrived ethnic groups and they 'are not afraid to defy social conventions, and [are] social activists, ready to intervene when they see something going wrong and quick to respond to perceived injustice' (Labov, 2012, location 413). Ultimately the change from below hits public consciousness, and irregular correction begins as the new variant competes with the existing overtly prestigious variant (Labov, 2001, p. 518). These leaders of linguistic innovation are also involved in the momentous series of vowel sound changes occurring around the Great Lakes region of the United States known as the Northern Cities Chain Shift, which is discussed further in Chapter 10, section 10.5 of the present book. (Remember also, as noted at the end of Chapter 6, that Labov's 1966 survey of New York City found women to be especially sensitive to the connections between linguistic variants and upwards social mobility, though the variants in question there were considered to have overt prestige. And one more point: in the Milroys' discussions of social networks, they argue that stable, close-knit, working class communities provide an environment in which non-standard linguistic features are fostered and maintained, offering researchers a different explanation for the persistent vitality of these forms from that presented by the covert-prestige perspective.)

9.3.1   The matched-guise technique and accommodation theory

Meanwhile, back in the 1960s, Labov's new 'ingenious devices' for examining speakers' hidden, internalized feelings about language variation helped stimulate a new strand of dialect study. Sociolinguists (including Labov in Harlem and Philadelphia) started to make use of a methodological procedure devised in the late 1950s by the psychologist Wallace Lambert and his colleagues at McGill University in Montreal, Canada, which was designed to tap into subjects' unconscious attitudes towards languages and dialects. This was the 'matched-guise' technique, in which listeners/respondents were exposed to short audio recordings of the same passage of speech performed by the same speaker in different guises, that is, speaking different languages such as Canadian English and Canadian French (Lambert et al., 1960; Anisfeld and Lambert, 1964; Lambert, 1967) or Arabic and Hebrew (Lambert et al., 1965), or different dialects such as African-American English and Standard American English (Tucker and Lambert, 1969). The respondents or 'judges' (as Lambert called them) were not told that the speaker was in fact the same speaker performing in different guises, and the speaker's guises were interspersed with other speakers' performances of the passage. The aim, from the researcher's point of view, was to eliminate unwanted variables from the experiment, so that the only variable being rated by the judges was the language or the dialect used in each recording, and not the speaker or the subject matter of the passage, for that was the same for each matched guise. The experiment required a speaker who was able to perform each guise – each language or dialect – with native-speaker proficiency. The speech passages would be rated by the judges according to their perceptions of the speaker in terms of traits such as friendliness, honesty, intelligence, and the like. In their early work on English and French in the greater Montreal region of Canada, for example, Lambert and his colleagues found that both English Canadian and French Canadian judges 'saw a bilingual person using his French language guise as being less intelligent, less trustworthy, shorter and less attractive (and so forth) than he was when using his English language guise' (Lambert, 1979, p. 187). From this we can see that the technique has the potential to expose the hidden connotations attached by communities to different languages and dialects. In Lambert's 1969 collaboration with Richard Tucker, which tested a number of northern, southern, and educated varieties of American English, it was found that the majority of respondents rated the so-called Network Standard American English most favourably on all of the 15 traits used in the survey (including, for example, upbringing, ambition, and 'faith in God', as well as the three mentioned above), whereas there was a racial split among the respondents regarding the least-favoured dialect.

Matched-guise studies by sociolinguists and social psychologists followed in other countries, including Australia (Ball, 1983, and Ball et al., 1989, for example), and Britain, where a prolonged investigation of attitudes towards linguistic varieties has been carried out by a group of scholars based at Cardiff University's Language and Communication section, among them Justine Coupland, Nikolas Coupland, Peter Garrett, Howard Giles, and Angie Williams. In the early 1970s, Howard Giles undertook several studies of evaluations of accents of British English (reviewed in Giles and Powesland, 1975, pp. 28–37, 68–73). In one study (Giles, 1971), groups of judges from Somerset and South Wales rated the matched guises of two speakers performing a passage in RP, Somerset, and South Welsh English accents. While the RP speakers were perceived as more ambitious, determined, industrious, intelligent, and self-confident, the non-standard speakers were perceived to have more personal integrity and greater social attractiveness (Giles and Powesland, 1975, p. 68). Giles and Powesland (p. 69) imply that there might be a mutually sustaining relationship between non-standard accents and such positive traits. Although they do not express this view in terms of covert prestige, one can see a potential connection between the two ideas. Howard Giles went on to become Professor of Psychology and Brain Sciences at the University of California, Santa Barbara, and is also known for developing the 'social psychological model of speech diversity' (Giles and Powesland, 1975, pp. 154–81) known as **accommodation theory**. Taking its cue from John L. Fischer's proto-sociolinguistic notion of a 'comparative idiolectology' (1958, p. 487; see my Chapter 6, section 6.3), accommodation theory attempts to codify aspects of linguistic diversity that arise in interpersonal communication. Put more simply, it attempts to model how we change our speech as a result of our perceptions of the person we are conversing with. It is a theory that emerges quite naturally from the matched-guise body of work. It also links with the theme of linguistic change.

Now, interpersonal communication is a very various phenomenon, and since its first proposals in the early 1970s (see Giles, 1973; Giles et al., 1973; Giles and Powesland, 1975) the accommodation model has specified numerous ways and circumstances in which accommodation would or would not happen, but its basic insights are as follows. A speaker wishing to accommodate towards her or his interlocutor, that is, actively to reduce the social distance between them, might adjust her or his own speech so that it sounds more like that of the interlocutor. This can be a conscious act, but it need not be. Where different languages are involved, one speaker – for example, an English speaker – might attempt some words or sentences in the language of the interlocutor – for example, a Greek speaker. Where different accents or dialects of the same language are involved, one speaker, such as a non-standard English speaker, might modify her or his accent or dialect in the direction of the other, such as an RP speaker. This could happen, say, in the context of a job interview, where the non-standard-speaking interviewee wants to gain the approval of the RP-speaking interviewer by moving towards the more prestigious accent. This is an example of **upward accent convergence** (Giles and Powesland, 1975, pp. 174–5). When an RP speaker accommodates towards a non-standard speaker, as he or she might in the context of a conversation in a pub or bar, this would be **downward convergence** (pp. 174–6). As well as convergence, **divergence** is possible. This occurs when a speaker wishes to emphasize her or his distinctive identity in relation to an interlocutor, to increase the social distance between them, and divergence too occurs in upward and downward versions, in the model proposed in 1975 by Giles and Powesland. Figure 9.3 gives their diagram of these basic types of convergence and divergence, with **acrolect** referring to the most prestigious speech form and **basilect** to the least prestigious.

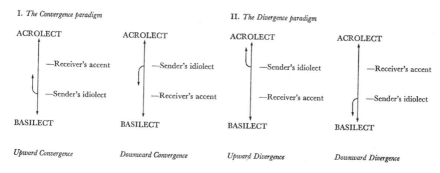

Figure 9.3 'Directions of accent mobility', an early accommodation model from Giles and Powesland (1975, p. 175).

There are numerous ways in which to modify this basic model. For example, convergence can be symmetrical, that is, both parties can converge towards each other. Downward convergence might be interpreted by the listener as condescending and she or he might respond negatively. Speakers might vary their accommodation strategies during the course of an interaction, and of course a conversation involving more than two participants requires a more elaborate model. Nevertheless, accommodation theory adds a signifi- cant interactional component to dialect study, as well as a further twist to Labov's observer's paradox – conversations between informants and dialect investigators do not possess any immunity from convergence and divergence. Furthermore, one can see accommodation as a miniature, snapshot instance of linguistic change, and one can see large-scale linguistic change (whether it involves languages, dialects, or particular features) as an accumulation of accommodation events. As a group phenomenon over a period of time, convergence may lead to a decline in the use of or even the loss of a feature or a dialect or a language, while divergence may sustain minority forms.

9.4   Perceptual dialectology

By the late 1990s, the Cardiff group of scholars had moved on from the highly controlled recordings of the matched-guise approach, instead playing to respondents recordings of authentic speakers telling personal narratives (Garrett et al., 2003; Giles and Bourhis had used a similar method as early as 1975), on the basis that matched-guise recordings are open to the charge of being idealized and stereotypical representations of accents and dialects. This modification is sometimes known as the **verbal-guise technique**. The Cardiff group were also exploring the potential of another strand of attitudes research, **perceptual dialectology** (Coupland et al., 1999; Garrett et al., 2003). The best-known practitioner and proponent of the perceptual dialectology of English is the American linguist Dennis R. Preston. In 1989 (p. 3), Preston succinctly pointed out what he considered to be a conspicuous omission in the methodology of most language attitude research: 'there are few studies in which the amazingly simple task "tell me where you think this voice is from" was made a part of the research'. In other words, although respondents were being asked to rate different accents and dialects according to certain criteria like friendliness and intelligence, the accent/dialect categories themselves (for example, Mississippi, Somerset, South Welsh, and so on) were chosen and identified by the researcher. Were respondents working with the same mental pictures of accent/dialect categories and areas? 'This', Preston added (1989, p. 4), 'is surely one area where overt linguistic knowledge should supplement the elicitation of covert responses.' The for-the-most-part unacknowledged assumption by investigators had been that respondents and researchers possessed essentially the same dialect taxonomy, that is, that they had in mind pretty much the same catalogue of regional speech areas. We could go further and say that even the existence of this assumption had not been greatly explored. Preston's message was one of, well, hang on, it is about time we looked into these matters. Perceptual dialectology aims to find out directly from speakers themselves about their knowledge and awareness of dialect areas. It is a form of **folk linguistics**, in which the 'folk' are all those not trained in specialist language study. In fact, although Preston (2010b, p. 121) believes that it was he who coined the term *perceptual dialectology* in 1981, he subsequently expressed (2010b, p. 121) a preference for **folk dialectology**, which makes clearer the relationship with folk linguistics. However, *perceptual dialectology* is the label that has stuck. In addition, Preston claims (1989, p. 4) an allegiance in spirit with the **ethnography of speaking**, that brand of anthropological sociolinguistics that stresses the study of language within the context of cultural norms and beliefs (see also my Chapter 6, section 6.3).

Perceptual dialectology is concerned with 'what people believe about the distribution and character of linguistic objects in space rather than the facts of such distribution' (Preston, 2010b, p. 121). It is concerned with speakers' beliefs about the geographical patterning of speech, their beliefs about standard varieties and notions of correctness, their perceptions about degrees of difference between dialects, and their accounts of how such beliefs and perceptions arise and persist (Preston, 1989, pp. 2–4). Specific lines of enquiry have asked respondents to hand-draw maps of dialect areas, to rate and locate dialect areas, and to rate individual speakers and identify where they come from by listening to voice samples. Once again there is a link with the study of linguistic change. Preston argues (1989, p. 2) that folk perceptions of the English language, its use, and its varieties (standard and non-standard) are likely to 'have influence on the shape of the language itself, that is, be important factors in change'. The perceptual stance can also encourage those who *are* trained in specialist language study to examine their own assumptions about the taxonomy of dialect areas. As Ronald Butters put it (1991, p. 296) in a review of Preston (1989), this work raises the question 'of just how much dialectologists' supposedly scientific determination of dialect areas may be artifacts of the dialectologists' own cultural biases and even the semiotics of the labels they select'. In support of this, Butters compares the different semantic effects of scholars' labelling the chief dialect regions of the eastern United States as *Northern, North Midland, South Midland,* and *Southern* (the older, conventional names) compared with *Upper North, Lower North, Upper South,* and *Lower South* (as decided by Craig Carver (1986, 1987)). The former taxonomy gives a greater impression of geographical continuity than the latter. Perceptual dialectology, then, has the potential to call into question some fundamental assumptions in dialect study and to provide a new kind of valuable data on linguistic diversity and linguistic change.

Now for some illustrations of perceptual dialectology.

9.4.1   Mental mapping in perceptual dialectology

Dennis Preston's published output in perceptual dialectology began in 1981, with a project inspired by the device of **mental mapping** as practised in **perceptual geography**, an approach which had been around since the early 1960s, paying attention to non-experts' sensitivity to their geographical environment. In particular, Preston cites (2010a, p. 184; 1989, pp. 14–15, 22, 48) the geographers Peter Gould and Rodney White's *Mental Maps* (1974), which describes, justifies, and exemplifies their discipline's interest in studying people's mental images of space and place. They are especially interested in how an individual's perception of the distance between themselves and a given place contributes to their mental imagery of geographical space (Gould and White, 1974, p. 17). For example, a positive perception can reduce the effect of distance, 'just as you will travel further to visit a good friend than you will to visit a more casual acquaintance' (p. 17). By getting individuals to externalize their mental imagery of specific places (especially their likes and dislikes of these places), Gould and White believed that they could arrive at a better understanding of spatial behaviour and population movements (1974, pp. 17–18). Such knowledge could have practical benefits, such as informing urban planning. An individual's state of knowledge about a given place clearly is a major factor in their mental image of that place, and this means that communal and cultural beliefs, as well as the influence of the mass media, all have some relevance to mental mapping. In his early work, Preston sought to import this research programme into dialectology, and to do so by using a very

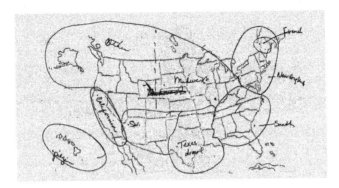

Figure 9.4   A Hawai'i respondent's hand-drawn map of US regional speech, as reproduced in Preston (2010a, p. 185).

straightforward methodology: have individuals draw a map. While he was a visiting professor at the University of Hawai'i at Manoa in 1980–81, he gave out a map of the United States showing only state lines to 35 students (not linguistics students) and asked them to draw on it and label whatever dialect regions they believed to exist (see Preston 1981, 1982, 1989). Figure 9.4 is a map filled in by one Hawai'i respondent.

Notice that the hand-drawn boundaries do not always follow state lines, and include some interesting labelling. Figure 9.5 is another example of this kind of map from a project later in the 1980s, this time mapping the American dialect regions from the viewpoint of respondents in south Indiana and south-eastern Michigan.

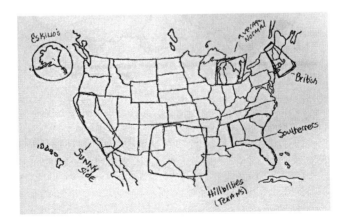

Figure 9.5   Hand-drawn map of US dialect regions by a young, university-enrolled south-eastern Michigan respondent (from Preston, 2010b, p. 129 (Map 0610 in Lameli et al., 2010b)).

It is in the nature of such an exercise that the focus is on the individual's perceptions, and such maps are on the face of it very individual and idiosyncratic. Yet they are also permeated by cultural, communal, and stereotypical opinion, and furthermore each one can be seen as the expression of an individual contribution to communal opinion. By 1988, Preston had developed techniques for producing composite maps combining individual hand-drawn maps. Doing this by hand, by copying each map's outline of the given regions onto a separate, composite map and keeping a tally where there was bundling of perceptual isoglosses was illuminating but cumbersome, and in fact not as informative as Preston required (1988, pp. 378–82). Like a true sociolinguist, Preston wanted to perform quantitative analyses, and to scrutinize his data according to different sub-groups of respondents, divided by age, ethnicity, sex, and social status. Digital technology provided him with the means to do this. Using a digitizing pad, Preston traced the outline of each respondent's dialect areas. The process activated each cell which fell within the boundaries of each area. The data could then be combined in the required ways to produce digital composite maps. For example, Figure 9.6 (taken from 1988, p. 384) uses responses digitized into cell activations from the south Indiana group to show their amalgamated perceptions of a southern United States dialect area. The contour lines show percentages of cell activation for the group, that is, the 80 per cent line encloses activations made by 80 per cent of the group, the 20 per cent line encloses activations by only 20 per cent of the group, and so on. In this way, one is given a picture of the 'core' perception of the southern dialect area, as well as the fullest possible extent of the area. If a perceptual dialect area has contours that lie closely together, one would

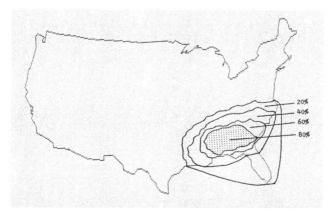

Figure 9.6   South Indiana respondents' perceptions of the southern dialect area of the United States at 20 per cent, 40 per cent, 60 per cent, and 80 per cent cell activation levels (from Preston, 1988, p. 384).

surmise that it is a well-defined area in the minds of respondents, whereas Figure 9.6 shows a rather more hazy perceptual area.

This kind of technique allows the researcher to return to the data again and again, to explore the folk-linguistic perceptions of females, males, elderly, young, and other groupings. Preston's method (which was first announced in Preston and Howe, 1987) opened up the possibility of versatile perceptual atlases, which could be compared with 'production' atlases. However, while the IT and digital revolution has galvanized and enabled much in dialect study, it is also characterized by exciting and rapid change coupled with a process of annoying and swift obsolescence, and, as Montgomery and Stoeckle (2013, p. 53) report, the specific technology used by Preston in 1987 and 1988 quickly became obsolete. Naturally, it has been superseded by other tools, and we will catch up with some of these before the end of Chapter 9.

9.4.2   Other perceptual techniques, and Preston's predecessors

Also by 1988, Preston had become aware that his perceptual dialectology was actually, up to a point, a revival rather than a total innovation. The Belgian dialectologist Willem A. Grootaers had brought to his attention work on dialect perceptions done in the Netherlands from the late 1930s (though in fact it had antecedents there going back to the late nineteenth century (Preston, 2010b, p. 123)) and in Japan from the late 1950s. In both territories, the research had looked into respondents' perceptions of differences and similarities between their own dialect and that of nearby localities. The early work in Japan (Sibata, 1959) was in its aims a little more complex, aiming to show degrees of difference (Preston, 2010b, p. 124), whereas in the Netherlands, in a 1939 survey by the Department of Dialects at the Royal Academy of Sciences and Letters at Amsterdam (see Daan, 1969, p. 10 (as reproduced in Preston, 1999a)), respondents were asked: 'In which location(s) in your region is the same or almost the same dialect spoken as in your own? In which location(s) in your area is a dialect spoken which is clearly different from the one spoken in your own? Can you name a few differences?' (Daan, 1969, p. 18). In 1946, the prolific Dutch dialectologist Antonius Weijnen introduced the 'little-arrow method' [*Pfeilchenmethode*] in order to map similarities between dialect localities in the Netherlands, using data collected by the above 'same/different' questions. In this method, the base of the arrow indicates the home site of a respondent and the head of the arrow indicates a site which the respondent named as dialectally the same. Two-headed arrows are sometimes used to mark reciprocal judgements by differently sited respondents. So as to show perceptual dialect areas, isoglosses can be drawn through the blank spaces left between clusters of connecting arrows. Figure 9.7 is a portion of such a map from Weijnen (1946).

Figure 9.7   Westernmost section of the North Brabant province of the Netherlands, showing the 'little arrows' of respondents' similarity perceptions and perceptual isoglosses (from Weijnen, 1946, reproduced in Preston, 1999b, p. xxvii).

You will have noticed that the little-arrow map bears a resemblance to Louis-Lucien Bonaparte's 1876 map of English dialects (see Figure 5.6 in this book), which used red lines to connect local varieties which belonged (according to Bonaparte's research) to the same dialect area, and certainly perceptual dialectology is both a return to and a development of dialect cartography. It is also, one might say, a kind of head-on attempt to deal with 'the map *is not* the territory' phenomenon outlined in Chapter 3, section 3.3.2 of the present book, in that it aims to map people's perceptual experiences of the (dialectal) world rather than to map 'production' facts as gathered by researchers.

From 1988 onwards, Preston began routinely to cite and summarize the work of his predecessors in Europe and Japan, and Volume 1 of his 1999 *Handbook of Perceptual Dialectology* contains translations of key examples of this work. His Introduction (1999b, pp. xxiii–xl) to this volume contains a five-point overview of the techniques he developed in the 1980s, together with comments on his general findings (xxxiv–xxxv), which I condense and occasionally illustrate as follows:

1. *Draw-a-map.* As exemplified by the studies with respondents from Hawai'i, Indiana, and Michigan. Respondents are especially sensitive to stigmatized and nearby local areas.

2. *Degree of difference.* Respondents rank regions on a scale of one to four (1 = *same*, 2 = *a little different*, 3 = *different*, 4 = *unintelligibly different*) for the perceived degree of dialect difference from the home locality. This technique follows earlier versions in the Netherlands and Japan. Rankings of difference can correlate with rankings of 'correctness' and 'pleasantness': for example, respondents who rank their home area as uniquely correct and most pleasant find regions of most difference from their home area also to be least correct and least pleasant; respondents who rate their home area as most pleasant but not most correct do not associate their degree of difference ratings in a consistent pattern with their correctness and pleasantness ratings.

3. *'Correct' and 'pleasant'.* Respondents rank regions for correct and pleasant speech, as Preston (1988, pp. 387–9) did with the Indiana and Michigan respondents. This technique is a development from earlier versions in perceptual geography and language attitude studies. Preston (1999b, p. xxxiv) equates respondents who rank their home area as uniquely correct and most pleasant with high linguistic security, and respondents who rate their home area as most pleasant but not most correct with linguistic insecurity. (The *Business Insider* survey that we looked at above is a market-research, opinion-poll version of this kind of exercise.)

4. *Dialect identification.* Respondents listen to voices located on a 'dialect continuum', with the voice recordings presented in a scrambled order. For example, the Indiana and Michigan respondents were asked to match nine voices with nine localities running north to south from the Great Lakes to Alabama, the intention being to gauge their sensitivity to northern and southern dialect areas (Preston, 1988, pp. 390–2). In this technique, respondents were instructed to assign each voice to the site where they think it belongs, and then simple calculations were made that showed how far north or south each respondent placed each voice. Mean north/ south scores per recording for each group of respondents as a whole were worked out, and where a significant gap in the score for adjacent localities emerged, a perceived major dialect boundary was assumed by Preston to exist, on the basis that the scores evinced a clear distinction being heard by the respondents. In general, Preston (1999b, p. xxxv) found that respondents from different areas 'hear' boundaries at different locations, and are able to make more distinctions closer to their home area.

5. *Qualitative data.* Respondents are questioned about the tasks they have carried out and are engaged in open-ended conversations about language varieties, speakers, and related topics. This data indicates that face-to-face

contacts have more influence on perceptions than the mass media, that overt identification of particular linguistic details (especially phonological details) of other varieties is weak (though respondents can mimic other varieties convincingly), and that 'correctness' is the most frequently occurring concern of respondents.

Subsequent to Preston's work in the 1980s, perceptual dialectology grew.

9.4.3   The growth of perceptual dialectology

In the 1990s and early twenty-first century, the sub-discipline evolved and diversified, with studies tackling many linguistic territories. The second volume of Preston and Daniel's *Handbook* (2002), for example, contains research on perceptions of variation in Dutch, French, Hungarian, Korean, Japanese, Spanish, Turkish, the languages of Mali, as well as studies on English in Canada, England, and the United States. The 2012 collection on concepts of linguistic space edited by Hansen et al. contains perceptual work on the Finnish-Swedish border, northern England, and London and Birmingham. The draw-a-map technique was applied to individual states in the United States by, for example, Bucholtz et al. (2007, 2008) on California, Evans (2011) on Washington, and Cukor-Avila et al. (2012) on Texas. The Cardiff group (Coupland et al., 1999; Garrett et al., 2003) administered a draw-a-map, labelling, and rating survey to secondary schoolteachers which produced seven perceptual dialect regions and ratings of dynamism, pleasantness, prestige, and 'Welshness' for varieties of Welsh English. The Japanese dialectologist Fumio Inoue published (1996, p. 149) a composite map of perceptual regions of British English from a draw-a-map study carried out from Essex University, in which each respondent's map was coded for digitization. The composite map, shown here as Figure 9.8, contrasts considerably with the Cardiff group's results with regard to Wales. Here Wales is a single dialect region. So is Ireland, and so is Scotland. Although Inoue's respondents were drawn from 'several universities in Great Britain' (Inoue, 1996, p. 144), one intuits that at least the majority if not all of them were English.

Inoue also (1995, 1996) applied to British English a radical technique of mental mapping he had used previously for analysing perceptions of Japanese dialects, which he called the study of **dialect images**. He argued (1996, p. 142) that 'subjects formed a dialect image without a specific map in mind'. First, he used a version of the **Semantic Differential Test** put forward by the psychologist Charles Egerton Osgood in the 1950s. The SD Test measures where a respondent's attitudes lie on a scale between two polarities, such as *good-bad*, *strong-weak*, and so forth. In Inoue's procedure, evaluative words for the dialects of the area under consideration (Britain) were first collected from respondents (British university students) and were then assembled into

Figure 9.8   Subjective Dialect Division of Great Britain, based on draw-a-map data collected in 1989 by Fumio Inoue (from Inoue, 1996, p. 149).

groups of semantic similarity. Inoue concluded that there were four groupings of words which could be placed at the extremes of two axes (one at each end): a vertical axis and a horizontal axis. Each axis represented a continuum along which dialects could be rated, and both axes could be shown in the same analytical space, as in Figure 9.9, from Inoue (1995, as reprinted in Preston, 1999a, p. 153). This is an instance of **multidimensional scaling**, each axis being a dimension along which a perceptual object (dialect) can be ranked. (Thinking back a few pages, and as an experiment, you might want to see how well the evaluations *broad, dissonant, distracting, marked, overwhelming, strong,* and *thick* fit into these word-groupings.)

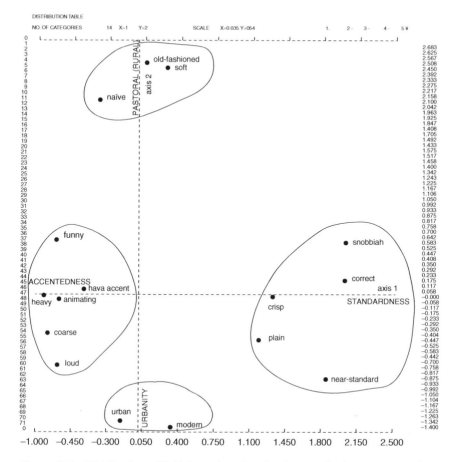

Figure 9.9 Distribution of British students' evaluative words along two axes by Inoue (1995/1999, p. 153).

The two scales here Inoue called 'standardness – accentedness' (right to left on the horizontal axis) and 'urbanity – ruralness' (bottom to top on the vertical axis). These are the factors that dialect images are composed of for British respondents, according to Inoue (1995/1999, 1996). (In the case of Japanese dialects, he had found images to be composed of an *intellectual* factor and an *emotional* factor.) Selected dialects were then rated with reference to these scales, producing the graph in Figure 9.10.

If we look at the centre of this graph, where the two axes cross, we see the dialects rated most neutrally by the respondents in this exercise: Hawaii, Own, and BBC. The dialects labelled Australia, Liverpool, and Western USA are rated slightly towards the urban on the vertical axis, but are considered very non-standard on the horizontal axis. And so on. As Preston (2010a, p. 189) puts it,

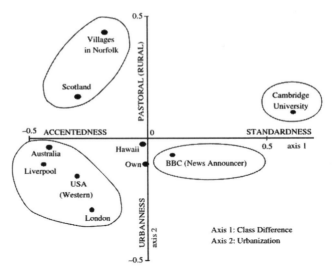

Figure 9.10 Distribution of dialects by British students according to dialect images (from Inoue, 1995/1999, p. 154).

'This is indeed a mental map that does not correspond to geographical space at all.' Rather, it indicates what are arguably the most salient factors in British respondents' mental imprints of different dialects.

The perceptual dialectology of British English yielded another innovative technique in Chris Montgomery's 2007 study on the perception by northern English respondents of (mainly northern) varieties of British English. In the placement-of-voices stage of his research, Montgomery made use of **starburst charts**. In this method, the (northern) respondent was played a voice sample and then asked to mark with an 'x' on a blank map where he or she believed the speaker in the sample came from. Using a digitizing pad, each respondent's 'x' for each voice sample was computerized. This enabled the production of maps on which the provenance of the voice sample was linked with a straight line to each placement made by a respondent. Using the drawing tools of Microsoft PowerPoint and other graphics-editing software, the base map was removed and replaced with a circular or 'starburst' chart, allowing the clear scaling of the distances between speech sample provenance and speech sample placement by each respondent. Figure 9.11 is one example of a starburst chart from Montgomery (2007), showing the group of Carlisle respondents' placements of the voice sample from Preston (not Dennis this time, but the city of Preston in the north-west of England).

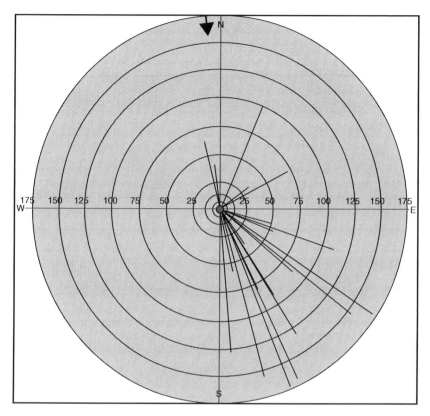

Figure 9.11   Carlisle respondents' placement of a Preston voice sample, from Montgomery (2007, p. 292).

The grey dot in the middle is the provenance of the voice sample (Preston). The chart is aligned with the points of the compass, and the concentric circles mark distance in miles. The arrow at the top indicates the position of Carlisle (in the far north-west of England) relative to Preston. The starburst chart is a particularly lucid vehicle for displaying the distance and direction of placements relative to provenance, whether for individuals or groups of respondents. In his summing-up (2007, pp. 330–44), Montgomery highlighted three factors influencing his respondents' perceptions: *cultural salience*, that is, 'the prominence of certain population centres in the national consciousness' (p. 331); *claiming/denial*, which is the phenomenon of respondents' placing voices that they like in their home area (claiming) and voices that they do not like away from their home area (denial) – compare this with Dennis Preston's general findings about difference and pleasantness, above; and *proximity*, that is, respondents' greater ability to achieve a finer reading of dialects closer to their home area.

9.5   Conclusion

In conclusion, then, what do we say about perceptual dialectology? It has acquired its own acronym: PD. It is now established as an integral subject area in the revival of linguistic geography – see, for example, the Foreword to the first edition in 2013 of the eagerly anticipated digital *Journal of Linguistic Geography*, edited by William Labov and Dennis Preston. In encouraging submissions on the perception of speech, they say (p. 2): 'We are interested in both how linguistic varieties across and within regions are heard and processed and how nonlinguists perceive the spatial distribution of varieties, particularly when such studies shed light on the linguistic and social characteristics of language variation and change.' This first edition also contains an article by Chris Montgomery and Philipp Stoeckle (pp. 52–85) which describes the advantages of using Geographic Information Systems (GIS) software in PD, as it can 'geoprocess' and 'georeference' data from linguistic studies (that is, the data can be handled, treated, and linked via coordinate systems to the earth's surface) in order to generate a variety of digital maps, including composite maps. As elsewhere in dialect study, developments in technology can facilitate research, and here GIS offers a way to do statistical analysis by combining and processing perceptual data quickly and easily. The revival of linguistic geography is also tied closely to the advent of **geolinguistics** in dialect study from around 1980 onwards. The perceptual approach has made an impact on geolinguistics, the primary aim of which is to improve the understanding of linguistic change. Geolinguistics is the subject of the final chapter of the present book.

So while there have been criticisms of perceptual dialectology (for example, Craig Carver, in his 1991 review of Preston (1989), highlights unreliable generalizations founded on inconsistent data, calls the use by Preston of his university students as respondents 'opportunistic' and 'not a good practice' (p. 436), and wonders whether the respondents are really rating places rather than speech), and its potential to inform educational planning and policy remains so far more promise than realization, PD is now an established part of contemporary dialect study. A detailed picture is being assembled of what the 'folk' in many parts of the world believe about language variation. The data and findings can be compared fruitfully with 'production' information on language variation (as done by Erica Benson (2003) for Ohio State), and with perceptual information gathered by other specialisms such as geography, market research (like the *Business Insider* survey of 2013, perhaps), and psychology. Preston's methods have been refined and appreciably augmented, and the incorporation of folk perceptions into geolinguistic studies is commonplace. Take, for example, on a local scale, the intensive community-based project by Barbara

Johnstone et al. (2006), which looks at the evolution of 'Pittsburghese' as a marker of communal identity. Employing both semiotic and sociolinguistic theory, Johnstone and her collaborators make extensive use of media output and informants' opinions about local speech and local identity. On a wider scale, the prestigious *Atlas of North American English* (Labov et al., 2006) has a perceptual component built into it, from data collection to map production, by means of the simple method of not only eliciting minimal pairs from informants but also then asking them if they thought the words sounded the same or different.

This takes us tidily to the next, and final, chapter, on geolinguistics.

9.6   Brief commentary on terms

Just one quick point to make here. When Dennis Preston decided in 1981 on the name *perceptual dialectology*, it was the first part of the phrase that he was in a dilemma over: whether to choose *folk* or *perceptual* (Preston, 2010b, p. 121). This shows some faith in the term *dialectology* at what was a difficult time in its history, when to many it signified an older, outdated approach to the study of regional speech compared with *sociolinguistics*. At almost the same time, Jack Chambers and Peter Trudgill (1980, p. 206) were suggesting that *dialectology* was not the best term for the discipline in its modern form (even though it was the title of their book). They advocated *geolinguistics*. As it has turned out, both terms are in currency. The term *dialectology* has itself been 'modernized', partly because of its association with contemporary IT-powered researches, but perhaps also in part because of its use in the name of Preston's sub-discipline.

9.7   What you can do

Here is one of my former students, Alexander Morris, summarizing the undergraduate dissertation that he completed in 2012:

I'm interested in people, psychology, and language in use, so I chose to focus on perceptual dialectology. It was Montgomery (2007) who was my main inspiration. My aim was to investigate the general accuracy of placement of English dialects, and to see if any patterns regarding geography and opinion emerged. I started by trawling the literature that separates England and Wales into dialect areas, and amalgamated the maps into one. Then I set about getting audio from each area. To save time, I used pre-recorded clips from the British Library and, once edited, played them to my respondents, as many as I could get from each area, in order to get a fair spread. While listening, they were subjected to an electronic questionnaire about their opinions, and a nearly blank map on which they were asked to mark their perceived location of each speaker in the audio clips. I compiled the results into 'starburst' diagrams, which showed all the placements, colour coded by area, for each audio clip. My results, in summary, showed that overall accuracy was poor, with some clips having over half of the placements hundreds of miles away from their origin! The relationship between geographical location, strength of feeling towards the audio clip, and north/south polarizations, showed some measure of correlation with degree of accuracy.

As is usually the case in dialect research, Alex's study, which was ambitious in its scope, also generates ideas for further work, which might involve a series of studies, each one focusing in more detail on the perceptions of respondents from one region at a time. As we have seen in the chapter above, research into attitudes and perceptions has produced quite a range of methodologies suited to small-scale studies. Matched- and verbal-guise techniques, draw-a-map, degree of difference, correctness and pleasantness, dialect identification, dialect image – all of these procedures, and Labov's subjective reaction, self-evaluation, and linguistic insecurity tests, offer methods that can be used and modified (and combined) by further surveys.

Resources and further reading

Dennis Preston has written a number of essays (for example, 2002, 2005, 2010a, 2010b, 2013) reviewing the origins, precursors, and development of perceptual dialectology. You could either read these in chronological order for a fuller experience or skip to the most recent (in Chambers and Schilling, 2013) for a quicker update. He also edited, with Daniel Long, the invaluable two-volume *Handbook of Perceptual Dialectology* (1999, 2002), which contains a wide range of older and newer examples of perceptual research (including pieces by Daan, Sibata, Grootaers, Weijnen, W. G. Rensink, Inoue, Paul Kerswill, and the Cardiff group), as well as another overview by Preston. His 1989 book, *Perceptual Dialectology: Nonlinguists' Views of Areal Linguistics*, assembles Preston's 1980s work. In addition, Preston's web-pages make available a large selection of his writings on perceptual dialectology: https://english.okstate. edu/173-lsa-institute-2015. For an overview perspective other than Preston's, see the excellent 'Perceptual Dialectology' (2011) by Chris Montgomery and Joan Beal in *Analysing Variation in English*, edited by Warren Maguire and April

McMahon. Montgomery's enterprising doctoral dissertation is available in full at: http://etheses.whiterose.ac.uk/1203/2/Montgomery,_C.pdf. Peter Garrett's *Attitudes to Language* (2010) is a thorough discussion of research since the 1960s on attitudes to linguistic varieties, covering matched- and verbal-guise techniques, accommodation theory, and perceptual dialectology. Shorter summaries of the domain of attitudes research are provided by Sonja Vandermeeren's 'Research on Language Attitudes' and Garrett's 'Attitude Measurements' in Volume 2 of *Sociolinguistics: An International Handbook* (2005), edited by Ammon et al. Many of Wallace Lambert's articles are available electronically, and a selection of his earlier work is collected in *Language, Psychology, and Culture* (1972), edited by Anwar Dil. *Speech Style and Social Evaluation* (1975) by Howard Giles and Peter Powesland presents an early accommodation model and reviews matched-guise research. *Language and Social Psychology* (1979) is a valuable collection of essays edited by Howard Giles and Robert St Clair, including Giles and Philip Smith on accommodation theory, a piece by Wallace E. Lambert, and the much-cited 'Why Do Low-Prestige Language Varieties Persist?' by Ellen Bouchard Ryan. By the 1990s a considerable body of work using the ideas of accommodation theory had been produced, and the collection *Contexts of Accommodation* (1991), edited by Howard Giles, Justine Coupland and Nikolas Coupland, surveys the achievements and potential of the approach. Subsequently, a *Handbook* and then a *New Handbook of Language and Social Psychology* (Robinson and Giles, 1990, 2001) have been published, and a short overview of the field by Giles and Jennifer Fortman is in Volume 1 of Ammon et al. (2004). For a chronicle of attitude-building in relation to dialects and accents of English, see *Images of English: A Cultural History of the Language* (1991), by Richard W. Bailey, and *'Talking Proper': The Rise of Accent as Social Symbol* (2nd edn, 2003), by Lynda Mugglestone.

10 Geolinguistics

This chapter includes the following:

- Discussion of the origins and phases of modern geolinguistics.
- Guide to models of innovation diffusion: *urban hierarchical, contra-hierarchical, wave,* and *cultural hearth*.
- The story of Northern Cities Chain Shift.
- Explanation of the *gravity model, regional dialect levelling* and the *community of practice* approach.

10.1 Introduction

At the time of writing, one can find in the *Oxford English Dictionary* (*OED*) Online entries for *geobiology, geobotany, geochemistry, geochronology, geodesy, geodynamics, geoengineering, geography, geohistory, geohydrology, geology, geomaly, geomancy, geomathematics, geomatics, geometry, geomorphology, geophagy, geophysics, geopolitics, geopony, geoscience, geoscopy, geosophy, geotechnology,* and *geothermometry,* but no entry for *geolinguistics.* This is strange, especially as one or two of these terms are quite obscure (*geomaly,* for example, which means, 'The tendency of an organism to grow symmetrically in a lateral or horizontal plane'), while *geolinguistics* has been used in the literature of dialect study for some four decades or more. In the present book, I have taken an interest in terms and from time to time in their etymologies. The name *geolinguistics* presents as knotty an issue as any in the catalogue of labels for types of dialect study, and only partly because it does not yet feature in the *OED*. Discussion of the name creates an opportunity for me to link back to the beginnings of dialectology, and so for that reason we will return to it at the end of this chapter, the last chapter of this book. For now, what we need to know is that the name has become well known in the twenty-first century and refers to a relatively young mode of dialect study. That said, nothing is utterly new in present-day dialect study. Twenty-first-century geolinguistics began to develop out of Labovian variationist sociolinguistics in the 1970s, and also it seeks to reconnect with the traditional linguistic geography that preceded sociolinguistics. However, one of its leading proponents, David Britain (a British geolinguist), argues that in its twenty-first-century mani-festation, geolinguistics differs significantly from and improves meaning-fully upon the earlier approaches of sociolinguistics and linguistic geography (Britain, 2010a, 2010b). There is no dispute of GADS (Great Argument in Dialect Study) proportions, but the case he makes is at times reminiscent of that late-twentieth century upheaval.

10.2   The two phases (so far) of geolinguistics

I will say just a little more here about the term and what it means before we look at some examples of geolinguistics in action. As a general definition, we can say that geolinguistics marries a geographical perspective to variationist sociolinguistics, with an added awareness of the achievements of linguistic geography thrown into the mix. Modern geolinguistics can be divided into two phases insofar as it relates to dialect study. The first phase was signalled by Jack Chambers and Peter Trudgill in 1980, who called the final chapter (pp. 205–8) of the first edition of their *Dialectology* textbook, 'Toward geolin-guistics'. At the time, they saw the term as one that they could import from the works of French and Italian dialectologists into English in order to use it for the new version of dialect study that they envisaged. They anticipated (p. 206) a 'unified discipline' which would be the confluence of three streams: 'dialect geography, urban dialectology, and human geography'. The first two streams refer to the older dialectology and the newer variationist sociolinguistics, respectively. Chambers and Trudgill were already interested in models developed by geographers in the 1950s and 1960s that sought to explain how social and technological innovations spread or **diffused** through geographical space, and their 1980 textbook summarizes (pp. 182–204) their own work to date on the **spatial diffusion of linguistic innovations**. Their initial foray into this kind of human-geography-inspired study was Trudgill (1974b). The first phase of geolinguistics is characterized in particular by work on innovation diffusion, looking at how some linguistic forms disperse gradually from a point of origin across geographical space thereby causing changes in local speech. Work on diffusion continues into the second phase of geolinguistics, but as the older models that inspired Chambers and Trudgill were superseded in human geography in the 1980s, so gradually did geolinguistics move towards subtler and more comprehensive readings of the complex and dynamic relationship between language use, linguistic change, and geographical space. By the late 1980s, says David Britain (2010b, p. 75), after a period caught up in the 'quantitative revolution' that also infused variationist sociolinguistics, human geography began considering geographical regions as 'dynamic entities, in which social and economic processes are constantly being played out through a geographically differentiated filter'. In other words, geographers were recognizing that geographical space is in an active and changing relationship with human society, a relationship that shapes both space and society. Second-phase geolinguistics attempts to bring this way of thinking into dialect study, drawing also on observations from perceptual studies, because, 'Space also exists at a psychological level – our perceptions of the physical and socialized spaces around us can lead us to act and behave in differing ways' (Britain, 2010b, p. 71). Britain takes the 1980 manifesto of Chambers and Trudgill further, in that, firstly, he is critical of Labovian variationist sociolinguistics, saying that 'the urban turn in dialectology represented an anti-spatial turn too, a turn which has in many respects lasted right to the present day' (2010b, p. 74). Labov and those who followed him examined language in specific urban localities, but, argues Britain (p. 74), the 'internal geographies' of these localities were 'largely ignored'. Secondly, the geolinguistics he advocates is 'a spatially sensitive dialectology' (p. 70) that he believes is more conscious than Chambers and Trudgill were in 1980 that geographical space 'is *socially produced*' (italics in original) and 'is a process not a fixed canvas on which social processes are enacted'. He is also more sympathetic to traditional dialectology than were Chambers and Trudgill in 1980, pointing out that 'in terms of the accumulation of descriptive material, this era is still, in many ways, unrivalled' (p. 73). In Britain's vision, geolinguistics is a return to spatial interests, but armed with a methodology more aware of and responsive to the processes of linguistic interaction (humans speaking to each other) than that possessed by the old linguistic geography. (Just in case I have given the impression above that things have moved on since Labov's work, well, they have if we are referring to his early work and those studies that followed in similar style. However, Labov himself has also 'moved on' and has been a principal contributor to second-phase geolinguistics, as we shall see in section 10.5 below. And as we witnessed in Chapter 7, section 2, the quantitative variationist approach has not stood still either.)

What we need next are some details. In concise form, then, there follow some selected illustrations of geolinguistics, beginning with Trudgill's opening piece from 1974.

10.3   Peter Trudgill, diffusion, urban hierarchy, and gravity

Published in the sixth edition of the leading sociolinguistics journal, *Language in Society*, Trudgill's article uses data from his researches on dialects of Norwegian in Brunlanes, a peninsula on the south coast of Norway, and on dialects of English in East Anglia, England. It should by now be no surprise when I say that the main theme of the piece is the goal of understanding linguistic change. In this case, the topic is the process or processes that occur when linguistic changes appear to spread geographically across a region over a period of time. For example, working-class London speech is '*h*-less', that is to say, the initial *h* in words like *happy* and *home* is not articulated. Among other things, Trudgill was interested in the extent, character, and ongoing progress of the spread of '*h*-deletion' outwards from London into East Anglia (an issue which we shall return to shortly). His 1974 article is thus an inquiry into the spatial or geographical diffusion of linguistic change or innovation.

His particular inspiration was the work in the 1950s and 1960s of the Swedish geographer Torsten Hägerstrand on the geographical diffusion of new technologies, such as the spread of motorcar ownership through southern Sweden in the early twentieth century (Hägerstrand, 1952). Following Hägerstrand, Trudgill placed a grid of equally sized cells across a map of Brunlanes, in Norway, and then chose a locality from each cell and, with his collaborator Arne Kjell Foldvik, recorded a sample of the population at each locality, with a view to investigating variants of the /æ/ vowel phoneme of Norwegian in this region. The 40 informants were not randomly sampled, but did comprise a range of ages, and the recordings contained 'several thousand' tokens of pronunciations of the (æ) variable (Trudgill, 1974b, p. 227). Preliminary research had suggested that, in the Brunlanes region, a phonetic change was in progress, from a tendency for older speakers to use a high [ε] variant to a tendency for younger speakers to use a lowered and slightly back [a] variant (p. 226). By using the **apparent-time methodology** of comparing data from different age-groups, Trudgill was able to confirm that this change was occurring, but, in addition, by mapping his statistics using Hägerstrand's grid system, he was able to reveal something else, that is, the geographical distribution of the change in progress. What his maps (pp. 230–1) suggest, in summary, is that change was spreading outwards from the main town of Larvik into neighbouring areas, but also jumping from Larvik to other centres of population in Brunlanes, affecting the intervening areas at a slower rate. This pattern can be explained by improvements in the road network between the centres, plus increasing centralization of education, leading to rising contact between the centres over time. Put simply, the linguistic innovation was spreading more quickly along these comparatively well-travelled routes between well-connected centres than it was into the intervening country-side. Subsequently, a number of studies in a number of territories have found similar patterns, and the model of explanation pioneered by Trudgill has become known as the **urban hierarchical model** (sometimes called **cascade diffusion**), in which innovations descend down a hierarchy of population centres, from large city to city to large town to town, village, and countryside. As Britain put it (2002a, p. 623), 'whilst distance plays some role, interaction between urban centers in modern societies is likely to be greater, and there-fore a more frequent and effective conduit for accommodation and transmis-sion of innovations, than between urban and rural'. Britain himself found *l*-vocalization (in which /l/ becomes a vowel or semi-vowel, so that *himself* sounds like *himsewf*) pursuing a hierarchical path in the East Anglian Fens of eastern England (Britain, 2002a, p. 623), and Bailey et al. (1993, pp. 368–71), using data from the Survey of Oklahoma Dialects (begun in 1991), found the unrounding of /ɔ/ to [ɑ] in words like *hawk* showing a hierarchical pattern in Oklahoma State. A rather overlooked but excellent study with hierarchical findings is David North's analysis (1985) of the diffusion from London into south-east England of stressed monophthongal long [æ:] vowels in words such as *about* and *house*. Drawing on historical evidence from A. J. Ellis (1889), and using data from the SED and his own doctoral research at Leeds University (1982b), North produced maps (pp. 91–2) which indicated that the innova-tion cascaded down transport routes from London to Dover, Hastings, and Brighton, and radiated outwards from each of these centres.

Back in 1974, Trudgill added another component to his investigation, namely the predictive **gravity model**. The gravity model again comes from human geography (ultimately from physics, of course), where it is used to predict the movement of people and ideas between two places. The basic idea is that centres of population exercise something like a 'gravitational pull', and the gravity model attempts to calculate by means of a simple mathematical formula the gravitational pull that two centres have on each other. It assigns a score to the interaction or bond between two centres. Size of population and distance are the components of the formula, which goes as follows: the population of city/town *A* is multiplied by the population of city/town *B*, and the result is divided by the distance between the two centres squared. In itself, the final figure from this exercise means little, for its usefulness comes from comparing it with bonds between other centres, such as between cities *C* and *D*, or indeed between *A* and *C*, *A* and *D*, and so on. The reasoning is that the formula reveals the strength of interaction between centres, and the stronger the bond, the greater the likelihood of innovations travelling between them. Trudgill saw that the gravity model had the potential to predict the degree of linguistic influence of one centre upon another, and to predict the speed and direction of the geographical diffusion of linguistic innovations, and, having made four important adjustments to the formula, he applied it to his Norwegian and East Anglian data.

The four adjustments were due to the following factors:

1. *Prior-existing linguistic similarity* (Trudgill, 1974b, p. 234). It is likely that it is easier for a community to adopt linguistic features from accents and dialects that are already similar to its own (in other respects) than from ones that are less similar (even if these less similar accents and dialects are geographically nearer).

2. *The need to measure uni-directional influence* (pp. 234–5). The formula was adjusted to show the influence of one centre upon the other, rather than the interaction between the two.

3. *The need to allow the inclusion of competing pressures from other centres* (pp. 235–6). For example, Norwich in East Anglia was absorbing influence from London (leading to *h*-deletion), but other smaller centres in East Anglia, such as Lowestoft, were subject to influence from London, Norwich, and the other local centres, King's Lynn and Yarmouth. Trudgill's calculations showed the influence of the local centres on Lowestoft outscoring influence from London.

4. *The need to build in a time-lag* (p. 236). For example, as long as Norwich remained *h*-pronouncing, Lowestoft (and the other local urban centres) were not likely to become *h*-less, despite some influence from London. But once Norwich becomes *h*-less (under influence from London), *h*-lessness was more likely to diffuse to the smaller towns.

Later studies of *h*-dropping in East Anglia bore out Trudgill's analysis (Britain, 2010a, p. 144), and the combination of the urban hierarchical and gravity models proved influential. However, bearing in mind later criticisms of this approach, it is worth noting Trudgill's own awareness in 1974 of its limitations (pp. 241–45). He points out that it would need somehow to factor in the level of prestige (including covert prestige) a diffusing feature possesses, and to include information on the social-group origin of a feature as well as its geographical origin. The model might have to take into account the make-up of the receiving linguistic system, as this could conceivably lead to some resistance to or slowing down of an innovation. For example, if a phonetic innovation in one set of words turned one or more of those words into homonyms of other, existing words, as happens when *howl* becomes '*owl*, causing some loss of phonological contrast overall, this possibly could affect the speed of innovation.

10.4   More types of diffusion

We have dwelt a while on Trudgill's initial exploration of spatial diffusion because it gives us a useful indication of the issues facing geolinguistics. He acknowledges the shortcomings of his 1974 model, but looks forward hopefully to a 'dynamic dialectology' (p. 245) that can cope with studying 'language as a dynamic phenomenon'. (p. 243). These sentiments sound similar to those of David Britain three decades on, but before we take a look at a few examples of the later geolinguistics, I should mention three other types of innovation diffusion revealed by studies carried out in the wake of Trudgill's article.

As well as finding evidence of urban hierarchical diffusion in their early 1990s study, Guy Bailey et al. (1993) suggested that **wave diffusion** and **contra-hierarchical diffusion** were operating in Oklahoma State. In fact, we have come across the former before (in Chapter 4), for the wave theory of linguistic change (which pictures innovations as radiating outwards over time from a central point) goes back to the heyday of the nineteenth-century philologists. It is also now sometimes known as **contagion diffusion**. Another linguist called Bailey – Charles-James N. Bailey – had revived and modified the wave theory in a volume called *Variation and Linguistic Theory*, published in 1973, which argued in favour of a conception of language based on studying the dynamic relationship between spatial and temporal variability. In 1993, Guy Bailey et al. (pp. 371–4) proposed that the quasi-modal form *fixin to* (used to express the intention that one is about to do something or that it is in the process of being done, as in *I'm fixin' to read all of this sentence*; in grammatical analysis *modality* refers to the mood or attitude expressed by a verb form) was spreading in wave fashion in Oklahoma, saying that the diffusion of the form 'seems to be contagious rather than hierarchical: it seems to spread outward from [rural] areas of intense concentration much like waves in a pond when a rock is thrown into the water' (p. 374). And although the hierarchical model seemed at first not to pertain to *fixin to*, when the apparent-time methodology was applied in more detail, *fixin to* also exhibited a contra-hierarchical diffusion. Comparison of age-groups suggested that the form was also spreading 'from intense concentrations in rural areas to small towns and then to larger cities and metropolises' (p. 374). In other words, as well as spreading in a wave pattern it was diffusing against the urban hierarchy too. Further, separate instances of wave diffusion and of contra-hierarchical diffusion have been found by other studies in England and the United States.

The third type of innovation diffusion is called by Britain (2010a, p. 148) **cultural hearth diffusion**, as found by Barbara Horvath (a sociolinguist) and Ronald Horvath (a geographer) in their studies (1997, 2001, 2002) of ongoing *l*-vocalization in Australian English and New Zealand English – though Britain's definition of this label ('the innovation gains a foothold in both town and country in one particular region before diffusing to other parts of the country') puts a fairly uncomplicated spin on the Horvaths' findings. The historian David Hackett Fischer used the phrase *cultural hearth* in his 1989 book *Albion's Seed*, which describes the persistence of traditional British regional identities in the development of the United States, and which has had some bearing on William Labov's account (2010, 2012) of the historical and social reasons for the Northern Cities Chain Shift of vowels in the Inland North dialect region of America, which we will discuss in section 10.5 below. The phrase was also used by Craig Carver in 1987 for the coastal centres 'from which most American dialects developed' (p. 7). (It is likely that the term *culture hearth* was introduced into cultural geography by Carl Sauer in 1952.) The Horvaths' research is an intricate and detailed phonetic, sociolinguistic, statistical, and geolinguistic enquiry, embracing nine urban localities in two countries (Australia and New Zealand). The nine localities showed varying amounts of *l*-vocalization, with the three New Zealand cities of Christchurch (South Island), Wellington, and Auckland (both North Island) exhibiting the highest scores. Christchurch had the top score, followed in descending order by the latter two, respectively, and the east Australian city of Brisbane showed the lowest score of the nine (Horvath and Horvath, 2002, p. 335). Based on these tallies, the 'straightforward interpretation' (2002, p. 335) of the geographical origin and direction of the change is that Christchurch led and then it moved northwards through New Zealand. Its apparent 'leap' over to Australia looks strange, however, as it is the two most western of the six Australian localities, Adelaide and Mount Gambier (which are the furthest from New Zealand), that take the lead there. Sydney, Hobart, Melbourne, and Brisbane follow, in that order, so that the direction of change appears to move east to the coast, then from there southwards to Tasmania, then back northwards to Melbourne, and from there northeast up the coast again (see Figure 10.1 for a map). As Horvath and Horvath observed in their 2001 article, 'the geographical pattern does not even faintly resemble either the diffusion pattern down the urban hierarchy or the contrary pattern from the smaller to the larger cities' (2001, p. 51), and 'a gravity model centered in the Antipodes does not account for the diffusion of /l/ vocalization' (p. 52).

In their search for a model that can explain this seemingly quite haphazard path, the Horvaths call upon the notion of **place effects**. The term refers to the collection of possible particular linguistic and social conditions that can affect each locality, with the result that change could be either accelerated or held up. Place effects include the specific social and historical forces at work in each locality, heavy migration into a locality, and changes in the political relationships between places that lead to divergent behaviour. One of the place effects that Horvath and Horvath (2002, pp. 338–9) explore is the 'vigorousness' of *l*-vocalization in each place, and they find that this does correlate up to

Figure 10.1   Bundles of isoglosses separating the nine cities in Horvath and Horvath's study of *l*-vocalization in Australia and New Zealand (2002, p. 342).

a point with their 'straightforward interpretation' above. They measure vigorousness by comparing old and young age-groups for their respective amounts of *l*-vocalization in each place. This comparison has Christchurch showing the most vigorous rate of adoption, and Adelaide and the Tasmanian capital Hobart scoring fairly highly and on a par with Wellington and Auckland. But the scores for the older age-group by themselves suggest that Auckland led the change, followed by Wellington then Christchurch, followed in turn by Mount Gambier and Adelaide. Thus it seems that there are place effects which have accelerated the rate of innovation in Christchurch and slowed it down in Mount Gambier. Set against this more ambitious and complex kind of study, the earlier diffusion models look quite unwieldy and ill-equipped to factor in locality-specific social, perceptual, and structural contexts (as pointed out by Britain (2010a, 2010b) and acknowledged earlier by Trudgill (1974b)), and the Horvaths' work is a good example of geolinguists attempting to improve the sensitivity, scope, and detail of their investigations.

Another aspect of their work is a 'reconceptualization' (2002, p. 341) of the traditional isogloss of linguistic geography, in order to map geographically differences in the ensemble of sociolinguistic and phonetic variations that occur in each locality. Their aim is to depict 'sociolinguistic variability that is also geographically variable' (2002, pp. 321, 341). In addition to the 'classic isogloss' marking a boundary between one variant and another, they propose the **variable isogloss**, 'which is a line on a map indicating a change in the pattern of variation between speech localities' (2002, p. 341). A variable isogloss is thus drawn when statistical analysis of the amount or rate of a feature or set of features shows a substantial gap or discontinuity between the localities being compared (2001, p. 47). Figure 10.1 amalgamates a total of 12 isoglosses (one classic, and 11 variable) which reveal five major 'bundles' separating the nine cities surveyed.

10.5   The diversification of geolinguistics

In its second phase (as I have called it), especially from the mid 1990s onwards, geolinguistics diversifies in its approaches as it grapples with the elaborate relationship between linguistic change and geographical space. It also reconnects more explicitly and confidently with older, pre-sociolinguistics linguistic geography, as illustrated vividly by the decision to name the major online journal of geolinguistics, launched in 2013, the *Journal of Linguistic Geography*. The high-profile *Atlas of North American English* (Labov et al., 2006) is probably the leading example of the revival of dialect cartography in geolinguistics (as Britain notes, 2010a, pp. 155–6).

Evolving out of William Labov's and others' continuing interest in phonological change in North American dialects, the *ANAE* combined state-of-the-art cartography with modern sociolinguistic sampling of informants (via Telsur, a 1990s telephone survey of over 760 speakers from nearly 300 communities representing '68 percent of the population of North America' (Labov et al., 2006, p. 3)) in order to chart the extent of important sound changes in progress in urban English in the United States and Canada. (For fans of Chapter 6, section 4.2.1 of the present book, those stats yield an informant-to-total-population ratio of 1 to 246,745.) As the authors put it (p. 3), the *ANAE* 'builds on the work of American dialectologists from 1933 to the present', but it also 'represents new departures', by mapping phonemic categories and phonological systems as well as phonetic forms, perception as well as production data, and computerized acoustic analyses of sounds. It also plots visually the systematic sound changes in progress in the regional dialects of North America, such as Canadian Shift, Northern Cities Shift, and Southern Shift, all of which affect vowel sounds. Figure 10.2 is a screen grab of one of the digital maps that can be accessed via the CD-ROM version of the *ANAE*.

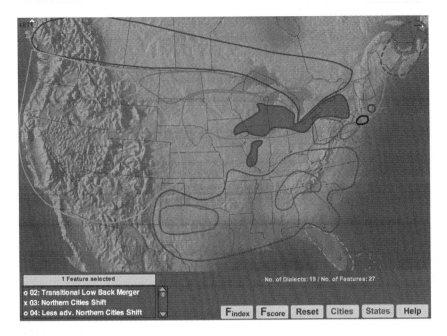

Figure 10.2   Map showing the main dialect regions of North American English, with the area affected by Northern Cities Shift shaded in (from Labov et al., 2006, CD-ROM version).

10.5.1   The story of Northern Cities Shift

The map in Figure 10.2 shows the main dialect regions of North American English as discovered by the *ANAE* survey, and the version of it captured by my screen grab has the area most affected by the **Northern Cities Shift (NCS)** shaded in. (The original version is in colour, with colour-coded dialect boundaries.) We came across two other, more historical sound shifts in Chapter 4 of the present book, those being the First and Second Germanic Consonant Shifts. NCS affects vowels, not consonants, and it is also a **chain shift**, that is, a series of connected changes. The basic principle in such an event, which takes place gradually through time, geographical space, and social groupings, is that a sound that is common to a group of words changes or moves in pronunciation into a different sound, with the consequence that it pushes another sound (which it has become identical with) in another group of words to change also, which in turn has the same effect on another sound in another group, and so on. Alternatively, a changed sound may vacate a space in the phonological/lexical system allowing another sound to change and move into the vacated space, creating another vacated space elsewhere in the system, and so on. In this section, I shall talk about the NCS and the research that has investigated it, describing the insights and methods of Labov and others, and using this narrative as a springboard to summarize some other key work in modern geolinguistics.

The NCS has affected the articulation of a number of mostly short vowels (that is, comparatively short in duration of pronunciation) in the Inland North dialect region of the United States, from New York State to Iowa, so that, as Kretzschmar (2004, p. 54) summarizes it, 'each of the following words might be heard and interpreted as something else by speakers from outside the area: *Ann* as *Ian*, *bit* as *bet*, *bet* as *bat* or *but*, *lunch* as *launch*, *talk* as *tuck*, *locks* as *lax*'. Kretzschmar's overarching summary emphasizes the new homophones (and confusions) that arise for outsiders listening to NCS-affected speakers. Labov has outlined the chronological order in which the elements of the NCS took place (Labov, 2010, 2012; Labov et al., 2006), as in this passage (2012, location 1709), where he is talking about how the sequencing played out among the youngsters observed in Penelope Eckert's influential 1980s study in a Detroit high school (Eckert, 1989, 2000), as follows: '[first] the shift of short-*a* in *bat* toward the vowel of *yeah* [described as *Ann* to *Ian* in Kretzschmar's summary, which illustrates the most extreme form of this particular change], [then] the shift of short-*o* in *got* toward *bat* [*locks* to *lax* in Kretzschmar], the shift of long open-*o* in *bought* toward *got* [*talk* to *tuck*; both *tuck* and *tock* are possible outcomes of this change], the shift of short-*e* in *bet* toward *but* [*bet* to *but*], and [last] the shift of short-*u* in *but* toward *bought* [*lunch* to *launch*]'. Each of the cited words in these summaries represents a whole group of words. For example, *bat* stands for all words with short-*a*: *Ann, attitude, bad, cap, cat, happen, that*, and so forth. If you look closely, you see that the first three shifts in Labov's chronology involve 'vacating' changes in the chain and the last two are 'pushing' changes. Actually, the first change, as well as 'vacating' the short-*a* space, also has a 'pushing' effect on short-*e*. Labov (1994) describes the NCS as a 'pull chain', because it was set in motion by a vacating short-*a* shift which pulled short-*o* into its vacated space. Kretzschmar's summary mentions a couple of possibilities not covered in Labov's, these being *bit* to *bet* (chronologically the final stage of the NCS, so far), and *bet* to *bat*, an alternative outcome for the *bet* stage. But maybe, as you try hard to construct a mental picture of exactly what is going in this game of vowelly musical chairs, a more general and familiar thought occurs: that what Labov, his collaborators, and other researchers of North American English are engaged in here is a quite neogrammarian enterprise, in that they are investigating the regularity of sound change. Before I amplify that a little, and say a bit more about Figure 10.2, here is a diagram that is indeed a picture of the main components of the NCS (Figure 10.3).

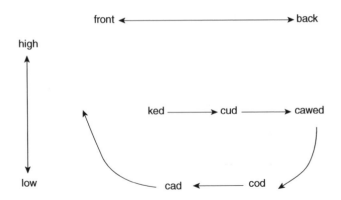

Figure 10.3 Directions of the main sound changes in the Northern Cities Shift using a diagram based on the vowel chart of the International Phonetic Alphabet (Labov, 2012, Figure 5, location 356).

This diagram is based on the principles of the vowel chart of the International Phonetic Alphabet, which provides a rather abstract picture of the different positions in the mouth of the tongue when different vowels are articulated. You have to imagine that the diagram offers a profile view of the human mouth from a left perspective, in which the tongue is lying along the bottom of the diagram, with its front or tip at the left of the diagram and its back at the right. The low-high dimension in the diagram indicates how high the tongue is when it articulates each vowel, and the front-back dimension shows which part of the tongue is highest for each vowel. Thus, for example, the vowel of *ked* can be called a mid-high, front vowel, because the front of the tongue is quite high when it articulates the -*e*- in *ked*. What the diagram makes crystal clear is that the NCS is phonologically a highly structured set of changes, because not one component takes place in isolation.

The first explicit evidence of the NCS was found in Detroit (by Fasold, 1967, according to Wolfram and Schilling-Estes, 2008, p. 360) and Chicago in the late 1960s and early 1970s (see also Labov, Yaeger and Steiner, 1972), followed by further data from Buffalo and Rochester, giving a regional spread stretching from Illinois at its western edge to New York State in the east. Labov (1994, p. 178) also notes supporting evidence in the earlier works of American linguistic geography. When Labov delivered his lectures in the Page-Barbour series at the University of Virginia in 2009 (Labov, 2012), he summed up what had been discovered about the NCS in the following four decades, as well as reviewing his explanation of its historical roots. The NCS characterizes the speech of the Inland North dialect region of the United States, as defined by the shaded area in Figure 10.2, which arcs around the south of the Great Lakes, stretching westward as far east Iowa, southern Wisconsin, and Illinois, and eastward into most of New York State. The NCS is found in every city in this extensive region, which Labov describes as a vast conurbation with a population of over 34 million (2012, location 493). Later research has shown the NCS diffusing into rural areas of Michigan (Gordon, 2001) and the Inland North fringe in New York State (Dinkin, 2009). Labov points out (2012, locations 442–93) that the Inland North is a sub-area of the North dialect region of the United States, as identified by Hans Kurath in 1949 in his atlas of regional vocabulary in the Atlantic states, and corroborated by Kurath's and McDavid's pronunciation atlas in 1961. Drawing on D. H. Fischer's *cultural hearth* view (1989), Labov also notes that the North dialect region 'is the area of original Yankee settlement from southeastern England' (2012, location 455). Not until the publication of the *ANAE* (Labov et al., 2006) had the mapping of English pronunciation patterns been extended from the Atlantic states westwards into the interior of America, and what the *ANAE* showed was a general correspondence with the three big traditional dialect/accent areas identified by Kurath: North, Midland, and South. Figure 10.4 is another version of the map shown in Figure 10.2, this time from the main *ANAE* volume, with the dialect regions named (the original again is colour-coded).

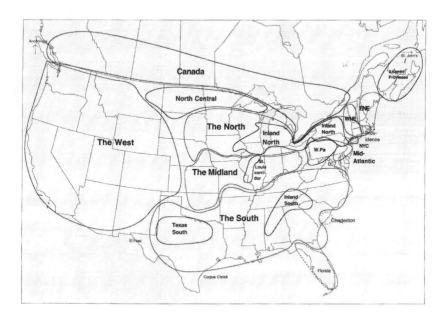

Figure 10.4   Map showing the main dialect regions of North American English and their labels (from Labov et al., 2006, p. 148). W. Pa = West Pennsylvania, WNE = Western New England, ENE = East New England, NYC = New York City.

These big regions not only persisted in similar (though not absolutely identical) form, but expanded well into the interior, which is 'the result of the steady westward orientation of streams of settlement in the 19th century' (Labov, 2012, location 469).

The last two quotes from Labov, about Yankee settlement and its westward expansion, give us a taste of his cultural hearth explanation of the roots of the NCS and Inland North region, which we shall get to soon. And I will come back to my neogrammarian comment soon as well. But the outline above also leads into a few short diversions which further highlight aspects of second-phase geolinguistics.

10.5.2   Some short diversions on second-phase geolinguistics

First, the NCS story has been exposed by both large-scale (Telsur, *ANAE*) and more localized, smaller operations (for example, Gordon, 2000, 2001; Dinkin, 2009, 2013) which propel a developed sociolinguistic methodology into a geographical context, and which gladly build on and refer back to the work of the linguistic geographers (for example, Kurath, McDavid).

Second, another type of localized research has also contributed, this being the **community of practice** approach as done by Penelope Eckert in Detroit in the early 1980s, mentioned above. Eckert defines a *community of practice* as 'an aggregate of people who come together around mutual engagement in some common endeavor' (page at Eckert's website: http://web.stanford. edu/~eckert/csofp.html; accessed 21 October 2014). She says that, 'Ways of doing things, ways of talking, beliefs, values, power relations – in short, practices – emerge in the course of their [people's] joint activity around that endeavor.' In this approach, the focus is on the function of speech in constructing individuals' identities as they participate in social groups, groups which in turn are constructed by their members' behaviours, including their speech behaviours. The focus here is on the dynamic, constructive relationship between speech and identity. The approach evolved out of Labov's work, and out of social network theory, and the emphasis shifts away from variables and social classes towards styles of speech and mutually defining communities. For example, in her Detroit study, Eckert spent two years observing the behaviour of two communities of practice in five suburban schools, especially one which she calls 'Belten High'. The two communities are called *jocks* and *burnouts*. 'The jocks are a school-oriented community of practice, embodying middle class culture. The burnouts are a locally-oriented community of practice, embodying working class culture' (Eckert's website: http://web.stanford. edu/~eckert/jb.html). The jocks engage positively with the school institution, while the burnouts engage positively with suburban and urban culture, and are alienated from the school. Each community gravitates to different spaces, the jocks to spaces that are central to school life, the burnouts to marginal suburban spaces such as parking lots and city streets (Eckert, 2010, pp. 171–2). And each community invests itself in different speech styles, the jocks veering away from non-standard grammar and urban phonology, the burnouts making significantly greater use of sound changes emanating from the urban centre (Eckert, 2010, p. 172), with the burnout females in particular leading the way in the use of new variants (Eckert, 2000, p. 219). In terms of the NCS, it was a group of females exhibiting the most extreme burnout behaviour – *burned-out burnouts* – who were in the vanguard, leading in the use of the latest shift at the time, that of short-*u* in *but* to *bought*. In his 2012 description of Eckert's research, Labov says (location 1722) that the advanced forms of sound change carry social meaning and 'originate specifically as features of local identification of the nonconformist group, and then spread to other portions of the social network who take the Burnouts as a reference group'. (Eckert has also explored the community of practice in relation to language and gender, with her collaborator Sally McConnell-Ginet (see Eckert and McConnell-Ginet, 1992, 2003).)

My third short diversion is about **dialect supralocalization** or **regional dialect levelling**. The two terms are pretty much synonymous and refer to processes whereby relatively distinct local varieties show some degree of convergence, exhibiting a greater number of features in common than before, and form a larger more homogeneous regional variety. Use of the term *supra-local* in connection with such phenomena goes back to a 1994 article by Milroy et al., which investigated the spread of the glottal stop in varieties of British English, and the phrase *dialect supralocalization* was launched by David Britain in 2002 (Britain, 2002b), the same year that Kerswill suggested the label *regional dialect levelling* (Kerswill, 2002). (Let's note also the term *supra-regional variety*, used in a similar sense by Hickey in 1999.) For David Britain, dialect supralocalization is caused by greater mobility of speakers within regions (and also therefore more intra-regional contact) which is breaking down the more local varieties of English in those regions and creating a smaller number of geographically larger regional varieties (Britain, 2010a, p. 152). These are regional **koines**: 'leveled supralocal varieties which are replacing some of the linguistic diversity that once reigned within individual regions' (Britain, 2010a, p. 152). *Supra-local* means literally 'above the local', that is, occurring at more than a local level. Standard English is a supra-local dialect, indeed a supra-regional dialect, but the features under investigation with regard to supralocalization are non-standard features, like use of the glottal stop for /p, t, k/. For Torgersen and Kerswill (2004, p. 3), *dialect levelling* occurs when two or more local varieties are in sustained contact and some of their more distinctive variant features are lost. When this levelling occurs over a relatively large geographical area (such as the south-east of England), then it can be called *regional dialect levelling* (Kerswill, 2002, p. 187). The geolinguistic studies that have investigated these phenomena have tended to focus on phonology. Northern Cities Shift can be interpreted as an example of supralocalization in that it is occurring with considerable uniformity over a large territory and is the foremost diagnostic of the Inland North dialect region. Labov et al. (2006, p. 119) state that the linguistic changes in progress in North America are leading to the large regional dialects becoming more differentiated from each other, but that diversity within each region is decreasing. In England, Torgersen and Kerswill (2004) investigated regional dialect levelling in the south-east. By sampling a total of 27 informants in two age-groups (14–15 years old, and speakers in their seventies and eighties), they discovered that the previously somewhat different short vowel systems of the towns of Reading (about 40 miles to the west of London) and Ashford (60 miles to the south-east of London) were converging. They found that Ashford was participating in a short vowel chain shift affecting much of south-east England. This brought Ashford pronunciations closer to Reading pronunciations, despite the fact that Reading was not participating in the chain shift. In Reading, 'the front vowels already had the positions in the vowel space which were the targets for the change farther east in London, Kent and East Anglia' (Torgersen and Kerswill, 2004, p. 27), though there was evidence of some Reading short vowels adjusting to the south-east change. Making use of accommodation theory (see Chapter 9, section 3), Torgersen and Kerswill (p. 27) say that the cause of this regional levelling is persistent intra-regional contact, with London influence figuring large.

Like those studying the NCS, Torgersen and Kerswill utilize the earlier linguistic geographers in reaching their conclusions, especially the Survey of English Dialects. And David Britain points out (2010a, p. 153) that supralocalization in south-east England was observed by A. J. Ellis in 1889 – not that he used the term (and neither does this undermine the view that such processes are on the increase). Here are some brief examples of Ellis's comments:

[T]he enormous congeries of persons from different parts of the kingdom and from different countries, and the generality of school education, render dialect nearly impossible.

(1889, p. 225)

For the rural portions of the SE district, I have very slender information. My informants find a shifting population, and nothing distinctive to record. They imagine that if there is nothing different to their hearing than uneducated London speech, there is nothing to report.

(1889, pp. 234–5; my thanks to David Britain for drawing my attention to these and other remarks in Ellis, 1889)

It is also worth reminding ourselves that while regional homogenization of dialects may be a growing characteristic of English in Britain and the United States, it does not mean that dialectal diversity is simply ebbing away. The NCS, for example, is increasing the divergence of the Inland North from other large regional varieties of American English. Labov (2012, location 587) reports 'vigorous new sound changes' taking place in other areas of North America, thereby increasing differences, while on the other hand the 'dialects of many smaller cities have receded in favor of the new regional patterns'. He says (location 615): 'The general picture of North American dialects shows both convergence and divergence.' And as far as the south-east of England is concerned, David Britain tells us (2010a, p. 153) that local varieties still exist within the larger **regiolect**, and that studies provide evidence both of ongoing linguistic homogenization and continuing linguistic diversity. Britain's own research in the Fens of East Anglia has shown the perseverance of historical local dialect boundaries for many features, while the most recent innovations from London ignore and sweep over these local boundaries (Britain, 2010a, p. 154). The research by Torgersen and Kerswill mentioned above formed part of a three-year project (2004–7) called Linguistic Innovators, which explored the English of adolescents in London (see: http://www.lancaster.ac.uk/fss/projects/linguistics/innovators/index.htm), and in which Jenny Cheshire, Sue Fox, and Arfaan Khan were the other collaborators. This project uncovered some interesting complexity within the bigger picture of south-eastern levelling. Torgersen et al. (2006), using data collected from adolescent and elderly age-groups in Hackney (inner London) and Havering (east outer London) which they compared with prior-existing data from London, found that some of their informants were involved in divergence rather than levelling in their vowels. While some features showed shared participation in south-east levelling, other vowel variants did not, and these latter were found particularly among inner-city speakers of Afro-Caribbean and other 'non-Anglo' backgrounds (Torgersen et al., 2006, pp. 12–13). To take one specific example, the vowel in the *foot* group of words, /ʊ/, is **fronted** in south-east levelling (that is, the highest part of the tongue during articulation is further forward than previously was the case), but this fronting had not occurred in Hackney, possibly because of the influence of West Indian varieties of English. Cheshire et al. (2005) also found innovations in the diphthong system of inner London which were not found elsewhere in the south-east.

Not only did the scholars involved in the Linguistic Innovators project (i) compare the Trudgillean diffusion-model with the levelling-model (they found evidence of both diffusion outwards from London and of levelling at the peripheries outside London (Kerswill et al., 2007)), (ii) invoke Labov's work on principles of vowel change (Labov, 1994), and (iii) use insights derived from community of practice and social network theory (Fox, 2007;

Cheshire et al., 2008), but they also (iv) couched their enquiry in an explicitly neogrammarian context (Kerswill et al., 2007; see also Kerswill, 2002). That is to say, they measured their own findings against the neogrammarian ideal of the regular nature of sound change in a common phonological environment and throughout a speech community. Their conclusion with regard to a series of changes affecting the vowels in the *face*, *goat*, *mouth*, and *price* groups of words is that in the long view there is evidence of regularity, but 'the social and phonetic detail is extremely messy' (Kerswill et al., 2007, slide 57). To add a little more detail to this: the diphthongs in these word groups have been involved in a sound shift in south-east England that has been noted for a long time, going back to A. J. Ellis (1889, as acknowledged by Kerswill et al., 2008, p. 453), but the recent data for young speakers in inner London shows divergence from or non-participation in this diphthong shift (Fox, 2007; Kerswill et al., 2008). The full detail is indeed untidy, but there are patterns, and factors which appear to shape the patterns: non-Anglo youngsters lead the non-participation; Anglo speakers with a multi-ethnic friendship network follow; male non-Anglo speakers lead female non-Anglo speakers; and there is some evidence of diffusion of this 'diphthong shift reversal' outwards from inner London (Kerswill et al., 2008, pp. 483–4). In summary, such sound shifts appear to have an inbuilt drive towards the goal of regularity, but the speech communities in which they are enacted are in a continual state of flux created by the interplay of ethnicity, social networks, age, gender, geographical space, and speaker mobility, and this can accelerate, halt, reverse, or otherwise disrupt that basic drive. Modern geolinguistics is developing and refining an array of methods that grapple with this societal flux.

10.5.3   And finally back to Northern Cities Shift

Figures 10.2 and 10.4, taken from the CD-ROM and main volume parts of *The Atlas of North American English* (Labov et al., 2006), respectively, show the greatest regional extent of the NCS. Labov has often emphasized the uniformity of this Inland North region in NCS terms: an extensive geographical area with a population of many millions participating in a single set of connected sound changes. This strongly suggests a drive towards regularity. But we have already seen that in its history some groups of speakers will be at a more advanced stage of the NCS than others, and, moreover, Labov et al. observe (2006, p. 191) that the sequencing of the component changes of the NCS might be different for different locations and different social groups. Both Figures 10.2 and 10.4 also show a dialect region immediately to the east of the Inland North. This region is labelled Western New England (WNE) in Figure 10.4. If you play around with the interactivity of the CD-ROM version of the map, you will find that WNE is characterized by 'less advanced NCS', and, when you add the colour-coded circles that represent each Telsur informant, you will find a minority in each region (about nine per cent overall) who are not participating in the NCS. In a meticulous, detailed study published in 2013, Aaron J. Dinkin interviewed a total of 98 speakers in 12 cities and towns lying between the *ANAE*'s Inland North and WNE regions, with a view to clarifying both the extent of NCS adoption and the dialect boundaries in the area. Following *ANAE* sampling procedures, and doing computer acoustic analysis of digital recordings using Praat software (see http://www.fon.hum.uva.nl/praat/), and presentation of this analysis using Labov's Plotnik program (http://www.ling.upenn.edu/~wlabov/Plotnik.html), Dinkin tentatively suggests the existence of an additional Hudson Valley dialect region between the Inland North and Southwestern New England. This Hudson Valley area shows only partial NCS characteristics, but it shows a partial NCS that is different from the partial NCS of WNE. In addition, Labov's work (2010, 2012) has shown that perceptions of NCS-affected pronunciations do not match exactly with the production data. Speakers leading the NCS in Chicago were audio recorded and then they listened to the recordings (along with recordings of other dialects). When NCS-affected words were played in isolation they tended to mishear them. For example, 'block' in the phrase 'senior citizens living on one block' was misheard as 'black' by 98 per cent of the Chicago listeners when played back in isolation (Labov, 2012, location 318). One more significant point: the NCS is overwhelmingly affecting the speech of white Americans only. African Americans 'participate only marginally in these sound changes' (Labov, 2012, location 614). What I am saying here is that, as with the Linguistic Innovators project, there is regularity and then there is 'messiness' in the details, with neither characteristic negating the other.

Labov has taken his explanation of linguistic change further by attempting to discover the deep-seated historical reasons why such a major swathe of the north-eastern United States is participating in the NCS. He argues (2012, location 1729) that 'no local mechanism can be driving the NCS in the same direction with the same results over this vast area', adding that if there is a social motivation involved, then 'it cannot depend on face-to-face contact between the speakers involved' (location 1744). This seems to rule out the kind of diffusion and levelling explanations that we have encountered so far. Instead Labov seeks to establish that there is in the white, English-speaking community of the Inland North dialect region a common sense of cultural identity at work. Beginning with D. H. Fischer's *cultural hearth* concept (which itself is influenced by W. G. Sumner's (1906) *folkways* notion), Labov builds a picture of a region possessing a striking degree of cultural cohesion in the historical development of its religious and political character (see Chapter 7 of Labov, 2012). The core of his argument is that this cohesion is also reflected in mass participation in the NCS.

In Labov's account, the origins of the NCS go back as far as the early nine-teenth century. A key event which created the conditions for the NCS was the building of the Erie Canal, from 1817 to 1825, connecting the Hudson River with the Great Lakes. Construction of the canal required large numbers of labourers, which led to high immigration into upstate New York. This brought together a variety of pronunciation systems from a variety of dialect origins in the population mix that resulted, including different systems for the pronun-ciation of short-*a* in the *bat* group of words, and, in an instance of koineiza-tion, the mixture produced a new system in which short-*a* was raised, yielding the first stage of the NCS. This new system moved westwards by means of an unusual form of population migration: again referencing Fischer (1989), Labov tells us that the northern 'Yankees' moved whole populations of communities westwards, sometimes up to 20,000 people at a go. 'This created the environ-ment in which generation after generation of child language learners trans-mitted the system intact, steadily incrementing the changes in a constant direction' (Labov, 2012, location 1797). Thus the 'cultural hearth' moved steadily westwards, and the phonetic structural push-and-pull dynamics set in motion by the shift of short-*a* words ensured that a chain shift came about. Dinkin's 2013 study again adds some local detail to this. The partial-NCS Hudson Valley dialect region that Dinkin proposes matches the region recognized in 1949 by Hans Kurath based on lexical data. The early settlement history of this region is different from that of the localities to its immediate west, where NCS is found. Those latter were settled mainly by migration from Western New England, whereas Dinkin's Hudson Valley localities 'all drew settlers from the original Dutch New Netherland population' (Dinkin, 2013, p. 23). Thus Dutch and German remained the principal languages in Hudson Valley communities until the early nineteenth century, leading eventually to structurally different short vowel systems in English which have proved more resistant to the full set of NCS changes.

10.6   Conclusion

Here then we reach the ending point for this history of the study of English dialects. Modern geolinguistics is a recent phase in dialect study, but it is not a break with the past. In fact, it involves a reaffirmation of the past, a return to the work of even the earliest dialectologists of the late nineteenth century, who themselves built on the achievements of their predecessors. In recent geolin-guistic work, methods, aims, and hypotheses are much refined in comparison with earlier approaches, but these refinements are infused with a willingness to make use of and acknowledge the earlier work. There is continuity, too, connecting the most recent work with the earliest. This continuity is found in the exploitation of technological advances that aid data collection and analysis, in the belief in the value of data to linguistic description and theory, and in the unbroken thread of two inseparable themes: understanding linguistic diversity and understanding linguistic change.

10.7   Brief commentary on terms

As I write the final sections of this chapter, I can report that the term *geolinguistics* still cannot be found in the *OED Online*. However, if you Google it (the verb *to Google* is in the *OED*) you will quickly come across an application of the term not mentioned in the chapter above. This is in the name the American Society of Geolinguistics (http://www.geolinguistics.org/), which was founded in 1965 by Mario A. Pei. The society has an interest in dialectology, linguistic geography, and sociolinguistics, but it applies the term *geolinguistics* to a wider remit than in the work described above. The society was set up to disseminate and explain linguistic research on the world's present-day languages, their use, distribution, and histories, to the wider public, with an emphasis on language education and language planning.

Another usage not discussed in the chapter above is when modern-day scholars sometimes apply the term retrospectively to earlier work in dialect study, as a kind of rewriting or effacing of previous terms like *linguistic geography*. You will come across this. Maybe it is not such a bad thing. The term *geolinguistics* is made up of *geo-*, which is used to form words relating to the earth, plus *linguistics*, giving the literal sense 'the study of language and the earth'. It is probably sensible also to see it as a contraction of *geographical linguistics*, and, if you have read Chapter 5 of the present book, that phrase will ring a bell. For there you will find a quotation from a presentation delivered to the Philological Society in London on 7 April 1876 (p. 577) by the pioneer of English linguistic geography, Prince Louis-Lucien Bonaparte, in which he describes his work as being that of 'the geographical linguist'.

10.8   What you can do

If you go to Penelope Eckert's web-pages (https://web.stanford.edu/~eckert/index.html), you can download a paper delivered by her on 28 October 2011 to the 40th New Ways of Analyzing Variation conference (NWAV40), entitled 'The Future of Variation Studies'. In it Eckert says, 'the availability of speech recognition and analysis technology … is moving the study of variation onto a completely new level' (Eckert, 2011, p. 2). She continues, 'The internet and communicative technology provide access to varied speech and written samples, in the form of large corpora and media of all sorts', adding, 'As a result of all these innovations, we can now take a far broader range of social and linguistic variables into consideration, and interpret the patterns we find.' Her short paper celebrates the wider opportunities opening up for the study of language variation, at a stage when the field as a whole has become an amalgam of methods refined and augmented through approximately 150 years of systematic research (if we take early comparative philology as our starting point), and when the ambition of the project as a whole (going back to before comparative philology to, say, John Ray) is now matched by sufficiently powerful technological tools and aids. As we have seen in the chapter above, Eckert's individual work has contributed to the bigger picture of sound shifts in North American English. Thus the combination of easier collection, storage, and processing of data, plus the greater availability of pre-existing, 'ready-made' data, plus the wealth of existing studies that can be used for comparative purposes, and the variety of models that one can draw upon to help explain linguistic variation and change, means that even very small-scale studies can make a contribution to the big stories and themes of dialect study.

Resources and further reading

One thing that you might notice as you progress through your further reading programme is that several of the overviews of perceptual dialectology written by Dennis Preston turn up in the same collections that have overviews of modern geolinguistics written by David Britain. As with Preston's output on PD, Britain's reviews (2002a, 2004, 2010a, 2010b, 2013) are the first locations to start deepening your acquaintance with the antecedents, scope, aims, methods, and achievements of geolinguistics. William Labov's *Dialect Diversity in America* (2012) is a good place to get an accessible summing up and discussion of what is known about the Northern Cities Chain Shift. For some time now, *The Atlas of North American English* (Labov et al., 2006) has been available in a free Kindle edition – check to see if this is still the case, and if so, download it immediately. There are other free materials and writings relevant to this and other chapters of the present book at Labov's web-pages. See also the web-pages of Penelope Eckert, Matthew J. Gordon, and Aaron J. Dinkin for more information on and explanations of their work, plus some downloads. A wealth of Paul Kerswill's work can be accessed via his pages at York and Lancaster Universities, and the website of the Linguistic Innovators project (2004–7) has information and downloads of articles and presentations. There is an assessment by Miriam Meyerhoff and Anna Strycharz of the communities of practice framework in the very useful second edition (2013) of *The Handbook of Language Variation and Change*, edited by J. K. Chambers and Natalie Schilling. The 1999 collection of essays on accents of British English, *Urban Voices*, edited by Paul Foulkes and Gerard Docherty, although not presenting itself under the label *geolinguistics*, contains a couple of interesting early reports on dialect levelling, by Dominic Watt and Lesley Milroy (on the north-east of England), and Ann Williams and Paul Kerswill (on the two southern centres of Reading and Milton Keynes and the northern city of Hull). For an up-to-date comprehensive collection of essays on the broad sweep of present-day dialectology, go to *The Handbook of Dialectology* (2017), edited by Charles Boberg, John Nerbonne and Dominic Watt. Finally, two videos that are well worth watching: a long interview done in November 2012 by Alan Macfarlane of Peter Trudgill on his life and work, in the Cambridge Film Interviews with Leading Thinkers series (http://www.sms.cam.ac.uk/media/1382735); and a lecture on 'The Relation of Social to Structural Factors in the Explanation of Linguistic Change' given by William Labov in June 2013 at York University (https://www.youtube.com/watch?v=qCJh8nFXBUE), in which he sums up his thinking on linguistic diversity and change in North American English.

Bibliography

Online items are listed in the Webography, which follows this Bibliography. Some electronic versions of items are also mentioned in Bibliography entries.

Adams, G. Brendan (ed.) (1964) *Ulster Dialects: An Introductory Symposium* (Cultra Manor, Holywood, County Down: Ulster Folk Museum).

Adams, G. Brendan, Barry, Michael V. and Tilling, Philip M. (1976) *A Tape-recorded Survey of Hiberno-English, Questionnaire* (Belfast: privately published, no publisher details given).

Adams, G. Brendan, Barry, Michael V. and Tilling, Philip M. (1985) 'The Tape-recorded Survey of Hiberno-English Speech: A Reappraisal of the Techniques of Traditional Dialect Geography'. In Kirk, Sanderson and Widdowson (eds) (1985), pp. 67–80.

Aitken, A. J. (1967, 2015) 'Quiet Scot Who Was a Master of Words'. In *Collected Writings on the Scots Language* (2015, online), by A. J. Aitken, edited by Caroline Macafee, Scots Language Centre: http://medio.scotslanguage.com/library/document/aitken/Quiet_ Scot_who_was_a_master_of_words_(1967). Originally published in *The Glasgow Herald*, 12 August 1967, p. 8. Online: http://news.google.com/newspapers?id=D1xAA AAAIBAJ&sjid=c6MMAAAAIBAJ&pg=3963%2C1856099.

Aitken, A. J. (1984) 'Scots and English in Scotland'. In *Language in the British Isles* (1st edn), edited by Peter Trudgill (Cambridge: Cambridge University Press), pp. 517–32.

Aitken, A. J. (1987) 'The Period Dictionaries'. In Burchfield (ed.) (1987), pp. 94–116.

Aitken, A. J. (1996, 2015) 'James Murray, Master of Scots', *Review of Scottish Culture*, No. 9 (1996), 14–34. Also in revised form online in *Collected Writings on the Scots Language* (2015), by A. J. Aitken, edited by Caroline Macafee, Scots Language Centre: http://media. scotslanguage.com/library/document/aitken/James_Murray,_master_of_Scots_(1996).

Aitken, A. J., Stevenson, James A. C., Watson, H. D. et al. (eds) (1931–2002) *A Dictionary of the Older Scottish Tongue: From the Twelfth Century to the End of the Seventeenth.* Founded on the collections of Sir William A. Craigie. Vols I–XII. (London: Oxford

University Press). *DOST* had 18 editors in all. See also Webography entry for *Dictionary of the Scots Language (DSL)*.

Alexander, Henry (1940) 'Linguistic Geography', *Queen's Quarterly*, Vol. 47, 38–47.

Allan, Scott (1990) 'The Rise of New Zealand Intonation'. In *New Zealand Ways of Speaking English*, edited by Allan Bell and Janet Holmes (Clevedon, Avon, UK and Bristol, Pennsylvania, USA: Multilingual Matters; Wellington: Victoria University Press), pp. 115–28.

Allen, Harold B. (1971) 'Some Problems in Editing the Linguistic Atlas of the Upper Midwest'. In *Dialectology: Problems and Perspectives*, edited by Lorraine Hall Burghardt (Knoxville, Tennessee: University of Tennessee), pp. 54–78.

Allen, Harold B. (1973) *The Linguistic Atlas of the Upper Midwest*. Vol. 1: *The Project and the Lexicon* (Minneapolis: University of Minnesota Press).

Allen, Harold B. (1973–6) *The Linguistic Atlas of the Upper Midwest*. Three vols. (Minneapolis: University of Minnesota Press).

Allen, Harold B. (1977) 'Regional Dialects, 1945–1974', *American Speech*, Vol. 52, No. 3/4, 163–261.

Allsopp, Richard (ed.), with a French and Spanish supplement edited by Jeannette Allsopp (1996) *Dictionary of Caribbean English Usage* (Oxford: Oxford University Press).

Ammon, Ulrich, Dittmar, Norbert, Mattheier, Klaus J. and Trudgill, Peter (eds) (2004–6) *Sociolinguistics: An International Handbook of the Science of Language and Society*. Three vols. (Berlin and New York: Walter de Gruyter, 2nd revised and extended edns).

Anderson, Peter M. (1987) *A Structural Atlas of the English Dialects* (London: Croom Helm).

Anisfeld, Elizabeth and Lambert, Wallace E. (1964) 'Evaluational Reactions of Bilingual and Monolingual Children to Spoken Languages', *Journal of Abnormal and Social Psychology*, Vol. 69, No. 1, 89–97.

Atwood, Elmer Bagby (1953) *A Survey of Verb Forms in the Eastern United States* (Studies in American English, No. 2) (Ann Arbor: University of Michigan Press).

Atwood, Elmer Bagby (1962) *The Regional Vocabulary of Texas* (Austin, Texas: University of Texas Press).

Atwood, Elmer Bagby (1963) 'The Methods of American Dialectology'. In *Dialect and Language Variation*, edited by Harold B. Allen and Michael D. Linn (Orlando, Florida: Academic Press, 1986), pp. 63–97. Reprinted from *Zeitschrift für Mundartforschung*, Vol. 30, No. 1 (October, 1963), 1–30.

Auer, Peter and Schmidt, Jürgen Erich (eds) (2010) *Language and Space: An International Handbook of Linguistic Variation*. Vol. 1: *Theories and Methods*. (Berlin and New York: De Gruyter Mouton).

Avis, Walter S. (ed.-in-chief), Crate, Charles, Drysdale, Patrick, Leechman, Douglas, Scargill, Matthew H. and Lovell, Charles J. (eds) (1967) *A Dictionary of Canadianisms on Historical Principles* (Toronto: W. J. Gage). See Webography entry for Dollinger, Stefan et al. (2013) for online edition.

Axon, William E. A. (ed.) (1883) *English Dialect Words of the Eighteenth Century as shown in the 'Universal Etymological Dictionary' of Nathaniel Bailey* (London: Published for The English Dialect Society by Trübner).

Bailey, Charles-James Nice (1973) *Variation and Linguistic Theory* (Arlington, Virginia: Center for Applied Linguistics).

Bailey, Charles-James Nice (1982) *The Yin and Yang Nature of Language* (Ann Arbor, Michigan: Karoma).

Bailey, Charles-James Nice (1987) 'Variation Theory and So-Called "Sociolinguistic Grammars"', *Language and Communication*, Vol. 7, No. 4, 269–91.

Bailey, Charles-James Nice (1996) *Essays on Time-Based Linguistic Analysis* (Oxford: Clarendon Press).

Bailey, Guy, Wikle, Tom, Tillery, Jan and Sand, Lori (1993) 'Some Patterns of Linguistic Diffusion', *Language Variation and Change*, Vol. 5, pp. 359–90.

Bailey, Nathaniel [Nathan] (1721–7) *An Universal Etymological Dictionary*. Two vols. (London: Printed for E. Bell).

Bailey, Richard W. (1991) *Images of English: A Cultural History of the Language* (Cambridge: Cambridge University Press).

Ball, Martin J. (ed.) (2010) *The Routledge Handbook of Sociolinguistics Around the World* (Abingdon, UK and New York: Routledge).

Ball, Peter (1983) 'Stereotypes of Anglo-Saxon and Non-Anglo-Saxon Accents: Some Exploratory Australian Studies with the Matched-Guise Technique', *Language Sciences*, Vol. 5, No. 2, 163–83.

Ball, Peter, Gallois, C. and Callan, V. J. (1989) 'Language Attitudes: A Perspective from Social Psychology'. In *Australian English: The Language of a New Society*, edited by P. Collins and D. Blair (Brisbane: University of Queensland Press), pp. 89–102.

Barbieri, Federica (2005) 'Quotative Use in American English: A Corpus-Based, Cross-Register Comparison', *Journal of English Linguistics*, Vol. 33, No. 3, 222–56.

Barbiers, Sjef (2005) 'Word Order Variation in Three-Verb Clusters and the Division of Labour Between Generative Linguistics and Sociolinguistics'. In Cornips and Corrigan (eds) (2005a), pp. 233–64.

Barbiers, Sjef (2010) 'Language and Space: Structuralist and Generative Approaches'. In Auer and Schmidt (eds) (2010), pp. 125–42.

Barnes, William (1844) *Poems of Rural Life, in the Dorset Dialect: With a Dissertation on the Folk Speech, and a Glossary of Dorset Words* (London: J. R. Smith).

Barnes, William (1859) *The Song of Solomon in the Dorset Dialect; From the Authorised English Version* (London: George Barclay). See also entry for Bonaparte (1862).

Barnes, William (1863) *A Grammar and Glossary of the Dorset Dialect, with the History of the Outspreading and Bearings of the South-Western English* (Berlin: A. Asher for the Philological Society).

Barnes, William (1886) *A Glossary of the Dorset Dialect with a Grammar of its Word Shapening And Wording* (Dorchester: M. and E. Case; London: Trübner). Republished in 1970 by The Toucan Press (Mount Durand, St Peter Port, Guernsey: Stevens-Cox).

Barry, Michael V. (1980) 'The Southern Boundaries of Northern Hiberno-English Speech'. In *Linguistic Studies in Honour of Paul Christophersen*, edited by R. Thelwall (Coleraine: The New University of Ulster), pp. 105–52.

Barry, Michael V. (ed.) (1981) *Aspects of English Dialects in Ireland*. Vol. 1: *Papers Arising from the Tape-Recorded Survey of Hiberno-English Speech* (Belfast: The Institute of Irish Studies).

Baumgarten, Rolf and Sommerfelt, Alf (1974) 'Alf Sommerfelt's Proposals for an Irish Linguistic Survey, 1941', *Studia Hibernica*, No. 14, 124–39.

Bayley, Robert (2013) 'The Quantitative Paradigm'. In Chambers and Schilling (eds) (2013), pp. 85–107.

Beckman, Mary E., and Ayers Elam, Gayle (1997) *Guidelines for ToBI Labelling* (version 3.0, March 1997) (The Ohio State University Research Foundation). Available at: http://www.ling.ohio-state.edu/~tobi/ame_tobi/labelling_guide_v3.pdf. Also at: http://www.ling.ohio-state.edu/research/phonetics/E_ToBI/. See also Webography entry for ToBI.

Beckman, Mary E., Hirschberg, Julia, and Shattuck-Hufnagel, Stefanie (2005) 'The Original ToBI System and the Evolution of the ToBI Framework'. In *Prosodic Typology: The Phonology of Intonation and Phrasing*, edited by Sun-Ah Jun (Oxford: Oxford University Press), pp. 9–54.

Bell, Allan and Holmes, Janet (eds) (1990) *New Zealand Ways of Speaking English* (Clevedon, Avon and Philadelphia: Multilingual Matters).

Bell, Allan and Kuiper, Koenraad (eds.) (2000) *New Zealand English* (Varieties of English Around the World, General Series, Vol. 25) (Amsterdam/Philadelphia: John Benjamins).

Benson, Erica J. (2003) 'Folk Linguistic Perceptions and the Mapping of Dialect Boundaries', *American Speech*, Vol. 78, No. 3, 307–30.

Bernhardi, Karl (1844, though drawn in 1843) *Sprachkarte von Deutschland. Als Versuch entworfen und erläutert von Karl Bernhardi* (Kassel: Bohné). Map reproduced in Lameli et al. (eds) (2010b, Map 0802).

Bickerton, Derek (1975) Review of *The Social Differentiation of English in Norwich* by Peter Trudgill, *Journal of Linguistics*, Vol. 11, No. 2, 299–308.

Biondelli, Bernardino (1841) *Atlante Linguistico d'Europa* (Milan: Chiusi). Available online at the Munich Digitization Center (MDZ) of the Bavarian State Library (BSB): http://daten.digitale-sammlungen.de/0000/bsb00003936/images/index.html?fip=193.174.98.30&id=00003936&seite=4.

Blair, David and Collins, Peter (eds) (2001) *English in Australia* (Varieties of English Around the World, General Series, Vol. 26) (Amsterdam/Philadelphia: John Benjamins).

Bobbin, Tim – see entries for John Collier.

Boberg, Charles (2005) 'The North American Regional Vocabulary Survey: Renewing the Study of Lexical Variation in North American English', *American Speech*, Vol. 80, No. 1, 22–60.

Boberg, Charles (2008) 'Regional Phonetic Differentiation in Standard Canadian English', *Journal of English Linguistics*, Vol. 36, No. 2, 129–54.

Boberg, Charles (2010) *The English Language in Canada: Status, History and Comparative Analysis* (Cambridge: Cambridge University Press).

Boberg, Charles, Nerbonne, John and Watt, Dominic (eds) (2017) *The Handbook of Dialectology* (Hoboken, New Jersey, Chichester and Oxford: Wiley-Blackwell).

Boersma and Weenink (1992–2016): see Webography entry for *Praat*.

Bonaparte, Louis-Lucien (1862) *The Song of Solomon in Twenty-Four English Dialects*, Printed at the Expense of His Imperial Highness, Prince Louis-Lucien Bonaparte (London: Sold by Bernard Quaritch). Includes: *Cumberland, the Dialect of, from the Authorised English Version*, by John Rayson (1858); *Dorset Dialect, from the Authorised English Version*, by the Rev. William Barnes (1859). See also Webography entry for Bonaparte (1858–63).

Bonaparte, Louis-Lucien (1873) 'A Small Map of the Counties of England Shewing [sic] the Principal English Dialects' (London), which accompanies: 'Classification des Dialects Anglais Modernes, Présentée a la Société Philologique de Londres, par Le Prince Louis-Lucien Bonaparte, son Membre Honoraire, Le 20 Juin 1873.'

Bonaparte, Louis-Lucien (1875) 'A Small Map of the Counties of England Shewing the Approximate Delimitation of their Dialects and the Enumeration of their Sub-dialects and Principal Varieties' (London).

Bonaparte, Louis-Lucien (1877) 'On the Dialects of Monmouthshire, Gloucestershire, Herefordshire, Worcestershire, Berkshire, Oxfordshire, South Warwickshire, South Northamptonshire, Buckinghamshire, Hertfordshire, Middlesex, and Surrey, with a New Classification of the English Dialects. (With Two Maps.)' Read before the Philological Society, 7 April 1876. *Transactions of the Philological Society*, 1875–6, Part III, 570–9. Published in 1877.

Bridges, Kevin (2010) *The Story So Far ... Live in Glasgow* (DVD, Universal Pictures UK).

Bright, Elizabeth (1971) *A Word Geography of California and Nevada* (Berkeley and Los Angeles: University of California Press).

Bright, William (ed.) (1966) *Sociolinguistics: Proceedings of the UCLA Sociolinguistics Conference, 1964* (The Hague: Mouton and Company).

Britain, David (2000) '*As far as* Analysing Grammatical Variation and Change in New Zealand English with Relatively Few Tokens <*is concerned/Ø*>'. In *New Zealand English*, edited by Allan Bell and Koenraad Kuiper (Amsterdam/Philadelphia: John Benjamins), pp. 198–220.

Britain, David (2002a) 'Space and Spatial Diffusion'. In Chambers, Trudgill and Schilling-Estes (eds) (2002), pp. 603–37.

Britain, David (2002b) 'Phoenix From the Ashes?: The Death, Contact, and Birth of Dialects in England', *Essex Research Reports in Linguistics*, No. 41, 42–73.

Britain, David (2004) 'Geolinguistics – Diffusion of Language'. In *Sociolinguistics: An International Handbook of the Science of Language and Society*, Vol. 1, edited by Ulrich Ammon, Norbert Dittmar, Klaus J. Mattheier and Peter Trudgill (Berlin and New York: Walter de Gruyter, 2nd revised and extended edn), pp. 34–48.

Britain, David (2010a) 'Language and Space: The Variationist Approach'. In Auer and Schmidt (eds) (2010), pp. 142–63.

Britain, David (2010b) 'Conceptualizations of Geographic Space in Linguistics'. In Lameli et al. (eds) (2010a), pp. 69–97.

Britain, David (2013) 'Space, Diffusion and Mobility'. In Chambers and Schilling (eds) (2013), pp. 471–500.

Brotton, Jerry (2012) *A History of the World in Twelve Maps* (London: Allen Lane).

Brough, J. and Scott, N. C. (1955) 'Philological Society: Secretaries' Annual Report for 1953', *Transactions of the Philological Society*, 1954 (published 1955), 206–7.

Brugmann, Karl and Osthoff, Hermann (1878) – see entry for Osthoff and Brugmann (1878).

Brown, Felicity (2009) – see entry in Webography.

Bucholtz, Mary, Bermudez, Nancy, Fung, Victor, Edwards, Lisa and Vargas, Rosalva (2007) 'Hella Nor Cal or Totally So Cal? The Perceptual Dialectology of California', *Journal of English Linguistics*, Vol. 35, No. 4, 325–52.

Bucholtz, Mary, Bermudez, Nancy, Fung, Victor, Vargas, Rosalva and Edwards, Lisa (2008) 'The Normative North and the Stigmatized South: Ideology and Methodology in the Perceptual Dialectology of California', *Journal of English Linguistics*, Vol. 36, No. 1, 62–87.

Burchfield, Robert (ed.) *Studies in Lexicography* (Oxford: Clarendon Press, 1987).

Burkette, Allison (2015) Private email communication, November 2015.

Burgess, Anthony (1978) 'The People's English': Review of *The Linguistic Atlas of England*, *Times Literary Supplement*, 27 October 1978, p. 1255.

Butters, Ronald (1991) Review of *Perceptual Dialectology: Nonlinguists' Views of Areal Linguistics* by Dennis R. Preston, *Language in Society*, Vol. 20, No. 2, 294–9.

Byrne, David (1985) 'Give Me Back My Name' (Talking Heads, *Little Creatures*; New York City: Sire Records).

Calt, Stephen (2009) *Barrelhouse Words: A Blues Dialect Dictionary* (Champaign: University of Illinois Press).

Carver, Craig M. (1986) 'The Influence of the Mississippi River on Northern Dialect Boundaries', *American Speech*, Vol. 61, No. 3, 245–61.

Carver, Craig M. (1987) *American Regional Dialects: A Word Geography* (Ann Arbor: The University of Michigan Press).

Carver, Craig M. (1991) Review: 'In Pursuit of the Subjective Dialect Region: *Perceptual Dialectology: Nonlinguists' Views of Areal Linguistics* by Dennis Preston', *American Speech*, Vol. 66, No. 4, 432–7.

Cassidy, Frederic G. (1948) 'On Collecting American Dialect', *American Speech*, Vol. 23, No. 3/4, 185–93.

Cassidy, Frederic G. (1959) 'English Language Studies in the Caribbean', *American Speech*, Vol. 34, No. 3, 163–71.

Cassidy, Frederic G. (ed.) 1985) *Dictionary of American Regional English*. Vol. I: *Introduction and A–C*. (Cambridge, Massachusetts: (Belknap Press of) Harvard University Press).

Cassidy, Frederic G. (1987) 'The *Dictionary of American Regional English* as a Resource for Language Study'. In Burchfield (ed.) (1987), pp. 117–35.

Cassidy, Frederic G. and Hall, Joan Houston (eds) (1985–2013) *Dictionary of American Regional English*. Vols I–VI. (Cambridge, Massachusetts: (Belknap Press of) Harvard University Press). See also The Digital *Dictionary of American Regional English* (2014), edited by Hall (Harvard UP): http://www.daredictionary.com/.

Cassidy, Frederic G. and Le Page, Robert Brock (eds) (1967) *Dictionary of Jamaican English* (Cambridge: Cambridge University Press). (2nd edn, 1980, CUP.)

Catford, J. C. (1937) 'Scottish Dialects and the Proposed Linguistic Atlas of Scotland'. Paper delivered at the International Association for European Ethnology and Folklore, Edinburgh Congress, 14–21 July 1937. Cited by Matheson (1937).

Catford, J. C. (1957) 'Vowel-Systems of Scots Dialects', *Transactions of the Philological Society*, 1957 (published 1958), 107–17.

Cedergren, Henrietta J. (1973) *The Interplay of Social and Linguistic Factors in Panama* (Cornell University, PhD dissertation).

Cedergren, Henrietta J. (1984) 'Panama Revisited: Sound Change in Real Time'. Paper given at NWAV 13 conference, University of Philadelphia.

Cedergren, Henrietta J. and Sankoff, David (1974) 'Variable Rules: Performance as a Statistical Reflection of Competence', *Language*, Vol. 50, No. 2, 333–55.

Celata, Chiara and Calamai, Silvia (eds) (2014) *Advances in Sociophonetics* (Amsterdam/ Philadelphia: John Benjamins).

Chambers, J. K. (1994) 'An Introduction to Dialect Topography', *English World-Wide*, Vol. 15, No. 1, 35–53.

Chambers, J. K. (1995, 2009) *Sociolinguistic Theory: Linguistic Variation and its Social Significance* (Cambridge, Massachusetts: Blackwell, 1st edn; Malden, Massachusetts, Oxford and Chichester: Wiley Blackwell, 3rd edn).

Chambers, J. K. (2008) 'Louis Gauchat, Proto-Variationist', *Historiographia Linguistica*, Vol. 35, No. 1/2, 215–25. Part of Jack Chambers, Sarah Cummins and Jeff Tennant (2008) 'Louis Gauchat – Patriarch of Variationist Linguistics', *Historiographia Linguistica*, Vol. 35, No. 1/2, 213–74.

Chambers, J. K. and Schilling, Natalie (eds) (2013) *The Handbook of Language Variation and Change*, 2nd edn (Malden, Massachusetts, Oxford and Chichester: Wiley-Blackwell).

Chambers, J. K. and Trudgill, Peter (1980, 1998) *Dialectology*, 1st and 2nd edns (Cambridge: Cambridge University Press).

Chambers, J. K., Trudgill, Peter and Schilling-Estes, Natalie (eds) (2002) *The Handbook of Language Variation and Change*, 1st edn (Malden, Massachusetts and Oxford: Blackwell).

Chapple, William – see entry for Devoniensis.

Chen, Chaomei (2003) *Mapping Scientific Frontiers: The Quest for Knowledge Visualization* (London: Springer).

Cheshire, Jenny (1982) *Variation in an English Dialect: A Sociolinguistic Study* (Cambridge: Cambridge University Press).

Cheshire, Jenny, Edwards, Viv and Whittle, Pamela (1993) 'Non-standard English and Dialect Levelling'. In *Real English: The Grammar of English Dialects in the British Isles*, edited by James Milroy and Lesley Milroy (London and New York: Longman), pp. 53–96.

Cheshire, Jenny and Fox, Sue (2009) 'New Perspectives on *was/were* Variation in London', *Language Variation and Change*, Vol. 21, No. 1, 1–38.

Cheshire, Jenny, Fox, Sue, Kerswill, Paul and Torgersen, Eivind (2005) 'Reversing "Drift": Changes in the London Diphthong System'. Paper given at the 5th UK Language Variation and Change conference, University of Aberdeen.

Cheshire, Jenny, Fox, Sue, Kerswill, Paul and Torgersen, Eivind (2008) 'Ethnicity, Friendship Network and Social Practices as the Motor of Dialect Change: Linguistic Innovation in London', *Sociolinguistica*, Vol. 22, 1–23. Special issue on Dialect Sociology, edited by Alexandra Lenz and Klaus J. Mattheier.

Cheshire, Jenny, Kerswill, Paul and Williams, Ann (2005) 'Phonology, Grammar, and Discourse in Dialect Convergence'. In *Dialect Change: Convergence and Divergence in European Languages*, edited by P. Auer, F. Hinskens and P. Kerswill (Cambridge: Cambridge University Press), pp. 135–67.

Chesters, Anne, Upton, Clive and Parry, David (1968) *A Questionnaire for a Linguistic Atlas of England, Modified for Use in Welsh Localities* (Swansea: privately published). See also entry for Dieth and Orton (1962).

Chomsky, Noam (1957) *Syntactic Structures* (The Hague: Mouton).

Chomsky, Noam (1965) *Aspects of the Theory of Syntax* (Cambridge, Massachusetts: The MIT Press).

Chomsky, Noam (1981) *Lectures on Government and Binding* (Dordrecht: Foris).

Chomsky, Noam (1986) *Knowledge of Language: Its Nature, Origin, and Use* (Westport, Connecticut: Praeger).

Chomsky, Noam (1996) *Silent Children, New Language*: Noam Chomsky interviewed by anonymous interviewer, BBC, Fall 1996. No page numbers. Available at: https://chomsky.info/1996___/.

Chomsky, Noam (2000) *The Architecture of Language*, edited by N. Mukherji, B. N. Patnaik and R. K. Agnihotri (New Delhi: Oxford University Press).

Chomsky, Noam and Gliedman, John (1983) 'Things No Amount of Learning Can Teach: Noam Chomsky Interviewed by John Gliedman', *Omni*, 6:11 (November). Available at: https://chomsky.info/198311__/.

Clark, Urszula (2007) *Studying Language* (Perspectives on the English Language Series) (Basingstoke, Hampshire: Palgrave Macmillan).

Clarke, Sandra (ed.) (1993) *Focus on Canada* (Varieties of English Around the World, General Series, Vol. 11) (Amsterdam/Philadelphia: John Benjamins).

Clopper, Cynthia G. and Pisoni, David B. (2006) 'The Nationwide Speech Project: A New Corpus of American English Dialects', *Speech Communication*, Vol. 48, No. 6, 633–44.

Clopper, Cynthia G. and Smiljanic, Rajka (2011) 'Effects of Gender and Regional Dialect on Prosodic Patterns in American English', *Journal of Phonetics*, Vol. 39, No. 2, 237–45.

Cochrane, G. R. (1959) 'The Australian English Vowels as a Diasystem', *Word: Journal of the Linguistic Circle of New York*, Vol. 15, 69–88.

Cockeram, Henry (1623) *The English Dictionarie* (London: Nathaniel Butter). (Scolar Press facsimile reprint, 1968, Menston, England).

Cofer, Thomas Michael (1972) *Linguistic Variability in a Philadelphia Speech Community* (University of Pennsylvania, doctoral dissertation; supervised by William Labov.) Available at: http://search.proquest.com.openathens-proxy.swan.ac.uk/pqdt/docvie w/302727715/4B01EA0FD5EA4983PQ/2?accountid=14680.

Coleman, Julie (2015) 'Slang Dictionaries'. In Durkin (ed.) (2015), pp. 325–37.

Coles, Elisha (1676) *An English Dictionary* (London: S. Crouch) (Scolar Press facsimile reprint, 1971, Menston, England).

Collier, John [pseudonym Tim Bobbin] (1746a) *A View of the Lancashire Dialect* (Manchester). 1850 edn: *Dialect of South Lancashire or Tim Bobbin's Tummus and Meary, Revised and Corrected, with his Rhymes, and an Enlarged and Amended Glossary of Words and Phrases, Chiefly Used by the Rural Population of the Manufacturing Districts of South Lancashire*, published by Samuel Bamford (Manchester), available at: http://gerald-massey.org.uk/bamford/b_tim_bobbin.htm.

Collier, John [pseudonym Tim Bobbin] (1746b) 'Vocabulary of the Lancashire Dialect', *The Gentleman's Magazine*, Vol. 16, 527–8.

Collins, Victor (1894) *Attempt at a Catalogue of the Library of the Late Prince Louis-Lucien Bonaparte* (London: Henry Sotheran and Company).

Collins, Victor (1902) *A Catalogue of All the Publications (so far as they can be traced) of the Late Prince Louis-Lucien Bonaparte, To Aid in the Comparative Study of European Languages, Compiled from the Prince's Own Catalogues and from Other Material Left by H. I. H.* (Paris: Printed by Charles Lépice).

Considine, John (2015) 'A Chronology of Major Events in the History of Lexicography'. In Durkin (ed.) (2015), pp. 605–15.

Cooper, Christopher (1687) *The English Teacher* (London: Printed by John Richardson for George Coniers). Also published as Bertil Sundby (ed.) (1953) *Christopher Cooper's 'English Teacher'* (Lund Studies in English XXII) (Copenhagen: Lund). The latter is the edition that I used.

Coote, Edmund (1596) *The English Schoole-Maister*. A Scolar Press Facsimile, selected and edited by R. C. Alston; No. 98. Reproduced (original size) by permission of Trinity College Library, Dublin. (Menston, England: The Scolar Press Limited, 1968). The original was printed 'by the Widow Orwin, for Ralph Jackson and Robert Dexter', at London.

Cornips, Leonie (Elise Alexandra) and Corrigan, Karen P. (eds) (2005a) *Syntax and Variation: Reconciling the Biological and the Social* (Amsterdam/Philadelphia: John Benjamins).

Cornips, Leonie and Corrigan, Karen P. (2005b) 'Toward an Integrated Approach to Syntactic Variation: A Retrospective and Prospective Synopsis'. In Cornips and Corrigan (eds) (2010a), pp.1–30.

Corrigan, Karen P. (2010) *Irish English*. Vol. 1: *Northern Ireland* (Edinburgh: Edinburgh University Press).

Coupland, Nikolas and Jaworski, Adam (eds) (2009) *The New Sociolinguistics Reader* (London: Palgrave Macmillan).

Coupland, Nikolas, Williams, Angie, and Garrett, Peter (1999) '"Welshness" and "Englishness" as Attitudinal Dimensions of English Language Varieties in Wales'. In Preston (ed.) (1999a), pp. 333–43.

Cowie, A. P. (ed.) (2009) *The Oxford History of English Lexicography*. Two vols. (Oxford: Oxford University Press).

Craigie, W. A. – see Aitken, A. J. et al. (1931–2002).

Crystal, David (2015) *The Disappearing Dictionary: A Treasury of Lost English Dialect Words* (London: Macmillan). I used the Kindle edition. See also Webography entry.

Cukor-Avila, Patricia, Jeon, Lisa, Rector, Patrícia C., Tiwari, Chetan and Shelton, Zak (2012) '"Texas – It's Like a Whole Nuther Country": Mapping Texans' Perceptions of Dialect Variation in the Lone Star State', *Texas Linguistics Forum*, No. 55, 10–19. (*Proceedings of the Twentieth Annual Symposium about Language and Society*, Austin, 13–15 April 2012.)

Currie, Haver C. (1952) 'A Projection of Socio-linguistics: The Relationship of Speech to Social Status', *Southern Speech Journal*, Vol. 18, No. 1, 28–37.

Daan, Jo C. (1969) 'Dialects'. Reproduced in *Handbook of Perceptual Dialectology*, Vol. 1, edited by Dennis R. Preston (Amsterdam/Philadelphia: John Benjamins, 1999), pp. 9–30. English translation by Karen Bouwer. Original: (1969) 'Dialekten.' In *Van Randstad tot Landrand, Bijdragen en Mededelingen der Dialectencommissie van de Koninklijke Nederlandse Akademie van Wettenschappen te Amsterdam*, No. 37, by Jo Daan and D. P. Blok, 9–43.

Dannenberg, Clare J., Locklear, Hayes A., Schilling-Estes, Natalie and Wolfram, Walt (1996) *A Dialect Dictionary of Lumbee English* (Raleigh: North Carolina Language and Life Project at North Carolina State University). Online version at: http://www. learnnc.org/lp/editions/nc-american-indians/5760.

Dartnell, George Edward and Goddard, Rev. Edward Hungerford (1893) [*Wiltshire Words:*] *A Glossary of Words used in the County of Wiltshire* (London: Henry Frowde,

Oxford University Press Warehouse, for the English Dialect Society). Facsimile edn, with an Introduction and Notes by Norman Rogers, and two Supplementary Articles (Avebury, Wiltshire: The Wiltshire Life Society, 1991).

Dauzat, Albert (1939) 'Le Nouvel Atlas Linguistique de la France par régions', *Le Français Moderne*, Vol. 7, 97–101, 289–92.

Davies, Samantha (2016) *To What Extent Have the Phonological Differences in Spoken English Between North and South Gower Changed Over Time?* (Swansea University, BA dissertation).

Davis, Alva L. (1949) *A Word Atlas of the Great Lakes Region* (University of Michigan, PhD dissertation).

Davis, Alva L., McDavid Jr., Raven I. and McDavid, Virginia G. (1969) *A Compilation of the Work Sheets of the Linguistic Atlas of the United States and Canada and Associated Projects* (Chicago and London: The University of Chicago Press). This is the 2nd edn; the 1st was a small mimeographed edn published in 1951.

Davis, Lawrence M. (1971) 'Work sheets and Their Variants', *American Speech*, Vol. 46, No. 1/2, 27–33.

Davis, Lawrence M. (1982) 'American Social Dialectology: A Statistical Appraisal', *American Speech*, Vol. 57, No. 2, 83–94.

Davis, Lawrence M. (1983) *English Dialectology: An Introduction* (Alabama: The University of Alabama Press).

Davis, Lawrence M. (1986) 'Sampling and Statistical Inference in Dialectology', *Journal of English Linguistics*, Vol. 19, No. 1, 42–8.

Davis, Lawrence M. (1990) *Statistics in Dialectology* (Tuscaloosa, Alabama: University of Alabama Press).

Dawkins, Richard (1998) *Unweaving the Rainbow: Science, Delusion and the Appetite for Wonder* (London: Penguin).

DeCamp, David (1968) 'The Field of Creole Language Studies', *Studia Anglica Posnaniensia*, Vol. 1, 29–51.

Delbridge, Arthur, Bernard, J. R. L., Blair, D., Ramson, W. S., Peters, P., Yallop, Colin and Butler, Susan (eds) (1981, 1991, 1997, 2005, 2009, 2013) *Macquarie Dictionary* (of Australian English). 1st–6th edns. (Sydney: The Macquarie Library, 1st–5th edns; Sydney: Pan Macmillan, 6th edn). See Webography entry for Macquarie for online edition.

Dell'Aquila, Vittorio (2010) 'GIS and Sociolinguistics'. In Lameli et al. (eds) (2010a), pp. 458–82.

Devoniensis (William Chapple) (1746) 'An Exmoor Vocabulary', *The Gentleman's Magazine*, Vol. 16, 405–8. Full title: 'A Vocabulary of the Exmoor Dialect, containing all such Words in the *Exmoor Scolding* and *Courtship*, the Meaning of which does not appear by the Sense; with the Addition of some others; all accented on their proper Syllables, to shew the Method of their Pronunciation (with Notes)'.

Dieth, Eugen (1932) *A Grammar of the Buchan Dialect (Aberdeenshire), Descriptive and Historical*. Vol. I: *Phonology and Accidence* (Cambridge: Cambridge University Press).

Dieth, Eugen (1946) 'A New Survey of English Dialects', *Essays and Studies by Members of the English Association*, Vol. 32, 74–104.

Dieth, Eugen (1951) – see entry for Orton and Dieth (1951).

Dieth, Eugen and Orton, Harold (1962) *A Questionnaire for a Linguistic Atlas of England*. In *Survey of English Dialects* (A) *Introduction*, by Harold Orton (Leeds: E. J. Arnold and Son), pp. 40–113. Reprint, with alterations and additions (6th version), of the edition published by the Leeds Philosophical and Literary Society, January, 1952.

Dil, Anwar S. (ed.) (1972) *Language, Psychology, and Culture: Essays by Wallace E. Lambert* (selected and introduced by Dil) (Stanford, California: Stanford University Press).

Dinkin, Aaron J. (2009) *Dialect Boundaries and Phonological Change in Upstate New York* (University of Pennsylvania, PhD dissertation; supervised by William Labov).

Dinkin, Aaron J. (2013) 'Settlement Patterns and the Eastern Boundary of the Northern Cities Shift', *Journal of Linguistic Geography*, Vol. 1, No. 1, 4–30.

Dittmar, Norbert (2010) 'Areal Variation and Discourse'. In Auer and Schmidt (eds) (2010), pp. 865–77.

Dobson, E. J. (1957) *English Pronunciation 1500–1700*. Vol. I: *Survey of the Sources* (Oxford: Clarendon Press, OUP).

Dollinger, Stefan (2006) 'Towards a Fully Revised and Extended Edition of the *Dictionary of Canadianisms on Historical Principles* (*DCHP-2*): Background, Challenges, Prospects', *Historical Sociolinguistics/Sociohistorical Linguistics* (Leiden, Netherlands), No. 6: http://www.let.leidenuniv.nl/hsl_shl/DCHP-2/DCHP-2/DCHP-2.htm.

Dollinger, Stefan (2015) 'National Dictionaries and Cultural Identity: Insights from Austrian German and Canadian English'. In Durkin (ed.) (2015), pp. 590–603.

Durkin, Philip (ed.) (2015) *The Oxford Handbook of Lexicography* (Oxford: Oxford University Press).

Durrell, Martin (2004) 'Linguistic Variable – Linguistic Variant'. In *Sociolinguistics: An International Handbook of the Science of Language and Society*, Vol. 1, edited by Ulrich Ammon, Norbert Dittmar, Klaus J. Mattheier and Peter Trudgill (Berlin and New York: Walter de Gruyter, 2nd revised and extended edn), pp. 195–200.

Dylan, Bob (2000) *Things Have Changed* (New York City: Columbia Records).

Dziubalska-Kołaczyk, Katarzyna and Przedlacka, Joanna (eds) (2008) *English Pronunciation Models: A Changing Scene*, 2nd edn (Frankfurt am Main: Peter Lang).

Eckert, Penelope (1989) *Jocks and Burnouts: Social Categories and Identity in the High School* (New York: Teachers College Press).

Eckert, Penelope (2000) *Linguistic Variation as Social Practice: The Linguistic Construction of Identity in Belten High* (Malden, Massachusetts, and Oxford: Blackwell).

Eckert, Penelope (2010) 'Who's There? Language and Space in Social Anthropology and Interactional Sociolinguistics'. In Auer and Schmidt (eds) (2010), pp. 163–78.

Eckert, Penelope (2011) – see entry in Webography.

Eckert, Penelope and McConnell-Ginet, Sally (1992) 'Think Practically and Look Locally: Language and Gender as Community-Based Practice', *Annual Review of Anthropology*, Vol. 21, 461–90.

Eckert, Penelope and McConnell-Ginet, Sally (2003) *Language and Gender* (New York: Cambridge University Press).

Edmondston, Thomas (1866) *An Etymological Glossary of the Shetland and Orkney Dialect With Some Derivations of Names of Places in Shetland* (Partly Read at Two Meetings of the Philological Society in the Spring of 1866) (London and Berlin: Asher; and Edinburgh: Adam and Charles Black).

Edwards, Viv K., Trudgill, Peter and Weltens, Bert (1984) *The Grammar of English Dialect: A Survey of Research.* A Report to the ESRC Education and Human Development Committee. (London: Economic and Social Research Council).

Edwards, Viv and Weltens, Bert (1985) 'Research on Non-standard Dialects of British English: Progress and Prospects'. In *Focus On: England and Wales,* edited by Wolfgang Viereck (Amsterdam/Philadelphia: John Benjamins), pp. 97–139.

Ellis, Alexander J. (1869) *On Early English Pronunciation, with Especial Reference to Shakspere and Chaucer.* Part I. (London: Trübner for the Early English Text Society).

Ellis, Alexander J. (1874) 'Third Annual Address of the President to the Philological Society, Delivered at the Anniversary Meeting, Friday, 15th May, 1874: The President on English Dialectology', *Transactions of the Philological Society,* 1873–4, Part III, 447–51.

Ellis, Alexander J. (1876) *Syllabus of a Lecture on English Dialects, Their Classes and Sounds on Thursday, March 9, 1876* (London: London Institute).

Ellis, Alexander J. (1882) 'Eleventh Annual Address of the President to the Philological Society, Delivered at the Anniversary Meeting, Friday, 19th May, 1882', *Transactions of the Philological Society,* 1882–4, 1–148. Includes Ellis's review of Georg Wenker's 1881 Atlas: 'On Dialect, Language, Orthoepy and Dr. G. Wenker's German Speech-Atlas', 20–32.

Ellis, Alexander J. (1889) *On Early English Pronunciation, with Especial Reference to Shakspere and Chaucer. Part V: Existing Dialectal As Compared With West Saxon Pronunciation.* (London: Trübner for the Philological Society, the Early English Text Society, and the Chaucer Society). See also Webography entry for An Atlas of Alexander J. Ellis: http://www.lel.ed.ac.uk/EllisAtlas/Index.html.

Ellis, Stanley (1952) *A Study of the Living Dialects of Lincolnshire Based on an Investigation by Questionnaire* (University of Leeds, MA dissertation).

Ellis, Stanley (1962) Review: '*Cockney Phonology* by Eva Sivertsen', *The Review of English Studies,* New Series, Vol. 13, No. 51, 323–5.

Ellis, Stanley (1976) 'Regional, Social and Economic Influences on Speech: Leeds University Studies'. In *Sprachliches Handeln, Soziales Verhalten: Ein Reader zur Pragmalinguistik und Soziolinguistik,* edited by Wolfgang Viereck (Munich: W. Fink), pp. 93–103.

Elmer, William (1999) 'The Phonetic Database Project (PDP) – A New Tool for the Dialectologist', *Leeds Studies in English,* New Series, Vol. 30, 31–58. Available at: http://digital.library.leeds.ac.uk/385/1/LSE_1999_pp31-58_Elmer_article.pdf.

Elworthy, Frederic Thomas (1877) *An Outline of the Grammar of the Dialect of West Somerset* (From the *Transactions of the Philological Society* for 1877–9, Part II, 143–257.) (London: For the English Dialect Society, Trübner and Company).

Elworthy, Frederic Thomas (1886) *The West Somerset Word-Book: A Glossary of Dialectal and Archaic Words and Phrases used in the West of Somerset and East Devon* (London: For the English Dialect Society, Trübner and Company).

English World-Wide: A Journal of Varieties of English (Amsterdam/Philadelphia: John Benjamins).

Eustace, Sinclair S. (1969) 'The Meaning of the Palaeotype in A. J. Ellis's *On Early English Pronunciation,* 1869–89', *Transactions of the Philological Society,* Vol. 68, No. 1, 31–79.

Evans, Betsy E. (2011) – see entry in Webography.

Fasold, Ralph W. (1967) *A Sociolinguistic Study of the Pronunciation of Three Vowels in Detroit* (Washington, D.C.: Center for Applied Linguistics, unpublished manuscript). 1967 is the date given by Walt Wolfram to this 'manuscript which was literally cut and pasted with Scotch tape', in his interview with Natalie Schilling-Estes (Wolfram and Schilling-Estes, 2008, p. 7). Labov (1994) gives the date as 1969.

Fasold, Ralph W. (1991) 'The Quiet Demise of Variable Rules', *American Speech*, Vol. 66, No. 1, 3–21.

Fasold, Ralph W. (2013) 'Variation and Syntactic Theory'. In Chambers and Schilling (eds) (2013), pp. 185–202.

Feagin, Crawford (1979) *Variation and Change in Alabama English: A Sociolinguistic Study of the White Community* (Washington, D.C.: Georgetown University Press).

Feagin, Crawford (2013) 'Entering the Community: Fieldwork'. In Chambers and Schilling (eds) (2013), pp. 19–37.

Fees, Craig (1991a) *The Imperilled Inheritance: Dialect and Folklife Studies at the University of Leeds 1946–1962*. Part 1: *Harold Orton and the English Dialect Survey* (Folklore Society Library Publications No. 6) (London: Folklore Society Library). Also available from: http://craigfees.com/documents/1991-imperilled_inheritance.pdf.

Fees, Craig (1991b) 'The Historiography of Dialectology', *Lore and Language*, Vol. 10, No. 2, 67–74. Also available from: http://craigfees.com/cv/publications/folk-life-studies/1991-historiography-of-dialectology/.

Filppula, Markku (1999) *The Grammar of Irish English: Language in Hibernian Style* (London: Routledge).

Fischer, Andreas and Amman, Daniel (1991) *An Index to Dialect Maps of Great Britain* (Varieties of English Around the World General Series, Vol. G10) (Amsterdam/Philadelphia: John Benjamins).

Fischer, David Hackett (1989) *Albion's Seed: Four British Folkways in America* (New York and Oxford: Oxford University Press).

Fischer, John L. (1958) 'Social Influences on the Choice of a Linguistic Variant', *Word*, Vol. 14, 47–56, reprinted in *Language in Culture and Society: A Reader in Linguistics and Anthropology*, edited by Dell Hymes (New York: Harper and Row, 1964), pp. 483–8. I used the reprint.

Foulkes, Paul and Docherty, Gerard J. (eds) (1999) *Urban Voices: Accent Studies in the British Isles* (London: Arnold).

Fox, Susan (2007) *The Demise of Cockneys? Language Change in London's 'Traditional' East End* (University of Essex, PhD thesis).

Francis, W. Nelson (1968) 'Modal *daren't* and *durstn't* in Dialectal English', *Leeds Studies in English*, New Series, Vol. II (1968), *Studies in Honour of Harold Orton on the Occasion of his Seventieth Birthday*, edited by Stanley Ellis (Leeds: School of English, University of Leeds), pp. 145–63.

Francis, W. Nelson (1983) *Dialectology: An Introduction* (London and New York: Longman).

Franklin, Michael J. (2006) 'Pluralism Celebrated and Desecrated: A Mughal and British Imperial "Romantic" Legacy', *Journal of The Asiatic Society*, Vol. 48, No. 2, 69–90.

Fridland, Valerie (1999) 'The Southern Shift in Memphis, Tennessee', *Language Variation and Change*, Vol. 11, No. 3, 267–85.

Fudge, Erik C. (1967) 'The Nature of Phonological Primes', *Journal of Linguistics*, Vol. 3, No. 1, 1–36.

Fudge, Erik C. (1969) 'Mutation Rules and Ordering in Phonology', *Journal of Linguistics*, Vol. 5, No. 1, 23–38.

Garfield, Simon (2012) *On The Map: Why the World Looks the Way it Does* (London: Profile Books).

Garrett, Peter (2005) 'Attitude Measurements'. In *Sociolinguistics: An International Handbook of the Science of Language and Society*, Vol. 2, edited by Ulrich Ammon, Norbert Dittmar, Klaus J. Mattheier and Peter Trudgill (Berlin and New York: Walter de Gruyter, 2nd revised and extended edn), pp. 1251–60.

Garrett, Peter (2010) *Attitudes to Language* (Cambridge: Cambridge University Press).

Garrett, Peter, Coupland, Nikolas and Williams, Angie (2003) *Investigating Language Attitudes: Social Meanings of Dialect, Ethnicity and Performance* (Cardiff: University of Wales Press).

Gaskell, Elizabeth (1854) *Mary Barton; A Tale of Manchester Life*, 5th edn (London: Chapman and Hall). To which are appended 'Two Lectures on The Lancashire Dialect', by the Reverend William Gaskell, 27 pp. The 'Two Lectures' are reprinted as Appendix C (pp. 384–414) of the Oxford World's Classics edn (2006) of *Mary Barton* edited by Shirley Foster (Oxford: Oxford University Press).

Gaskell, William (1854) – see entry above.

Gauchat, Louis (1905) 'L'unité phonétique dans le patois d'une commune'. Originally published in *Aus romanischen Sprachen und Literaturen: Festschrift für Heinrich Morf zur Feier seiner fünfundzwanzigjährigen Lehrtätigkeit von seinen Schülern dargebracht*, edited by Ernest Bovet, Louis Gauchat, Jakob Jud and many others [26 in total] (Halle/ Saale: Max Niemeyer, 1905), pp. 175–232. English translation 'Phonetic Unity in the Dialect of a Single Village' by Sarah Cummins, *Historiographia Linguistica*, Vol. 35, No. 1/2 (2008), 226–74. Part of Jack Chambers, Sarah Cummins and Jeff Tennant (2008) 'Louis Gauchat – Patriarch of Variationist Linguistics', *Historiographia Linguistica*, Vol. 35, No. 1/2 (2008), 213–74.

The Gentleman's Magazine – see entries for Collier (1746b), Devoniensis, and Hole.

Gil, Alexander (1619) *Logonomia Anglica* (London: Printed by Iohannes Beale).

Giles, Howard (1971) 'Patterns of Evaluation in Reactions to R.P., South Welsh and Somerset Accented Speech', *British Journal of Social and Clinical Psychology*, Vol. 10, 280–1.

Giles, Howard (1973) 'Accent Mobility: A Model and Some Data', *Anthropological Linguistics*, Vol. 15, 87–105.

Giles, Howard and Bourhis, Richard Y. (1975) 'Linguistic Assimilation: West Indians in Cardiff', *Language Sciences*, No. 38, 9–12.

Giles, Howard, Coupland, Justine and Coupland, Nikolas (eds) (1991) *Contexts of Accommodation: Developments in Applied Sociolinguistics* (Cambridge: Cambridge University Press).

Giles, Howard and Fortman, Jennifer (2004) 'The Social Psychology of Language'. In *Sociolinguistics: An International Handbook of the Science of Language and Society*, Vol. 1, edited by Ulrich Ammon, Norbert Dittmar, Klaus J. Mattheier and Peter Trudgill (Berlin and New York: Walter de Gruyter, 2nd revised and extended edn), pp. 99–108.

Giles, Howard and Powesland, Peter F. (1975) *Speech Style and Social Evaluation* (London and New York: Academic Press in cooperation with the European Association of Experimental Social Psychology).

Giles, Howard and Robinson, W. Peter (eds) (1990) *Handbook of Language and Social Psychology* (Chichester and New York: Wiley). See also entry for Robinson and Giles (2001).

Giles, Howard and St Clair, Robert N. (eds) (1979) *Language and Social Psychology* (Oxford: Basil Blackwell).

Giles, Howard and Smith, Philip M. (1979) 'Accommodation Theory: Optimal Levels of Convergence'. In Giles and St Clair (eds) (1979), pp. 45–65.

Giles, Howard, Taylor, Donald M. and Bourhis, Richard Y. (1973) 'Towards a Theory of Interpersonal Accommodation Through Language: Some Canadian Data', *Language in Society*, Vol. 2, No. 2, 177–92.

Gilles, Peter and Siebenhaar, Beat (2010a) 'Areal Variation in Segmental Phonetics and Phonology'. In Auer and Schmidt (eds) (2010), pp. 760–86.

Gilles, Peter and Siebenhaar, Beat (2010b) 'Areal Variation in Prosody'. In Auer and Schmidt (eds) (2010), pp. 786–804.

Gilliéron, Jules (1880) *Petit Atlas Phonétique du Valais Roman (Sud du Rhône)* (Paris: Champion).

Gilliéron, Jules and Edmont, Edmond (1902–10) *Atlas Linguistique de la France.* Nine vols. (Paris: Champion).

Gilliéron, Jules and Edmont, Edmond (1902) *Atlas Linguistique de la France: Notice servant a l'intelligence des cartes* (Paris: Honoré Champion. Authors not named. Available as a reprint: Bologna: Forni, 1968). Also available at: https://archive.org/details/atlaslinguistnot00gilluoft.

Gilliéron, Jules and Edmont, Edmond (1914–15) *Atlas Linguistique de la France. Corse.* Two vols. (Paris: Champion).

Gilliéron, Jules and Mongin, J. (1905) *Scier dans la Gaule Romance du Sud et de l'Est* (Paris: Champion). Also available via: http://onlinebooks.library.upenn.edu/webbin/book/browse?type=lcsubc&key=Romance%20languages%20–%20Dialects%20–%20Switzerland&c=x.

Glauser, Beat (1985) 'Linguistic Atlases and Generative Phonology'. In Kirk, Sanderson and Widdowson (eds) (1985), pp. 113–29.

Goebl, Hans (2010) 'Dialectometry and Quantitative Mapping'. In Lameli et al. (eds) (2010a), pp. 433–57.

Gordon, Matthew J. (2000) 'Tales of the Northern Cities', *American Speech*, Vol. 75, No. 4, 412–14.

Gordon, Matthew J. (2001) *Small-Town Values, Big-City Vowels: A Study of the Northern Cities Shift in Michigan* (Durham, North Carolina: Duke University Press).

Gordon, Matthew J. (2013) *Labov: A Guide for the Perplexed* (London: Bloomsbury Academic).

Gould, Peter and White, Rodney (1974) *Mental Maps* (Harmondsworth: Penguin).

Grabe, Esther (2004) 'Intonational Variation in Urban Dialects of English Spoken in the British Isles'. In *Regional Variation in Intonation*, edited by P. Gilles and J. Peters (Tübingen: Niemeyer), pp. 9–31.

Grabe, Esther, Kochanski, Greg and Coleman, John (2008) 'The Intonation of Native Accent Varieties in the British Isles: Potential for Miscommunication?' In *English Pronunciation Models: A Changing Scene*, 2nd edn, edited by Katarzyna Dziubalska-Kołaczyk and Joanna Przedlacka (Frankfurt am Main: Peter Lang), pp. 311–37.

Graham, Alison (2013) 'Television: The Voice of Reason', *Radio Times*, 27 July–2 August, 51.

Graham, John J. (1993a) *The Shetland Dictionary*, revised 3rd edn (Lerwick: Shetland Times). Also in 1st, 2nd, and 4th edns (1979, 1984, 2009).

Graham, John J. (1993b) 'The Survival of a Tongue on the Margins of Scots', *Fortnight*, No. 318, Supplement: *Talking Scots* (June, 1993), 18–19.

Granovetter, Mark S. (1973) 'The Strength of Weak Ties', *American Journal of Sociology*, Vol. 78, No. 6, 1360–80.

Grant, William (1909) *What Still Remains to be Done for the Scottish Dialects* (The English Association, Leaflet No. 11, June 1909).

Grant, William and Murison, David D. (eds) (1931–76) *The Scottish National Dictionary*. Vols I–X. (Edinburgh: The Scottish National Dictionary Association). See also Webography entry for *Dictionary of the Scots Language* (*DSL*).

Gregg, Robert J. (1963) *The Boundaries of the Scotch-Irish Dialects in Ulster* (University of Edinburgh, PhD dissertation). Published as *The Scotch-Irish Dialect Boundaries in the Province of Ulster* (Ottawa: Canadian Federation for the Humanities, 1985).

Gregg, Robert J. (1964) 'Scotch-Irish Urban Speech in Ulster'. In *Ulster Dialects: An Introductory Symposium*, edited by G. Brendan Adams (Cultra Manor, Holywood, County Down: Ulster Folk Museum), pp. 163–92.

Gregg, Robert J. (1972) 'The Scotch-Irish Dialect Boundaries in Ulster'. In *Patterns in the Folk Speech of the British Isles*, edited by Martyn F. Wakelin (London: The Athlone Press, University of London), pp. 109–39.

Griffiths, Bill (2004, 2005, 2011) *A Dictionary of North East Dialect*, 1st, 2nd, 3rd edns (Newcastle upon Tyne: Northumbria University Press).

Griffiths, Bill (2007) *Pitmatic: The Talk of the North East Coalfield* (Newcastle upon Tyne: Northumbria University Press).

Griffiths, Bill (2008) *Fishing and Folk: Life and Dialect on the North Sea Coast* (Newcastle upon Tyne: Northumbria University Press).

Griffiths, Dennis, Hughes, James Vernon and Buckley Young People's Cultural Association (1969) *Talk of My Town* (Buckley: Buckley Young People's Cultural Association).

Grigg, D. B. (1980) *Population Growth and Agrarian Change: An Historical Perspective* (Cambridge: Cambridge University Press).

Grimm, Jacob (1822) *Deutsche Grammatik*. Vol. 1, 2nd edn. (Göttingen: Dieterich).

Grose, Francis (1787) *A Provincial Glossary, with a Collection of Local Proverbs and Popular Superstitions* (London: Printed for S. Hooper). 2nd corrected and enlarged edn (1790) (London: Printed for S. Hooper). 1839 edn, *A Glossary of Provincial And Local Words Used in England*, incorporating a Supplement by Samuel Pegge (the younger) (London: John Russell Smith).

Guy, Gregory, Horvath, Barbara, Vonwiller, Julia, Daisley, Elaine and Rogers, Inge (1986) 'An Intonational Change in Progress in Australian English', *Language in Society*, Vol. 15, No. 1, 23–51.

Hägerstrand, Torsten (1952) *The Propagation of Innovation Waves* (Lund Studies in Geography, Series B: Human Geography, Vol. 4) (Lund: Royal University of Lund, Department of Geography).

Halliwell, James Orchard (1847) *A Dictionary of Archaic and Provincial Words, Obsolete Phrases, Proverbs, and Ancient Customs, From The Fourteenth Century* (London: John Russell Smith). 2nd edn (1850) (London: John Russell Smith); 8th edn (1874) (London: John Russell Smith).

Hankey, Clyde T. (1960) *A Colorado Word Geography* (Publications of the American Dialect Society No. 34) (Tuscaloosa, Alabama: University of Alabama Press).

Hansen, Sandra, Schwarz, Christian, Stoeckle, Philipp and Streck, Tobias (eds) (2012) *Dialectological and Folk Dialectological Concepts of Space: Current Methods and Perspectives in Sociolinguistic Research on Dialect Change* (linguae & litterae: Publications of the School of Language and Literature, Freiburg Institute for Advanced Studies, Vol. 17) (Berlin and Boston: Walter de Gruyter).

Hargreaves, Roger (1971) *Mr. Tickle*, 1st edn (London: Thurman).

Harris, P. Valentine (1960, 1974) *Pembrokeshire Place-Names and Dialect*, 1st and 2nd edns (Tenby: H. G. Walters).

Haugen, Einar (1951) 'Directions in Modern Linguistics', *Language*, Vol. 27, No. 3, 211–22.

Heath, Christopher D. (1980) *The Pronunciation of English in Cannock, Staffordshire: A Socio-Linguistic Survey of an Urban Speech-Community* (Oxford: Basil Blackwell, for The Philological Society).

Hempl, George (1894) 'American Dialect', *Modern Language Notes*, Vol. 9, No. 5, 155–7.

Hempl, George (1896a) 'American Speech-Maps', *Dialect Notes*, Vol. 1 (Parts I–IX, 1890–96), Part VII, 315–18.

Hempl, George (1896b) '*Grease* and *Greasy*', *Dialect Notes*, Vol. 1 (Parts I–IX, 1890–96), Part IX, 438–44.

Hempl, George (1902) 'Stovepipes and Funnels', *Dialect Notes*, Vol. 2 (Parts I–VI, 1900–04), Part IV, 250–6.

Henry, Patrick Leo (1958) 'A Linguistic Survey of Ireland: Preliminary Report', *Lochlann: Review of Celtic Studies*, Vol. 1, 49–208. [Supplement to the Norsk Tidsskrift for Sprogvidenskap.]

Henry, Patrick Leo (1985) 'Linguistic Atlases and Vocabulary: The Linguistic Survey of Anglo-Irish'. In Kirk, Sanderson and Widdowson (eds) (1985), pp. 157–71.

Hensel, Gottfried (1741) *Synopsis Universae Philologiae* (Nuremberg: Homann).

Hernández, Nuria, Kolbe, Daniela and Schulz, Monika Edith (eds) (2011) *A Comparative Grammar of British English Dialects: Modals, Pronouns and Complement Clauses*. Vol. 2 of *A Comparative Grammar of British English Dialects*. (Berlin/New York: De Gruyter).

Herrgen, Joachim (2010) 'The *Digital Wenker Atlas* (www.diwa.info): An Online Research Tool for Modern Dialectology', *Dialectologia*, Special Issue I, 89–95.

Herzog, Marvin, Kiefer, Ulrike, Neumann, Robert, Putschke, Wolfgang and Sunshine, Andrew, with Hartweg, Frédéric (eds) (2008) *EYDES: Evidence of Yiddish Documented in European Societies: The Language and Culture Atlas of Ashkenazic Jewry* (Tübingen: Max Niemeyer).

Hickey, Raymond (1999) 'Dublin English: Current Changes and Their Motivation'. In Foulkes and Docherty (eds) (1999), pp. 265–81.

Hickey, Raymond (2002) *A Source Book for Irish English* (Amsterdam/Philadelphia: John Benjamins). See also entry for Hickey's Irish English Resource Centre in Webography.

Hickey, Raymond (2004) *A Sound Atlas of Irish English* (Berlin and New York: Mouton de Gruyter). Includes DVD.

Hickey, Raymond (2005) *Dublin English: Evolution and Change* (Amsterdam/Philadelphia: John Benjamins). Includes CD-ROM. See also entry in Webography.

Hickey, Raymond (2007) *Irish English: History and Present-Day Forms* (Cambridge: Cambridge University Press).

Hickey, Raymond (ed.) (2010) *Varieties of English in Writing: The Written Word as Linguistic Evidence* (Varieties of English Around the World, Vol. G41) (Amsterdam/Philadelphia: John Benjamins).

Hickey, Raymond (ed.) (2012) *Standards of English: Codified Varieties Around the World* (Cambridge: Cambridge University Press).

Hickey, Walter (2013) – see entry in Webography.

Hodson, Thomas C. (1939) 'Socio-linguistics in India', *Man in India*, Vol. 19, 94–8.

Hole, Reverend William (1746a and 1746b) 'Exmoor Courtship: A Provincial Dialogue', *The Gentleman's Magazine*, Vol. 16, 297–300; 'An Exmoor Scolding', *The Gentleman's Magazine*, Vol. 16, 352–5.

Holmes, Janet, Bell, Allan and Boyce, Mary (1991) *Variation and Change in New Zealand English: A Social Dialect Investigation*. Project Report to the Social Sciences Committee of the Foundation for Research, Science and Technology. (Wellington, New Zealand: Victoria University of Wellington).

Horvath, Barbara M. (1985) *Variation in Australian English: The Sociolects of Sydney* (Cambridge: Cambridge University Press).

Horvath, Barbara M. and Horvath, Ronald J. (1997) 'The Geolinguistics of a Sound Change in Progress: /l/ Vocalization in Australia'. In *Working Papers in Linguistics: A Selection of Papers from NWAVE 25*, edited by Charles Boberg, Miriam Meyerhoff, Stephanie Strassel and the P[enn]WPL editorial board (Alexis Dimitriadis, Laura Siegel, Clarissa Surek-Clark, and Alexander Williams) (Philadelphia: University of Pennsylvania), pp. 105–24.

Horvath, Barbara M. and Horvath, Ronald J. (2001) 'A Multilocality Study of a Sound Change in Progress: The Case of /l/ Vocalization in New Zealand and Australian English', *Language Variation and Change*, Vol. 13, No. 1, 37–57.

Horvath, Barbara M. and Horvath, Ronald J. (2002) 'The Geolinguistics of /l/ Vocalization in Australia and New Zealand', *Journal of Sociolinguistics*, Vol. 6, No. 3, 319–46.

Horvath, Barbara and Sankoff, David (1987) 'Delimiting the Sydney Speech Community', *Language in Society*, Vol. 16, No. 2, 179–204.

Houck, Charles L. (1968) 'Methodology of an Urban Speech Survey', *Leeds Studies in English*, New Series, Vol. II (1968), *Studies in Honour of Harold Orton on the Occasion of his Seventieth Birthday*, edited by Stanley Ellis (Leeds: School of English, University of Leeds), pp. 115–28. Electronic copy available at: http://digital.library.leeds. ac.uk/94/1/LSE1968_pp115-28_Houck_article.pdf.

Humboldt, Wilhelm von (1811) *Essai sur les Langues du Nouveau Continent* ['Essay on the Languages of the New Continent']. In *Gesammelte Schriften* ['Collected Writings'], Vol. III, edited by Albert Leitzmann (Berlin: Behr, 1904), pp. 300–41. See also Webography entry.

Hundt, Marianne (1998) *New Zealand English Grammar: Fact or Fiction? A Corpus-Based Study in Morphosyntactic Variation* (Varieties of English Around the World, General Series, Vol. 23) (Amsterdam/Philadelphia: John Benjamins).

Hunter, Reverend Joseph (1829) *The Hallamshire Glossary* (London: William Pickering). There is also a facsimile edition with an Introduction by J. D. A. Widdowson and P. S. Smith (Sheffield: Centre for English Cultural Tradition and Language, University of Sheffield, and The Hunter Archaeological Society, 1983).

Hymes, Dell (1979) 'The Origin of "Sociolinguistics"', *Language in Society*, Vol. 8, No. 1, 141.

Ihalainen, Ossi (1976) 'Periphrastic *do* in Affirmative Sentences in the Dialect of East Somerset', *Neuphilologische Mitteilungen*, Vol. 77, No. 4, 608–22. In revised and abbreviated form in Trudgill and Chambers (eds) (1991), pp. 148–60.

Inoue, Fumio (1995) 'Classification of Dialects by Image: English and Japanese'. In *Verhandlungen des Internationalen Dialektologenkongresses: Bamberg, 29.7.–4.8.1990* ['Proceedings of the International Congress of Dialectologists: Bamberg, 29 July–4 August 1990'], Vol. 4, edited by Wolfgang Viereck (Stuttgart: Steiner), pp. 355–68. Reprinted in Preston (ed.) (1999a), pp. 147–59. I used the reprint.

Inoue, Fumio (1996) 'Subjective Dialect Division in Great Britain', *American Speech*, Vol. 71, No. 2, 142–61. Reprinted in Preston (ed.) (1999a), pp. 161–76.

International Phonetic Association (1999) *Handbook of the International Phonetic Association: A Guide to the Use of the International Phonetic Alphabet* (Cambridge: Cambridge University Press).

Jaberg, Karl and Jud, Jakob (1928–40) *Sprach- und Sachatlas Italiens und der Südschweiz*. Eight vols, plus an index published in 1960. (Zofingen: Ringier). Reprint edn by Kraus Reprint, Nendeln, Liechtenstein (1971–81). See also Webography entry for *AIS*, *NavigAIS*: http://www3.pd.istc.cnr.it/navigais/.

Jackson, Georgina F. (1879) *Shropshire Word-Book: A Glossary of Archaic and Provincial Words, Etc., Used in the County* (London: Trübner).

Jakobsen, Jakob (1928–32) *An Etymological Dictionary of the Norn Language in Shetland*. Two vols. (Copenhagen: Vilhelm Prior). Republished by Shetland Folk Society, Lerwick (1985).

Jakobsen, Jakob (1897) *The Dialect and Place Names of Shetland: Two Popular Lectures* (Lerwick: T. & J. Manson).

Johnstone, Barbara, Andrus, Jennifer and Danielson, Andrew E. (2006) 'Mobility, Indexicality, and the Enregisterment of "Pittsburghese"', *Journal of English Linguistics*, Vol. 34, No. 2, 77–104.

Jones, Daniel (1926) *English Pronouncing Dictionary*, 3rd edn (London: J. M. Dent and Sons).

Jones, Val (1978) *Some Problems in the Computation of Sociolinguistic Data* (University of Newcastle upon Tyne, PhD thesis). Available from EThOS e-theses online service, British Library, at: https://ethos.bl.uk/Logon.do;jsessionid=A55BD3C88BE6D7B8392 3590927578F4D.

Jones, Val (1985) 'Tyneside Syntax: A Presentation of Some Data from the Tyneside Linguistic Survey'. In *Focus On: England and Wales*, edited by Wolfgang Viereck (Amsterdam/Philadelphia: John Benjamins), pp. 163–77.

Jones, W. E. (1952) 'The Definite Article in Living Yorkshire Dialect', *Leeds Studies in English*, Vol. 7–8, 81–91. Electronic copy available at: http://digital.library.leeds. ac.uk/72/1/LSE1952_pp81-91_Jones_article.pdf.

Jones, William (1786) 'The Third Anniversary Discourse, Delivered 2nd February, 1786', *Asiatic Researches; or, Transactions of the Society, Instituted in Bengal, for Inquiring into the History and Antiquities, the Arts, Sciences, and Literature of Asia*, Vol. I (1799), 415–31. Also Chapter 1 in *A Reader in Nineteenth Century Historical Indo-European Linguistics*, edited by Winfred P. Lehmann (Bloomington: Indiana University Press, 1st edn, 1967; Austin, Texas: Linguistics Research Center of the University of Texas at Austin, online edition, 2006). The 2006 online version is available at: https://liberalarts.utexas.edu/ lrc/resources/books/reader/index.php.

Jones-Sargent, Val (1983) *Tyne Bytes. A Computerised Sociolinguistic Study of Tyneside* (Frankfurt am Main: Peter Lang).

Joseph, John E. (2002) *From Whitney to Chomsky: Essays in the History of American Linguistics* (Amsterdam/Philadelphia: John Benjamins).

Journal of Linguistic Geography (Cambridge: Cambridge University Press): https://www. cambridge.org/core/journals/journal-of-linguistic-geography.

Kallen, Jeffrey L. (2013) *Irish English*. Vol. 2: *The Republic of Ireland* (Berlin: De Gruyter Mouton).

Kate, Lambert ten (1723) *Aenleiding Tot de Kennisse van het Verhevene Deel der Nederduitsche Sprake* ['Guidance to the Knowledge of the Higher Part of the Low German Language']. Two vols. (Amsterdam: Rudolph and Gerard Wetstein). Available at MDZ: http:// reader.digitale-sammlungen.de/en/fs1/object/display/bsb10523049_00001.html.

Keil, Gerald C. (1969) *Survey of English Dialects: Scheme for Computerization*. Unpublished notes (dated 14 January 1969) of a meeting held on 11 January 1969 between Keil, Harold Orton, and Stewart Sanderson.

Kemp, W. (1981) 'Major Sociolinguistic Patterns in Montreal French' In *Variation Omnibus*, edited by D. Sankoff and H. Cedergren (Edmonton: Linguistic Research), pp. 3–16.

Kent, Roland G. (1931) 'Linguistic Society of America: Record of the Linguistic Institute, Fourth Session, June 29 to August 7, 1931', *Language*, Vol. 7, No. 3, Bulletin No. 8, 3–7, 12–16.

Kerswill, Paul (2002) 'A Dialect with "Great Inner Strength"?: The Perception of Nativeness in the Bergen Speech Community'. In Preston and Long (eds) (2002), pp. 151–71.

Kerswill, Paul (2002) 'Models of Linguistic Change and Diffusion: New Evidence from Dialect Levelling in British English', *Reading Working Papers in Linguistics*, Vol. 6, 187–216.

Kerswill, Paul, Torgersen, Eivind Ness and Fox, Susan (2007) 'Phonological Innovation in London Teenage Speech: Ethnicity as the Driver of Change in a Metropolis', Oxford Graduate Seminar, 12 November 2007. Available at: http://www.lancaster.ac.uk/fss/ projects/linguistics/innovators/documents/Oxford_Kerswill_Nov07_000.ppt.

Kerswill, Paul, Torgersen, Eivind Ness and Fox, Susan (2008) 'Reversing "Drift": Innovation and Diffusion in the London Diphthong System', *Language Variation and Change*, Vol. 20, No. 3, 451–91.

Khusrau, Amīr (1318) – see Webography entry.

Kirk, John M., Sanderson, Stewart and Widdowson, J. D. A. (eds) (1985) *Studies in Linguistic Geography: The Dialects of English in Britain and Ireland* (London: Croom Helm).

Klaproth, Julius (1823) *Asia Polyglotta: Sprachatlas* (Paris: Heideloff and Campe). Map reproduced in Lameli et al. (eds) (2010b, Map 0001).

Klemola, Juhani (1994) 'Periphrastic DO in South-Western Dialects of British English: A Reassessment', *Dialectologia et Geolinguistica*, No. 2, 33–51.

Klemola, Juhani (1996) *Non-standard Perisphrastic DO: A Study in Variation and Change* (University of Essex, PhD thesis).

Klemola, Juhani (2002) 'Periphrastic DO: Dialectal Distribution and Origins'. In *The Celtic Roots of English* (Studies in Languages 37), edited by Markku Filppula, Juhani Klemola and Heli Pitkänen (Joensuu: University of Joensuu, Faculty of Humanities), pp. 199–210.

Klemola, Juhani and Jones, Mark J. (1999) 'The Leeds Corpus of English Dialects – Project', *Leeds Studies in English*, New Series, Vol. 30, 17–30. Available at: http://digital.library. leeds.ac.uk/381/1/LSE_1999_pp17-30_Klemola_Jones_article.pdf.

Klerk, Vivian de (ed.) (1996) *Focus on South Africa* (Varieties of English Around the World, General Series, Vol. 15) (Amsterdam/Philadelphia: John Benjamins).

Koerner, E. F. Konrad (1991) 'Toward a History of Modern Sociolinguistics', *American Speech*, Vol. 66, No. 1, 57–70.

Koerner, E. F. Konrad (2004) 'Myths in the History of Linguistics: The Case of the Goals of Georg Wenker's Dialectology'. In *Essays in the History of Linguistics*, by E. F. K. Koerner (Amsterdam/Philadelphia: John Benjamins), pp. 43–64.

Kolb, Eduard (1966) *Linguistic Atlas of England: Phonological Atlas of the Northern Region: The Six Northern Counties, North Lincolnshire and the Isle of Man* (Bern: Francke Verlag).

Kolb, Eduard, Glauser, Beat, Elmer, Willy and Stamm, Renate (1979) *Atlas of English Sounds* (Bern: Francke).

Kortmann, Bernd, Herrmann, Tanja, Pietsch, Lukas and Wagner, Susanne (eds) (2005) *A Comparative Grammar of British English Dialects: Agreement, Gender, Relative Clauses.* Vol 1. (Berlin/New York: De Gruyter).

Kortmann, Bernd and Lunkenheimer, Kerstin (eds) (2012) *The Mouton World Atlas of Variation in English* (Berlin/New York: De Gruyter). Also known as *pWAVE*.

Kortmann, Bernd and Lunkenheimer, Kerstin (eds.) (2013) – see Entry in Webography.

Kortmann, Bernd, and Schneider, Edgar W., with Kate Burridge, Rajend Mesthrie and Clive Upton (eds) (2004) *A Handbook of Varieties of English.* Vol. 1: *Phonology.* Vol. 2: *Morphology and Syntax.* Includes CD-ROM. (Berlin/New York: Mouton de Gruyter).

Kortmann, Bernd and Schneider, Edgar W., with Kate Burridge, Rajend Mesthrie, and Clive Upton (eds) (2008) *Varieties of English.* Vols 1–4. Includes CD-ROM. (Berlin/New York: Mouton de Gruyter).

Korzybski, Alfred (1933, 1994) *Science and Sanity: An Introduction to Non-Aristotelian Systems and General Semantics* (Lancaster, Pennsylvania: Science Press Printing Company, 1st edn; New York: Institute of General Semantics, 5th edn). Preface to the 5th edn by Robert P. Pula. I used the 5th edn.

Kretzschmar Jr., William A. (1996) 'Quantitative Areal Analysis of Dialect Features', *Language Variation and Change*, Vol. 8, No. 1, 13–39.

Kretzschmar Jr., William A. (2002) 'Dialectology and the History of the English Language'. In *Studies in the History of the English Language: A Millennial Perspective*, edited by Donka Minkova and Robert Stockwell (Berlin: Mouton de Gruyter), pp. 79–108.

Kretzschmar Jr., William A. (2004) 'Regional Varieties of American English'. In *Language in the USA*, 2nd edn, edited by Edward Finegan and John Rickford (Cambridge: Cambridge University Press), pp. 39–57. Reprinted in *Making Sense of Language: Readings in Culture and Communication*, edited by S. Blum (New York: Oxford University Press, 2013), pp. 357–71.

Kretzschmar Jr., William A., Andres, Claire, Votta, Rachel and Johnson, Sasha (2006) *Roswell Voices, Phase 2* (Roswell: Roswell Folk and Heritage Bureau). Booklet and CD.

Kretzschmar Jr., William A., Childs, Becky, Anderson, Bridget and Lanehart, Sonja (2004) *Roswell Voices* (Roswell: Roswell Folk and Heritage Bureau). Booklet and CD.

Kretzschmar Jr., William A., McDavid, Virginia G., Lerud, Theodore K. and Johnson, Ellen (eds) (1993) *Handbook of the Linguistic Atlas of the Middle and South Atlantic States* (Chicago and London: The University of Chicago Press).

Kretzschmar Jr., William A. and Schneider, Edgar W. (1996) *Introduction to Quantitative Analysis of Linguistic Survey Data. An Atlas by Numbers* (Thousand Oaks, California, London and New Delhi: Sage).

Krug, Manfred and Schlüter, Julia (eds) 2013) *Research Methods in Language Variation and Change* (Cambridge: Cambridge University Press). See also Webography for companion website.

Kurath, Hans (1936) 'The Linguistic Atlas of the United States and Canada'. In *Proceedings of the Second International Congress of Phonetic Sciences*, edited by Daniel Jones and D. B. Fry (Cambridge: Cambridge University Press), pp. 18–22.

Kurath, Hans (1949) *A Word Geography of the Eastern United States*. (Ann Arbor, Michigan: University of Michigan Press; reprinted 1966).

Kurath, Hans (1963) Review of the Survey of English Dialects, *American Speech*, Vol. 38, No. 2, 124–9.

Kurath, Hans (1972) *Studies in Area Linguistics* (Bloomington and London: Indiana University Press).

Kurath, Hans, Hanley, Miles L., Bloch, Bernard, Lowman Jr., Guy S. and Hansen, Marcus L. (1939–43) *Linguistic Atlas of the US and Canada: Linguistic Atlas of New England*. Three double vols. (Providence, Rhode Island: Brown University for the American Council of Learned Societies). Reprinted 1972 (New York: AMS Press).

Kurath, Hans, with the collaboration of Marcus L. Hansen, Julia Bloch and Bernard Bloch (1939) *Handbook of the Linguistic Geography of New England* (Providence, Rhode Island: Brown University for the American Council of Learned Societies).

Kurath, Hans and Lowman Jr., Guy S. (1970) *The Dialectal Structure of Southern England: Phonological Evidence* (Publications of the American Dialect Society, No. 54) (Alabama: University of Alabama Press).

Kurath, Hans and McDavid Jr., Raven I. (1961) *The Pronunciation of English in the Atlantic States* (Ann Arbor, Michigan: University of Michigan Press).

Labov, William (1963) 'The Social Motivation of a Sound Change', *Word*, Vol. 19, 273–309. Reprinted as Chapter 1 of Labov (1972a), *Sociolinguistic Patterns*, pp. 1–42.

Labov, William (1966/2006) *The Social Stratification of English in New York City* (Washington, D.C.: Center for Applied Linguistics, 1st edn; Cambridge: Cambridge University Press, 2nd edn). I used the 2nd edn. An electronic version of Labov's original PhD dissertation (1964) is available via ProQuest Dissertations and Theses.

Labov, William (1966b) 'Hypercorrection by the Lower Middle Class as a Factor in Linguistic Change'. In *Sociolinguistics: Proceedings of the UCLA Sociolinguistics*

Conference, 1964, edited by William Bright (The Hague: Mouton, 1966), pp. 84–113. Reprinted as Chapter 5 of Labov (1972a), *Sociolinguistic Patterns*, pp. 122–42.

Labov, William (1966c) 'The Linguistic Variable as a Structural Unit', *Washington Linguistics Review*, Vol. 3, 4–22. Available at: http://eric.ed.gov/?q=labov&ft=on&pg =2&id=ED010871.

Labov, William (1967a) 'Some Sources of Reading Problems for Negro Speakers of Non-Standard English'. In *New Directions in Elementary English*, edited by Alexander Frazier (Champaign, Illinois: National Council of Teachers of English), pp. 140–67. Also published as 'Some Sources of Reading Problems for Speakers of the Black English Vernacular', Chapter 1 of Labov (1972c), *Language in the Inner City*, pp. 3–35. Submitted to the Bureau of Curriculum Research of the Board of Education of the City of New York.

Labov, William (1967b) 'The Non-Standard Vernacular of the Negro Community – Some Practical Suggestions'. Seminar in English and Language Arts, Temple University, 17 May 1967. Available at: http://eric.ed.gov/?q=labov&ft=on&pg=2&id=ED016947. Also published as: 'The Non-Standard Negro Vernacular: Some Practical Suggestions'. In *Position Papers from Language Education for the Disadvantaged* (Report 3 of National Defense Education Act National Institute for Advanced Study in Teaching Disadvantaged Youth), pp. 4–7.

Labov, William (1968) 'Contraction, Deletion, and Inherent Variability of the English Copula'. Paper presented at The Annual Meeting of the Linguistic Society of America, Chicago, Illinois, December 1967. Available at: http://eric.ed.gov/?q=labov&ft=on& pg=3&id=ED027514. Also published as: Labov (1969) 'Contraction, Deletion, and Inherent Variability of the English Copula', *Language*, Vol. 45, No. 4 (December, 1969), 715–62, and in revised form as Chapter 9 of Labov (1972c), *Language in the Inner City*, pp. 65–129.

Labov, William (1969) – see preceding entry.

Labov, William (1972a) *Sociolinguistic Patterns* (Philadelphia: University of Pennsylvania Press).

Labov, William (1972b) 'Some Principles of Linguistic Methodology', *Language in Society*, Vol. 1, No. 1, 97–120.

Labov, William (1972c) *Language in the Inner City* (Philadelphia: University of Pennsylvania Press).

Labov, William (1973) 'The Linguistic Consequences of Being a Lame', *Language in Society*, Vol. 2, No. 1, 81–115.

Labov, William (1981a) 'Resolving the Neogrammarian Controversy', *Language*, Vol. 57, No. 2, 267–308.

Labov, William (1981b) 'Field Methods of the Project on Linguistic Change and Variation', *Sociolinguistic Working Paper*, No. 31 (Austin, Texas: Southwest Educational Development Laboratory; sponsored by the National Institute of Education, Washington, D.C.). Available at: http://files.eric.ed.gov/fulltext/ED250938.pdf.

Labov, William (1982a) 'Building on Empirical Foundations'. In *Perspectives on Historical Linguistics: Papers From a Conference Held at the Meeting of the Language Theory Division, Modern Language Association: San Francisco, 27–30 December 1979*, edited by Winfred P. Lehmann and Yakov Malkiel (Amsterdam/Philadelphia: John Benjamins, 1982), pp. 17–92.

Labov, William (1982b) 'Objectivity and Commitment in Linguistic Science: The Case of the Black English Trial in Ann Arbor', *Language in Society*, Vol. 11, No. 2, 165–201.

Labov, William (1994) *Principles of Linguistic Change*. Vol. 1: *Internal Factors*. (Cambridge, Massachusetts and Oxford: Blackwell).

Labov, William (1997) Testimony on 'Ebonics' given by William Labov, Professor of Linguistics at the University of Pennsylvania, Past President of the Linguistic Society of America, member of the National Academy of Science, 23 January 1997, before the Subcommittee on Labor, Health and Human Services and Education of the Senate Appropriations Committee. Available at: http://www.ling.upenn.edu/~wlabov/ Papers/Ebonic%20testimony.pdf.

Labov, William (2001) *Principles of Linguistic Change*. Vol. 2: *Social Factors*. (Malden, Massachusetts and Oxford: Blackwell; digital edn, 2006).

Labov, William (2008a) 'Is a Structural Dialectology Practical? Re-deploying Weinreich's Approach to Diasystems'. In *EYDES: Evidence of Yiddish Documented in European Societies: The Language and Culture Atlas of Ashkenazic Jewry*, edited by Marvin Herzog, Ulrike Kiefer, Robert Neumann, Wolfgang Putschke and Andrew Sunshine, with Frédéric Hartweg (Berlin: Max Niemeyer), pp. 217–29.

Labov, William (2008b) Private email communication, August 2008.

Labov, William (2010) *Principles of Linguistic Change*. Vol. 3: *Cognitive and Cultural Factors* (Malden, Massachusetts, Oxford and Chichester: Wiley-Blackwell; digital edn, 2011). Chapters 1–17 of Volume 3 are also available from: http://www.ling.upenn. edu/phonoatlas/PLC3/PLC3.html.

Labov, William (1994–2010) *Principles of Linguistic Change*. Three vols. (Malden, Massachusetts, Oxford and Chichester: Wiley-Blackwell).

Labov, William (2002–11) – see entry in Webography for *Plotnik* software.

Labov, William (2012) *Dialect Diversity in America: The Politics of Language Change* (Page-Barbour Lectures for 2009) (Charlottesville and London: University of Virginia Press). Kindle edn, no page numbers.

Labov, William et al. (2008) *Summary Statement on African-American Vernacular English*. Submitted by Nine Linguists to the California Curriculum Commission on 10 February 2008. William Labov, H. Samy Alim, Guy Bailey, John Baugh, Anne H. Charity, Lisa J. Green, Tracey Weldon, Walt Wolfram. Appendix to Labov (2012), locations 2126–2269.

Labov, William, Ash, Sharon and Boberg, Charles (2006) *The Atlas of North American English: Phonetics, Phonology and Sound Change. A Multimedia Reference Tool* (Berlin and New York: Mouton de Gruyter). Print edn includes CD-ROM.

Labov, William, Ash, Sharon, Boberg, Charles, Baranowski, Maciej and Barrow, Janet (1997) *Phonological Atlas of North America*, at: http://www.ling.upenn.edu/phono_ atlas/home.html#staff.

Labov, William and Cohen, Paul (1967a) 'Systematic Relations of Standard and Non-standard Rules in the Grammars of Negro Speakers'. Report presented at the 7th Project Literacy Conference, Cambridge, Massachusetts, 25 May 1967; appears in *Project Literacy Reports*, No. 8, 66–84 (Ithaca, New Jersey: Cornell University). Available at: http://files.eric.ed.gov/fulltext/ED016946.pdf.

Labov, William and Cohen, Paul (1967b) 'Some Suggestions for Teaching Standard English to Speakers of Non-standard Dialects'. Paper submitted to the Bureau of Curriculum Research of the New York City Board of Education for their use in preparing a manual for language art skills in Grades 5 to 12. Available at: http://eric. ed.gov/?q=labov&ft=on&pg=3&id=ED016948. Published as 'Some Suggestions for Teaching Standard English to Speakers of Non-standard Urban Dialects'. In *Language, Society and Education: A Profile of Black English*, edited by Johanna S. DeStefano (Worthington, Ohio: C. A. Jones, 1973), pp. 218–37.

Labov, William, Cohen, Paul and Robins, Clarence (1965) *A Preliminary Study of the Structure of English used by Negro and Puerto Rican Speakers in New York City*. Cooperative Research Report No. 3091. (ERIC No. ED003819, available through Center for Applied Linguistics, Washington, D.C.).

Labov, William, Cohen, Paul, Robins, Clarence and Lewis, John (1968a) *A Study of the Non-Standard English of Negro and Puerto Rican Speakers in New York City*. Vol. I: *Phonological and Grammatical Analysis*. (Supported by the Cooperative Research Program/Project of the Office of Education, US Department of Health, Education and Welfare, Washington, D.C.; Philadelphia: US Regional Survey, Linguistics Laboratory, University of Pennsylvania). Available at: http://eric.ed.gov/?q=labov&ft=on&pg=3 &id=ED028423.

Labov, William, Cohen, Paul, Robins, Clarence and Lewis, John (1968b) *A Study of the Non-Standard English of Negro and Puerto Rican Speakers in New York City*. Vol. II: *The Use of Language in the Speech Community*. (Cooperative Research Project, Report 3288; Philadelphia: US Regional Survey, Linguistics Laboratory, University of Pennsylvania). Available at: http://eric.ed.gov/?q=labov&ft=on&pg=3&id=ED028424.

Labov, William and Preston, Dennis R. (2013) 'Foreword', *Journal of Linguistic Geography*, Vol. 1, No. 1, 1–3.

Labov, William and Robins, Clarence (1969) 'A Note on the Relation of Reading Failure to Peer-group Status in Urban Ghettos', *The Teachers College Record*, Vol. 70, No. 5, 395–406. A Progress Report of the Cooperative Research Project. Available at: http:// eric.ed.gov/?q=labov&ft=on&pg=3&id=ED018343.

Labov, William and Waletzky, Joshua (1967) 'Narrative Analysis: Oral Versions of Personal Experience'. In *Essays on the Verbal and Visual Arts: Proceedings of the 1966 Annual Spring Meeting of the American Ethnological Society*, edited by June Helm (Seattle: University of Washington Press), pp. 12–44. Reprinted in *Journal of Narrative and Life History*, Vol. 7, Nos 1–4 (1997), 3–38.

Labov, William, Yaeger, Malcah and Steiner, Richard (1972) *A Quantitative Study of Sound Change in Progress*. Report on National Science Foundation Project No. GS-3287. Two vols. (Philadelphia: US Regional Survey).

Laing, Margaret (2013) – see entry in Webography.

Lambert, Wallace E. (1967) 'A Social Psychology of Bilingualism', *Journal of Social Issues*, Vol. 23, No. 2, 91–109.

Lambert, Wallace E. (1979) 'Language as a Factor in Intergroup Relations'. In *Language and Social Psychology*, edited by Howard Giles and Robert N. St Clair (Oxford: Basil Blackwell), pp. 186–92.

Lambert, Wallace E., Anisfeld, Moshe and Yeni-Komshian, Grace (1965) 'Evaluational Reactions of Jewish and Arab Adolescents to Dialect and Language Variations', *Journal of Personality and Social Psychology*, Vol. 2, No. 1, 84–90.

Lambert, Wallace E., Hodgson, R. C., Gardner, R. C. and Fillenbaum, S. (1960) 'Evaluational Reactions to Spoken Languages', *Journal of Abnormal and Social Psychology*, Vol. 60, No. 1, 44–51.

Lameli, Alfred (2010) 'Linguistic Atlases – Traditional and Modern'. In Auer and Schmidt (eds) (2010), pp. 567–92.

Lameli, Alfred, Kehrein, Roland and Rabanus, Stefan (eds) (2010a) *Language and Space: An International Handbook of Linguistic Variation*. Vol. 2: *Language Mapping*, Part I: text (Berlin and New York: De Gruyter Mouton).

Lameli, Alfred, Kehrein, Roland and Rabanus, Stefan (eds) (2010b) *Language and Space: An International Handbook of Linguistic Variation*. Vol. 2: *Language Mapping*, Part II: *Maps* (Berlin and New York: De Gruyter Mouton).

Lanehart, Sonja L. (ed.) (2001) *Sociocultural and Historical Contexts of African American English* (Varieties of English Around the World, General Series, Vol. 27) (Amsterdam/ Philadelphia: John Benjamins).

Language in Society (Cambridge: Cambridge University Press).

Language Magazine: The Journal of Communication and Education (California): http://languagemagazine.com/.

Language Variation and Change (Cambridge: Cambridge University Press).

Le Dû, Jean (2001–2) *Nouvel Atlas Linguistique de la Basse-Bretagne*. Two vols. (Brest: Centre de Recherche Bretonne et Celtique, Université de Bretagne Occidentale.)

Lehmann, Winfred P. (1962, 1973) *Historical Linguistics: An Introduction*, 1st edn, 2nd edn (New York: Holt, Rinehart and Winston). I used the 2nd edn.

Lehmann, Winfred P. (ed.) (1967, 2006) *A Reader in Nineteenth Century Historical Indo-European Linguistics* (Bloomington: Indiana University Press, 1st edn, 1967; Austin, Texas: Linguistics Research Center of the University of Texas at Austin, online edition, 2006). Online version (no page numbers) edited by Jonathan Slocum, available at: https://liberalarts.utexas.edu/lrc/resources/books/reader/index.php.

Lehmann, Winfred P. and Malkiel, Yakov (eds) (1982) *Perspectives on Historical Linguistics: Papers From a Conference Held at the Meeting of the Language Theory Division, Modern Language Association: San Francisco, 27–30 December 1979* (Amsterdam Studies in the Theory and History of Linguistic Science, Series IV: Current Issues in Linguistic Theory, Vol. 24) (Amsterdam/Philadelphia: John Benjamins, 1982), pp. 17–92.

Leskien, August (1876) *Die Declination im Slavisch-Litauischen und Germanischen* (Leipzig: S. Hirzel).

Linn, Michael D. (1983) 'Informant Selection in Dialectology', *American Speech*, Vol. 58, No. 3, 225–43.

Local, J. K. (1983) 'Making a Transcription: The Evolution of A. J. Ellis's Palaeotype', *Journal of the International Phonetic Association*, Vol. 13, No. 1, 2–12.

Macafee, Caroline (ed.) (1996) *A Concise Ulster Dictionary* (Oxford: Oxford University Press).

Macaulay, Ronald K. S. (1970) Review of *A Sociolinguistic Description of Detroit Negro Speech* by Walter A. Wolfram, *Language*, Vol. 46, No. 3, 764–73.

Macaulay, Ronald K. S. (1976) Review of *The Social Differentiation of English in Norwich* by Peter Trudgill, *Language*, Vol. 52, No. 1, 266–270.

Macaulay, Ronald K. S. (1980) Review of *The Linguistic Atlas of England* by Orton, Sanderson and Widdowson, *Language*, Vol. 56, No. 1, 230.

Macaulay, Ronald K. S. (1985) 'Linguistic Maps: Visual Aid or Abstract Art?' In Kirk, Sanderson and Widdowson (eds) (1985), pp. 172–85.

Macaulay, Ronald K. S. (1988) 'What Happened to Sociolinguistics?', *English World-Wide*, Vol. 9, No. 2, 153–69.

Macaulay, Ronald K. S. (2002) 'Discourse Variation'. In Chambers, Trudgill and Schilling-Estes (eds) (2002), pp. 283–305.

Macaulay, Ronald K. S. (2013) 'Discourse Variation'. In Chambers and Schilling (eds) (2013), pp. 220–36.

Macaulay, Ronald K. S. and Trevelyan, G. D. (1973) *Language, Education and Employment in Glasgow* (Report to the Social Science Research Council) (Edinburgh: Scottish Council for Research in Education).

Macaulay, Ronald K. S., with the assistance of G. D. Trevelyan (1977) *Language, Social Class and Education: A Glasgow Study* (Edinburgh: Edinburgh University Press).

McCormick, Kay (1989) *English and Afrikaans in District Six: A Sociolinguistic Study* (University of Cape Town, PhD thesis).

McCormick, Kay (2003) *Language in Cape Town's District Six* (Oxford: Oxford University Press).

McDavid Jr., Raven I. (1948) 'Post-vocalic /r/ in South Carolina: A Social Analysis', *American Speech*, Vol. 23, No. 3/4, 194–203.

McDavid Jr., Raven I. (1968) 'Two Studies of Dialects of English', *Leeds Studies in English*, New Series, Vol. II (1968), *Studies in Honour of Harold Orton on the Occasion of his Seventieth Birthday*, edited by Stanley Ellis (Leeds: School of English, University of Leeds), pp. 23–45. Electronic copy available from the University of Leeds Digital Library: http://digital.library.leeds.ac.uk/.

McDavid Jr., Raven I. (1981) Review of *The Linguistic Atlas of England* by Orton, Sanderson and Widdowson, *American Speech*, Vol. 56, No. 3, 219–34.

McDavid Jr., Raven I. (1985) 'Eliciting: Direct, Indirect, and Oblique', *American Speech*, Vol. 60, No. 4, 309–17.

McDavid Jr., Raven I. and McDavid, Virginia G. (1956) 'Regional Linguistic Atlases in the United States', *Orbis: Bulletin International de Documentation Linguistique*, Vol. 5, No. 2, 349–86.

McDavid Jr., Raven I., McDavid, Virginia G., Kretzschmar Jr., William A., Lerud, Theodore and Ratliff, Martha (1986) 'Inside a Linguistic Atlas', *Proceedings of the American Philosophical Society*, Vol. 130, No. 4, 390–405.

McDavid Jr., Raven I. and O'Cain, Raymond (1973) 'Sociolinguistics and Linguistic Geography', *Kansas Journal of Sociology*, Vol. 9, No. 2, 137–56.

Macfarlane, Robert (2015) *Landmarks* (London: Hamish Hamilton). I used the Kindle edition.

McGovern, Stephanie (2013) 'Point of View: Don't Judge Me' ['I may be northern – but I'm not stupid'], *Radio Times*, 20–26 July, 9.

McIntosh, Angus (1952) *An Introduction to a Survey of Scottish Dialects* (University of Edinburgh Linguistic Survey of Scotland Monographs, No. 1) (Edinburgh: Thomas Nelson and Sons for the University of Edinburgh).

McIntosh, Angus, Samuels, Michael Louis and Benskin, Michael, with the assistance of Margaret Laing and Keith Williamson (1986) *A Linguistic Atlas of Late Mediaeval English, 1350–1450* (Aberdeen: Aberdeen University Press; Edinburgh: Mercat Press). See also Webography entry for electronic version.

McMahon, April M. S. (1994) *Understanding Language Change* (Cambridge: Cambridge University Press).

Maguire, Warren (2012) 'Mapping The Existing Phonology of English Dialects', *Dialectologia et Geolinguistica*, Vol. 20, No. 1, 84–107.

Maguire, Warren and McMahon, April (eds) (2011) *Analysing Variation in English* (Cambridge and New York: Cambridge University Press).

Malkiel, Yakov (1984) 'Revisionist Dialectology and Mainstream Linguistics' (Review Article), *Language in Society*, Vol. 13, No. 1, 29–66.

Malmesbury, William of (1125) *De Gestis Pontificum Anglorum* (*Deeds of the English Pontiffs*), Prologue to Book III, edited from the Autograph Manuscript by N. E. S. A. Hamilton (London: Longman, and Trübner; Oxford: Parker; and Cambridge: Macmillan, 1870).

Man journal – see entry for Matheson (1937).

Marckwardt, Albert H. (1947) 'Nowell's *Vocabularium Saxonicum* and Somner's *Dictionarium*', *Philological Quarterly*, Vol. 26, 345–51.

Marckwardt, Albert H. (ed.) (1952) *Laurence Nowell's* Vocabularium Saxonicum (Ann Arbor: University of Michigan Press).

Marckwardt, Albert H. (1957) 'Principal and Subsidiary Dialect Areas in the North-Central States', *Publications of the American Dialect Society*, No. 27, 3–15.

Markus, Manfred (2007) – see Webography entry.

Markus, Manfred (2012) 'How Can Joseph Wright's *English Dialect Dictionary* be Used as a Corpus?', *Language and Computers*, Vol. 75, No. 1, 97–108. (*Corpus Linguistics and Variation in English: Theory and Description*, edited by Joybrato Mukherjee and Magnus Huber (Amsterdam: Rodopi).)

Markus, Manfred, Upton, Clive and Heuberger, Reinhard (eds) (2010) *Joseph Wright's English Dialect Dictionary and Beyond: Studies in Late Modern English Dialectology* (Frankfurt am Main: Peter Lang).

Mather, James Y. and Speitel, Hans-Henning (eds.), cartography by G. W. Leslie (1975, 1977, 1986) *The Linguistic Atlas of Scotland: Scots Section*. Three vols. (London: Croom Helm).

Mather, Patrick-André (2012) 'The Social Stratification of /r/ in New York City: Labov's Department Store Study Revisited', *Journal of English Linguistics*, Vol. 40, No. 4, 338–56.

Matheson, Hilda (1937) 'Report on the International Association for European Ethnology and Folklore: Edinburgh Congress, 14–21 July, 1937', *Man: A Monthly Record of Anthropological Science*, Vol. 37, 165. The author is given only as 'H.M.', but judging by the Volume Information (Vol. 37, January, 1937, i–viii) it seems likely that the author was Matheson.

Mazzoni, Dannenberg et al. (1999–2016) – see Webography entry for *Audacity*.

Meillet, Antoine (1921) 'L'état actuel des études de linguistique générale', opening lecture for a course on comparative linguistics at the Collège de France, 13 February 1906, reprinted in *Linguistique Historique et Linguistique Générale* (Paris: Champion, and La Société Linguistique de Paris, 1921), pp. 1–18.

Melchers, Gunnel (1996) '"Now, will that do for you?" On the Value of the SED Recordings of Spontaneous Speech'. In *Speech Past and Present: Studies in English Dialectology in Memory of Ossi Ihalainen*, edited by Juhani Klemola, Merja Kytö and Matti Rissanen (Frankfurt am Main: Peter Lang, 1996), pp. 152–68.

Mesthrie, Rajend (2000) 'Regional Dialectology'. In Mesthrie et al. (eds) (2000), pp. 44–75.

Mesthrie, Rajend (2009) 'Social Dialectology'. In Mesthrie et al. (eds) (2009), pp. 74–108.

Mesthrie, Rajend, Swann, Joan, Deumert, Ana and Leap, William L. (2000, 2009) *Introducing Sociolinguistics* (Edinburgh: Edinburgh University Press, 1st and 2nd edns).

Meyerhoff, Miriam and Strycharz, Anna (2013) 'Communities of Practice'. In Chambers and Schilling (eds) (2013), pp. 428–47.

Milroy, James (1992) *Linguistic Variation and Change: On the Historical Sociolinguistics of English* (Oxford: Blackwell).

Milroy, James and Milroy, Lesley (1978) 'Belfast: Change and Variation in an Urban Vernacular'. In *Sociolinguistic Patterns in British English*, edited by Peter Trudgill (London: Edward Arnold), pp. 19–36.

Milroy, James and Milroy, Lesley (1985) 'Linguistic Change, Social Network and Speaker Innovation', *Journal of Linguistics*, Vol. 21, No. 2, 339–84.

Milroy, James and Milroy, Lesley (eds) (1993) *Real English: The Grammar of English Dialects in the British Isles* (London and New York: Longman). Reprinted in 2013 by Routledge (Abingdon, Oxfordshire and New York).

Milroy, James, Milroy, Lesley and Hartley, Sue (1994) 'Local and Supra-Local Change in British English: The Case of Glottalisation', *English World-Wide*, Vol. 15, No. 1, 1–33.

Milroy, Lesley (1980) *Language and Social Networks* (Oxford: Basil Blackwell).

Milroy, Lesley and Llamas, Carmen ((2013) 'Social Networks'. In Chambers and Schilling (eds) (2013), pp. 409–27.

Milroy, Lesley and Milroy, James (1992) 'Social Network and Social Class: Toward an Integrated Sociolinguistic Model', *Language in Society*, Vol. 21, No. 1, 1–26.

Mitzka, Walther and Schmitt, Ludwig Erich, under the direction of Reiner Hildebrandt (1951–80) *Deutscher Wortatlas*. 22 vols. (Gießen: Schmitz).

Mobilization for Youth Program (MFY) (1962) *A Proposal for the Prevention and Control of Delinquency by Expanding Opportunities*, 2nd edn (New York: Mobilization for Youth, Inc.).

Montgomery, Christopher (2007) – see entry in Webography.

Montgomery, Christopher and Beal, Joan (2011) 'Perceptual Dialectology'. In *Analysing Variation in English*, edited by Warren Maguire and April McMahon (Cambridge and New York: Cambridge University Press), pp. 121–48.

Montgomery, Christopher and Stoeckle, Philipp (2013) 'Geographic Information Systems and Perceptual Dialectology: A Method for Processing Draw-A-Map Data', *Journal of Linguistic Geography*, Vol. 1, No. 1, 52–85.

Moulin, Claudine (2010) 'Dialect Dictionaries – Traditional and Modern'. In Auer and Schmidt (eds) (2010), pp. 592–612.

Moulton, W. G. (1960) 'The Short Vowel Systems of Northern Switzerland. A Study in Structural Dialectology', *Word: Journal of the Linguistic Circle of New York*, Vol. 16, 155–82.

Moulton, W. G. (1962) 'Dialect Geography and the Concept of Phonological Space', *Word: Journal of the Linguistic Circle of New York*, Vol. 18, 23–32.

Moulton, William G. (1968) 'Structural Dialectology', *Language*, Vol. 44, No. 3, 451–66.

Mugglestone, Lynda (2003) *'Talking Proper': The Rise of Accent as Social Symbol* (Oxford: Oxford University Press).

Murray, James A. H. (1873) *The Dialect of the Southern Counties of Scotland: Its Pronunciation, Grammar, and Historical Relations. With An Appendix on the Present Limits of the Gaelic and Lowland Scotch, and the Dialectical Divisions of the Lowland Tongue. And a Linguistical Map of Scotland* (London and Berlin: Published for the Philological Society by Asher and Company). Also in *Transactions of the Philological Society*, 1870–2, Part II, 1–251 (published in 1873).

Murray, James, Bradley, Henry, Craigie, William and Onions, C. T. (eds) (1884–1933) *The Oxford English Dictionary, or A New English Dictionary on Historical Principles*, 1st edn and Supplement. 13 vols. (Oxford: Clarendon Press). See also the entry for *Oxford English Dictionary*.

Muysken, Pieter (2005) 'A Modular Approach to Sociolinguistic Variation in Syntax: The Gerund in Ecuadorian Spanish'. In Cornips and Corrigan (eds) (2005a), pp. 31–53.

Nida, Eugene A. (1949) *Morphology: The Descriptive Analysis of Words*, 2nd edn (Ann Arbor: The University of Michigan Press). This 2nd edn is 'a complete revision of a work of the same title published in 1946' (p. v) as Vol. 2 of the series University of Michigan Publications in Linguistics.

North, David J. (1982a) 'The Importance of Local Systems in Dialectology', *Papers in Folk Life Studies*, No. 2 (Leeds: The School of English, University of Leeds).

North, David J. (1982b) *Aspects of the Phonology and Agricultural Terminology of the Rural Dialects of Surrey, Kent and Sussex* (University of Leeds, PhD thesis).

North, David J. (1983) *Studies in Anglo-Cornish Phonology: Aspects of the History and Geography of English Pronunciation in Cornwall* (Redruth: Institute of Cornish Studies).

North, David J. (1985) 'Spatial Aspects of Linguistic Change in Surrey, Kent and Sussex'. In *Focus On: England and Wales*, edited by W. Viereck (Amsterdam: John Benjamins), pp. 79–96.

North, David J. and Sharpe, Adam (1980) *A Word-Geography of Cornwall* (Redruth: Institute of Cornish Studies).

Nowell, Laurence (*circa* 1565) *Vocabularium Saxonicum* – see entry for Marckwardt (ed.) (1952).

Ó Dochartaigh, Cathair (ed.) (1994–7) *Survey of the Gaelic Dialects of Scotland: Questionnaire Materials Collected for the Linguistic Survey of Scotland 1–5*. Five vols. (Dublin: School of Celtic Studies, Dublin Institute for Advanced Studies).

Orr, John (1936) Memorandum on a Linguistic Survey of Scotland for the Language Survey Committee of the Scottish Archive for Ethnological, Folkloristic and Linguistic Studies. Copy held in the files of the LSS, Edinburgh.

Orsman, H. W. (ed.) (1997) *The Dictionary of New Zealand English: A Dictionary of New Zealandisms on Historical Principles* (Auckland and Oxford: Oxford University Press).

Orton, Harold (1930) 'The Dialects of Northumberland', *Transactions of the Yorkshire Dialect Society*, Part XXXI, Vol. 5, 14–25.

Orton, Harold (1933) *The Phonology of a South Durham Dialect: Descriptive, Historical, and Comparative* (London: Kegan Paul). Reprinted in 2015 (Abingdon, Oxfordshire and New York: Routledge).

Orton, Harold (1937) 'Northumberland Dialect Research: First Report', *Proceedings of the University of Durham Philosophical Society*, Vol. 8, 127–35.

Orton, Harold (1947) *Dialectal English and the Student*. Pamphlet, reprinted from *Transactions of the Yorkshire Dialect Society*, Part XLVII, Vol. 7, 27–38, being the transcript of a lecture delivered to a meeting of the Yorkshire Dialect Society at the University of Sheffield on 11 May 1946.

Orton, Harold (1962) *Survey of English Dialects* (A) *Introduction* (Leeds: E. J. Arnold and Son).

Orton, Harold and Dieth, Eugen (1951) 'The New Survey of Dialectal English'. In *English Studies To-day: Papers Read at the International Conference of University Professors of English held in Magdalen College, Oxford, August, 1950*, edited by C. L. Wrenn and G. Bullough (Oxford: Oxford University Press), pp. 63–73. Part I by Orton, pp. 63–8; Part II by Dieth, pp. 68–73.

Orton, Harold and Halliday, Wilfrid J. (eds) (1962) *Survey of English Dialects* (B) *The Basic Material*. Vol. 1: *The Six Northern Counties and the Isle of Man*, Part I. (Leeds: E. J. Arnold and Son).

Orton, Harold and Halliday, Wilfrid J. (eds) (1963) *Survey of English Dialects* (B) *The Basic Material*. Vol. 1: *The Six Northern Counties and the Isle of Man*, Part II, question IV.11.6. (Leeds: E. J. Arnold and Son).

Orton, Harold, Halliday, Wilfrid J., Barry, Michael V., Tilling, Philip M. and Wakelin, Martyn F. (eds) (1962–71) *Survey of English Dialects* (B) *The Basic Material*. Vols 1–4. (Leeds: E. J. Arnold and Son). Reprinted in 1998 (Abingdon, Oxfordshire: Routledge).

Orton, Harold, Sanderson, Stewart and Widdowson, John (eds) (1978) *The Linguistic Atlas of England* (London: Croom Helm).

Orton, Harold and Wakelin, Martyn F. (eds) (1968) *Survey of English Dialects* (B) *The Basic Material*. Vol. IV: *The Southern Counties*, Part III. (Leeds: E. J. Arnold and Son). With the assistance of Philip M. Tilling and Mary Hodges.

Orton, Harold and Wright, Nathalia (1974) *A Word Geography of England* (London and New York: Seminar Press).

Orton, Harold, Wright, Nathalia, with the assistance of Jean M. Jones (1972) *Questionnaire for the Investigation of American Regional English: Based on the Work Sheets of the Linguistic Atlas of the United States and Canada* (Knoxville: University of Tennessee).

Osthoff, Hermann and Brugmann, Karl (1878) Preface to *Morphological Investigations in the Sphere of the Indo-European Languages* I [*Morphologische Untersuchungen auf dem Gebiete der indogermanischen Sprachen* I] (Leipzig: S. Hirzel, 1878), pp. iii–xx. Also Chapter 14 in *A Reader in Nineteenth Century Historical Indo-European Linguistics*, edited by Winfred P. Lehmann (Bloomington: Indiana University Press, 1st edn, 1967; Austin, Texas: Linguistics Research Center of the University of Texas at Austin, online edition, 2006). I used the online version, which has no page numbers, available at: https://liberalarts.utexas.edu/lrc/resources/books/reader/index.php.

Oxford English Dictionary, or *A New English Dictionary on Historical Principles* (1884–1928), edited by James A. H. Murray et al., 13 vols, 1st edn (Oxford: Clarendon Press); 2nd edn, 20 vols, edited by John A. Simpson and Edmund S. C. Weiner (Oxford: Clarendon Press, 1989). Supplements and Additions were also published in 1933,

1972–86, and 1993–7. See also entry for Murray et al. (1884–1933), and Webography for the *OED Online*.

Paolillo, John C. (2001) *Analyzing Linguistic Variation: Statistical Models and Methods* (Stanford, California: Center for the Study of Language and Information, Leland Stanford Junior University).

Parry, David R. (ed.) (1977) *The Survey of Anglo-Welsh Dialects*. Vol. 1: *The South East*. (Swansea: privately published).

Parry, David R. (ed.) (1979) *The Survey of Anglo-Welsh Dialects*. Vol. 2: *The South West*. (Swansea: privately published).

Parry, David R. (1985) 'On Producing a Linguistic Atlas: The Survey of Anglo-Welsh Dialects'. In Kirk, Sanderson and Widdowson (eds) (1985), pp. 51–66.

Parry, David R. (ed.) (1999) *A Grammar and Glossary of the Conservative Anglo-Welsh Dialects of Rural Wales* (Sheffield: The National Centre for English Cultural Tradition, University of Sheffield).

Paulasto, Heli (2006) *Welsh English Syntax: Contact and Variation* (Joensuu: Joensuu University Press).

Paulston, Chistine Bratt and Tucker, G. Richard (eds) (2003a) *Sociolinguistics: The Essential Readings* (Malden, Massachusetts and Oxford: Blackwell).

Paulston, Christine Bratt and Tucker, G. Richard (2003b) Introduction to Part I: 'History of Sociolinguistics' in Paulston and Tucker (eds) (2003a), pp. 1–3.

Pederson, Lee (1977) 'Studies of American Pronunciation Since 1945', *American Speech*, Vol. 52, No. 3/4, 262–327.

Pederson, Lee, McDaniel, Susan L. and Adams, Carol M. (eds) (1986–92) *Linguistic Atlas of the Gulf States*. Seven vols. (Athens, Georgia: University of Georgia Press).

Pegge, Samuel (the elder) (1735–6) *An Alphabet of Kenticisms* (London: Published for The English Dialect Society by Trübner, 1876).

Pellowe, John (1967) *Studies Towards a Classification of Varieties of Spoken English* (University of Newcastle upon Tyne, MLitt thesis).

Pellowe, John (1991) *Studies in Theory and Method in Sociolinguistics* (University of Newcastle upon Tyne, PhD thesis). Available from Newcastle University eTheses: https://theses.ncl.ac.uk/dspace/handle/10443/607. Catalogue gives the date as 1991, though the title page says 1990.

Pellowe, John and Jones, Val (1978) 'On Intonational Variability in Tyneside Speech'. In *Sociolinguistic Patterns in British English*, edited by Peter Trudgill (London: Edward Arnold, 1978), pp. 101–21.

Pellowe, John, Nixon, Graham, Strang, Barabara, and McNeany, Vincent (1972) 'A Dynamic Modelling of Linguistic Variation: The Urban (Tyneside) Linguistic Survey', *Lingua*, Vol. 30, 1–30.

Penhallurick, R. J. (1982) 'Two Gower Accents: A Phonological Comparison of Penclawdd and Reynoldston', *Transactions of the Yorkshire Dialect Society*, Part LXXXII, Vol. XV, 29–41.

Penhallurick, Robert J. (1991) *The Anglo-Welsh Dialects of North Wales: A Survey of Conservative Rural Spoken English in the Counties of Gwynedd and Clwyd* (Frankfurt am Main: Peter Lang).

Penhallurick, Robert (1994) *Gowerland and Its Language: A History of the English Speech of the Gower Peninsula, South Wales* (Frankfurt am Main: Peter Lang).

Penhallurick, Rob (1996) 'The Grammar of Northern Welsh English: Progressive Verb Phrases'. In *Speech Past and Present: Studies in English Dialectology in Memory of Ossi Ihalainen*, edited by Juhani Klemola, Merja Kytö and Matti Rissanen (Frankfurt am Main: Peter Lang), pp. 308–42.

Penhallurick, Rob (ed.) (2000) *Debating Dialect: Essays on the Philosophy of Dialect Study* (Cardiff: University of Wales Press).

Penhallurick, Rob (2009) 'Dialect Dictionaries'. In *The Oxford History of English Lexicography*, Vol. II, edited by A. P. Cowie (Oxford: Oxford University Press), pp. 290–313.

Penhallurick, Rob (2010a) 'The Dialect Dictionary: What Is It Good For?' In *Proceedings of Methods XIII: Papers from the Thirteenth International Conference on Methods in Dialectology, 2008*, edited by Barry Heselwood and Clive Upton (Frankfurt am Main: Peter Lang), pp. 133–42.

Penhallurick, Rob (2010b) *Studying the English Language*, 2nd edn (Basingstoke: Palgrave Macmillan).

Penhallurick, Rob (2012) 'Welsh English'. In *The Mouton World Atlas of Variation in English*, edited by Bernd Kortmann and Kerstin Lunkenheimer (Berlin: De Gruyter), pp. 58–69.

Penhallurick, Rob (2013) '*Voices* in Wales: A New National Survey'. In *Analysing 21st Century British English: Conceptual and Methodological Aspects of the* Voices *Project*, edited by Clive Upton and Bethan L. Davies (Abingdon, Oxfordshire and New York: Routledge), pp. 124–35.

Penhallurick, Rob and Willmott, Adrian (2000) 'Dialect/"England's Dreaming"'. In Penhallurick (ed.) (2000), pp. 5–45.

Petyt, K. M. (1980) *The Study of Dialect: An Introduction to Dialectology* (London: André Deutsch).

Petyt, K. M. (1982) 'Who Is Really Doing Dialectology?' In *Linguistic Controversies: Essays in Linguistic Theory and Practice in Honour of F. R. Palmer*, edited by David Crystal (London: Edward Arnold), pp. 192–208.

Petyt, K. M. (1985) *Dialect and Accent in Industrial West Yorkshire* (Varieties of English Around the World, General Series, Vol. 6) (Amsterdam/Philadelphia: John Benjamins).

Pickford, Glenna Ruth (1956) 'American Linguistic Geography: A Sociological Appraisal', *Word*, Vol. 12, 211–33.

Plichta, Bartłomiej [Bartek] (2003–12) – see Webography entry for *Akustyk*.

Poole, Jacob (1867) *A Glossary, With Some Pieces of Verse, of the Old Dialect of the English Colony in the Baronies of Forth and Bargy, County of Wexford, Ireland, Formerly Collected by Jacob Poole* (London: John Russell Smith). This is the 1st edn, edited by William Barnes. The *Glossary* was compiled by Poole in the early nineteenth century. A new version, edited by Terrence P. Dolan and Diarmaid Ó Muirithe, was published in 1979 as *The Past: Organ of the Uí Cinsealagh Historical Society*, No. 13 (reprinted in 1996, Dublin: Four Courts Press).

Pop, Sever (1950 *La Dialectologie: Aperçu historique et méthodes d'enquêtes linguistiques* ['Dialectology: Historical overview and linguistic survey methods']. Two vols. (Louvain: University of Louvain).

Praxmarer, Christoph (2010a) 'Dialect Relations in the *English Dialect Dictionary*'. In *Proceedings of Methods XIII: Papers from the Thirteenth International Conference on*

Methods in Dialectology, 2008, edited by Barry Heselwood and Clive Upton (Frankfurt am Main: Peter Lang), pp. 153–9.

Praxmarer, Christoph (2010b) 'Joseph Wright's *EDD* and the Geographical Distribution of Dialects: A Visual Approach'. In *Joseph Wright's* English Dialect Dictionary *and Beyond: Studies in Late Modern English Dialectology*, edited by Manfred Markus, Clive Upton and Reinhard Heuberger (Frankfurt am Main: Peter Lang), pp. 61–76.

Preston, Dennis R. (1981) 'Perceptual Dialectology: Mental Maps of United States Dialects from a Hawaiian Perspective (Summary)'. In *Methods IV/Méthodes IV (Papers from the Fourth International Conference on Methods in Dialectology)*, edited by H. Warkentyne (Victoria, British Columbia: University of Victoria), pp. 192–8.

Preston, Dennis R. (1982) 'Perceptual Dialectology: Mental Maps of United States Dialects from a Hawaiian Perspective', *Hawaii Working Papers in Linguistics*, Vol. 14, No. 2 (edited by Dennis R. Preston), 5–49.

Preston, Dennis R. (1988) 'Methods in the Study of Dialect Perception'. In *Methods in Dialectology: Proceedings of the Sixth International Conference held at the University College of North Wales, 3rd–7th August 1987*, edited by Alan R. Thomas (Clevedon, Avon and Philadelphia: Multilingual Matters), pp. 373–95.

Preston, Dennis R. (1989) *Perceptual Dialectology: Nonlinguists' Views of Areal Linguistics* (Dordrecht: Foris).

Preston, Dennis R. (ed.) (1999a) *Handbook of Perceptual Dialectology*. Vol. 1. (Amsterdam/ Philadelphia: John Benjamins).

Preston, Dennis R. (1999b) Introduction to *Handbook of Perceptual Dialectology*. Vol. 1. (Amsterdam/Philadelphia: John Benjamins), pp. xxiii–xl.

Preston, Dennis R. (2002) 'Language with an Attitude'. In Chambers, Trudgill and Schilling-Estes (eds) (2002), pp. 40–66.

Preston, Dennis R. (2005) 'Perceptual Dialectology'. In *Sociolinguistics: An International Handbook of the Science of Language and Society*, Vol. 2, edited by Ulrich Ammon, Norbert Dittmar, Klaus J. Mattheier and Peter Trudgill (Berlin and New York: Walter de Gruyter, 2nd revised and extended edn), pp. 1683–96.

Preston, Dennis R. (2010a) 'Language, Space, and the Folk'. In Auer and Schmidt (eds) (2010), pp. 179–201.

Preston, Dennis R. (2010b) 'Mapping the Geolinguistic Spaces in Your Brain'. In Lameli et al. (eds) (2010a), pp. 121–40.

Preston, Dennis R. (2013) 'Language with an Attitude'. In Chambers and Schilling (eds) (2013), pp. 157–82.

Preston, Dennis R. and Howe, George M. (1987) 'Computerized Studies of Mental Dialect Maps'. In *Variation in Language: NWAV-XV at Stanford (Proceedings of the Fifteenth Annual Conference on New Ways of Analyzing Variation)*, edited by K. Denning, S. Inkelas, F. C. McNair-Knox and J. R. Rickford (Stanford, California: Department of Linguistics, Stanford University), pp. 361–78.

Preston, Dennis R. and Long, Daniel (eds) (2002) *Handbook of Perceptual Dialectology*. Vol. 2. (Amsterdam/Philadelphia: John Benjamins).

Preston, Dennis R. and Niedzielski, Nancy (eds) (2010) *A Reader in Sociophonetics* (New York: De Gruyter Mouton).

Pula, Robert P. (1994) Preface to the 5th edn of *Science and Sanity* by Alfred Korzybski (New York: Institute of General Semantics), pp. xiii–xxii.

Pulgram, Ernst (1964) 'Structural Comparison, Diasystems and Dialectology', *Linguistics*, Vol. 2, No. 4, 66–82.

Putnam, George N. and O'Hern, Edna M. (1955) *The Status Significance of an Isolated Urban Dialect*, *Language* Vol. 31, No. 4, Part II, supplement: *Language* Dissertation No. 53 (Oct.–Dec., 1955), v, 1–32.

Quaino, Stefano (2011) *The Intonation of Welsh English: The Case of Ceredigion and Gwynedd* (Alpen-Adria-University Klagenfurt, Faculty of Cultural Sciences / Institute of English and American Studies, PhD dissertation).

Ramisch, Heinrich (2010) 'Mapping British English'. In Lameli et al. (eds) (2010a), pp. 238–52.

Ramson, W. S. (1987) '*The Australian National Dictionary*: A Foretaste'. In Burchfield (ed.) (1987), pp. 136–55.

Ramson, W. S. (ed.) (1988) *The Australian National Dictionary: A Dictionary of Australianisms on Historical Principles* (Oxford: Oxford University Press). See entry for *Australian National Dictionary* in Webography for online edition.

Ray, John (1670) *A Collection of English Proverbs* (Cambridge: Printed by John Hayes for W. Morden).

Ray, John (1674) *A Collection of English Words Not Generally Used, with their Significations and Original, in two Alphabetical Catalogues* (London: Printed by H. Bruges for Thomas Burrell). 2nd edn (1691) (London: Christopher Wilkinson; Scolar Press facsimile reprint, Menston, England, 1969). Reprint by the English Dialect Society (London, 1874), rearranged and edited by Walter W. Skeat.

Rayson, John (1858) *The Song of Solomon in the Cumberland Dialect; From the Authorised English Version* (London: George Barclay). See also entry for Bonaparte (1862).

Reed, Carroll E. (1957) 'Word Geography of the Pacific Northwest', *Orbis*, Vol. 6, 86–93.

Reed, Carroll E. (1961) 'The Pronunciation of English in the Pacific Northwest', *Language*, Vol. 37, No. 4, 559–64.

Rensink, W. G. (1955) 'Informant Classification of Dialects' ['Dialectindeling Naar Opgaven van Medewerkers'], *Amsterdam Dialectbureau Bulletin*, No. 7, 20–23. English translation in Preston (ed.) (1999a), pp. 3–7. I used the English version.

Rickford, John R., Ball, Arnetha, Blake, Renee, Jackson, Raina and Martin, Nomi (1991) 'Rappin on the Copula Coffin: Theoretical and Methodological Issues in the Analysis of Copula Variation in African-American Vernacular English', *Language Variation and Change*, Vol. 3, No. 1, 103–32.

Robinson, Mairi (ed.-in-chief) (1985) *The Concise Scots Dictionary* (Aberdeen: Aberdeen University Press). I have the 2nd edn (1987).

Robinson, W. Peter and Giles, Howard (eds) (2001) *The New Handbook of Language and Social Psychology* (Chichester, England: Wiley). See also entry for Giles and Robinson (1990).

Romaine, Suzanne (1981) 'The Status of Variable Rules in Sociolinguistic Theory', *Journal of Linguistics*, Vol. 17, No. 1, 93–119.

Royle, Nicholas (2000) 'Dialectology and Deconstruction'. In Penhallurick (ed.) (2000), pp. 112–15.

Rudin, Ernst and Elmer, Willy (1998) 'PDP: A Recent Shift in Phonetic Performance', *SPELL: Swiss Papers in English Language and Literature*, Vol. 11, 171–84. Available from e-periodica, at: http://dx.doi.org/10.5169/seals-99963.

Ryan, Ellen Bouchard (1979) 'Why Do Low-Prestige Language Varieties Persist?' In *Language and Social Psychology*, edited by Howard Giles and Robert N. St Clair (Oxford: Basil Blackwell), pp. 145–57.

Sanders, Robert (1991) 'Alexander John Ellis (1814–1890): A Bibliography of his Writings, Part I: Studies in Phonetics, Spelling Reform, and Universal Language', *Regional Language Studies (Newfoundland)*, No. 13, 2–13.

Sanders, Robert (1993) 'Alexander John Ellis (1814–1890): A Bibliography of his Writings, Part II: Ellis's Philological Writings', *Regional Language Studies (Newfoundland)*, No. 14, 26–31.

Sanders, Robert (1994) 'Alexander John Ellis (1814–1890): A Bibliography of his Writings, Part III: Miscellaneous Publications, Studies in the Physics of Music, Studies in Mathematics', *Regional Language Studies (Newfoundland)*, No. 15, 2–10.

Sanderson, Stewart and Widdowson, J. D. A. (1985) 'Linguistic Geography in England: Progress and Prospects'. In Kirk, Sanderson and Widdowson (eds) (1985), pp. 34–50.

Sandys, William (1846) – see entry for Treenoodle, Uncle Jan.

Sankoff, David (ed.) (1986) *Diversity and Diachrony* (Amsterdam Studies in the Theory and History of Linguistic Science, Series IV: Current Issues in Linguistic Theory, Vol. 53) (Amsterdam/Philadelphia: John Benjamins).

Sankoff, David (2005) 'Variable Rules'. In *Sociolinguistics: An International Handbook of the Science of Language and Society*, Vol. 2, edited by Ulrich Ammon, Norbert Dittmar, Klaus J. Mattheier and Peter Trudgill (Berlin and New York: Walter de Gruyter, 2nd revised and extended edn), pp. 1150–63.

Sankoff, David and Labov, William (1979) 'On the Uses of Variable Rules', *Language in Society*, Vol. 8, No. 2, 189–222.

Sankoff, David and Sankoff, Gillian (1973) 'Sample Survey Methods and Computer-Assisted Analysis in the Study of Grammatical Variation'. In *Canadian Languages in their Social Context*, edited by Regna Darnell (Edmonton, Alberta: Linguistic Research), pp. 7–64.

Sankoff, Gillian and Blondeau, Hélène (2007) 'Language Change Across the Lifespan: /r/ in Montreal French', *Language*, Vol. 83, No. 3, 560–88.

Sauer, Carl (1952) *Agricultural Origins and Dispersals* (New York: American Geographical Society).

Saussure, Ferdinand de (1916) *Cours de linguistique générale*, edited by C. Bally and A. Sechehaye, in collaboration with A. Riedlinger (Paris: Éditions Payot). English translations (*Course in General Linguistics*) by W. Baskin (New York City: The Philosophical Library, 1960), and by R. Harris (London: Duckworth, 1983). I favour the 1960 translation.

Scargill, M. H. and Warkentyne, Henry J. (1972) 'The Survey of Canadian English: A Report', *English Quarterly*, Vol. 5, No. 3, 47–104.

Šafařik, Pavel Jozef [Paul Josef Schafarik] (1842) *Slovanský Zeměvid* (Prague: publisher not named). Map reproduced in Lameli et al. (eds) (2010b, Map 1501). Also available at: http://www.maproom.org/00/48/present.php?m=0015, as Plate 15 from *Die Bulgaren in ihren historischen, ethnographischen und politischen Grenzen*, by A. Ishirkoff and V. Zlatarski (Berlin: William Greve, 1917).

Scheuringer, Hermann (2010) 'Mapping the German Language'. In Lameli et al. (eds) (2010a), pp. 158–79.

Schleicher, August (1863) *Die Darwinsche Theorie und die Sprachwissenschaft* (Weimar: Hermann Böhlau). Available online at the Munich Digitization Center (MDZ) of the Bavarian State Library (BSB): http://reader.digitale-sammlungen.de/de/fs1/object/display/bsb10588615_00001.html.

Schmeller, Johann Andreas (1821) *Die Mundarten Bayerns grammatisch dargestellt* (München: Karl Thienemann). The volume's map of Bavarian dialects is reproduced in Lameli et al. (eds) (2010b, Map 0801).

Schmeller, Johann Andreas [though credited as 'Anonymous'] (1844) Review of *Sprachkarte von Deutschland; Slovanský Zemĕvid*, in *Gelehrte Anzeigen*, Vol. 18, Nos 69–71 (April 1844), 553–76.

Schmidt, Johannes (1872) *Die Verwandtschaftsverhältnisse der indogermanischen Sprachen* (Weimar: Hermann Böhlau).

Schneider, Edgar W. (2003) 'The Dynamics of New Englishes: From Identity Construction to Dialect Birth', *Language*, Vol. 79, No. 2, 233–81.

Schrambke, Renate (2010) 'Language and Space: Traditional Dialect Geography'. In Auer and Schmidt (eds) (2010), pp. 87–107.

Séguy, Jean (1973) *Atlas Linguistique de la Gascogne. Vol. 6. Artes. Notice explicative. Matrices dialectométriques.* (Paris: Centre National de la Recherche Scientifique).

Shorrocks, Graham (1985) 'Further Thoughts on the Labovian Interview', *Lore and Language*, Vol. 4, No. 1, 46–56.

Shorrocks, Graham (1991) 'A. J. Ellis as Dialectologist: A Reassessment', *Historiographia Linguistica*, Vol. 18, No. 2/3, 321–34.

Shorrocks, Graham (1996) 'Non-standard Dialect Literature and Popular Culture'. In *Speech Past and Present: Studies in English Dialectology in Memory of Ossi Ihalainen*, edited by Juhani Klemola, Meja Kytö and Matti Rissanen (Frankfurt am Main: Peter Lang), pp. 385–411.

Shorrocks, Graham (2000) 'Purpose, Theory and Method in English Dialectology: Towards a More Objective History of the Discipline'. In Penhallurick (ed.) (2000), pp. 84–107.

Shuy, Roger W. (1962) *The Northern-Midland Dialect Boundary in Illinois* (Publications of the American Dialect Society No. 38) (Tuscaloosa: University of Alabama Press).

Shuy, Roger W. (1969) 'Subjective Judgments in Sociolinguistic Analysis'. In *Report of the Twentieth Annual Round Table Meeting on Linguistics and Language Studies: Linguistics and the Teaching of Standard English To Speakers of Other Languages or Dialects* (Monograph Series on Languages and Linguistics, No. 22, 1969), edited by James E. Alatis (Washington, D.C.: Georgetown University Press), pp. 175–88. Includes discussion points by Joan Baratz, David DeCamp, Ralph Fasold, and William Labov.

Shuy, Roger W. (1990) 'A Brief History of American Sociolinguistics 1949–1989', *Historiographia Linguistica*, Vol. 17, No. 1/2, 183–209. Extracts reprinted in *Sociolinguistics: The Essential Readings*, edited by Christina Bratt Paulston and G. Richard Tucker (Oxford, and Malden, Massachusetts: Blackwell, 2003), pp. 4–16.

Shuy, Roger W., Baratz, Joan C. and Wolfram, Walter A. (1969) *Sociolinguistic Factors in Speech Identification* (National Institute of Mental Health Research Project Final Report No. MH 15048-01) (Washington, D.C.: Center for Applied Linguistics).

Shuy, Roger W., Wolfram, Walter A. and Riley, William K. (1968a) *A Study of Social Dialects in Detroit. Linguistic Correlates of Social Stratification in Detroit Speech.* (Final Report, Cooperative Research Project No. 6-1347) (Washington, D.C.: US Department of Health, Education, and Welfare; Office of Education, Bureau of Research). Available at: http://eric.ed.gov/?q=shuy&ft=on&pg=2&id=ED022187.

Shuy, Roger W., Wolfram, Walter A. and Riley, William K. (1968b) *Field Techniques in an Urban Language Study* (Washington, D.C.: Center for Applied Linguistics).

Sibata, Takesi (1959) 'Consciousness of Dialect Boundaries' ['Hôgen Kyôkai no Ishiki'], *Gengo Kenkyu: Journal of the Linguistic Society of Japan*, No. 36, 1–30. English translation in Preston (ed.) (1999a), pp. 39–62. I used the English version.

Silva, Penny, Dore, Wendy, Mantzel, Dorothea, Muller, Colin and Wright, Madeleine (eds) (1996) *A Dictionary of South African English on Historical Principles* (Oxford: Oxford University Press; and the Dictionary Unit for South African English (DSAE), Associate Institute of Rhodes University, South Africa). See Webography entry for Silva et al. (1996) for online edition.

Silverman, Kim, Beckman, Mary, Pitrelli, John, Ostendorf, Mari, Wightman, Colin, Price, Patti, Pierrehumbert, Janet and Hirschberg, Julia (1992) 'ToBI: A Standard for Labeling English Prosody'. In *Proceedings of the 1992 International Conference on Spoken Language Processing*, 12–16 October, Banff, Alberta, Canada (Alberta: University of Alberta), pp. 867–70.

Sivertsen, Eva (1960) *Cockney Phonology* (Oslo Studies in English, No. 8; Publications of the British Institute in the University of Oslo) (Oslo: Oslo University Press).

Sjölander and Beskow (2005–12) – see Webography entry for *WaveSurfer*.

Skeat, Walter W. (1896) *A Student's Pastime, Being A Select Series of Articles Reprinted From 'Notes and Queries'* (Oxford: Oxford University Press, at the Clarendon Press).

Skeat, Walter W. and Nodal, J. H. (eds) (1877) *A Bibliographical List of the Works that have been Published, or are Known to Exist in MS., Illustrative of the Various Dialects of English* (Compiled by Members of the English Dialect Society) (London: Published for the English Dialect Society by Trübner).

Skinner, Stephen (1671) *Etymologicon Linguæ Anglicanæ.* Edited by T. Henshaw. (London: H. Brome).

Somner, William (1659) *Dictionarium Saxonico-Latino-Anglicum* (London: Daniel White).

Spenser, Edmund (1590–1609) *The Faerie Queene* (London: William Ponsonby).

Story, G. M., Kirwin, W. J. and Widdowson, J. D. A. (eds) (1982, 1990, 1999) *Dictionary of Newfoundland English* (Toronto: University of Toronto Press). 1st edn, 2nd edn with Supplement, online edn (see also Webography).

Strang, Barbara (1968) 'The Tyneside Linguistic Survey' (Paper read at the International Congress of Dialectologists, 1965, Marburg), *Zeitschrift für Mundartforschung*, New Series, Vol. 4, 788–94.

Sumner, William Graham (1906) *Folkways: A Study of the Sociological Importance of Usages, Manners, Customs, Mores, and Morals* (Boston: Ginn and Company).

Sutton, Charles W. (1880) *Catalogue of the English Dialect Library, Free Reference Library, King Street, Manchester. Founded Under the Auspices of the English Dialect Society* (Manchester: Charles Sever).

Swiggers, Pierre (2010) 'Mapping the Romance Languages of Europe'. In Lameli et al. (eds) (2010a), pp. 269–300.

Szmrecsanyi, Benedikt (2013) *Grammatical Variation in British English Dialects: A Study in Corpus-Based Dialectometry* (Cambridge: Cambridge University Press).

Tagliamonte, Sali A. (2006) *Analysing Sociolinguistic Variation* (Cambridge: Cambridge University Press). See also Webography for companion website.

Tagliamonte, Sali A. (2012) *Variationist Sociolinguistics: Change, Observation, Interpretation* (Malden, Massachusetts, Oxford and Chichester: Wiley Blackwell).

Tagliamonte, Sali A. (2013) *Roots of English: Exploring the History of Dialects* (Cambridge: Cambridge University Press).

Tagliamonte, Sali A. (2016) *Making Waves: The Story of Variationist Sociolinguistics* (Malden, Massachusetts, Oxford and Chichester: Wiley Blackwell). See also Webography for companion website.

Thomas, Alan R. (1968) 'Generative Phonology in Dialectology', *Transactions of the Philological Society*, 1967, 179–203. Published in 1968.

Thomas, Alan R. (1973) *The Linguistic Geography of Wales* (Cardiff: University of Wales Press).

Thomas, Alan R. (ed.) (1988) *Methods in Dialectology: Proceedings of the Sixth International Conference held at the University College of North Wales, 3rd–7th August 1987* (Clevedon, Avon and Philadelphia: Multilingual Matters). Preface, p. v.

Thompson, Ann (2008) 'Joseph Wright's Slips', *Transactions of the Yorkshire Dialect Society*, Part CVIII, Vol. 21, 12–21.

Tillery, Jan and Bailey, Guy (1998) '*Yall* in Oklahoma', *American Speech*, Vol. 73, No. 3, 257–78.

Tolkien, J. R. R. (1954–5) *The Lord of the Rings* (London: George Allen and Unwin).

Tooley, R. V. and Bricker, Charles (1976) *Landmarks of Mapmaking: An Illustrated Survey of Maps and Mapmakers* (Oxford: Phaidon). Maps chosen and displayed by Tooley, text written by Bricker.

Torgersen, Eivind and Kerswill, Paul (2004) 'Internal and External Motivation in Phonetic Change: Dialect Levelling Outcomes for an English Vowel Shift', *Journal of Sociolinguistics*, Vol. 8, No. 1, 24–53. I used the pre-publication version from the School of Linguistics and Applied Language Studies, University of Reading, downloaded from Kerswill's Lancaster University web-pages: http://www.lancaster.ac.uk/fass/groups/LVLT/profiles/eprints/293/489/.

Torgersen, Eivind, Kerswill, Paul and Fox, Susan (2006) 'Ethnicity as a Source of Changes in the London Vowel System'. In *Language Variation – European Perspectives. Selected Papers from the Third International Conference on Language Variation in Europe (ICLaVE3)*, Amsterdam, June, 2005, edited by F. Hinskens (Amsterdam: John Benjamins), pp. 249–63. I used the online version from: http://www.lancaster.ac.uk/fss/projects/linguistics/innovators/output.htm.

Transactions of the Scottish Dialects Committee (1913–21), Numbers I–IV, edited by William Grant (1913, 1916, 1919, 1921).

Treenoodle, Uncle Jan (pseudonym of William Sandys) (1846) *Specimens of Cornish Provincial Dialect, Collected and Arranged by Uncle Jan Treenoodle, with some Introductory Remarks, and a Glossary, by an Antiquarian Friend, also a Selection of Songs and Other Pieces Connected with Cornwall* (London: John Russell Smith).

Trench, Richard Chenevix (1860) *On Some Deficiencies in our English Dictionaries. (Being the substance of two papers read before the Philological Society, Nov. 5, and Nov. 19, 1857).* Revised and enlarged 2nd edition. (London: John W. Parker and Son). Published also in Part II of the *Transactions of the Philological Society*, 1857. 1st edn published in 1858.

Trevisa, John of (1387) *Polychronicon Ranulphi Higden Monachi Cestrensis* ['Universal History by Ranulf Higden, monk of Chester']; *Together with the English Translations of John Trevisa and of an Unknown Writer of the Fifteenth Century.* Vol. II. Edited by Churchill Babington. (London: Longmans, Green, And Company, 1869). Also, 1527 edn of Trevisa's translation of the *Polychronicon* printed by Peter Treveris (London).

Trudgill, Peter ([1972/]1983) 'Sex and Covert Prestige: Linguistic Change in the Urban Dialect of Norwich'. In *On Dialect: Social and Geographical Perspectives*, Peter Trudgill (Oxford: Blackwell, 1983), pp. 169–85. Revised version of 'Sex, Covert Prestige and Linguistic Change in the Urban British English of Norwich', *Language in Society*, Vol. 1, No. 2 (October, 1972), 179–95.

Trudgill, Peter (1974a) *The Social Differentiation of English in Norwich* (Cambridge: Cambridge University Press).

Trudgill, Peter (1974b) 'Linguistic Change and Diffusion: Description and Explanation in Sociolinguistic Dialect Geography', *Language in Society*, Vol. 3, No. 2, 215–46.

Trudgill, Peter (ed.) (1978) *Sociolinguistic Patterns in British English* (London: Edward Arnold).

Trudgill, Peter (1988) 'Norwich Revisited: Recent Linguistic Changes in an English Urban Dialect', *English World-Wide*, Vol. 9, No. 1, 33–49.

Trudgill, Peter and Chambers, J. K. (eds) (1991) *Dialects of English: Studies in Grammatical Variation* (London and New York: Longman).

Tucker, G. Richard and Lambert, Wallace. E. (1969) 'White and Negro Listeners' Reactions to Various American-English Dialects', *Social Forces*, Vol. 47, No. 4, 463–8.

Underwood, Gary N. (1976) 'American English Dialectology: Alternatives for the Southwest', *International Journal of the Sociology of Language*, Vol. 2, 19–40.

Upton, Clive (2000) 'Maintaining the Standard'. In Penhallurick (ed.) (2000), pp. 66–83.

Upton, Clive (2010) 'Designing Maps for Non-linguists'. In Lameli et al. (eds) (2010a), pp. 142–57.

Upton, Clive (2015) 'Regional and Dialect Dictionaries'. In Durkin (ed.) (2015), pp. 381–92.

Upton, Clive and Davies, Bethan L. (eds) (2013) *Analysing 21st Century British English: Conceptual and Methodological Aspects of the Voices Project* (Abingdon, Oxfordshire and New York: Routledge). See also Webography for companion website.

Upton, Clive, Parry, David and Widdowson, J. D. A. (eds) (1994) *Survey of English Dialects: The Dictionary and Grammar* (London and New York: Routledge).

Upton, Clive, Sanderson, Stewart and Widdowson, John (1987) *Word Maps: A Dialect Atlas of England* (London: Croom Helm). Cartography by David Brophy.

Upton, Clive and Widdowson, J. D. A. (1996, 2006) *An Atlas of English Dialects*, 1st and 2nd edns (Oxford: Oxford University Press; and Abingdon, Oxfordshire: Routledge, respectively).

Vandermeeren, Sonja (2005) 'Research on Language Attitudes'. In *Sociolinguistics: An International Handbook of the Science of Language and Society*, Vol. 2, edited by Ulrich Ammon, Norbert Dittmar, Klaus J. Mattheier and Peter Trudgill (Berlin and New York: Walter de Gruyter, 2nd revised and extended edn), pp. 1318–32.

Verner, Karl (1875) 'Eine Ausnahme der ersten Lautverschiebung' ['An Exception to the First Sound Shift'], *Zeitschrift für vergleichende Sprachforschung auf dem Gebiete der Indogermanischen Sprachen*, Vol. 23, No. 2, 97–130.

Viereck, Wolfgang (1968) 'Guy S. Lowman's Contribution to British English Dialectology', *Transactions of the Yorkshire Dialect Society*, Part LXVIII, Vol. 12, 32–9.

Viereck, Wolfgang (1975) *Lexikalische und grammatische Ergebnisse des Lowman-Survey von Mittl- und Südengland*. Two vols. (Munich: Wilhelm Fink Verlag).

Viereck, Wolfgang (1980) 'The Dialectal Structure of British English: Lowman's Evidence', *English World-Wide*, Vol. 1, No. 1, 25–44. And *Angol Filológiai Tanulmányok / Hungarian Studies in English*, Vol. 12 (1979), 203–31.

Viereck, Wolfgang (1985a) 'On the Interrelationship of British and American English: Morphological Evidence'. In *Focus on England and Wales*, edited by Wolfgang Viereck (Amsterdam/Philadelphia: John Benjamins), pp. 247–300.

Viereck, Wolfgang (1985b) 'Linguistic Atlases and Dialectometry: The Survey of English Dialects'. In Kirk, Sanderson and Widdowson (eds) (1985), pp. 94–112.

Viereck, Wolfgang (ed.) (1985c) *Focus On: England and Wales* (Varieties of English Around the World, General Series, Vol. 4) (Amsterdam/Philadelphia: John Benjamins).

Viereck, Wolfgang (1991) 'Prince Louis-Lucien Bonaparte and English Dialectology'. In *Proceedings of the International Congress on Dialectology*, Bilbao, 21-25.X.1991, edited by G. Aurrekoetxea and C. Videgain (Bilbao: Euskaltzaindia, 1992), pp. 17–30.

Viereck, Wolfgang in collaboration with Ramisch, Heinrich (1991) *The Computer Developed Linguistic Atlas of England 1* (Tübingen: Niemeyer). Computational production by Harald Händler, Petra Hoffmann and Wolfgang Putschke.

Viereck, Wolfgang and Ramisch, Heinrich (1997) *The Computer Developed Linguistic Atlas of England 2* (Tübingen: Niemeyer). Computational production by Harald Händler and Christian Marx. With dialectometrical contributions by Sheila Embleton, Chitsuko Fukushima, Hans Goebl, Harald Händler, Fumio Inoue, Guillaume Schiltz, Alan R. Thomas, Wolfgang Viereck and Eric Wheeler.

Wagner, Heinrich (1958–69) *Linguistic Atlas and Survey of Irish Dialects*. Four vols. (Dublin: Dublin Institute for Advanced Studies).

Wagner, Susanne (2013) – see entry in Webography.

Wakelin, Martyn F. (ed.) (1972) *Patterns in the Folk Speech of the British Isles* (London: The Athlone Press, University of London).

Wakelin, Martyn F. (1977) *English Dialects: An Introduction*, revised edn (London: Athlone Press).

Wakelin, Martyn F. (1987) 'The Treatment of Dialect in English Dictionaries'. In Burchfield (ed.) (1987), pp. 156–77.

Walker, James A. (2015) *Canadian English: A Sociolinguistic Perspective* (New York and Abingdon, Oxfordshire: Routledge).

Walter, Henriette (1994) *French Inside Out: The World-Wide Development of the French Language in the Past, Present and the Future* (Abingdon, Oxfordshire and New York: Routledge). French edition: *Le français dans tous les sens* (Paris: Éditions Robert Laffont, 1988). English translation by Peter Fawcett.

Walters, J. Roderick (1999) *A Study of the Segmental and Suprasegmental Phonology of Rhondda Valleys English* (University of Glamorgan, PhD thesis). Available at: http://phonetics.research.glam.ac.uk.

Walters, J. Roderick (2001) 'English in Wales and a "Welsh Valleys accent"', *World Englishes*, Vol. 20, No. 3, 285–304.

Walters, J. Roderick (2003a) '"Celtic English": Influences on a South Wales Valleys Accent', *English World-Wide*, Vol. 24, No. 1, 63–87.

Walters, J. Roderick (2003b) 'On the Intonation of a South Wales "Valleys Accent" of English', *Journal of the International Phonetics Association*, Vol. 33, No. 2, 211–38.

Walters, J. Roderick (2003c) 'A Study of the Prosody of a South East Wales "Valleys Accent"'. In *The Celtic Englishes III*, edited by Hildegard L. C. Tristram (Heidelberg: Universitatsverlag Winter).

Wardhaugh, Ronald (2006) *An Introduction to Sociolinguistics*, 5th edn (Malden, Massachusetts and Oxford: Blackwell).

Wardhaugh, Ronald and Fuller, Janet M. (2015) *An Introduction to Sociolinguistics*, 7th edn (Malden, Massachusetts, Oxford and Chichester: Wiley Blackwell).

Warkentyne, H. J. (1971) 'Contemporary Canadian English: A Report of the Survey of Canadian English', *American Speech*, Vol. 46, No. 3/4, 193–9.

Warrack, Alexander (1911) *A Scots Dialect Dictionary Comprising the Words in Use from the Latter Part of the Seventeenth Century to the Present Day*. With an Introduction and a Dialect Map by William Grant. (London and Edinburgh: W. and R. Chambers).

Watt, Dominic and Milroy, Lesley (1999) 'Patterns of Variation and Change in Three Newcastle Vowels: Is This Dialect Levelling?' In Foulkes and Docherty (eds) (1999), pp. 25–46.

Webb, Victor N. (2002) *Language in South Africa: The Role of Language in National Transformation, Reconstruction and Development* (Amsterdam/Philadelphia: John Benjamins).

Webster, Noah Webster (1828) *An American Dictionary of the English Language*. Two vols. (New York: S. Converse).

Weijnen, Antonius A. (1946) 'De grenzen tussen de Oost-Noordbrabantse dialecten onderling' ['The borders between the dialects of eastern North Brabant']. In *OostNoordbrabantse dialectproblemen* ['Eastern North Brabant dialect problems'], edited by Antonius A. Weijnen, J. M. Renders, and Jac. van Ginneken (Bijdragen en Mededelingen der Dialectencommissie van de Koninklijke Nederlandse Akademie van Wetenschappen te Amsterdam No. 8 ['Contributions and Communications of the Dialect Committee of the Royal Dutch Academy of Sciences of Amsterdam']), 1–15.

Weinreich, Max (1923) *Studien zur Geschichte und dialektischen Gliederung der jiddischen Sprache* ['Studies in the History and Dialect Distribution of the Yiddish Language'] (University of Marburg, doctoral dissertation). Published in 1993 as *Geschichte der jiddischen Sprachforschung*, edited by Jerold C. Frakes (Atlanta, Georgia: Scholar's Press).

Weinreich, Uriel (1951) *Research Problems in Bilingualism, with Special Regard to Switzerland* (Columbia University, doctoral dissertation).

Weinreich, Uriel (1953) *Languages in Contact: Problems and Findings* (New York: Linguistic Circle of New York).

Weinreich, Uriel (1954) 'Is a Structural Dialectology Possible?' In *Linguistics Today: Published on the Occasion of the Columbia University Bicentennial*, edited by André Martinet and Uriel Weinreich (New York: Linguistic Circle of New York, Columbia University), pp. 268–80. Publications of the Linguistic Circle of New York, No. 2.

Weinreich, Uriel, Labov, William and Herzog, Marvin I. (1968) 'Empirical Foundations for a Theory of Language Change'. In *Directions for Historical Linguistics: A Symposium*, edited by Winfred P. Lehmann and Yakov Malkiel (Austin: University of Texas Press), pp. 95–195. Online version (2006; no page numbers), edited by Jonathan Slocum, available at: https://liberalarts.utexas.edu/lrc/resources/books/directions/5-weinreich.php. I used the online version.

Wells, J. C. (1978) Review of *The Linguistic Atlas of England*, *The Times Higher Education Supplement*, 1 December 1978, accessed 5 June 2016, at: http://www.phon.ucl.ac.uk/home/estuary/lae-revw.htm; no page numbers.

Wells, J. C. (1979) Review of *The Linguistic Atlas of England*, *Journal of the International Phonetic Association*, Vol. 9, 39–43.

Wells, J. C. (1982) *Accents of English*. Three vols. (Cambridge: Cambridge University Press). Recordings available at: http://www.phon.ucl.ac.uk/home/wells/accentsanddialects/.

Wenker, Georg (1877) *Sprach-Karte der Rheinprovinz nördlich der Mosel*. Part of: *Das rheinische Platt. Den Lehrern des Rheinlandes gewidmet*. ['The Low German of the Rhineland. Dedicated to the teachers of the Rhineland.'] (Düsseldorf: self-published).

Wenker, Georg (1878) *Sprachatlas der Rheinprovinz nördlich der Mosel sowie des Kreises Siegen. Nach systematisch aus circa 1500 Orten gesammeltem Material zusammengestellt, entworfen und gezeichnet*. Manuscript (hand-drafted onto printed base maps) held in the archives of the *Forschungszentrum Deutscher Sprachatlas*, Marburg.

Wenker, Georg (1881) *Sprach-Atlas von Nord- und Mitteldeutschland. Auf Grund von systematisch mit Hülfe der Volksschullehrer gesammeltem Material aus circa 30 000 Orten. Text. Einleitung*. (Strasbourg and London: Trübner).

Wenker, Georg (1885) *Sprachatlas von Nordwestdeutschland*. Manuscript (hand-drafted onto printed base maps) held in the archives of the *Forschungszentrum Deutscher Sprachatlas*, Marburg.

Wenker, Georg (1889–1923) *Sprachatlas des Deutschen Reichs*. Hand-drafted onto printed base maps by Emil Maurmann, Georg Wenker and Fredinand Wrede. Manuscript held in the archives of the *Forschungszentrum Deutscher Sprachatlas*, Marburg, and in the *Staatsbibliothek zu Berlin*.

Wenker: see also Webography entries for *DiWA*: http://www.diwa.info, and Regionalsprache.de (REDE): http://www.regionalsprache.de/.

Wentworth, Harold (1944) *American Dialect Dictionary* (New York: Thomas Y. Crowell).

Whitney, William Dwight (1867) *Language and the Study of Language* (New York: Scribner).

Wieling, Martijn (2013) '*Voices* Dialectometry at the University of Groningen'. In *Analysing 21st Century British English: Conceptual and Methodological Aspects of the Voices Project*, edited by Clive Upton and Bethan L. Davies (Abingdon, Oxfordshire and New York: Routledge), pp. 208–18. See also Webography entry for Wieling.

Wikle, Thomas A. and Bailey, Guy (2010) 'Mapping North American English'. In Lameli et al. (eds) (2010a), pp. 253–68.

Williams, Ann and Kerswill, Paul (1999) 'Dialect Levelling: Change and Continuity in Milton Keynes, Reading and Hull'. In Foulkes and Docherty (eds) (1999), pp. 141–62.

Williamson, Keith (2008–13) – see entry in Webography.

Wolfram, Walt (1969) *A Sociolinguistic Description of Detroit Negro Speech* (Washington, D.C.: Center for Applied Linguistics).

Wolfram, Walt (1976) 'Toward a Description of A-Prefixing in Appalachian English', *American Speech*, Vol. 51, No. 1/2, 45–56. Reprinted in Trudgill and Chambers (eds) (1991), pp. 229–40.

Wolfram, Walt and Schilling-Estes, Natalie (2008) Interview with Walt Wolfram, *Journal of English Linguistics*, Vol. 36, No. 4, 354–71.

Wolfram, Walt and Ward, Ben (eds) (2006) *American Voices: How Dialects Differ from Coast to Coast* (Malden, Massachusetts and Oxford: Blackwell).

Wood, Gordon R. (1970) *Word Dissemination: A Study of Regional Words in Eight of the Southern States* (Carbondale, Illinois: Southern Illinois University Press).

Wood, Gordon R. (1971a) *Vocabulary Change: A Study of Variation in Regional Words in Eight of the Southern States* (Carbondale and Edwardsville, Illinois: Southern Illinois University Press).

Wood, Gordon R. (1971b) 'Why Not a Computer as Editor?' In *Dialectology: Problems and Perspectives*, edited by Lorraine Hall Burghardt (Knoxville, Tennessee: University of Tennessee), pp. 41–53.

Woods, Howard Bruce (1979) *A Socio-dialectology Survey of the English Spoken in Ottawa: A Study of Sociological and Stylistic Variation in Canadian English* (University of British Columbia, doctoral dissertation) (Ann Arbor: UMI Dissertations Publishing).

Wrede, Ferdinand, Mitzka, Walther and Martin, Bernhard (eds) (1926–56) *Deutscher Sprachatlas, auf Grund des von Georg Wenker begründeten Sprachatlas des Deutschen Reichs* (Marburg: Elwert).

Wright, Elizabeth Mary (1913) *Rustic Speech and Folk-Lore* (London: Humphrey Milford, Oxford University Press).

Wright, Elizabeth Mary (1932) *The Life of Joseph Wright*. Two vols. (London: Humphrey Milford, Oxford University Press).

Wright, Joseph (1892) *A Grammar of the Dialect of Windhill in the West Riding of Yorkshire* (London: Kegan Paul, Trench, Trübner and Company for the English Dialect Society).

Wright, Joseph (ed.) (1898) *The English Dialect Dictionary*. Vol. I: *A–C*. (London: Henry Frowde, publisher to the English Dialect Society; New York: G. P. Putnam's Sons). Note: 1898 is the publication date given on the title page of Volume I, though E. M. Wright (1932, p. 397) states that it was published in July 1896, a date corroborated by reviews collected in Wright's scrapbook of press cuttings held at the Bodleian Library (MS Eng. lang. d. 107).

Wright, Joseph (ed.) (1898–1905) *The English Dialect Dictionary*. Six vols. (London: Henry Frowde).

Wright, Joseph (ed.) (1900) *The English Dialect Dictionary*. Vol. II: *D–G*. (London: Henry Frowde, publisher to the English Dialect Society; New York: G. P. Putnam's Sons).

Wright, Joseph (ed.) (1905a) *The English Dialect Dictionary*. Vol. IV: *M–Q*. (Oxford, London: Henry Frowde).

Wright, Joseph (ed.) (1905b) *The English Dialect Dictionary*. Vol. VI: *T–Z*. *Also Supplement, Bibliography and Grammar*. (London: Henry Frowde, publisher to the English Dialect Society; Oxford and New York: G. P. Putnam's Sons).

Wright, Joseph (1905c) *The English Dialect Grammar*, as appendix to *EDD* (London: Henry Frowde). Also published separately as *The English Dialect Grammar comprising the Dialects of England, of the Shetland and Orkney Islands, and of those Parts of Scotland, Ireland & Wales where English is Habitually Spoken* (Oxford, London, Edinburgh, Glasgow, New York and Toronto: Henry Frowde, 1905).

Wright, Joseph and Wright, Elizabeth Mary (1923) *An Elementary Middle English Grammar* (Oxford: Humphrey Milford, Oxford University Press).

Wright, Peter (1972) *Lanky Twang: How It Is Spoke* (Lancaster: Dalesman Books).

Wright, Peter (1974) *The Language of British Industry* (London and Basingstoke: Macmillan).

Wright, Peter (1980) *Cumbrian Dialect* (Lancaster: Dalesman Books).

Wright, Peter (1980) *The Yorkshireman's Dictionary* (Lancaster: Dalesman Books). Revised edn, 1990.

Wright, Peter and Rohrer, Fritz (1968) 'Early Work for the Survey of English Dialects: The Academic and Human Sides', *Leeds Studies in English*, New Series, Vol. 2 (1968), *Studies in Honour of Harold Orton on the Occasion of his Seventieth Birthday*, edited by Stanley Ellis (Leeds: School of English, University of Leeds), pp. 7–13. Available from the University of Leeds Digital Library: http://digital.library.leeds.ac.uk/.

Wright, Thomas (1857) *Dictionary of Obsolete And Provincial English* (London: H. G. Bohn).

Yule, Colonel Henry and Burnell, A. C. (1886) *Hobson-Jobson: A Glossary of Colloquial Anglo-Indian Words and Phrases, and of Kindred Terms, Etymological, Historical, Geographical and Discursive* (London: John Murray). *A Selected Edition*, edited by Kate Teltscher, was published in 2013 (Oxford: Oxford University Press).

Webography

Webography entries are ordered alphabetically by surname or main keyword. All information is correct at the time of writing.

AIS (*Sprach- und Sachatlas Italiens und der Südschweiz*), digital online version, *NavigAIS*: http://www3.pd.istc.cnr.it/navigais/. By Graziano G. Tisato (2009).

The Aitken Papers: A. J. Aitken, edited by Caroline Macafee, *Collected Writings on the Scots Language* (2015): http://www.scotslanguage.com/aitken-papers.

Akustyk: A Free Praat Plug-in for Sociolinguists: http://bartus.org/akustyk/. Bartłomiej [Bartek] Plichta (2003–12). Also: https://github.com/akustyk.

Laurence Anthony's *AntConc*: http://www.laurenceanthony.net/software/antconc/. (Tokyo: Waseda University).

Audacity: http://web.audacityteam.org/. Dominic Mazzoni and Roger Dannenberg and team (1999–2016), see: http://web.audacityteam.org/about/credits.

Australian Corpus of English (ACE; 1986), available via ICAME: http://clu.uni.no/icame/clarin/.

Australian National Corpus website: https://www.ausnc.org.au/.

The Australian National Dictionary: A Dictionary of Australianisms on Historical Principles (Ramson, 1988; online from 2008): http://andc.anu.edu.au/node/13927 and http://australiannationaldictionary.com.au/ (Oxford University Press Australia and New Zealand).

BBC News online: 'Language Plea by Sacred Heart School, Middlesbrough', at: http://www.bbc.co.uk/news/uk-england-tees-21340029, 5 February 2013, accessed 17 November 2014; 'Colley Lane School in Halesowen Bans Black Country Dialect', at: http://www.bbc.co.uk/news/uk-england-birmingham-24941692, 14 November 2013, accessed 17 November 2014.

BBC *Voices* – see entry at *Voices*.

Biddulph, Joseph (accessed 13 May 2016) *An Index of the Contents of the* Transactions of the Yorkshire Dialect Society, *1897–2009*: http://www.yorkshiredialectsociety.org.uk/dialect-research/.

Boersma and Weenink (1992–2016) – see Webography entry for *Praat*.

Bonaparte, Louis-Lucien (1858–63), dialect versions of *The Song of Solomon*, a list with bibliographical details available at the Internet Bible Catalog: http://bibles.wikidot. com/bonaparte#toc9.

The British Library's *Map Your Voice* project (2011): http://www.bl.uk/evolvingenglish/ maplisten.html.

The British Library's version of *Mr Tickle* (2010): http://www.bl.uk/pdf/tickle.pdf.

The British Library, 'Sociolinguistics: Sound Recordings': http://www.bl.uk/reshelp/ findhelpsubject/socsci/socioling/soundrec/sociolingsound.html.

The British Library's online dialect and accent archive at *Sounds* (2004 onwards): http://sounds.bl.uk/Accents-and-dialects.

The British Library's *Sounds Familiar?* website (2007 onwards): http://www.bl.uk/ learning/langlit/sounds/. Includes 'Regional Voices: Phonological Variation', at: http://www.bl.uk/learning/langlit/sounds/regional-voices/phonological-variation/.

British National Corpus (BNC; 1994 onwards): http://www.natcorp.ox.ac.uk/.

Brown Corpus of American English (1986 onwards), available via ICAME: http://clu. uni.no/icame/clarin/.

Brown, Felicity (2009) 'Percentage of Global Population Living in Cities, by Continent', *The Guardian* online, 24 August: http://www.theguardian.com/news/datablog/2009/ aug/18/percentage-population-living-cities.

Business Insider – see entry for Walter Hickey (2013).

Atlas of Canada section on languages: http://www.nrcan.gc.ca/earth-sciences/geography/ atlas-canada/selected-thematic-maps/16880.

J. C. Catford: *The Catford Tapes: Professor Catford's Life in Linguistics* (1985/2008): http://linguistlist.org/issues/19/19-492.html. Eight lectures given in 1985 by J. C. Catford; videos made available by the University of Michigan in 2008; digitization and publication supervised by Alan Pagliere.

Chambers, Jack and Pi, Tony (2006) *Atlas of Dialect Topography (On-Line)*: http://dialect. topography.chass.utoronto.ca/.

Chomsky.Info, The Noam Chomsky Website: https://chomsky.info/.

Chomsky, Noam (2013) 'What is Language and Why Does It Matter', lecture to the 2013 Linguistic Society of America Summer Institute at the University of Michigan: https://www.youtube.com/watch?v=-72JNZZBoVw.

Clarke, Sandra and Hiscock, Philip (directors) (2012) *Dialect Atlas of Newfoundland and Labrador*: http://www.dialectatlas.mun.ca/. Memorial University Dialect Atlas design and development team: Jamie Chang, Jane Costello, Donna Downey, Gerry Porter, Levin Meija, David Cantwell and Dale Conway.

Coal Mining Oral History Project: http://www.durhamintime.org.uk/coal_mining/ cd_rom/index.htm. Developed by Durham County Council's Durham Studies and funded by the Heritage Lottery Fund.

Tom Cobb's Compleat Lexical Tutor: http://www.lextutor.ca/. (Université du Québec à Montréal).

Crystal, David (2015): http://www.disappearingdictionary.com/. Companion website to the 2015 book.

Diachronic Electronic Corpus of Tyneside English (DECTE) – see Webography entry for Tyneside Linguistic Survey (TLS).

Atlas of Dialect Topography (On-Line): see entry for Chambers and Pi (2006).

Dictionary of American Regional English (DARE) website: http://dare.wisc.edu/.

The Digital *Dictionary of American Regional English* (2014), edited by Joan Houston Hall (Cambridge, Massachusetts: Harvard University Press): http://www.daredictionary.com/.

DARE pilot online survey of Wisconsin (2013–14) maps: http://dare.wisc.edu/surveys/OSWE-maps. By Evan Applegate at the University of Wisconsin–Cartography Lab. Audio: http://dare.wisc.edu/audio.

DiWA, the *Digitaler Wenker-Atlas*: http://www.diwa.info/. *DiWA*: Schmidt, Jürgen Erich and Herrgen, Joachim (eds) (2001–2009) *Digitaler Wenker-Atlas*. Compiled and prepared by Alfred Lameli, Tanja Giessler, Roland Kehrein, Alexandra Lenz, Karl-Heinz Müller, Jost Nickel, Christoph Purschke and Stefan Rabanus. Online publication. (Marburg: Forschungszentrum Deutscher Sprachatlas.)

Digital Public Library of America (DPLA): https://dp.la/.

Aaron J. Dinkin's home-page: http://www.ling.upenn.edu/~dinkin/.

Dollinger, Stefan (ed.-in-chief), Brinton, Laurel J. and Fee, Margery (eds) (2013) *DCHP-1 Online: A Dictionary of Canadianisms on Historical Principles Online*: http://dchp.ca/DCHP-1/ (Toronto: Nelson Education). Based on Avis et al. (eds) (1967). See also: http://faculty.arts.ubc.ca/sdollinger/dchp2.htm, for information on *DCHP-2: The Dictionary of Canadianisms on Historical Principles*, 2nd edn, online dictionary: http://dchp.ca/DCHP-2/, Stefan Dollinger (ed.-in-chief), Laurel J. Brinton (assoc. ed.) and Margery Fee (assoc. ed.). In preparation.

DSL: Dictionary of the Scots Language (2004) online: http://www.dsl.ac.uk/. The original project team included William Aitken, Grant Cunningham, Frances Phillips, Susan Rennie and Viktor Skretcowicz. The *DSL*2 Project Team includes Brian Aitken, Peter Bell, Ann Ferguson, Eileen Finlayson, Alison Grant and Pauline Cairns Speitel.

Durham and Tyneside Dialect Group: http://www.indigogroup.co.uk/durhamdialect/index.html.

Internet Library of Early Journals (such as *The Gentleman's Magazine*): http://www.bodley.ox.ac.uk/ilej/. An eLib (Electronic Libraries Programme) Project by the Universities of Birmingham, Leeds, Manchester and Oxford, completed in 1999.

Penelope Eckert's home-page: https://web.stanford.edu/~eckert/.

Eckert, Penelope (2011) 'The Future of Variation Studies'. Panel on the past, present, and future of NWAV and Variation Studies; NWAV40 conference, Georgetown University, 28 October. Available at: http://web.stanford.edu/~eckert/PDF/FutureOFVariation.pdf.

EDD Online at: http://www.uibk.ac.at/anglistik/projects/speed/startseite_edd_online.html. Originally part of the SPEED Project (Spoken English in Early Dialects), 2006–2010: see entry for SPEED. From April 2011: *EDD Online* Project, Manfred Markus and Reinhard Heuberger; Scientific Collaborators: Andrea Krapf, Regina Seiwald and Anna-Maria Waldner; Local Programmer: Joachim Masser; External Programmers: Thomas Burch and Dr. Hans-Werner Bartz, of the University of Trier.

An Atlas of Alexander J. Ellis's *The Existing Phonology of English Dialects (Æ)*: http://www.lel.ed.ac.uk/EllisAtlas/Index.html, developed by Warren Maguire from 2012 onwards. See also: Maguire, Warren (2012) 'Mapping The Existing Phonology of English Dialects', *Dialectologia et Geolinguistica*, Vol. 20, No. 1, 84–107.

English Dialects App: https://www.cam.ac.uk/research/news/do-you-say-splinter-spool-spile-or-spell-english-dialects-app-tries-to-guess-your-regional-accent.

ERIC (Education Resources Information Center, US Office of Education): http://eric.ed.gov/.

EThOS e-theses online service, British Library: http://ethos.bl.uk/Home.do.

European Dialect Syntax (Edisyn) project: http//www.dialectsyntax.org. See also: http://www.dialectsyntax.org/wiki/About_Edisyn.

Evans, Betsy E. (2011) *Seattle to Spokane: Mapping English in Washington State.* Available from the Seattle to Spokane website: http://depts.washington.edu/folkling/.

eWAVE, The Electronic World Atlas of Varieties of English – see entry below for Kortmann and Lunkenheimer (eds) (2013).

Express Scribe Transcription Software: http://www.nch.com.au/scribe/.

Craig Fees's website: http://craigfees.com/.

Fieldwork Forum, Department of Linguistics, University of California, Berkeley, Resources for Linguistic Fieldwork: http://linguistics.berkeley.edu/~fforum/resources.html.

Forgotten Books: http://www.forgottenbooks.com/.

Freiburg-Brown Corpus of American English (Frown; 1999 onwards), available via ICAME: http://clu.uni.no/icame/clarin/.

Freiburg English Dialect Corpus (FRED; 2000–2005): http://www2.anglistik.uni-freiburg.de/institut/lskortmann/FRED/.

Freiburg-LOB Corpus of British English (F-LOB; 1999 onwards), available via ICAME: http://clu.uni.no/icame/clarin/.

Dialect glossaries:

> *Australian Slang*, at: http://www.koalanet.com.au/australian-slang.html (Koala Net, 2011);
>
> *Boston to English Dictionary*, at: http://www.celebrateboston.com/culture/dictionary.htm (CelebrateBoston.com, 2016);
>
> *The Dialect Dictionary*, at: http://www.thedialectdictionary.com/;
>
> *Jamaican Patwah: Patois and Slang Dictionary*, at: http://jamaicanpatwah.com/dictionary;
>
> *A Dialect Dictionary of Lumbee English,* by Dannenberg et al. (1996), online version, http://www.learnnc.org/lp/editions/nc-american-indians/5760;
>
> *Pembrokeshire English,* at: http://www.pembrokeshirecoast.org.uk/?PID=218 (Pembrokeshire Coast National Park web-pages);
>
> *Pittsburghese*, at: http://www.pittsburghese.com/;
>
> *A Glossary of Quaint Southernisms* (of the USA), at: http://www.alphadictionary.com/articles/southernese.html, by Robert Beard (2014–15);
>
> *Talkin' Texan and Southern Slang: Howdy Get Rowdy*, at: https://truetexanliving.wordpress.com/2012/10/25/talkin-texan-and-southern-slang/, by Tyler Cole Stevens (2012);
>
> *Tok Pisin/English Dictionary*, at: http://www.tok-pisin.com/sort-tokpisin.php, part of Tok-Pisin.com;
>
> *Yorkshire Dictionary*, at: http://www.yorkshire-dialect.org/dictionary.htm, by Kevin Wilde.

Goldvarb (2005–15), available from: http://individual.utoronto.ca/tagliamonte/goldvarb.html, by David Sankoff, Sali A. Tagliamonte and Eric Smith.

Goldvarb Online Manual – see Webography entry for Rand and Sankoff (1990).

Matthew J. Gordon's home-page: https://english.missouri.edu/people/gordon.

Gordon, Matthew J. (2005) 'Language Change: Vowel Shifting', *Do You Speak American? What Lies Ahead?* pages on PBS website: http://www.pbs.org/speak/ahead/change/changin/.

Esther Grabe home-page (up to 2005): http://www.phon.ox.ac.uk/files/people/grabe/.

Project Gutenberg (founded by Michael Hart in 1971): http://www.gutenberg.org/wiki/Main_Page.

Rob Hagiwara's Monthly Mystery Spectrogram Webzone (2002–09): http://home.cc.umanitoba.ca/~robh/.

HathiTrust Digital Library: https://www.hathitrust.org/.

Hickey, Raymond, *Variation and Change in Dublin English* website, using research from the mid 1990s onwards: https://www.uni-due.de/VCDE/.

Hickey, Raymond (2015), Irish English Resource Centre: https://www.uni-due.de/IERC/.

Hickey, Walter (2013) 'Politics: Maps: A Poll Asked America which States were the Drunkest, the Hottest and which had the Silliest Accents', *Business Insider*, 20 August: http://www.businessinsider.com/poll-how-americans-feel-about-the-states-2013-8. Read more: http://www.businessinsider.com/poll-how-americans-feel-about-the-states-2013-8#ixzz3JKYPOjSZ.

Entry on Wilhelm von Humboldt in the online *Stanford Encyclopedia of Philosophy*, at: http://plato.stanford.edu/archives/sum2016/entries/wilhelm-humboldt/. Kurt Mueller-Vollmer and Markus Messling, 'Wilhelm von Humboldt', *The Stanford Encyclopedia of Philosophy* (Summer 2016 Edn), edited by Edward N. Zalta.

ICAME (International Computer Archive of Modern and Medieval English, 1977 onwards): http://clu.uni.no/icame/.

ICE (International Corpus of English, 1990 onwards): http://ice-corpora.net/ice/.

Indo-European Documentation Center, Linguistics Research Center of the University of Texas at Austin: from 2016 under Resources of the Linguistics Research Center, http://liberalarts.utexas.edu/lrc/resources/overview.php.

Internet Archive: https://archive.org/index.php.

Intonational Variation in English (IViE; 1997–2008): http://www.phon.ox.ac.uk/files/apps/IViE/index.php.

Jefferies, Julie (2005) *Focus On People and Migration: The UK Population: Past, Present and Future*, Office for National Statistics (ONS), moved to: http://ons.gov.uk/ons/rel/fertility-analysis/focus-on-people-and-migration/december-2005/index.html.

Jisc, Joint Information Systems Committee: https://www.jisc.ac.uk/.

Journal of Linguistic Geography (Cambridge: Cambridge University Press): https://www.cambridge.org/core/journals/journal-of-linguistic-geography.

JSTOR (Journal Storage): http://www.jstor.org/.

Paul Kerswill's home-page at York University: https://www.york.ac.uk/language/people/academic-research/paul-kerswill/. Older page at Lancaster University: http://www.research.lancs.ac.uk/portal/en/people/paul-kerswill(ea347f1d-3d8d-4b41-9e8c-0a682903baa4)/publications.html.

Amīr Khusrau (1318) *Nuh Sipihr* ['The Nine Heavens/Spheres']: 'The Third Sphere', at: http://persian.packhum.org/persian/main.

Kortmann, Bernd and Lunkenheimer, Kerstin (eds.) (2013) *The Electronic World Atlas of Varieties of English* (*eWAVE*; Leipzig: Max Planck Institute for Evolutionary

Anthropology). Available online at http://ewave-atlas.org, accessed on 14 January 2016. Original version launched 2011.

Krug, Manfred and Schlüter, Julia (eds) (2013) *Research Methods in Language Variation and Change* companion website: https://www.uni-bamberg.de/eng-ling/research-methods.

William Labov's home-page: http://www.ling.upenn.edu/~wlabov/.

Labov, William (2013) 'The Relation of Social to Structural Factors in the Explanation of Linguistic Change', lecture at the University of York, 19 June 2013: https://www.youtube.com/watch?v=qCJh8nFXBUE.

Labov, William, Ash, Sharon, Boberg, Charles, Baranowski, Maciej and Barrow, Janet (1997) *Phonological Atlas of North America*, at: http://www.ling.upenn.edu/phono_atlas/home.html#staff.

Laing, Margaret (2008–13) *A Linguistic Atlas of Early Middle English, 1150–1325*: http://www.amc.lel.ed.ac.uk/?page_id=492. (Edinburgh: University of Edinburgh; Version 3.2, 2013). Webscripts by Keith Williamson, Vasilis Karaiskos and Sherrylyn Branchaw.

Lancaster-Oslo/Bergen Corpus (LOB), available via ICAME: http://clu.uni.no/icame/clarin/.

Language Magazine: The Journal of Communication and Education (California): http://languagemagazine.com/.

Leeds Archive of Vernacular Culture (LAVC): https://library.leeds.ac.uk/special-collections/collection/61/the_leeds_archive_of_vernacular_culture. The Incidental Material of the SED: http://library.leeds.ac.uk/special-collections/collection/61/the_leeds_archive_of_vernacular_culture/74/incidental_material_documents_sed.

University of Leeds Digital Library: http://digital.library.leeds.ac.uk/.

Leeds Studies in English: http://www.leeds.ac.uk/lse/.

David W. Lightfoot's home-page: http://explore.georgetown.edu/people/lightd/?action=viewgeneral&PageTemplateID=360.

Linguistic Atlas Project of the USA and Canada (LAP) website (2011): http://www.lap.uga.edu/. Old LAP sites: http://old.lap.uga.edu/ (2005), and http://us.english.uga.edu/cgi-bin/lapsite.fcgi/old/index.html (1998).

Linguistic Innovators: The English of Adolescents in London (2004–7): http://www.lancaster.ac.uk/fss/projects/linguistics/innovators/index.htm. Jenny Cheshire, Sue Fox, Paul Kerswill and Eivind Torgersen.

Linguist List: http://linguistlist.org/indexfd.cfm.

Linguistics Research Center of the University of Texas at Austin: formerly, http://www.utexas.edu/cola/centers/lrc/; from 2016, http://liberalarts.utexas.edu/lrc/.

Greater London Authority's London DataStore web-pages: http://data.london.gov.uk/dataset/.

Angus McIntosh Centre for Historical Linguistics, University of Edinburgh: http://www.amc.lel.ed.ac.uk/.

McIntosh, Angus et al. (1986), revised online edn (2013) of *A Linguistic Atlas of Late Mediaeval English* (*eLALME*): http://www.amc.lel.ed.ac.uk/?page_id=490. Revised and supplemented by Michael Benskin and Margaret Laing; webscripts by Vasilis Karaiskos and Keith Williamson.

The Macquarie Dictionary Online (2003 onwards): https://www.macquariedictionary.com.au/ (Macmillan Australia). Edited by Susan Butler.

Manchester Libraries online: https://manchester.spydus.co.uk/cgi-bin/spydus.exe/ MSGTRN/OPAC/BSEARCH?HOMEPRMS=GENPARAMS.

Nick Wedd's maproom.org: http://www.maproom.org/.

Markus, Manfred (2007) 'Wright's *EDD* Computerised: Architecture and Retrieval Routine', online publication, Conference Dagstuhl, *Digital Historical Corpora*, 3–10 December 2006: http://drops.dagstuhl.de/opus/volltexte/2007/1052/pdf/06491.MarkusManfred. Paper.1052.pdf.

Mazzoni, Dannenberg et al. (1999–2016) – see Webography entry for *Audacity*.

Melissa (2007) 'Do You Like the Australian Accent?': https://answers.yahoo.com/ question/index?qid=20080329220731AAc9rxv. Accessed 17 November 2014.

Memorial University Digital Archives Initiative: http://collections.mun.ca/index.php.

Montgomery, Christopher (2007) *Northern English Dialects: A Perceptual Approach* (University of Sheffield, PhD dissertation, electronic publication at: http://etheses. whiterose.ac.uk/1203/2/Montgomery,_C.pdf).

Munich Digitization Center (MDZ; Münchener DigitalisierungsZentrum): http://www.muenchener-digitalisierungszentrum.de/index.html?c=startseite&l=en. MDZ handles the digitization and online publication of the cultural heritage preserved by the Bavarian State Library (Bayerische StaatsBibliothek) and by other institutions in Germany.

Newcastle Electronic Corpus of Tyneside English (NECTE) – see Webography entry for Tyneside Linguistic Survey.

NORM (The Vowel Normalization and Plotting Suite): http://lingtools.uoregon. edu/norm/. Thomas, Erik R. and Kendall, Tyler (2007). See also: Thomas, Erik R., Kendall, Tyler, Yeager-Dror, Malcah and Kretzschmar Jr., William A. (2007) 'Two Things Sociolinguists Should Know: Software Packages for Vowel Normalization, and Accessing Linguistic Atlas Data' (Workshop at New Ways of Analyzing Variation (NWAV) 36, University of Pennsylvania).

Office for National Statistics (ONS) web-pages: https://www.ons.gov.uk/. See also Webography entry for Jefferies (2005).

The Online Books Page, edited by John Mark Ockerbloom (1993 onwards): http://onlinebooks.library.upenn.edu/.

Oxford English Dictionary Online: http://www.oed.com/. Chief Editor: Michael Proffitt; Editorial Director of Dictionaries: Judy Pearsall; Deputy Chief Editors: Philip Durkin, Edmund Weiner; Editorial Project Director: Sarah Williams; Editorial Content Director: Graeme Diamond (Oxford: Oxford University Press).

Parry, David R. (2008) 'The Survey of Anglo-Welsh Dialects: History': http://www. swansea.ac.uk/riah/researchgroups/lrc/awe/storyofsawd/. Edited by Rob Penhallurick, and published on the Archive of Welsh English website.

Plichta (2003–12) – see Webography entry for *Akustyk*.

Plotnik software (Labov, 2002–11): http://www.ling.upenn.edu/~wlabov/Plotnik.html.

populstat: http://www.populstat.info/. Populstat website (1999–2006): Jan Lahmeyer.

Praat software: http://www.fon.hum.uva.nl/praat/. Boersma, Paul and Weenink, David (1992–2016), University of Amsterdam. Accessed 13 May 2016: 'Praat: Doing Phonetics by Computer [Computer Program]'.

Dennis Preston's home-page: https://english.okstate.edu/news/department-publications/11-faculty/47-dennis-r-preston.

Michael Quinion, *World Wide Words: Investigating the English Language Across the Globe* (1996 onwards): http://www.worldwidewords.org/index.htm.

R statistical software: https://www.r-project.org/.

Rand, David and Sankoff, David (1990) *GoldVarb, Version 2, A Variable Rule Application for the Macintosh, April 1990, Online Manual*: http://albuquerque.bioinformatics. uottawa.ca/goldVarb/GoldManual.dir/index.html.

Rbrul statistical software by Daniel Ezra Johnson: http://www.danielezrajohnson.com/ rbrul.html.

Regionalsprache.de (REDE): http://www.regionalsprache.de/. Schmidt, Jürgen Erich, Herrgen, Joachim and Kehrein, Roland (eds) (2008 onwards). Forschungsplattform zu den modernen Regionalsprachen des Deutschen ['Research platform of the modern regional dialects of German']. Edited by Dennis Bock, Brigitte Ganswindt, Heiko Girnth, Roland Kehrein, Alfred Lameli, Slawomir Messner, Christoph Purschke and Anna Wolańska (Marburg: Forschungszentrum Deutscher Sprachatlas, Phillipps University, in collaboration with the Academy of Science and Literature at Mainz).

Ian G. Roberts's home-page: http://www.mml.cam.ac.uk/professor-ian-roberts.

Roswell Voices [Bill Kretzschmar]: http://www.openlivinglabs.eu/livinglab/roswell-voices-ll.

R-Varb statistical software, John C. Paolillo (2002): http://paolillo.soic.indiana.edu/ index.php/ALV/RVarb.

Salamanca Corpus: Digital Archive of English Dialect Texts (2011 onwards): http://www.thesalamancacorpus.com/index.html.

David Sankoff's home-page: http://albuquerque.bioinformatics.uottawa.ca/.

Gillian Sankoff's home-page: http://www.ling.upenn.edu/~gillian/home.html.

Scots Language Centre/Centre for the Scots Leid: http://www.scotslanguage.com/. Run from the A. K. Bell Library, York Place, Perth.

Dictionary of the Scots Language online – see entry for *DSL*.

Shetland ForWirds website: http://www.shetlanddialect.org.uk/.

Roger Shuy's home-page: http://rogershuy.com/.

Silva, Penny, Dore, Wendy, Mantzel, Dorothea, Muller, Colin and Wright, Madeleine (eds) (1996) *A Dictionary of South African English on Historical Principles*, online (2014) at: dsae.co.za. (Oxford: Oxford University Press; and the Dictionary Unit for South African English (DSAE), Associate Institute of Rhodes University, South Africa).

Sjölander and Beskow (2005–12) – see Webography entry for *WaveSurfer*.

Jennifer L. Smith's Phonetics Resources (2000–2014) web-page: http://www.unc. edu/~jlsmith/pht-url.html#(5.

The History of Sound Recording: Technology, Culture, Commerce: http://www. recording-history.org/. Maintained by David Morton.

SPEED (Spoken English in Early Dialects), 2006–2010: https://www.uibk.ac.at/anglistik/ projects/speed/. Director: Manfred Markus; Deputy Director: Reinhard Heuberger; Project Manager: Alexander Onysko; Scientific Collaborators: Christian Peer and Christoph Praxmarer; Technical Collaborators: Günter Mühlberger and Raphael Unterweger.

Statistical Package for the Social Sciences (*SPSS*): http://www.ibm.com/analytics/us/en/ technology/spss/. IBM.

Story, G. M., Kirwin, W. J. and Widdowson, J. D. A. (1999) *Dictionary of Newfoundland English* online: http://www.heritage.nf.ca/dictionary/.

Benedikt Szmrecsanyi website: https://sites.google.com/site/bszmrecsanyi/.

Tomasz P. Szynalski's TypeIt website: http://ipa.typeit.org/.

Sali Tagliamonte's home-page: http://individual.utoronto.ca/tagliamonte/index.html.

Tagliamonte, Sali A. (2006) *Analysing Sociolinguistic Variation* companion website: http://www.cambridge.org/ca/academic/subjects/languages-linguistics/discourse-analysis/analysing-sociolinguistic-variation?format=PB#contentsTabAnchor.

Tagliamonte, Sali A. (2016) *Making Waves: The Story of Variationist Sociolinguistics* companion website: http://www.wiley.com//legacy/wileychi/tagliamonte/index.html?type=Home.

ToBI (Tones and Break Indices) transcription system, Ohio State University Department of Linguistics: http://www.ling.ohio-state.edu/~tobi/. See also: Beckman, Mary E. and Ayers Elam, Gayle (1997) *Guidelines for ToBI Labelling* (version 3.0): http://www.ling.ohio-state.edu/~tobi/ame_tobi/labelling_guide_v3.pdf. Also at: http://www.ling.ohio-state.edu/research/phonetics/E_ToBI/.

Peter Trudgill (2012) interviewed by Alan Macfarlane, University of Cambridge Film Interviews with Leading Thinkers: https://www.sms.cam.ac.uk/media/1382735.

Tyneside Linguistic Survey (TLS), see: http://research.ncl.ac.uk/necte/basecorpora.htm (Newcastle Electronic Corpus of Tyneside English (NECTE)); and: http://research.ncl.ac.uk/decte/index.htm (Diachronic Electronic Corpus of Tyneside English (DECTE)), which also incorporates the Talk of the Toon project: http://research.ncl.ac.uk/decte/toon/index.html.

The Ulster Dialect Archive of the Ulster Folk Museum: https://nmni.com/uftm/Collections/Library/Dialect-archive.

United States Census Bureau web-pages: https://www.census.gov/population/census-data/urpop0090.txt.

Upton, Clive and Davies, Bethan L. (eds) (2013) *Analysing 21st Century British English* companion website: http://routledgetextbooks.com/textbooks/_author/upton-9780415694438/. Routledge Access to Dialect and Region (2015).

Varbrul: see the entry for Cedergren and Sankoff (1974), and the Webography entry for *Goldvarb*.

VARIENG (Research Unit for the Study of Variation, Contacts and Change in English, University of Helsinki): https://www.helsinki.fi/en/researchgroups/varieng.

VARIENG: CoRD (Corpus Resource Database, 2007 onwards): http://www.helsinki.fi/varieng/CoRD/index.html.

BBC *Voices* (2005–14): http://www.bbc.co.uk/voices/.

BBC *Voices* from Cornwall: http://www.bbc.co.uk/cornwall/voices2005/stories/jan2005/voices_from_you2.shtml.

BBC *Voices* language survey kit: http://www.open.edu/openlearn/history-the-arts/culture/english-language/download-your-language-survey-kit.

Wagner, Susanne (2013) 'English Dialects in the Southwest of England'. In *The Electronic World Atlas of Varieties of English*, edited by Bernd Kortmann and Kerstin Lunkenheimer (Leipzig: Max Planck Institute for Evolutionary Anthropology). Available online at: http://ewave-atlas.org/languages/7, accessed on 15 January 2016.

WaveSurfer: http://www.speech.kth.se/wavesurfer/. Older site: http://www.speech.kth.se/wavesurfer/index2.html. Kåre Sjölander and Jonas Beskow (2005–12). Developed at the Centre for Speech Technology at the Kungliga Teknista Högskolan Royal Institute of Technology in Stockholm, Sweden.

Wellington Corpus of Spoken New Zealand English (WSC), and Wellington Corpus of Written New Zealand English (WWC), both available on CD from Victoria University of Wellington. Go to: http://www.victoria.ac.nz/lals/resources/corpora-default#wwc.

Wells, J. C. (1982) *Accents of English*. Three vols. (Cambridge: Cambridge University Press), audio recordings available at: http://www.phon.ucl.ac.uk/home/wells/accentsanddialects/.

Syntactic Atlas of Welsh Dialects project: http://lion.ling.cam.ac.uk/david/sawd/index.html. Project (2010–13, Department of Linguistics, University of Cambridge) conducted by David Willis, Maggie Tallerman and Bob Borsley. See also Webography entries for European Dialect Syntax project and David Willis.

Archive of Welsh English (2008): http://www.swansea.ac.uk/riah/researchgroups/lrc/awe/. Developed by Rob Penhallurick; technical assistance by Mostyn Jones.

Wieling, Martijn (2013 onwards) BBC *Voices* Explored: http://www.gabmap.nl/voices/.

Williamson, Keith (2008–13) *A Linguistic Atlas of Older Scots* (*LAOS*), *Phase 1, 1380–1500*: http://www.lel.ed.ac.uk/ihd/laos1/laos1.html. (Edinburgh: University of Edinburgh).

David Willis's home-page: http://www.mml.cam.ac.uk/dr-david-willis.

Walt Wolfram's home-page: https://english.chass.ncsu.edu/faculty_staff/wolfram.

York University: Resources web-pages of the Department of Language and Linguistic Science, University of York: http://www.york.ac.uk/language/current/resources/.

Yorkshire Dialect Society *Transactions of the Yorkshire Dialect Society* – see Webography entry for Biddulph.

Index

Note: Items in italics are example dialectal or other words discussed in the text. Book and journal titles are also shown in italics.

Printed in Great Britain
by Amazon